PRAISE FOR DOROTHY ROBERTS'S
KILLING THE BLACK BODY

"In asking us to acknowledge the centrality of reproductive justice to the larger quest for racial justice, and indeed liberty writ large, *Killing the Black Body* insists that the complex issues that define black women's path toward reproductive liberty constitute the precondition for understanding the entire field of women's reproductive rights." —Angela Davis

"Monumental. . . . An important contribution to the literature of civil rights, reproductive issues, racism and feminism."
—*San Francisco Chronicle*

"An important publication for new generations of scholars and activists who will be educated and inspired by Roberts's humanity, acumen and courage. *Killing the Black Body* draws back the curtain on a breathtakingly brutal legal assault."
—Harriet Washington, author of *Medical Apartheid*

"In this volume Dorothy Roberts delves deeply, brilliantly into questions that haunted the earliest moments of American history and remain deeply salient today. . . . This book should be read by all who are concerned with inequality in the United States." —William Jelani Cobb, author of *The Substance of Hope*

"Chilling. . . . It becomes difficult to reject the author's thesis . . . that there is a sustained, and in some quarters deliberate, campaign to punish Black women—especially the poor—for having children." —*The National Law Journal*

DOROTHY ROBERTS
KILLING THE
BLACK BODY

Dorothy Roberts is the George A. Weiss University Professor of Law and Sociology and the Raymond Pace and Sadie Tanner Mossell Alexander Professor of Civil Rights at the University of Pennsylvania. She is the author of three books of nonfiction, *Killing the Black Body*, *Shattered Bonds*, and *Fatal Invention*, and has coedited six works on constitutional law and gender. She lives in Philadelphia.

ALSO BY DOROTHY ROBERTS

Shattered Bonds:
The Color of Child Welfare

Fatal Invention: How Science, Politics,
and Big Business Re-create Race
in the Twenty-first Century

KILLING THE BLACK BODY

◆

Race, Reproduction,
and the Meaning
of Liberty

DOROTHY ROBERTS

Vintage Books
A Division of Penguin Random House LLC
New York

The Library of Congress has cataloged the Pantheon edition as follows:
Roberts, Dorothy, 1956–
Killing the black body : race, reproduction, and the meaning of liberty /
Dorothy Roberts.
p. cm.
Includes index.
1. Birth control—United States. 2. Afro-American women—Civil rights.
3. Welfare recipients—United States. 4. Race discrimination—
United States. I. Title.
HQ766.5.U5R58 1997 363.9'6W73-dc21 97-2383

Vintage Books Trade Paperback ISBN: 978-0-679-75869-3
eBook ISBN: 978-0-8041-5259-4

Author photograph © Chris Crisman

www.vintagebooks.com

Printed in the United States of America
32 34 33

To my precious children,
Amilcar, Camilo, Yaosca, and Dessalines

Contents

Contents

Acknowledgments

This book is the product of eight years of research and writing about race and reproductive freedom. I have countless people to thank for their comments as I have presented my ideas at workshops, conferences, and seminars over that period. Rutgers University School of Law, and Deans Peter Simmons and Roger Abrams, provided a wonderfully supportive environment for my work. Yale Law School's invitation to deliver the 1993 Thomas Lecture, which I entitled "Race and Reproduction," provided the spark. My fellowship at Harvard University's Program in Ethics and the Professions, directed by Dennis Thompson, gave me the opportunity to start writing this book. Martha Fineman's Feminism and Legal Theory Workshops at Columbia Law School and the Northeast Corridor of Black Women Law Professors were especially helpful.

I am indebted to numerous scholars who read and commented on papers that contributed to this book, including Taunya Banks, Joan Callahan, Norman Cantor, Rebecca Dresser, Nancy Ehrenreich, Judith Greenberg, Dwight Greene, Joel Handler, Kenneth Karst, Howard Latin, Nadine Taub, George Thomas, and Iris Marion Young. My thinking on welfare benefitted from conversations with Marion Smiley and Lucie White. Anita Allen, Regina Austin, Derrick Bell, Jerome Culp, Peggy Davis, Martha Fineman, Martha Minow, Jim Pope, and Susan Wolf deserve special recognition for their inspiration and support. Peggy Davis and Susan Wolf also generously commented on the final manuscript and improved it immensely.

One of the many privileges of being a law professor is having the benefit of research assistants. I would like to thank the following Rutgers Law School graduates whose invaluable research contributed to this book: Anita Brown, Decanda Faulk, Marianne Hatcher, Donna Jackson, Nina Loewenstein, Bronwen Mantlo, Elizabeth Marshall, Frederick Morton, Eric Pennington, Deborah Reid, Mavel Ruiz, Sandra Satchell, Valenicia Smith, Lysette Toro, Claudia Wernick, and Andrea Williams. I am also grateful to Simone Sandy, who provided research and friendship during my fellowship year at the Program in Ethics and the Professions. A team of Rutgers students (Elliot Monteverde-Torres, Melanie Routh, Margaret Hall, Kevin Kreisler, Theodora McCormick, and Eileen O'Toole) helped in the final stages of writing this book. Secretaries Bobbie Leach at Rutgers and Helen Hawkins at Harvard also provided important assistance.

I greatly appreciate the contributions of several organizations that generously sent me court papers, newsletters, and other information: ACLU Reproductive Freedom and Women's Rights Projects, ACLU of Chicago, Center for Reproductive Law and Policy, National Black Women's Health Project, National Women's Health Network, NOW Legal Defense and Education Fund, Planned Parenthood Federation, and Puerto Rican Legal Defense and Education Fund. I am also grateful to Wendy Chavkin, Sherrill Cohen, Deb Ellis, Lori Valencia Greene, Alexandra Halkin, Mary Faith Marshall, Lynn Paltrow, Nina Perales, Julia Scott, and Judith Scully for discussions and interviews.

I am indebted to several people who helped me turn my years of research into a book. Jane Alexander encouraged me to take the book to a broader audience and suggested my agent and publisher. My agent, Kathy Robbins, and my editor at Pantheon, Erroll McDonald, believed in this project from the start and gave me sound advice. Marya Van't Hul at Beacon Press and Bruce Nichols at The Free Press also encouraged me early on.

I could not have completed this book without the loving embrace of friends and family, who discussed my ideas, endured my preoccupation with writing, and watched my children. I am deeply grateful to Brenda and Alva Drakes, Michael Hanchard, Sheryl Jackson, Lela Jackson, Debra and Major Jennings, Sonya Smith, Nancy Tart, and Pamela Tyler for all their support. I appreciate the prayers of Rev. Michael Harriot and my friends at St. Mark's United Methodist Church. My parents, sisters, husband, and children have blessed me with the most incredible love and commitment.

Some of the material in this book previously appeared in the following law review articles: "Punishing Drug Addicts Who Have Babies: Women of Color, Equality, and the Right of Privacy," *Harvard Law Review* 104 (1991), p. 1419; "The Genetic Tie," *University of Chicago Law Review* 62 (1995), p. 209; "Irrationality and Sacrifice in the Welfare Reform Consensus," *Virginia Law Review* 81 (1995), p. 2607; "Welfare and the Problem of Black Citizenship," *Yale Law Journal* 105 (1996), p. 1563; and "Race and the New Reproduction," *Hastings Law Journal* 47 (1996), p. 935.

Preface to the Vintage Books Edition (2017)

In the late 1980s, I began to notice news stories about prosecutions of women for using drugs while pregnant. District attorneys across the country concocted an assortment of charges to punish these women for fetal crimes—child neglect, distribution of drugs to a minor, assault with a deadly weapon, and attempted murder. How did a public health problem become a criminal justice matter to be solved by locking up women instead of providing them with better health care? I was sure of three things about the prosecutions: they primarily targeted Black women, they punished these women for having babies, and they were a form of both race and gender oppression. Yet, at the time, mainstream reproductive rights organizations such as Planned Parenthood and National Abortion Rights Action League largely ignored the role of racism in these fetal crime charges, and failed to make the connection between the prosecutions of pregnant women who wanted to bear a child and laws denying women access to abortion. Both were affronts to the reproductive freedom of Black women; yet civil rights organizations failed to put these violations on their racial justice agendas.

As I investigated the prosecutions, I began to link them to a long history of regulation of Black women's bodies—a history that was crucial to reproductive and racial politics in America. *Killing the Black Body: Race, Reproduction, and the Meaning of Liberty* was the product of my mission to explain how the legacy of punishing Black motherhood was vital to the very meaning of reproductive freedom. The book was also the foundation for my work with a burgeoning network of women of color activists to build a movement for reproductive justice that put Black women's organizing at the forefront.

Twenty years have passed since *Killing the Black Body* was first published. My reflections on the state of reproductive freedom in America during the intervening decades evoke a mixture of exasperation and expectation. All the devaluing ideologies, laws, and policies I wrote about not only persist, but have expanded in new guises to inflict even more injury on even more women and their families and communities. Indeed, this book's claim about the pivotal role policing Black women's bodies has played in the U.S. racial regime rings even truer today.

Yet there is hope: the exciting rise of reproductive justice activism over the last two decades has provided a new framework and potential for resistance.

THE EXPANSION OF REPRODUCTIVE OPPRESSION

One of the most potent images used to justify the control of Black motherhood in the 1990s—and turn drug use during pregnancy into a crime—was the "crack baby." In the last twenty years, medical researchers have definitively discredited this myth: the babies exposed to crack cocaine in utero during that era grew up and were not the monsters the media predicted. The negative outcomes they exhibited as newborns, originally attributed to crack, actually resulted from structural inequities experienced by Black children.[1] But the caricature of crack babies—trembling in tiny hospital beds, permanently brain damaged, and on their way to becoming criminals—remains etched in many Americans' psyches, available to rationalize continued infringements of Black women's bodies.

Equally devastating, the legal apparatus crafted two decades ago to criminalize pregnant Black women set the stage for a new and more widespread surge of fetal harm prosecutions. Women across the country have been arrested for risking fetal health not only by using drugs while pregnant, but also by falling down stairs, attempting suicide, driving drunk, and botching self-induced abortions. The targets of prosecution extend from Black women accused of smoking crack cocaine during pregnancy to pregnant white women charged under laws intended to protect children from meth lab explosions. Since 1973—when *Roe v. Wade* was decided—more than seven hundred women have been arrested, detained, or subjected to forced medical interventions because of pregnancy-related accusations.[2] African American women in particular were significantly more likely to be reported by hospital staff, arrested, and charged with crimes.

The 2001 conviction of Regina McKnight, a twenty-one-year-old African American woman living in South Carolina, for "homicide by child abuse" paved the way for prosecuting women who suffered a miscarriage or stillbirth. The state claimed McKnight's drug use caused her baby's stillbirth, despite never being able to prove the link. She served eight years of a twelve-year sentence before the South Carolina Supreme Court overturned her conviction because her lawyer at trial failed to call experts who could have refuted the state's outdated evidence against her. Similarly, in Indiana in 2015, Purvi Patel, an Indian

American woman, was convicted of feticide and child neglect following her miscarriage and sentenced to twenty years. Prosecutors alleged she had attempted an abortion and was guilty both of killing the fetus and failing to seek medical care for her newborn. In July 2016, the Indiana Court of Appeals overturned her conviction for feticide as a misinterpretation of the criminal law, but left standing her child neglect conviction.

When this book was first published, prosecutors had to invent novel interpretations of existing child abuse, homicide, and drug laws to persuade courts to apply them to fetuses. Since then, state legislatures have enacted fetal protection laws that directly criminalize pregnant women by giving fetuses the same legal status as an already born child.[3] For example, Alabama revised its homicide laws in 2006 to include "an unborn child in utero at any stage of development, regardless of viability" as a "person" or "human being." And in *Ex parte Ankrom* (2013), the Alabama Supreme Court held that the state's chemical endangerment law applied to pregnant women who exposed "an unborn child" to controlled substances—not only by ingesting illegal drugs, but even by entering places where they are manufactured or sold. In 2014, Tennessee became the first state in the nation to pass a law making it a crime for women to use illegal narcotics while pregnant. Law enforcement authorities have used the law to arrest pregnant women for a broader range of illegal conduct, including infractions as minor as driving without a seat belt.[4]

As states have expanded prosecutions for fetal crimes during the past two decades, they have simultaneously escalated their assault on women's access to abortion. State legislatures have passed hundreds of laws restricting abortion, in effect stripping millions of women of their constitutional right to terminate a pregnancy. The escalation has been striking: a quarter of the state abortion restrictions on the books were enacted in the five years between 2010 and 2015.[5] The variety of tactics is mind-boggling: the banning of abortion after twelve weeks, so-called partial birth abortions, and abortions after fetal heartbeat or fetal pain can be detected; closing clinics via targeted regulation of abortion providers (TRAP laws), including requiring that clinics employ doctors who have hospital admitting privileges, conduct special procedures, and maintain unnecessary equipment; imposing mandatory counseling, vaginal ultrasounds, waiting periods, and involvement of pregnant teens' parents; and limiting medication abortions and private insurance coverage for the procedure. Only after the Texas TRAP statute threatened to shut down almost all clinics in the state did the U.S. Supreme Court, in *Whole Women's Health v. Hellerstedt* (2016), find an unconstitutional burden on women's rights.

The controversial Hyde Amendment, banning federal funding of abortions except in very limited circumstances, has survived for two more decades. Most states continue to refuse Medicaid payments for abortion services, and many states fund pregnancy crisis centers aimed at discouraging women from seeking abortions. The 2010 Patient Protection and Affordable Care Act ("ACA") became a missed opportunity for challenging the Hyde Amendment and making abortion and other reproductive health services universally accessible. Nor has the U.S. Supreme Court reconsidered its 1980 decision, *Harris v. McRae*, which upholds the constitutionality of Hyde despite its blatant discrimination against women.

Black women have been at the center of the contemporary battle around abortion rights. To begin with, Black women have the highest abortion rates because they are the most likely to have an unintended pregnancy. According to the Centers for Disease Control and Prevention, Black women account for 36 percent of abortions in the United States, although Blacks comprise less than 13 percent of the national population.[6] Black women, because they are disproportionately cash poor and face a host of structural barriers to accessing reproductive health services, are more likely to be deterred by restrictive abortion laws—and to risk injury and death as a result, both from unsafe pregnancies and unsafe abortions. For decades, Black women have died of pregnancy-related complications at far higher rates than white women and are now suffering the most from an escalating maternal mortality crisis.[7]

Black women's abortions also became a contentious tool of anti-abortion advocates. In February 2011, for Black History Month, the nonprofit antiabortion organizations Life Always and thatsabortion .com erected a giant billboard at the intersection of Sixth Avenue and Watts Street in New York City's Soho neighborhood.[8] The billboard displayed the image of a six-year-old African American girl beneath the words: "THE MOST DANGEROUS PLACE FOR AN AFRICAN AMERICAN IS IN THE WOMB." The billboard appeared during a nationwide campaign by the right-wing Radiance Foundation, which placed more than one hundred similar billboards targeting Black women in Arkansas, Atlanta, Chicago, Milwaukee, Los Angeles, and Texas. The campaign argued for defunding Planned Parenthood, accusing the group and its founder, Margaret Sanger, of committing genocide by locating its clinics in Black neighborhoods. Antiabortion legislators made political hay of the claim that abortion is a form of Black genocide: they introduced laws that banned race-selective abortions. The failed

Susan B. Anthony and Frederick Douglass Prenatal Nondiscrimina-tion Act (PreNDA), introduced in Congress in 2012 by Trent Franks (R-AZ), served as a model for state legislation that criminalized abor-tions provided to women of color supposedly because of the race or sex of the fetus.[9]

Far from grasping the dangers of the eugenics era, the abortion-as-black-genocide argument distorted that movement's history and, in fact, promoted its racist ideology. The billboards' statements declaring Black women's wombs unsafe recalled eugenicist rhetoric advocating sterilization of women deemed unfit to bear children. The antiabortion rhetoric diverted attention from the structural causes of racial disparities in abortion rates—poverty, lack of access to contraception, and inad-equate sex education—that result in unwanted pregnancies. Instead, the campaign demonized Black women by blaming them for "genocide" against their own communities and by suggesting they are incapable of making their own reproductive decisions.

SisterSong Women of Color Reproductive Justice Collective, SPARK Reproductive Justice NOW, Black Women's Health Impera-tive, and other Black women's organizations swiftly responded to the antiabortion campaign by forming the Trust Black Women Partner-ship. The partnership applied pressure that succeeded in bringing down many of the billboards, staving off the race-selective abortion bans, and sending the message that Black women should be trusted to make deci-sions for themselves, their families, and their communities.

The unified right-wing strategy of turning pregnant women into crim-inals while shutting down access to abortion services is now crystal clear. Women are arrested both for stillbirths and attempted abortions under the same laws—laws that were honed at the expense of Black women. Recent years have also uncovered more evidence of past sterilization abuse of Black women and its continuing presence in state programs. In 2013, North Carolina became the first state to pass a law providing monetary compensation for survivors of forced sterilizations after it was revealed that the state's Eugenics Board had approved the sterilizations of more than seven thousand people between 1933 and 1976.[10] In its final decade of operation, the board victimized primarily Black women receiv-ing public assistance. Meanwhile, an investigative report published in July 2013 disclosed a program of unapproved and coerced steriliza-tions of women incarcerated in California state prisons. The physician in charge, Dr. James Heinrich, justified spending $147,460 on the pro-cedures over a ten-year period "compared to what you save in welfare paying for these unwanted children—as they procreated more."[11]

SYSTEMIC PUNISHMENT OF BLACK MOTHERS
AND THE U.S. POLITICAL REGIME

Killing the Black Body focuses on how a sustained assault on Black women's childbearing has shaped the meaning of reproductive freedom in America. Since its publication, I have thought more about how this assault is critical to the entire U.S. political order. My work in the last twenty years has examined how the contemporary intersection of the welfare, prison, and foster care systems in Black mothers' lives not only extends the history I wrote about in this book but also works to bolster the white supremacist, patriarchal, and capitalist regime in the United States in a neoliberal age.[12] State regulation of Black women's bodies, already devalued by a long history of reproductive regulation and derogatory stereotypes of maternal irresponsibility, makes excessive policing by punitive state systems seem necessary in order to protect the public from harm. Blaming Black mothers for structural inequities has the added effect of obscuring the need for radical social change.

In *Killing the Black Body*, I described how the Personal Responsibility and Work Opportunity Reconciliation Act of 1996 (PRWORA) relied on stereotypes of Black women, especially the "Welfare Queen," that were at once sexist and racist—and implemented policies targeted specifically at them as the vilified beneficiaries of state largess. Key to these policies are workfare rules that force recipients into low-wage jobs, as well as provisions punishing their childbearing and pressuring them to get married. As Black women gained welfare rights in the 1960s and composed a larger and larger share of recipients, benefits became stingier, more stigmatized, and tied to harsher regulation. In 1996, welfare ceased being an entitlement and became instead a behavior modification program to control the sexual and reproductive decisions of cash poor mothers.[13]

Once the 1996 law was in place, more states rushed to enact "child exclusions" or "family caps" that aim to deter women receiving public assistance from having babies by denying them any increment in their benefits, infringing on their reproductive autonomy and denying their families income needed to survive. By 1999, twenty states with caps "contained about half of the national TANF [Temporary Assistance to Needy Families] caseload and roughly half of all poor families with children."[14] Congress noted in its 2001 TANF reauthorization bill that "[s]tates in which African Americans make up a higher proportion of recipients are statistically more likely to adopt family cap policies," and studies have found that caps influenced Black women's reproductive decisions the most out of all women. Challenges from reproductive justice, civil liberties, and civil rights organizations have pushed several states to repeal their benefits caps, but progress is slow. California ended its cap, called the Maximum Family Grant rule, in June 2016—increasing the monthly payment for an additional child, but only by about $130.[15]

Like welfare, the prison and foster care systems are marked by glaring race, gender, and class disparities.[16] Poor and low-income Black mothers are disproportionately involved in both systems. Thousands of Black women in prison today—mostly for nonviolent offenses—need treatment for substance abuse, support for their children, or safety from violent relationships, not criminal punishment. Locking up astronomical numbers of Black men and women is a powerful way of restricting reproductive liberty and transferring political inequality to the next generation.

Prisons cruelly devalue incarcerated mothers by shackling pregnant inmates during childbirth. In many states, when incarcerated women go into labor, they are shackled to the hospital bed, their legs, wrists, and abdomens chained during the entire delivery of their babies.[17] In the vast majority of states, inmates' newborns are automatically placed in foster care immediately after delivery. Moreover, federal law governing child welfare practice encourages the termination of incarcerated mothers' parental rights, and local policies do too little to keep these mothers in contact with their children or to support their families after they are released from prison. On the contrary, the collateral penalties routinely inflicted on convicted women, including monetary sanctions and bans on welfare benefits, public housing, post-secondary financial aid, and professional licenses, place affirmative barriers to maintaining a relationship with their children.[18]

If you go into dependency court in Chicago, New York, or San Francisco without any preconceptions about its purpose, you might conclude that the child welfare system is designed to monitor, regulate, and punish Black mothers. The 1996 abolition of the welfare safety net coincided with the passage of the Adoption and Safe Families Act (ASFA) in 1997, which emphasized adoption as the solution to the rising foster care population. ASFA was promoted by racially explicit appeals to "free" Black children for adoption by speeding up termination of their mothers' rights. By attributing Black families' hardships to maternal deficits, the child welfare system hides their systemic causes, devalues Black children's bonds with their families, and prescribes foster care and adoption in place of resources and social change. The scale of the multibillion-dollar foster care apparatus, which entails extreme disruption and surveillance of families, is often overlooked, but it is a vital aspect of the U.S. neoliberal carceral state that brutally intervenes in the very communities most devastated by the evisceration of public resources.

THE RACIAL BIOPOLITICS OF HIGH-TECH REPRODUCTION: A NEW REPRODUCTIVE DYSTOPIA?

Killing the Black Body contrasted policies that penalize Black women's childbearing with the high-tech fertility industry that mainly promotes childbearing by more affluent white women. Later, I tied them together in relation to a neoliberal trend of placing reproductive duties on women that privatize remedies for illness and social inequities. Like punishment of Black women's childbearing, pressure to use reproduction assisting technologies that involve genetic selection—reprogenetics—also shifts responsibility for promoting well-being from government to individual women by making them responsible for ensuring the genetic fitness of their children.[19] I also reconsidered reproductive dystopia scenarios that had cast white women as the only consumers of reproductive technologies. The recent expansion of both reproductive genetic screening and race-based biomedicine signals a dramatic change in the racial politics of reproductive technologies.[20]

To be sure, the racist assumption that whiteness, intelligence, and talent are connected and hereditary remains robust in the reprogenetic industry. Black babies still figure in media coverage of high-tech reproduction only in sperm bank mix-up stories that portray them as defective merchandise precisely because of their race.[21] But some clinics that offer high-tech reproductive services now explicitly appeal to clients of color. As more people of color buy and sell reprogenetic goods and services, race is considered an essential way of grouping reproductive commodities. Advertisements on Craigslist, for example, explicitly solicit egg donors by race and ethnicity. Happy Beginnings, LLC, advertised, "Egg Donors Wanted All Ethnic Backgrounds," specifying, "We have a very high demand for Jewish, East Indian, Middle Eastern, Asian, Italian, and blonde donors."

Moreover, the expanding role of genetic screening, which makes women responsible for ensuring the health of their children by reducing genetic risk, may support the wider incorporation of reprogenetic technologies into the neoliberal health care system. Cash poor women, especially Black women, currently face financial and other barriers to receiving reproduction assisting services, such as in vitro fertilization

(IVF). Because genetic screening is now considered an essential part of preventive medicine, however, these technologies are becoming integrated into social welfare systems and private insurance schemes and are likely to become increasingly available to low-income women. It is not hard to imagine a regime in the near future that integrates prenatal genetic screening into social welfare systems so everyone, including Black women, are encouraged to select out certain disfavored traits. Unlike IVF, whose primary purpose is to increase fertility, genetic screening aims to avoid having a baby or starting a pregnancy with undesirable genes. Reprogenetics incorporates a seemingly benign form of eugenicist thinking in its reliance on reproductive strategies to eliminate genetic risk, rather than social strategies to eliminate structural inequities, including discrimination against people with disabilities.

The expectation of genetic self-regulation may fall especially harshly on Black women, who are stereotypically defined as hyperfertile and lacking the capacity for self-control. The neoliberal reification of market logic is also likely to support paying these women to gestate fetuses or to produce eggs for genetic research, even as they are encouraged to use genetic technologies to screen their own children. Thus, a reproductive dystopia for the twenty-first century can no longer exclude Black women from the market for high-tech reprogenetics. Their inclusion does not eradicate the racial hierarchy underlying today's reproductive caste system that values some women's childbearing more than others'; rather, it transplants racial hierarchy into the high-tech genomic age.

TOWARD NEW SUNS: REPRODUCTIVE JUSTICE

I concluded *Killing the Black Body* by proposing a "radical vision of reproductive justice." I called on theorists "to explore how social justice could be made central to their conception of rights, of harms, and of the value of procreation." At the time I wrote those words, a movement led by women of color reproductive health activists was forming—a movement grounded in a long legacy of women of color organizing for reproductive freedom, health equity, and racial justice.[22]

A caucus of Black feminists at a 1994 pro-choice conference coined the term "reproductive justice," a framework that included not only the human right not to have a child, but also the right to have children and to raise them with dignity in safe, healthy, and supportive environments. For too long, the rhetoric of "choice" had privileged predominantly white middle-class women who have had the ability to choose from reproductive options that are unavailable to low-income women and women of color. The caucus's 1994 framework positioned reproductive rights in a political context of intersecting race, gender, and class oppressions. The caucus recognized that their activism had to be linked to social justice organizing in order to gain the power, resources, and structural changes needed for improving the well-being of all women. SisterSong Women of Color Reproductive Health (now Justice) Collective, founded in 1997, pulled together a national coalition of sixteen women of color health organizations to put the reproductive justice framework into action.

I remember being filled with euphoric confidence that we would win the battle for reproductive freedom when I linked arms with Black women activists at a march in Washington, D.C., in 2004.[23] My elation stemmed partly from SisterSong's success in shifting the march's focus from "choice" to "social justice." This shift was dramatically symbolized by deleting the words "freedom of choice" from the march's original name — Save Women's Lives: March for Freedom of Choice — to rename it the March for Women's Lives. SisterSong, Black Women's Health Imperative, National Latina Institute for Reproductive Health, and National Asian Pacific American Women's Forum brought a reproductive justice approach to the march's leadership and helped to mobilize busloads of newly energized, diverse supporters, making the march one of the largest of its kind in U.S. history.

In one sense, reproductive justice has enjoyed a remarkable rise in the consciousness of activists and scholars alike. Zakiya Luna and Kristin Luker found numerous examples of its adoption: "altered titles of law school courses, new research centers at major universities, and the outlines of a coherent field of scholarship on the topic," as well as public claims by established pro-choice organizations that their work is in line with a reproductive justice approach.[24] A Google search of the term in 2007 yielded more than 1.2 million hits.[25]

Yet a resilient pernicious strain of thinking within liberal politics continues to view birth control as a primary means of addressing problems like poverty, overpopulation, and environmental protection. On one hand, the right has recently exploited the history of eugenics to falsely portray abortion as a form of Black "genocide." On the other hand, however, the left has yet to purge its advocacy of family planning of some of its racist and eugenicist roots, still promoting birth control as a way to save taxpayer money spent on unintended, welfare-dependent children, rather than a way for women to have greater control over their lives. For example, public health experts have recently recommended increased use of provider-controlled long-acting reversible contraception (LARC) by "at risk" Black and Latina teens in order to reduce poverty, high school drop-out rates, and Medicaid costs. Framing birth control as a cost-reducing and problem-solving measure masks its potential for racial and class bias and coercion, as well as the structural inequities that are actually responsible for teen girls' limited opportunities.[26]

A social justice focus provides a concrete basis for building radical coalitions between reproductive rights activists and organizations fighting for racial, economic, and environmental justice, for immigrant, queer, and disabled people, and for systemic change in law enforcement, health care, and education.[27] True reproductive freedom requires a living wage, universal health care, and the abolition of prisons. Black women see the police slaughter of unarmed people in their communities as a reproductive justice issue. At their core, reproductive justice and Black Lives Matter both insist that U.S. society must begin to value Black people's humanity.

The great science fiction novelist Octavia Butler wrote, "There is nothing new under the sun, but there are new suns." In the face of withering state repression, the reproductive justice movement continues Black women's long struggle for liberation that has always pointed the way to new suns.

KILLING THE
BLACK BODY

Introduction

The painful, patient, and silent toil of mothers to gain a fee simple title to the bodies of their daughters, the despairing fight, as of an entrapped tigress, to keep hallowed their own persons, would furnish material for epics.

ANNA JULIA COOPER, 1893[1]

In 1989, officials in Charleston, South Carolina, initiated a policy of arresting pregnant women whose prenatal tests revealed they were smoking crack. In some cases, a team of police tracked down expectant mothers in the city's poorest neighborhoods. In others, officers invaded the maternity ward to haul away patients in handcuffs and leg irons, hours after giving birth. One woman spent the final weeks of pregnancy detained in a dingy cell in the Charleston County Jail. When she went into labor, she was transported in chains to the hospital, and remained shackled to the bed during the entire delivery. All but one of the four dozen women arrested for prenatal crimes in Charleston were Black.

We are in the midst of an explosion of rhetoric and policies that degrade Black women's reproductive decisions. Poor Black mothers are blamed for perpetuating social problems by transmitting defective genes, irreparable crack damage, and a deviant lifestyle to their children. A controversial editorial in the *Philadelphia Inquirer* suggested coerced contraception as a solution to the Black underclass. Noting that "[t]he main reason more black children are living in poverty is that the people having the most children are the ones least capable of supporting them," the editorial proposed reducing the number of children born to poor Black women by implanting them with the long-acting contraceptive Norplant. This thinking was supported by the best-selling book *The Bell Curve*, which claims that social disparities stem from the higher fertility rates of genetically less intelligent groups, including Blacks.

Along with this disparagement of Black motherhood, policymakers have initiated a new wave of reproductive regulation. The targeting of

Black women who use drugs during pregnancy is only one example. State legislatures across the country are considering measures designed to keep women on welfare from having babies—a goal also advanced by Newt Gingrich's Contract with America and then incorporated in the newly enacted federal welfare law. The plans range from denying benefits to children born to welfare mothers to mandatory insertion of Norplant as a condition of receiving aid. Many family-planning clinics, with the support of Medicaid, are already encouraging young Black women to keep the risky device implanted in their arms. The emerging agenda is reminiscent of government-sponsored programs as late as the 1970s that coerced poor Black women by the thousands into being sterilized. Meanwhile, a fertility business devoted to helping white middle-class couples to have children is booming.

How can we possibly confront racial injustice in America without tackling this assault on Black women's procreative freedom? How can we possibly talk about reproductive health policy without addressing race, as well as gender? Yet books on racial justice tend to neglect the subject of reproductive rights; and books on reproductive freedom tend to neglect the influence of race. Few, if any, have addressed the many dimensions of governmental regulation of Black women's childbearing or the impact this repression has had on the way Americans think about reproductive liberty.

The story I tell about reproductive rights differs dramatically from the standard one. In contrast to the account of American women's increasing control over their reproductive decisions, centered on the right to an abortion, this book describes a long experience of dehumanizing attempts to control Black women's reproductive lives. The systematic, institutionalized denial of reproductive freedom has uniquely marked Black women's history in America. Considering this history—from slave masters' economic stake in bonded women's fertility to the racist strains of early birth control policy to sterilization abuse of Black women during the 1960s and 1970s to the current campaign to inject Norplant and Depo-Provera in the arms of Black teenagers and welfare mothers—paints a powerful picture of the link between race and reproductive freedom in America.

Several years ago I spoke at a forum in a neighborhood church entitled "Civil Rights Under Attack: Recent Supreme Court Decisions," sponsored by several civil rights organizations. I chose to focus on how the Supreme Court's decision in *Webster v. Reproductive Health Services*, which weakened the holding in *Roe v. Wade* and denied women a right to abortion in publicly funded hospitals, hurt Black women. I linked the decision to a series of current attacks on Black women's reproductive autonomy, including the growing trend to prosecute poor Black mothers for smoking crack while pregnant. When it came time for questions, I was immediately assailed by a man in the audience for risking solidarity around racial issues by interjecting the controversial issue of reproduction. He thought it was dangerous to mention the word "abortion." He said that reproductive rights was a "white woman's issue," and he advised me to stick to traditional civil rights concerns, such as affirmative action, voting rights, and criminal justice.

While this man felt that the civil rights agenda should leave out reproductive health concerns, the mainstream reproductive rights agenda has neglected Black women's concerns. Public and scholarly debate about reproductive freedom has centered on abortion, often ignoring other important reproductive health policies that are most likely to affect Black women. Yet I came to grasp the importance of women's reproductive autonomy, not from the mainstream abortion rights movement, but from studying the lives of slave women, like those described by Anna Julia Cooper, who fought to retain control over their reproductive lives. The feminist focus on gender and identification of male domination as the source of reproductive repression often overlooks the importance of racism in shaping our understanding of reproductive liberty and the degree of "choice" that women really have.

I want this book to convince readers that reproduction is an important topic and that it is especially important to Black people. It is important not only because the policies I discuss keep Black women from having children but because these policies persuade people that racial inequality is perpetuated by Black people themselves. The belief that Black procreation is the problem remains a major barrier to radical change in America. It is my hope that by exposing its multiple reincarnations, this book will help to put this dangerous fallacy to rest. I also want this book to convince readers to think about reproduction in a new way. These policies affect not only Black Americans but also the very meaning of reproductive freedom.

My objective is to place these issues in their broader political context by exploring how the denial of Black reproductive autonomy serves the interests of white supremacy. I am also interested in the way in which the dominant understanding of reproductive rights has been shaped by racist assumptions about Black procreation. Three central themes, then, run through the chapters of this book. The first is that *regulating Black women's reproductive decisions has been a central aspect of racial oppression in America*. Not only do these policies injure individual Black women, but they also are a principal means of justifying the perpetuation of a racist social structure. Second, *the control of Black women's reproduction has shaped the meaning of reproductive liberty in America*. The traditional understanding of reproductive freedom has had to accommodate practices that blatantly deny Black women control over critical decisions about their bodies. Highlighting the racial dimensions of contemporary debates such as welfare reform, the safety of Norplant, public funding of abortion, and the morality of new reproductive technologies is like shaking up a kaleidoscope and taking another look.

Finally, in light of the first two themes, *we need to reconsider the meaning of reproductive liberty to take into account its relationship to racial oppression*. While Black women's stories are sometimes inserted as an aside in deliberations about reproductive issues, I place them at the center of this reconstructive project. How does Black women's experience change the current interpretation of reproductive freedom? The dominant notion of reproductive liberty is flawed in several ways. It is limited by the liberal ideals of individual autonomy and freedom from government interference; it is primarily concerned with the interests of white, middle-class women; and it is focused on the right to abortion. The full extent of many Americans' conception of reproductive freedom is the Constitution's protection against laws that ban abortion. I suggest an expanded and less individualistic conception of reproductive liberty that recognizes control of reproduction as a critical means of racial oppression and liberation in America. I do not deny the importance of autonomy over one's own reproductive life, but I also recognize that reproductive policy affects the status of entire groups. Reproductive liberty must encompass more than the protection of an individual woman's choice to end her pregnancy. It must encompass the full range of procreative activities, including the ability to bear a child, and it must acknowledge that we make reproductive decisions within a social context, including inequalities of wealth and power. *Reproductive freedom is a matter of social justice*, not individual choice.

Black women's earliest experience in America was one of brutal denial of autonomy over reproduction. In Chapter 1, I describe the exploitation of slave women's capacity to produce more slaves and the denial of their rights as mothers. After Emancipation, racism continued to corrupt notions of reproductive liberty, helping to direct the birth control movement which emerged early in this century. Chapter 2 explores the alliances between birth control advocates and eugenicists during the 1920s and 1930s, as well as the rampant sterilization abuse of Black women in later decades. It also considers the debate about family planning and genocide that took place within the Black community throughout this period. In Chapters 3 through 5, I demonstrate that a panoply of policies continue to degrade Black women's reproductive decisions. Plans to distribute Norplant in Black communities as a means of addressing their poverty, law enforcement practices that penalize Black women for bearing a child, and welfare reform measures that cut off assistance for children born to welfare mothers all proclaim the same message: The key to solving America's social problems is to curtail Black women's birth rates. In Chapter 6, I argue that race also determines the use and popularity of technologies designed to enable people to have children.

Finally, Chapter 7 presents a reconception of liberty that takes into account this relationship between race and reproduction. The book ends by proposing an approach to reproductive rights that acknowledges the complementary and overlapping qualities of the Constitution's guarantees of liberty and equality. This approach recognizes the connection between the dehumanization of the individual and the repression of the group. It provides a positive claim to state support for poor women's procreative decisions that counters proposals to cut funding both for children born to women on welfare and for abortion. It also adds a compelling dimension to the feminist claim that reproductive liberty is essential to women's political and social citizenship. Thus, I hope to show that, while racism has perverted dominant notions of reproductive freedom, the quest to secure Black women's reproductive autonomy can transform the meaning of liberty for everyone.

The greatest risk in writing a book about reproductive domination is that it will leave the false impression that Black women have been no more than passive puppets in a unidimensional plot to control their actions. I try to avoid that perception by showing throughout this book Black women's activism in the struggle to control their own bodies. The full story of Black women's resistance and its impact on the national movement for reproductive freedom is long overdue. As Anna Julia Cooper recognized a century ago, this "fight, as of an entrapped tigress, . . . would furnish material for epics."

"BEARERS OF 'INCURABLE IMMORALITY'"

Before turning to the history of reproductive regulation, it is important to recognize the images of Black women that form its backdrop. America has always viewed unregulated Black reproduction as dangerous. For three centuries, Black mothers have been thought to pass down to their offspring the traits that marked them as inferior to any white person. Along with this biological impairment, it is believed that Black mothers transfer a deviant lifestyle to their children that dooms each succeeding generation to a life of poverty, delinquency, and despair. A persistent objective of American social policy has been to monitor and restrain this corrupting tendency of Black motherhood.

Regulating Black women's fertility seems so imperative because of the powerful stereotypes that propel these policies. A popular mythology that portrays Black women as unfit to be mothers has left a lasting impression on the American psyche. Although these attitudes are not universally held, they influence the way many Americans think about reproduction. Myths are more than made-up stories. They are also firmly held beliefs that represent and attempt to explain what we perceive to be the truth. They can become more credible than reality, holding fast even in the face of airtight statistics and rational argument to the contrary. American culture is replete with derogatory icons of Black women—Jezebel, Mammy, Tragic Mulatto, Aunt Jemima, Sapphire, Matriarch, and Welfare Queen. Over the centuries these myths have made Black women seem like "nothing more than the bearers of 'incurable immorality.'"[2] In this introduction, I focus on those images that have justified the restrictions on Black women's childbearing explored in subsequent chapters.

Reproduction as Degeneracy

The degrading mythology about Black mothers is one aspect of a complex set of stereotypes that deny Black humanity in order to rationalize white supremacy.[3] The white founding fathers justified their exclusion of Blacks from the new republic by imbuing them with a set of attributes that made them unfit for citizenship. The men who crafted the nation's government, such as Thomas Jefferson, claimed that Blacks lacked the capacity for rational thought, independence, and self-control that was essential for self-governance.[4] Racist thinking dictates that Black bodies, intellect, character, and culture are all inherently vulgar.[5] It reflects a pattern of oppositional categories in which whites are associated with positive characteristics (industrious, intelligent, responsible), while Blacks are associated with the opposite, negative qualities (lazy, ignorant, shiftless).[6] These disparaging stereotypes of Black people all proclaim a common message: it is the depraved, self-perpetuating character of Blacks themselves that leads to their inferior social status.

Scientific racism understands racial variation as a biological distinction that determines superiority and inferiority.[7] Only a theory rooted in nature could systematically account for the anomaly of slavery existing in a republic founded on a radical commitment to liberty, equality, and natural rights. Whites invented the hereditary trait of race and endowed it with the concept of racial superiority and inferiority to resolve the contradiction between slavery and liberty. Scientific racism explained domination by one group over another as the natural order of things: Blacks were biologically destined to be slaves, and whites were destined to be their masters. It also forged an indelible link between race and policies governing reproduction. Because race was defined as an inheritable trait, preserving racial distinctions required policing reproduction. *Reproductive politics in America inevitably involves racial politics.*

As both biological and social reproducers, it is only natural that Black mothers would be a key focus of this racist ideology. White childbearing is generally thought to be a beneficial activity: it brings personal joy and allows the nation to flourish. Black reproduction, on the other hand, is treated as a form of *degeneracy*. Black mothers are seen to corrupt the reproduction process at every stage. Black mothers, it is believed, transmit inferior physical traits to the product of conception through their genes. They damage their babies in the womb through their bad habits during pregnancy. Then they impart a deviant lifestyle to their children through their example. This damaging behavior on the part of Black mothers—not arrangements of power—explains the persistence of Black poverty and marginality. Thus it warrants strict measures to control Black women's childbearing rather than wasting resources on useless social programs.

George Frederickson's description of the rationale for Jim Crow laws parallels the welfare and crime reform rhetoric we hear today:

> If the blacks were a degenerating race with no future, the problem ceased to be one of how to prepare them for citizenship or

even how to make them more productive and useful members of the community. The new prognosis pointed rather to the need to segregate or quarantine a race liable to be a source of contamination and social danger to the white community, as it sank ever deeper into the slough of disease, vice, and criminality.[8]

Blaming Black mothers, then, is a way of subjugating the Black race as a whole. At the same time, devaluing motherhood is particularly damaging to Black women. As Simone de Beauvoir wrote in *The Second Sex*, "It was as Mother that woman was fearsome; it is in maternity that she must be transfigured and enslaved." [9] Being a mother is considered a woman's major social role. Society defines all women as mothers or potential mothers. Motherhood is compulsory for women: most little girls expect to become mothers, and women who do not are considered deviant. Because women have been defined in terms of motherhood, devaluing this aspect of a woman's identity is especially devastating. It cuts to the heart of what it means to be valued as a woman.

Jezebel and the Immoral Black Mother

From the moment they set foot in this country as slaves, Black women have fallen outside the American ideal of womanhood.[10] This contradiction became especially pronounced during the Victorian era. The nineteenth-century image of the True Woman was delicate, refined, and chaste. Although she was considered physically and intellectually inferior to men, she was morally superior to them. She was perfectly suited to the home, where she served as mother and wife. All of her attributes were precisely the opposite of those that characterized Black women. "Judged by the evolving nineteenth-century ideology of femininity," Black activist Angela Davis observed, "Black women were practically anomalies." [11]

Not only were Black women exiled from the norm of true womanhood, but their maternity was blamed for Black people's problems. Contrary to the ideal white mother, Black mothers had their own repertory of images that portrayed them as immoral, careless, domineering, and devious.

One of the most prevalent images of slave women was the character of Jezebel, named after the biblical wife of King Ahab. Jezebel was a purely lascivious creature: not only was she governed by her erotic desires, but her sexual prowess led men to wanton passion.[12] As early as 1736, the South Carolina *Gazette* described "African Ladies" as women "of 'strong robust constitution' who were 'not easily jaded out' but able to serve their lovers 'by Night as well as Day.' " Jezebel was diametrically opposed to the prevailing vision of the True Woman, who was chaste, pure, and white. As an unidentified Southern white woman wrote in *The Independent* in 1904, "I cannot imagine such a creature as a virtuous black woman." [13] This construct of the licentious temptress served to justify white men's sexual abuse of Black women. The stereotype of Black women as sexually promiscuous also defined them as bad mothers.

The myth of the lascivious Black woman was systematically perpetuated after slavery ended.[14] While white women were placed on moral pedestals, "[e]very black woman was, by definition, a slut according to this racist mythology," writes historian Gerda Lerner. Lerner notes a number of practices that reinforced this view: "the laws against intermarriage; the denial of the title 'Miss' or 'Mrs.' to any black woman; the taboos against respectable social mixing of the races; the refusal to let black women customers try on clothing in stores before making a purchase; the assigning of a single toilet to both sexes of Blacks." [15]

Historian Philip A. Bruce's book *The Plantation Negro as a Freeman*, published in 1889, strengthened popular views of both Black male and Black female degeneracy. True to the "retrogressionist" ideology of the time, Bruce argued that, without the moral discipline imposed by slave masters, free Blacks were regressing to their naturally immoral state.[16] He devoted two chapters to an exposition of Black women's lascivious impulses, which he claimed had been loosened by Emancipation. Bruce explained Blacks' sexual promiscuity by the fact that "the procreative instinct being the most passionate that nature has implanted" was especially potent in Negroes. He traced the alleged propensity of the Black man to rape white women to "the sexual laxness of plantation women as a class." [17] According to Bruce, Black men lacked any understanding of sexual violation because their women were always eager to engage in sex.

Bruce explicitly tied Black women's sexual impurity to their dangerous mothering. He reasoned that Black women's promiscuity not only provoked Black men to rape white women but also led the entire Black family into depravity. Black women raised their children to follow their own licentious lifestyle: "[T]heir mothers do not endeavor to teach them, systematically, those moral lessons that they peculiarly need as members of the female sex; they learn to sew in a rude way, to wash, to iron, and to cook, but no principle is steadily instilled that makes them solicitous and resolute to preserve their reputations untarnished." [18] Because it was women who "really molded the institution of marriage among the plantation negroes," Bruce explained, "to them its present degradation is chiefly ascribable." Other authors of the period similarly blamed the immoral example set by Black mothers for Black criminality. For example, Howard Odum, a professor at the University of North Carolina, wrote a chapter, "The Home Life, Diseases and Morals of the Negro," in which he attributed Blacks' poor home life partly to the sexual and domestic laxity of Black mothers.[19] Decadent Black mothers, then, were responsible for the menace that Blacks posed for American social order.

A corollary of the myth of Black promiscuity is the belief that Black women procreate with abandon. According to a prominent treatise on reproductive behavior published in 1958, most Blacks regarded "coitus . . . as [an] inevitable, natural, and desirable activity to be enjoyed both in and out of marriage; contraception is little known and considered at best a nuisance and at worst dangerous or unnatural; and pregnancy is accepted as an inevitable part of life." [20]

The myth of Black people's innate hyperfertility has been given currency by J. Philippe Rushton, a psychology professor at the University of Western Ontario. In *Race, Evolution, and Behavior: A Life History Perspective*, recently reviewed with *The Bell Curve* in the *New York Times Book Review*, Rushton traces the evolutionary origins of physical differences between the races, including brain and genital size.[21] Blacks adapted to Africa's unpredictable environment, he argues, by developing high fertility rates, bearing more children but nurturing each one less. Rushton claims that Black women ovulate more often and mature sexually faster than white women while "sperm competition" among sexually indiscriminate Black males "leads to enlarged penises and testes to make deeper and more voluminous ejaculations possible." Rushton denied he was a racist to *Rolling Stone* reporter Adam Miller, saying, "it's a trade-off; more brain or more penis. You can't have everything." [22] While Rushton's propositions may be extreme, the view of unrestrained Black childbearing is commonly held and bolsters efforts to impose family-planning regimes on Black communities. Lacking the inclination to control their own fertility, it is thought, Black women require government regulation.

Mammy and the Negligent Black Mother

If the "bad" Black Jezebel represented the opposite of the ideal mother, the asexual and maternal Mammy was the embodiment of the ideal Black woman. The image of Mammy was based on the Black female house servant who cared for her master's children. Pictured as rotund and handkerchiefed, Mammy was both the perfect mother and the perfect slave: whites saw her as a "passive nurturer, a mother figure who gave all without expectation of return, who not only acknowledged her inferiority to whites but who loved them."[23] It is important to recognize, however, that Mammy did not reflect any virtue in Black motherhood. The ideology of Mammy placed no value on Black women as the mothers of their own children. Rather, whites claimed Mammy's total devotion to the master's children, without regard to the fate of Mammy's own offspring. What's more, Mammy, while she cared for the master's children, remained under the constant supervision of her white mistress.[24] She had no real authority over either the white children she raised or the Black children she bore.

During the Jim Crow era, Mammy became a cult figure. In a period of brutal racial repression her image served as a valuable symbol of a good Black woman. White citizens created a "Black Mammy Memorial Association" in Athens, Georgia, in 1910 to solicit support for a Black vocational school modeled after Booker T. Washington's Tuskegee Institute. The association's promotional pamphlet asked, "Did you not have an 'Old Black Mammy' who loved and cared for you?" The "Black Mammy Memorial Institute," named by the chancellor of the University of Georgia, was established to train the Negro "in the arts and industries that made the 'old Black Mammy' valuable and worthy . . . where men and women learn to work, how to work and to love their work."[25]

Mammy also appeared in great American novels, including works by Washington Irving, James Fenimore Cooper, William Faulkner, and Robert Penn Warren. She was embodied in Aunt Jemima for the Chicago Columbia Exposition in 1893 and appeared on pancake boxes for decades.[26] Perhaps the best evidence of Mammy's rise to cult figure status was her prominence in American motion pictures, which usually portrayed her as inept, subservient, and comical.[27] Hattie McDaniel won an Oscar for her memorable 1939 performance as Scarlett O'Hara's Mammy in *Gone with the Wind*.

While whites adored Mammy, who dutifully nurtured white children, they portrayed Black slave mothers as careless and unable to care for their *own* children. Whites described Black women as bad mothers not only because of immorality but also because of incompetence. The scapegoating of Black mothers dates back to slavery days, when mothers were blamed for the devastating effects of bondage on their children. When a one-month-old slave girl named Harriet died in the Abbeville District of South Carolina on December 9, 1849, the census marshal reported the cause of death as "[s]mothered by carelessness of [her] mother." [28] This report's attribution of a Black infant death to accidental suffocation by the mother was typical of the U.S. census mortality schedules in the South. Census marshal Charles M. Pelot explained: "I wish it to be distinctly understood that nearly all the accidents occur in the negro population, which goes clearly to prove their great carelessness & total inability to take care of themselves." It now appears that the true cause of these deaths was infant illness, due to the hard physical work, poor nutrition, and abuse that their mothers endured during pregnancy.[29]

Whites believed that Black mothers needed the moral guidance that slavery once afforded. Eleanor Tayleur, for example, argued that deprived of the intimate contact with their morally superior white mistresses, freed Black women displayed uncontrolled passion and ignorance. "The modern negro woman," Tayleur complained, "has no such object-lesson in morality or modesty, and she wants none." According to Tayleur, Black women exhibited a purely animal passion toward their children, which often led to horrible abuses:

When they are little, she indulges them blindly when she is in good humor, and beats them cruelly when she is angry; and once past their childhood her affection for them appears to be exhausted. She exhibits none of the brooding mother-love and anxiety which the white woman sends after her children as long as they live. Infanticide is not regarded as a crime among negroes, but it is so appallingly common that if the statistics could be obtained on this subject they would send a shudder through the world.[30]

The conception of Black women as unfit for motherhood was reinforced by their working lives. The virtuous mother depended on her husband for support, while women who worked for wages were considered deviant and neglectful. The conception of motherhood confined to the home and opposed to wage labor never applied to Black women. While Victorian roles required white women to be nurturing mothers, dutiful housekeepers, and gentle companions to their husbands, slave women's role required backbreaking work in the fields.

Even after Emancipation, political and economic conditions forced many Black mothers to earn a living outside the home.[31] At the turn of the century nearly all Black women worked long days as sharecroppers, laundresses, or domestic servants in white people's homes. There was a dramatic racial disparity among married women who worked for wages at that time. In 1870, in the rural South, more than 40 percent of married Black women had jobs, mostly as field laborers, while over 98 percent of white wives were homemakers.[32] In Southern cities, Black married women worked outside the home five times more often than white married women.

The demands of work within white homes undermined Black women's own roles as mothers and homemakers.[33] Black domestics returned home late at night (if not on weekends alone) and had to entrust their young children to the care of a neighbor, relative, or older sibling. Sometimes older children had to be left to wander the neighborhood. The great civil rights leader W. E. B. Du Bois, a passionate defender of Black women's honor, recognized the irony of Mammy's care for white children rather than her own. "Let the present-day mammies suckle their own children. Let them walk in the sunshine with their own toddling boys and girls and put their own sleepy little brothers and sisters to bed," he declared in a 1912 issue of his monthly paper, *The Crisis*.[34] Americans have expected Black mothers to look like Aunt Jemima—dressed in an apron and headrag and working in a white family's kitchen. American culture reveres no Black madonna. It upholds no popular image of a Black mother tenderly nurturing her child.

The Matriarch and the Black Unwed Mother

White sociologists during the 1920s and 1930s elaborated on the theory of a Negro pathology stemming from sexual depravity by focusing on family structure. Sociological studies of Black family life claimed that Black women's independence promoted Black male jealousy and irresponsibility.[35] In *The Negro Family in the United States*, Black sociologist E. Franklin Frazier reiterated the thesis that dominant Black women, by perpetuating the slave legacy of unwed motherhood, were the cause of family instability.[36] Frazier saw Black people's redemption in their adoption of white family patterns. These sociologists held Black families up against a white middle-class model and declared that they were defective.

This theory was reincarnated in the 1960s in the myth of the Black matriarch, the domineering female head of the Black family. White sociologists once again held Black mothers responsible for the disintegration of the Black family and the consequent failure of Black people to achieve success in America. This thinking held that Black matriarchs damaged their families in two ways: they demoralized Black men and they transmitted a pathological lifestyle to their children, perpetuating poverty and antisocial behavior from one generation to the next.

Daniel Patrick Moynihan popularized this thesis in his 1965 report, *The Negro Family: The Case for National Action.*[37] Moynihan, then assistant secretary of labor and director of the Office of Policy Planning and Research under President Lyndon Johnson, argued that reforming the Black family was vital to President Johnson's War on Poverty. Playing on the theme of degeneracy, Moynihan described Black culture as a "tangle of pathology" that is "capable of perpetuating itself without assistance from the white world." The chief culprit, Moynihan asserted, was Blacks' matriarchal family structure. According to Moynihan:

> At the heart of the deterioration of the fabric of the Negro society is the deterioration of the Negro family. It is the fundamental cause of the weakness of the Negro community. . . . In essence, the Negro community has been forced into a matriarchal structure, which, because it is so out of line with the rest of the American society, seriously retards the progress of the group as a whole.

Moynihan thus endowed poor Black women—the most subordinated members of society—with the power of a matriarch.

The last two decades have witnessed a revival of this castigation of Black single mothers. In a 1986 CBS special report, "The Vanishing Family: Crisis in Black America," host Bill Moyers lent liberal authority to Americans' fears about the moral depravity of Black childbearing.[38] The report featured scenes from a housing project in Newark, where young welfare mothers and the estranged fathers of their children epitomized the Black stereotypes of sexual promiscuity and laziness. Recent rhetoric casts single motherhood literally as the cause of all social problems. According to American Enterprise Institute fellow Charles Murray, "Illegitimacy is the most important social problem of our time—more important than crime, drugs, poverty, illiteracy, welfare, or homelessness because it drives everything else." [39] Former education secretary William Bennett called it "the single most destructive social pathology in modern American society." [40]

While Blacks have the highest rate of unwed motherhood, the rate among whites has grown most dramatically, from 3 percent to 22 percent since 1965.[41] Today, there are more white babies than Black babies born to single mothers. Still, single motherhood is viewed as a Black cultural trait that is creeping into white homes. "White illegitimacy was generally not perceived as a 'cultural' or racial defect, or as a public expense, so the stigma suffered by the white unwed mother was individual and familial," Rickie Solinger observes in her history of single pregnancy between World War II and *Roe v. Wade*.[42] Black unwed motherhood, on the other hand, was seen as a major social problem: "Black women, illegitimately pregnant, were not shamed but simply blamed. . . . There was no redemption possible for these women, only the retribution of sterilization, harassment by welfare officials, and public policies that threatened to starve them." Charles Murray hammered in this point in his *Wall Street Journal* editorial, "The Coming White Underclass," which warns white Americans that their rising illegitimacy rate threatens to spread to white neighborhoods the same crime, drugs, and "drop out from the labor force" that now infects Black communities.[43]

The Welfare Queen and the Devious Black Mother

The myths about immoral, neglectful, and domineering Black mothers have been supplemented by the contemporary image of the welfare queen—the lazy mother on public assistance who deliberately breeds children at the expense of taxpayers to fatten her monthly check. The picture of reckless Black fertility is made all the more frightening by a more devious notion of Black women's childbearing. Poor Black mothers do not simply procreate irresponsibly; they purposely have more and more children to manipulate taxpayers into giving them more money. A 1990 study found that 78 percent of white Americans thought that Blacks preferred to live on welfare.[44] In a chapter of *Welfare Mothers Speak Out*, entitled "Welfare Mythology," the Milwaukee County Welfare Rights Organization depicts a common sentiment about welfare mothers:

> You give those lazy, shiftless good-for-nothings an inch and they'll take a mile. You have to make it tougher on them. They're getting away with murder now. You have to catch all those cheaters and put them to work or put them in jail. Get them off the welfare rolls. I'm tired of those niggers coming to our state to get on welfare. I'm tired of paying their bills just so they can sit around home having babies, watching their color televisions, and driving Cadillacs.[45]

Bob Grant, the popular New York radio talk show host, appealed to his listeners' stereotypes by imitating a welfare mother, using an exaggerated Black accent: " 'I don't have no job, how'm I gonna feed my family?' I wonder if they've ever figured out how they multiply like that," Grant railed over the airwaves. "It's like maggots on a hot day. You look one minute and there are so many there, and you look again and, wow, they've tripled!"[46] Grant calls his welfare reform proposal the "Bob Grant Mandatory Sterilization Act."

Modern-day racist ideology, then, seems to have shed the assumption that Black people are entirely incapable of rational decisionmaking. Rather, Blacks are more likely to be blamed for the poor choices they make. Charles Murray, for example, argued in *Losing Ground* that Black Americans' deviant family structure stemmed from Black women's rational responses to welfare incentives.[47] Black mothers are portrayed less as inept or reckless reproducers in need of moral supervision, and more as calculating parasites deserving of harsh discipline.

According to this view, far from helping children, welfare payments to Black single mothers merely encourage their transgenerational pathology. As Princeton English professor Wahneema Lubiano powerfully depicts this rhetoric, "She is the agent of destruction, the creator of the pathological, black, urban, poor family from which all ills flow; a monster creating crack dealers, addicts, muggers, and rapists — men who become those things because of being immersed in *her* culture of poverty."[48] The media often connect the welfare debate to notorious cases of neglectful mothers, leaving the impression that all welfare mothers squander their benefits on their own bad habits rather than caring for their children. In February 1994, Chicago police conducting a raid found nineteen barely clothed Black children living in a filthy, rat- and roach-infested apartment with little more to nourish them than cans of corn and Kool-Aid. The mothers of these children were five sisters who were all unmarried and living on welfare.

"The Chicago 19" soon became the leading portrait of families supported by welfare.[49] As President Bill Clinton announced his proposals for welfare reform, for example, ABC's *World News Tonight* ran footage of the story as the backdrop. A reporter introduced the topic of welfare reform by stating, "Here's an example of the problem. When the police found nineteen children living in squalor in a Chicago apartment last winter, it was a shocking symbol of all that is wrong with the system. Their mothers received more than $5,000 a month in welfare." This bizarre family came to represent welfare mothers rather than the far more representative women who devote themselves to making ends meet for the sake of their children.

THE NEW BIO-UNDERCLASS

Along with these disparaging images of Black mothers, the media increasingly portray Black children as incapable of contributing anything positive to society. Many Americans believe not only that Black mothers are likely to corrupt their children, but that Black children are predisposed to corruption. This trend is epitomized by the panic over "crack babies," Black infants irreparably damaged by their mothers' use of crack during pregnancy. It was erroneously reported that these children sustained neurological injuries that warped their emotional development, making them unresponsive as babies and uncontrollable as toddlers. Newspaper stories warned of a horde of Black children about to descend on inner-city kindergartens in need of high-cost special services.[50] But the brain damage crack babies sustained was supposed to cut even deeper: lacking an innate social conscience, crack babies were destined to grow up to be criminals.

As I discuss in Chapter 4, there is no good evidence to support this caricature of the crack baby. Nevertheless, the frightening image spawned a cottage industry of angry letters to the editor calling for harsh measures to keep crack addicts from having babies. "Reducing her welfare payments will not stop this woman from having babies," wrote one commentator. "The only way to stop her is the dreaded 'S' word—involuntary sterilization, either surgically or with Norplant. The other alternative is to allocate our resources to caring for unlimited numbers of crack babies while other children continue to be without health care."[51] The figures cited are so astronomical that it seems as if most Black children in America are crack babies impaired by a host of defects. "By the end of the 1990s the first 'crack babies' will be entering their teens," a Michigan prosecutor predicted. "It is estimated that by the year 2000 about 4,000,000 citizens of the United States will have experienced *in utero* exposure to controlled substances."[52]

The stories about hopelessly defective crack babies represent a new kind of biodeterminism. Instead of transmitting immutable deficiencies through their genes, these poor Black mothers inflict similar damage *in utero*, "callously dooming a new generation to 'a life of certain suffering, of probable deviance, of permanent inferiority.'"[53] These negative predictions easily become self-fulfilling prophecies when adoptive parents are afraid to take home a crack baby, teachers expect the children to be incapable of learning, and legislators believe it is pointless to waste money on programs for children who cannot possibly achieve. The upshot of this version of Black biological inferiority is the same as its hereditary cousin, exemplified by *The Bell Curve*: since these children are unalterably defective, any attempt to improve their lives through social spending will be futile. Indeed, John Silber, the influential president of Boston University, "went so far as to lament the expenditure of so many health care dollars on 'crack babies who won't ever achieve the intellectual development to have consciousness of God.'"[54]

The new biodeterminism presents drugs, poverty, and race as interchangeable marks that inevitably consign Black children to a worthless future. The stories about crack babies always depict Black children and they often assume they are on welfare. As one reporter wrote, "Call them 'welfare babies,' 'crack babies,' 'at-risk babies,' or 'deficit babies'—by whatever term, they constitute a new '*bio-underclass*' of infants who are disadvantaged almost from the moment of conception."[55] In this author's mind, children exposed to crack, receiving welfare, or living a disadvantaged lifestyle are all the same and they are all biologically inferior—and they are all perceived to be Black. The primary concern of this sort of rhetoric is typically the huge cost these children impose on taxpayers, rather than the children's welfare. A letter on the editorial pages of the *Atlanta Journal*, for example, noted that, in addition to burdening society with the cost of hospital care, "[c]rack babies most often grow up in a culture of

welfare dependency; there's the cost of adding their names to the welfare rolls."[56]

The powerful Western image of childhood innocence does not
seem to benefit Black children. Black children are born guilty. The
new bio-underclass constitutes nothing but a menace to society —
criminals, crackheads, and welfare cheats waiting to happen. Blaming
Black women for bringing up a next generation of degeneracy stigmatizes not only mothers but their children as well.

∞

Black motherhood has borne the weight of centuries of disgrace manufactured in both popular culture and academic circles. A lurid
mythology of Black mothers' unfitness, along with a science devoted
to proving Black biological inferiority, cast Black childbearing as a
dangerous activity. This view has justified the regulation of every aspect of Black women's fertility, policies I describe in the next six
chapters. It has also induced a deep suspicion in the minds of many
Black Americans that white-dominated family-planning programs are
a form of racial genocide. But the objective of reproductive control
has never been primarily to reduce the numbers of Black children
born into the world. It perpetuates the view that racial inequality is
caused by Black people themselves and not by an unjust social order.

1

REPRODUCTION IN BONDAGE

When Rose Williams was sixteen years old, her master sent her to live in a cabin with a male slave named Rufus. It did not matter that Rose disliked Rufus "cause he a bully." At first Rose thought that her role was just to perform household chores for Rufus and a few other slaves. But she learned the true nature of her assignment when Rufus crawled into her bunk one night: "I says, 'What you means, you fool nigger?' He say for me to hush de mouth. 'Dis my bunk, too,' he say." When Rose fended off Rufus's sexual advances with a poker, she was reported to Master Hawkins. Hawkins made it clear that she had no choice in the matter:

> De nex' day de massa call me and tell me, "Woman, I's pay big money for you, and I's done dat for de cause I wants yous to raise me chillens. I's put you to live with Rufus for dat purpose. Now, if you doesn't want whippin' at de stake, yous do what I wants.

Rose reluctantly acceded to her master's demands:

> I thinks 'bout massa buyin' me offen de block and savin' me from bein' sep'rated from my folks and 'bout bein' whipped at de stake. Dere it am. What am I's to do? So I 'cides to do as de massa wish and so I yields.[1]

The story of control of Black reproduction begins with the experiences of slave women like Rose Williams. Black procreation helped to sustain slavery, giving slave masters an economic incentive to govern Black women's reproductive lives. Slave women's childbearing replenished the enslaved labor force: Black women bore children who belonged to the slaveowner from the moment of their conception. This feature of slavery made control of reproduction a central aspect of whites' subjugation of African people in America. It marked Black women from the beginning as objects whose decisions about reproduction should be subject to social regulation rather than to their own will.

For slave women, procreation had little to do with liberty. To the contrary, Black women's childbearing in bondage was largely a product of oppression rather than an expression of self-definition and personhood. As Henry Louis Gates, Jr., writes about the autobiography of a slave named Harriet Jacobs, it "charts in vivid detail precisely how the shape of her life and the choices she makes are defined by her reduction to a sexual object, an object to be raped, bred, or abused."[2] Even when whites did not interfere in reproduction so directly, this aspect of slave women's lives was dictated by their masters' economic stake in their labor. The brutal domination of slave women's procreation laid the foundation for centuries of reproductive regulation that continues today.

All of these violations were sanctioned by law. Racism created for white slaveowners the possibility of unrestrained reproductive control. The social order established by powerful white men was founded on two inseparable ingredients: the dehumanization of Africans on the basis of race, and the control of women's sexuality and reproduction. The American legal system is rooted in this monstrous combination of racial and gender domination. One of America's first laws concerned the status of children born to slave mothers and fathered by white men: a 1662 Virginia statute made these children slaves.[3]

Slave masters' control of Black women's reproduction illustrates better than any other example I know the importance of reproductive liberty to women's equality. Every indignity that comes from the denial of reproductive autonomy can be found in slave women's lives—the harms of treating women's wombs as procreative vessels, of policies that pit a mother's welfare against that of her unborn child, and of government attempts to manipulate women's childbearing decisions through threats and bribes. Studying the control of slave women's reproduction, then, not only discloses the origins of Black people's subjugation in America; it also bears witness to the horrible potential threatened by official denial of reproductive liberty.

REPRODUCING THE LABOR FORCE
The Vitality of Slavery

The essence of Black women's experience during slavery was the brutal denial of autonomy over reproduction. Female slaves were com-
mercially valuable to their masters not only for their labor, but also
for their ability to produce more slaves. The law made slave women's
children the property of the slaveowner. White masters therefore
could increase their wealth by controlling their slaves' reproductive
capacity. With owners expecting natural multiplication to generate as
much as 5 to 6 percent of their profit, they had a strong incentive to
maximize their slaves' fertility. An anonymous planter's calculations
made the point:

> I own a woman who cost me $400, when a girl, in 1827. Admit
> she made me nothing—only worth her victuals and clothing. She
> now has three children, worth over $3000 . . . I would not this
> night touch $700 for her. Her oldest boy is worth $1250 cash,
> and I can get it.[4]

Another report confirmed that "[a] breeding woman is worth from
one-sixth to one-fourth more than one that does not breed."[5] Slave
births and deaths were not recorded in the family Bible but in the
slaveholder's business ledger.

The ban on importing slaves after 1808 and the steady inflation in
their price made enslaved women's childbearing even more valuable.
Female slaves provided their masters with a ready future supply of
chattel. Black procreation not only benefitted each slave's particular
owner; it also more globally sustained the entire system of slavery.
Unlike most slave societies in the New World, which relied on the
massive importation of Africans, the slave population in the United
States maintained itself through reproduction.[6] As Massachusetts
senator Charles Sumner deplored, "Too well I know the vitality of
slavery with its infinite capacity of propagation."[7] Here lies one of
slavery's most odious features: it forced its victims to perpetuate the
very institution that subjugated them by bearing children who were
born the property of their masters.

To be sure, female slaves were primarily laborers and their capacity
to reproduce did not diminish their masters' interest in their work. As
we will see below, when a female slave's role as worker conflicted

with that of childbearer, concern for high productivity often outweighed concern for high fertility. Slaveholders were willing to overwork pregnant slaves at the expense of the health of both mother and child. But even if, as some historians contend, "slave childbearing and rearing were not among slaveowners' top priorities,"[8] there is convincing evidence that whites placed a premium on slave fertility and took steps to increase it. Indeed, it seems incredible that whites, who dominated every aspect of their slaves' existence, would neglect the attribute that produced their most vital resource—their workforce. Nor can we ignore the sentiments of slaveholders like Thomas Jefferson, who instructed his plantation manager in 1820, "I consider a woman who brings a child every two years as more profitable than the best man on the farm."[9] Slaveowners who overworked their pregnant slaves operated under general ignorance about prenatal health combined with stereotypes about Black women's natural propensity for childbirth. They were not fully aware of the extent of the damage their labor practices inflicted on their long-term human investment.

A more realistic assessment is that because female slaves served as both producers and reproducers, their masters tried to maximize both capacities as much as possible, with labor considerations often taking precedence. Even then, the grueling demands of field work constrained slave women's experience of pregnancy and child-rearing. Every aspect of slave women's reproductive lives was dictated by the economic interests of their white slave masters.

The Carrot and the Stick

Slaveholders devised a number of tactics to induce their female slaves to bear children. Although these methods were neither uniformly practiced nor uniformly successful, most slave masters used some techniques to enhance slave fertility. They rewarded pregnancy with relief from work in the field and additions of clothing and food, punished slave women who did not bear children, manipulated slave marital choices, and forced slaves to breed. The owner of one Georgia plantation, for example, gave slave families an extra weekly ration for the birth of a child; a Virginia planter rewarded new mothers with a small pig. Some women seemed especially to appreciate presents that recognized their femininity, such as a calico dress or hair ribbons. On P. C. Weston's estate, the *Plantation Manual* prescribed that "women with six children alive at any one time are allowed all Saturday to themselves."[10] Slave women were sometimes guaranteed freedom if they bore an especially large number of children. Rhoda Hunt's mother was promised manumission when she had her twelfth child, but died a month before the baby's due date.[11]

Even without these concrete rewards, slave women felt pressure to reproduce. Because a fertile woman was more valuable to her master, she was less likely to be sold to another owner. So women could reduce the chances of being separated from their loved ones if they had children early and frequently. In addition, women could expect some relief from their arduous work load in the final months of pregnancy. (Records show, however, that expectant mothers received little or no work relief before the fifth month.)[12] Although data are scanty, it appears that slave women had their first child at an earlier age than white women of the time. A Virginia slaveholder reported in the early 1860s that "the period of maternity is hastened, the average youth of negro mothers being nearly three years earlier than that of the free race."[13] The first generation of slaves born in America also had more children than their African mothers, who avoided pregnancy for two or more years while nursing their infants. It was natural increase, and not importation of slaves, that explained the enormous growth in the slave population to 1.75 million by 1825.

Women who did not produce children, on the other hand, were often sold off—or worse. Slaveholders, angered at the loss on their investment, inflicted cruel physical and psychological retribution on their barren female slaves. A report presented to the General Anti-Slavery Convention held in London in 1840 revealed:

Where fruitfulness is the greatest of virtues, barrenness will be regarded as worse than a misfortune, as a crime and the subjects of it will be exposed to every form of privation and affliction. Thus deficiency wholly beyond the slave's power becomes the occasion of inconceivable suffering.[14]

One witness testified that a North Carolina planter ordered a group of women into a barn, declaring he intended to flog them all to death. When the women asked what crime they had committed, the master replied, "Damn you I will let you know what you have done; you don't breed, I have not had a young one from one of you for several months." Slaveholders treated infertile slaves like damaged goods, often attempting to pawn them off on unsuspecting buyers. Southern courts established rules for dealing with sellers' misrepresentations about the fertility of slave women similar to rules governing the sale of other sorts of commodities.

Slave-Breeding

Another aspect of reproductive control made the common inducement of slave childbearing even more despicable. Some slaveowners also practiced *slave-breeding* by compelling slaves they considered "prime stock" to mate in the hopes of producing children especially suited for labor or sale. While slave masters' interest in enhancing slave fertility is well established, slave-breeding has been the subject of greater controversy. That debate, however, has revolved around the extent and purpose of the practice, not whether or not slaveholders engaged in it at all.

In their 1974 bombshell *Time on the Cross: The Economics of American Negro Slavery*, historians Robert Fogel and Stanley Engerman contested the key assumptions about the management of slaves, the material conditions of slaves' lives, and the efficiency of slave agriculture. Among the myths they debunked was "the thesis that *systematic* breeding of slaves for sale in the market accounted for a major share of the net income or profit of slaveholders, especially in the Old South."[15] Their disagreement with prevailing accounts of forced mating centered on the claim that whites widely employed livestock breeding techniques to raise slaves for market. Fogel and Engerman argued that such a practice was unsupported by plantation records and would have interfered with slave masters' overriding objective of maintaining a stable workforce. Unlike animals, slaves would rebel against massive breeding, the authors argued, thus wiping out any potential gain achieved by pushing their fertility rate to its biological peak. Rather, planters usually encouraged fertility through the positive economic incentives described above.

But Fogel and Engerman did not dispute evidence that slaveowners at least occasionally engaged in breeding to enhance the productivity of their own plantations and more rarely to increase their slaves' marketability. In her extensive review of slave narratives, for example, Thelma Jennings discovered that about 5 percent of the women and 10 percent of the men referred to slave-breeding.[16]

It is from slaves' stories, such as Rose Williams's experience with Rufus, that we learn of the indignities of forced mating. Frederick

Douglass recorded in his autobiography how Edward Covey purchased a twenty-year-old slave named Caroline as a "breeder." Covey
mated Caroline with a hired man and was pleased when a pair of
twins resulted. Douglass observed that the slaveowner was no more
criticized for buying a slave for breeding than "for buying a cow and
raising stock from her, and the same rules were observed, with a view
to increasing the number and quality of the one as of the other."[17]
Katie Darling, an ex-slave from Texas, described the practice in these
words: "massa pick out a p'otly man and a p'otly gal and just put 'em
together. What he want am the stock."[18]

Slaveholders had a financial stake in male slaves' marital choices,
as well, since the children of the union belonged to the *wife's* owner.
Although marrying "abroad" was common, some masters forbade
their male slaves to court a woman from another plantation. Nor
could a slave marry a free Black man or woman. The obstacles to
finding a mate of one's choosing led one slave to complain that Black
men "had a hell of a time gittin' a wife durin' slavery. If you didn't see
one on de place to suit you and chances was you didn't suit them, why
what could you do?"[19] Slave marriages were not recognized by law;
these were partnerships consecrated by slaves' own ceremonies and
customs.

Slaveholders' interference with bonded men's intimate lives was
often more blunt. Some masters rented men of exceptional physical
stature to serve as studs. Using terms such as "stockmen," "travelin'
niggers," and "breedin' niggers," slave men remembered being
"weighed and tested," then used like animals to sire chattel for their
masters.[20] Of course, this also meant forcing slave women to submit to
being impregnated by these hired men. Jeptha Choice recalled fulfill-
ing the role of stud: "The master was might careful about raisin'
healthy nigger families and used us strong, healthy young bucks to
stand the healthy nigger gals. When I was young they took care not to
strain me and I was as handsome as a speckled pup and was in demand for breedin'." Elige Davison similarly reported that his master
mated him with about fifteen different women; he believed that he
had fathered more than one hundred children.[21] Although this was
quite rare, some slaveholders also practiced a cruel form of negative
breeding. An ex-slave reported that "runty niggers" were castrated
"so dat dey can't have no little runty chilluns."[22]

VICTIMS OF "THE GROSSEST PASSION"

"Slavery is terrible for men," wrote Harriet Jacobs, "but it is far more terrible for women." Slave women's narratives often decried the added torment that women experienced under bondage on account of their sex. Female slaves were commonly victims of sexual exploitation at the hands of their masters and overseers. The classification of 10 percent of the slave population in 1860 as "mulatto" gives some indication of the extent of this abuse.[23] Most of these mixed-race children were the product of forced sex between slave women and white men. Of course, the incidence of sexual assault that did not end in pregnancy was far greater than these numbers reveal.

Black women's sexual vulnerability continued to be a primary concern of Black activists after Emancipation. A pamphlet entitled *The Black Woman of the South: Her Neglects and Her Needs*, published in 1881 by the prominent Black Episcopalian minister Alexander Crummel, emphasized the violation of female virtue:

> In her girlhood all the delicate tenderness of her sex has been rudely outraged. . . . No chance was given her for delicate reserve or tender modesty. From her childhood she was the doomed victim of the grossest passion. All the virtues of her sex were utterly ignored. If the instinct of chastity asserted itself, then she had to fight like a tiger for the ownership . . . of her own person. . . . When she reached maturity, all the tender instincts of her womanhood were ruthlessly violated.[24]

The law reinforced the sexual exploitation of slave women in two ways: it deemed any child who resulted from the rape to be a slave and it failed to recognize the rape of a slave woman as a crime.

Legislation giving the children of Black women and white men the status of slaves left female slaves vulnerable to sexual violation as a means of financial gain. Children born to slave women were slaves, regardless of the father's race or status. This meant, in short, that whenever a white man impregnated one of his slaves, the child produced by his assault was his property.

The fact that white men could profit from raping their female slaves does not mean that their motive was economic. The rape of slave women by their masters was primarily a weapon of terror that reinforced whites' domination over their human property.[25] Rape was an act of physical violence designed to stifle Black women's will to resist and to remind them of their servile status. In fact, as historian Claire Robertson points out, sexual harassment was more likely to have the immediate effect of interfering with the victim's productivity both physically and emotionally.[26] Its intended long-term effect, however, was the maintenance of a submissive workforce. Whites' sexual exploitation of their slaves, therefore, should not be viewed simply as either a method of slave-breeding or the fulfillment of slaveholders' sexual urges.

The racial injustice tied to rape is usually associated with Black men. We are more familiar with myths about Black men's propensity to rape white women, which served as the pretext for thousands of brutal lynchings in the South. In the words of Ida B. Wells, who crusaded against lynching during the nineteenth century, "white men used their ownership of the body of white female[s] as a terrain on which to lynch the black male."[27] But white men also exploited Black women sexually as a means of subjugating the entire Black community. After Emancipation, the Ku Klux Klan's terror included the rape of Black women, as well as the more commonly cited lynching of Black men. White sexual violence attacked not only freed Black men's masculinity by challenging their abilty to protect Black women; it also invaded freed Black women's dominion over their own bodies.[28]

I nevertheless think that sexual exploitation belongs in a discussion of reproductive control. Because rape can lead to pregnancy, it interferes with a woman's freedom to decide whether or not to have a child. In addition, forced sex and forced procreation are both degrading invasions of a woman's bodily integrity; both pursue the same ultimate end—the devaluation of their female victim. Although sexual assault and slave-breeding are distinguishable, both were part and parcel of whites' general campaign to control slave women's bodies. A contemporary example of this point is the rape of Muslim women by Serbian soldiers as part of the Serbians' "ethnic cleansing" campaign. Here, too, rape was a form of mass terrorism inflicted on a group of subjugated women. But there are reports that soldiers boasted to their victims, "You will have a Serbian child."[29]

The law also fostered the sexual exploitation of slave women by allowing white men to commit these assaults with impunity. Slaves were at the disposal of their masters. Owners had the right to treat their property however they wished, so long as the abuse did not kill the chattel. Conversely, slave women had no recognizable interest in preserving their own bodily integrity. After all, female slaves legally could be stripped, beaten, mutilated, bred, and compelled to toil alongside men. Forcing a slave to have sex against her will simply followed the pattern. This lack of protection was reinforced by the prevailing belief among whites that Black women could not be raped because they were naturally lascivious.

Louisiana's rape law explicitly excluded Black women from its protection.[30] Although the language of the Virginia rape law applied to all women victims, there is not a single reported eighteenth-century case in which a white man was prosecuted for raping a female slave.[31] Even if the criminal code did recognize the rape of a slave, the law would have prevented the victim from testifying in court about the assault. An evidentiary rule in most slave-holding states disqualified Blacks from testifying against a white person.[32] In short, for most of American history the crime of rape of a Black woman did not exist.

Nor could Black women be raped by Black men. When a slave named George was charged with having sex with a child under the age of ten, his lawyer argued that the criminal code did not apply because the victim was also a slave. The Mississippi court dismissed the indictment, adopting the lawyer's contention that "[t]he crime of rape does not exist in this State between African slaves."[33] The laws that regulated sexual intercourse among whites were not relevant to slaves: "Their intercourse is promiscuous" and "is left to be regulated by their owners," the court wrote. A similar crime committed against a white woman was a capital offense.

White Women's Fury

Although the law did not recognize a crime against the slave herself, some judges held that the rape of a female slave was grounds for divorce.[34] Southern white women often cited in their divorce actions their husbands' "affection" for slave women as the cause for the marital discord. The records from one divorce case revealed the husband's cruelty inflicted on both his wife and his house servant, whose presence in the house made her particularly vulnerable to abuse:

> Your petitioner states that shortly after her marriage with her present husband she discovered that he had taken up with one of his female slaves who acted as a cook and waited about the house. So regardless was her husband of her feelings, that he would before her eyes and in the very room in which your peti-

tioner slept go to bed to the said slave or cause the said slave to
come in and go to bed with him. Your petitioner states that without complaint, she submitted in silence to her husband's infidelity, and attempted to reclaim him by caresses and obedience
but in vain.[35]

In 1865, a former slave named Louisa was sworn as a witness (over
the defendant's objection) at her mistress's Georgia divorce trial.
Louisa testified that her master, James Odom, had offered her "two
dollars to feel her titties" when her mistress was out. She also told
how Odom repeatedly invaded her bedroom despite numerous tactics
to evade him, including bringing her children to bed with her, threatening to scream, and nailing up her windows.[36]
Southern women also frequently cited their husbands' sexual li-
aisons with slaves as a reason for their opposition to slavery. One of
the best known examples is Mary Boykin Chesnut, whose diary con-
tains many passages condemning this aspect of slavery.

[March 14, 1861] . . . God forgive us, but ours is a monstrous system, a wrong and an iniquity! Like the patriarchs of old, our
men live all in one house with their wives and their concubines;
and the mulattoes one sees in every family partly resemble the
white children.
[Aug. 22, 1861] I hate slavery. You say there are no more fallen
women on a plantation than in London, in proportion to numbers; but what do you say to this? A magnate who runs a
hideous black harem with its consequences under the same roof
with his lovely white wife and his beautiful and accomplished
daughters?[37]

Most white women who opposed this unseemly aspect of slavery appeared to be more concerned about their own humiliation than the injury to female slaves. Other passages of Chesnut's diaries reveal her
deep racism, such as criticism of Harriet Beecher Stowe's abolitionist
writings. Chesnut, like most women of her time, accepted slavery as a
necessary part of her life. Despite their private grumbling, Southern
white women failed to attack the entire system, which benefitted them
in many ways. "Slavery, with all its abuses, constituted the fabric of
their beloved country," explains Elizabeth Fox-Genovese, "the warp
and woof of their social position, their personal relations, their very
identities."[38] The white woman, socialized to view the African female

as an exotic temptress, was more likely to blame the slave woman for her husband's unfaithfulness. While some white wives made their husbands' infidelity public by suing for divorce, most kept it quiet. More common was the reaction of Matilda's mistress, who, upon hearing the thirteen-year-old girl was pregnant by the master, "run to her and crammed these socks in her mouth and say, 'don't you ever tell nobody. If you do, I'll skin you alive.'"[39] Bonded women often suffered the brunt of their mistresses' jealousy in the form of taunting, whippings, and other cruel mistreatment.[40]

SHATTERING THE BONDS OF MOTHERHOOD

The domination of slave women's reproduction continued after their children were born. Black women in bondage were systematically denied the rights of motherhood. Slavery so disrupted their relationship with their children that it may be more accurate to say that as far as slaveowners were concerned, they "were not mothers at all."[41]

Prenatal Property

Slave mothers had no legal claim to their children. Slave masters owned not only Black women but also their offspring, and their ownership of these children was automatic and immediate. In fact, the law granted to whites a devisable, *in futuro* interest in the potential children of their slaves. Wills frequently devised slave women's children before the children were born—or even conceived. In 1830, for example, a South Carolina slaveowner named Mary Kincaid bequeathed a slave woman named Sillar to her grandchild and Sillar's two children to other grandchildren. Mary's will provided that if Sillar should bear a third child, it was to go to yet another grandchild.[42] Sillar's future baby became the property of a white master before the child took its first breath!

An 1823 case, *Banks' Administrator v. Marksberry*, confirmed a master's property interest in the reproductive capacity of his female slaves.[43] The case involved the following clause in a deed executed by Samuel Marksberry, Sr.: "to Samuel Marksberry, my younger son, I do likewise give my negro wench, Pen; and her increase from this time, I do give to my daughter, Rachel Marksberry." The plaintiff challenged the gift of Pen's "increase" on the ground that the testator had nothing to give at the time he wrote the will. The court, however, sided with Rachel Marksberry:

> He who is the absolute owner of a thing, owns all its faculties for profits or increase, and he may, no doubt, grant the profits or increase, as well as the thing itself. Thus, it is every day's practice, to grant the future rents or profits of real estate; and it is held, that a man may grant the wool of a flock of sheep, for years. The interest which the donor's daughter, Rachel, took in the increase of Pen, must indeed, from its nature, have been contingent at the time of the gift; but as the children of Pen were thereafter born, they would, by the operation of the deed, vest in the donee, and her title thus become complete.[44]

The court viewed the slave Pen just like any other piece of property that produces offspring, crops, or other goods. Marksberry owned not only the piece of property itself but also the goods that she bore, as well as her potential to bear future goods. In this way, the law ensured that the relationship between the master and slave existed prior to the bond between mother and child. Owning a slave woman's future children was another way of cementing whites' control of reproduction.

The Auction Block

Perhaps the most tragic deprivation was the physical separation of enslaved women from their children. It has been estimated that nearly half a million Africans were transported to the North American mainland between 1700 and 1861. Many of these Africans purchased or kidnapped from their homelands lost track of their family members forever.

For slaves in America, the auction block became the agonizing site of slave mothers' separation from their children. Because it was in slaveowners' economic interest to maintain stable, productive families, they did not frequently tear young children from their homes. But the law permitted such disruptions when it became expedient. A nineteenth-century South Carolina court ruled, for example, that children could be sold away from their mothers no matter how young because "the young of the slaves . . . stand on the same footing as other animals."[45] A planter might decide to sell a mother or her children to pay off a debt or to get rid of an unruly slave. Slaves were devised in wills, wagered at horse races, and awarded in lawsuits. Bonded families were disbanded when the heirs of an estate decided not to continue the patriarch's business.

A mother's relationship with her children might also be shattered when young children were hired or apprenticed out to labor for others, sometimes for as long as ten years. Mothers often learned the heartbreaking news only when a new master appeared to take their children away. They might even be denied the chance to kiss their babies goodbye. As novelist Toni Morrison so vividly imagined the experience, most of slave women's loved ones "got rented out, loaned out, bought up, brought back, stored up, mortgaged, won, stolen or seized. . . . Nobody stopped playing checkers just because the pieces included [their] children."[46]

Most whites owned slaves to work for them, not to sell on the market. Some slaveowners, however, were in the business of purchasing or breeding human chattel for profit. A matter of dispute, the bulk of historical evidence indicates that the interstate slave trade often broke up slave families.[47] Professional slave traders fed, washed, and oiled the slaves they acquired, and marched the merchandise, chained together, to market. On the way, a crying baby might be snatched from his mother and sold on the spot to the first slave gang that approached.

The auction was often a government-sponsored event, taking place on the courthouse steps. In fact, government agents conducted half of the antebellum sales of slaves at sheriffs', probate, and equity court sales.[48] The South Carolina courts, for example, "acted as the state's greatest slave auctioneering firm."[49] The slaves were paraded before potential buyers, who inspected their teeth and pulled back their eyelids as if they were purchasing a horse. The auctioneer sold each slave to the highest bidder. At auction, families might be mercilessly torn apart, with parents and children sold to different buyers. Josiah Henson remembered the moving scene when, as a young child, his family was splintered on the auction block:

> My brothers and sisters were bid off first, and one by one, while my mother, paralyzed with grief, held me by the hand. Her turn came and she was bought by Isaac Riley of Montgomery County. Then I was offered. . . . My mother, half distracted with the thought of parting forever from all her children, pushed through the crowd while the bidding for me was going on, to the

spot where Riley was standing. She fell at his feet, and clung to his knees, entreating him in tones that a mother could only command, to buy her baby as well as herself, and spare to her one, at least, of her little ones. . . . This man disengag[ed] himself from her with . . . violent blows and kicks. . . . I must have been between five and six years old.[50]

The Working Mother

More insidious than the physical separation of mother and child was the slave masters' control over child-rearing. If an enslaved woman was fortunate enough to keep her children with her, she was deprived of the opportunity to nurture them. Becoming a mother did not change her primary task, which was physical labor for her master. Since most slave mothers worked all day, their children were watched by other slaves who were too weak, too old, or too young to join them in the fields.[51] A Florida plantation owner, for example, entrusted forty-two children to the care of an elderly man and woman, assisted by older youngsters. Caregivers were often too inexperienced or overwhelmed to give proper attention to the children in their charge.

Mothers were often forced to leave their nursing babies at home for hours while they worked in the field. Charlotte Brooks remembered how her baby suffered from her long absences: "When I did go I could hear my poor child crying long before I got to it. And la, me! my poor child would be so hungry when I'd get to it!"[52] All of Charlotte's children, like many slave children, died at an early age "for want of attention." The infant mortality rate among slaves in 1850 was twice that of whites, with fewer than two out of three Black children surviving to age ten.[53] Death from malnutrition and disease was more likely to snatch a mother's children than sale to a new owner.

Mothers who were not allowed time out from work to return to their cabins had to bring their infants with them to the field. Slave women ingeniously combined mothering and hard labor. One North Carolina slave woman, for example, strapped her infant to her back and "[w]hen it get hungry she just slip it around in front and feed it and go right on picking or hoeing."[54] On one plantation, the women dug a long trough in the ground to create a makeshift cradle, where they put their babies every morning while they toiled. A former slave named Ida Hutchinson recalled the tragic fate of those babies as their mothers picked cotton in the distance:

When [the mothers] were at the other end of the row, all at once a cloud no bigger than a small spot came up and it grew fast, and it thundered and lightened as if the world were coming to an end, and the rain just came down in great sheets. And when it got so they could go to the other end of the field, that trough was filled with water and every baby in it was floating round in the water, drowned. [The master] never got nary a lick of labor and nary a red penny for any of them babies.[55]

Ida understood that the deaths of the babies meant a financial loss to the slave master—the infants' gruesome demise denied him both their future labor and the money he might have gotten from selling them to another owner. No one recorded the horror their mothers must have felt upon discovering their precious babies floating lifeless in their makeshift cradle.

Stealing Authority over Children

Mothers could not shield their children from the harsh realities of slave existence. In *Stolen Childhood*, historian Wilma King concludes that "enslaved children virtually had no childhood."[56] It was the master's decision when a child should be put to work. So it is not surprising that children were sent to the fields at an early age, with most beginning work by age eleven and many working before they turned seven.[57] They were often initiated into field work as part of a "trash gang" or "children's squad" that pulled weeds, cleaned up, hoed, or picked cotton. By eighteen, children were classified as "prime field hands." The master dictated the slave child's daily routine—when to rise, when to work, when to play, when to eat, and when to sleep. Children who displeased a master or overseer were whipped, and their mothers were powerless to intercede. Adolescent girls who fell prey to sexual abuse had no one to turn to for help. Children were also forced to witness the brutal beatings of their parents, an experience we now know causes deep emotional trauma.

Slave law installed the white master as the head of an extended plantation family that included his slaves. The plantation family ruled by white slaveholders was considered the best institution to transmit moral precepts to uncivilized Africans.[58] Courts reasoned that the slaveowners' moral authority over the family was ordained by divine imperative. "The slave, to remain a slave, must be made sensible," a

North Carolina judge decreed in 1829. "There is no appeal from his master. . . . [H]is power is in no instance, usurped; but is conferred by the laws of man at least, if not by the law of God."[59]

The slave master's authority over children was reflected in slaves' names. A Black child often received the surname of his owner, which was also the name of his father. His name could change several times during his lifetime, depending on how many owners he had. As an anonymous slave explained, "A Negro has got no name. . . . If you belong to Mr. Jones and he sell you to Mr. Johnson, consequently you go by the name of your owner. Now where you get a name? We are wearing the name of our master. I was first a Hale; then my father was sold and then I was named Reed."[60] (Slaves commonly noted their lineage despite this rule by giving a newborn child the first name of a parent, grandparent, or another blood relation; some secretly kept a surname different from the owner's.[61]) Naming a slave after his owner reinforced the slave's lack of a separate identity apart from his master. It also emphasized the child's ultimate subservience to his white master rather than to his parents.

Law professor Peggy Cooper Davis sees the denial of slaves' right of family as a critical aspect of denying slaves political and moral autonomy.[62] The institution of slavery required that the political existence of slaves merge with that of their masters. To be a slave, wrote Lunsford Lane, was "[t]o know . . . that I was never to consult my own will, but was, while I lives, to be entirely under the control of another."[63] Whites tried to prevent slaves from constructing their own system of morals and acting according to their own chosen values. To usurp slaves' own moral independence, all sources of values other than the slave master had to be eliminated. The key transmitter of values to be destroyed was the family. As Senator James Harlan observed during the debates on the Thirteenth Amendment, "Another incident [of slavery] is the abolition practically of the parental relation. . . . This guardianship of the parent over his own children must be abrogated to secure the perpetuity of slavery."[64]

Slaveholding whites had to ensure that their human chattel were "bound more surely by ties of ownership than by ties of kinship."[65] Professor Davis elaborates this point:

> To the extent that the system of slave subordination worked according to its design, the values of the enslaved were not nurtured within an intimate, familial community structured by its adult members, but inscribed by authoritarian decree. The slave-

holding class imposed values upon the enslaved and assumed the power to own and to socialize slave children; the moral voice of the slave was therefore silenced in two ways. First, parents were prohibited from teaching freely chosen values to their children. Second, slave children were denied both the moral and social heritage of their families and the freedom to develop values in the more flexible and intimate environment of family.[66]

Slavery could only exist by nullifying Black parents' moral claim to their children.

SLAVE WOMEN'S CONFLICTING ROLES

The dual status of slave women as both producer and reproducer created tensions that perplexed their masters and injured their children. A slaveholder was caught in an impossible dilemma—how to maximize his immediate profits by extracting as much work as possible from his female slaves while at the same time protecting his long-term investment in the birth of a healthy child.[67] The two goals were simply incompatible. Pregnancy and infant care diminished time in the field or plantation house. Overwork hindered the chances of delivering a strong future workforce.

Bearing children who were their masters' property only compounded the contradictions that scarred slave women's reproductive lives. It separated mothers from their children immediately upon conception. This division between mother and child did not exist for white women of that era. The notion that a white mother and child were separable entities with contradictory interests was unthinkable, as was the idea of a white woman's work interfering with her maternal duties. Both violated the prevailing ideology of female domesticity that posited mothers as the natural caretakers for their children.

The First Maternal-Fetal Conflict

The conflict between mother and child was most dramatically expressed in the method of whipping pregnant slaves that was used throughout the South. Slaveholders forced women to lie face down in a depression in the ground while they were whipped. A former slave named Lizzie Williams recounted the beating of pregnant slave women on a Mississippi cotton plantation: "I[']s seen nigger women dat was fixin' to be confined do somethin' de white folks didn't like. Dey [the white folks] would dig a hole in de ground just big 'nuff fo' her stomach, make her lie face down an whip her on de back to keep from hurtin' de child."[68]

This description of the way in which pregnant slaves were beaten vividly illustrates the slaveowners' dual interest in Black women as both workers and childbearers. This was a procedure that enabled the master to protect the fetus while abusing the mother. It was the slave-holder's attempt to resolve the tough dilemma inherent in female bondage. As far as I can tell, the relationship between Black women and their unborn children created by slavery is the first example of maternal-fetal conflict in American history.

Feminists use the term "maternal-fetal conflict" to describe the way in which law, social policies, and medical practice sometimes treat a pregnant woman's interests in opposition to those of the fetus she is carrying. The miracles of modern medicine, for example, that em-power doctors to treat the fetus apart from the pregnant woman make it possible to imagine a contradiction between the two. If the mother opposes the physician's suggestions for the care of the fetus, courts often treat the standoff as an adversarial relationship between the pregnant woman and her unborn child. Pitting the mother's interests against those of the fetus, in turn, gives the government a reason to restrict the autonomy of pregnant women.

Some feminist scholars have refuted the maternal-fetal conflict by pointing to its relatively recent origin. Ann Kaplan has explored, for example, how current representations of motherhood in popular ma-terials, such as magazines, newspapers, television, and films, allow the public to imagine a separation between mother and fetus. She gives examples of the recent focus on the fetus as an independent subject — sensational pictures in *Life* magazine of fetal development during ges-tation or a *New York Times* enlarged image of the fetus floating in space, attached to an umbilical cord extending out of frame and dis-connected from the mother's body, which is not seen.[69] Rayna Rapp adds that these fetal images were not even possible fifty years ago: "Until well after World War II, there were no medical technologies for the description of fetuses independent of the woman in whose body a given pregnancy was growing. Now, sciences like 'perinatol-ogy' focus on the fetus itself, bypassing the consciousness of the mother, permitting [the] image of the fetus as a separate entity."[70]

Others have attributed the current attention to the fetus as a separate subject to a backlash against the successes of the women's movement during the 1960s and 1970s.

But the beating of pregnant slaves reveals that slave masters created just such a conflict between Black women and their unborn children to support their own economic interests. The Black mother's act of bearing a child profited the system that subjugated her. Even without the benefit of perinatology and advanced medical technologies, slaveowners perceived the Black fetus as a separate entity that would produce future profits or that could be parceled out to another owner before its birth. The whipping of pregnant slaves is the most powerful image of maternal-fetal conflict I have ever come across in all my research on reproductive rights. It is the most striking metaphor I know for the evils of policies that seek to protect the fetus while disregarding the humanity of the mother. It is also a vivid symbol of the convergent oppressions inflicted on slave women: they were subjugated at once as Blacks and as females.

The Cycles of Work and Childbirth

The tension between slave women's productive and reproductive roles also appeared in the fascinating interplay between annual cycles of crop production and the birth of children. It seems that slaves' procreative activities were subtly orchestrated by the nature of the work they performed. By studying the reproductive careers of nearly a thousand slave women, Cheryll Ann Cody discovered that many bore their children in strong seasonal patterns that tracked plantation work and planting calendars.[71] Slave births on the plantations she surveyed were concentrated in the late summer and early fall. On the Ravenal cotton plantations in South Carolina, for example, one-third of the slave children were born during the months of August, September, and October.

Consider the reproductive history of Cate, one of the Ravenal family's slaves. Cate was nineteen when she had her first child, Phillip, in September 1848. Her second child, who died in infancy, was born in August two years later, followed the next August by a third child. Between 1853 and 1859, Cate gave birth to six more children like clockwork—each born between September and January.

Why did slave women tend to give birth during this period? The timing of births, of course, relates back to the timing of conception. A large proportion of these women became pregnant during the months of November, December, and January when labor requirements were reduced owing to completion of the harvest and to harsh weather, giving slaves more time and energy to devote to their families. As an added factor, the more nutritious diet available after the fall harvest probably increased slave women's fecundity.

It turns out that the seasonality of conceptions and births had a devastating impact on the survival of slave infants. Late summer and early fall, when many slave women were in their last term of pregnancy, was also the time of the highest labor demand and the greatest sickness.[72] Slaves on cotton and rice plantations spent these months intensely harvesting the crop. There was also a heightened risk of contracting diseases such as typhus and malaria, particularly for slaves who worked in swampy rice fields—diseases that could damage the fetus. Although Cody focuses on the effects of hard work and disease on gestation, the season also took its toll on new mothers and their infants. A woman who gave birth during harvest time, when planters had the greatest need for workers, could expect to be called to the fields soon after the delivery. According to the records of an Alabama plantation, a slave named Fanny had a baby in early August 1844, and was back picking cotton by August 29.[73] Needless to say, Fanny's fragile baby could hardly have received the type of neonatal care required for healthy development.

Records reveal that season of birth made little difference on plantations with exceedingly high mortality rates: on the Ball rice plantation, for example, nearly half of all infants died before their first birthday, no matter when they were born. But on the Gaillard cotton plantation, "children born during the summer, when their mother's labor was in highest demand, suffered nearly twice the level of infant mortality as those born after the harvest."[74] Data collected by economist Richard Steckel from three large South Carolina and Alabama cotton plantations confirm this finding: Steckel discovered that the average probability of infant death from February to April (the plowing and planting season) and from September to November (harvest) was 40.6 percent—nearly four times greater than neonatal losses in other months.[75] In the conflict between slave women's service as producers and as reproducers, children ended up the losers.

Child Hostages

The tension that slavery created between mothers and their children continued after birth. Slaveowners used children as hostages to prevent slave women from running away or to lure escaped women back to the plantation. Owners could threaten unruly slave women with the sale of their children to make them more submissive. As a result, far fewer bonded women than men escaped. Only 19 percent of the runaways advertised in North Carolina from 1850 to 1860, for example, were women.[76] The same pattern was common throughout the South.

One of the main reasons more men than women fled slavery was that children tied mothers to their masters. It was also true that, because enslaved children were more likely to stay with their mothers, fathers were forced to run away more often to visit their families. Nevertheless, the typical runaway slave was a lone man between the ages of sixteen and thirty-five, who paid the price of losing all contact with his family.

Unwilling to leave their children permanently, women sometimes hid out in woods and rice swamps for varying periods of time before returning to the plantation. "Truancy," historian Deborah White concludes, "seems to have been the way many slave women reconciled their desire to flee and their need to stay."[77] Some slave women elected to take their children with them on the journey to freedom. Few deliberately abandoned their children in order to increase the chances of their escape. None of the 151 female runaways advertised in the 1850s New Orleans newpapers left children behind.[78] The same was true for most of the fugitive women publicized in the *Georgia Gazette* between 1763 and 1775 and 1783 and 1795; all reportedly took their children with them. The *Gazette* printed that only one runaway, a slave woman named Hannah, abandoned one of her children. The story quoted Hannah's owner as saying that, although she had taken her five-year-old daughter Lydia, "she had 'inhumanely' left 'a child at her breast.'"[79] The slaveholder castigated Hannah for shirking her maternal duty rather than condemning the system that necessitated Hannah's flight and enslaved Hannah's child.

Another slave, named Anna Baker, fled the sexual abuse of overseers, leaving her young children behind. After the Civil War, Anna returned to retrieve her children and told them why she had deserted them. Her daughter later explained, "It was 'count o' de Nigger overseers. . . . Dey kep'a-tryin' to mess 'roun' wid her an' she wouldn' have nothin' to do wid 'em." Once, when one of the overseers asked her to go to the woods with him, she offered to go ahead to find a nice spot, and she "jus kep' a'goin. She swum de river an' run away."[80]

Historian Elizabeth Fox-Genovese observes that slave mothers who absconded without their children exhibited an unusual independence, for "however much they may have loved their men and their children, [they] did not feel bound by conventional notions of domesticity and motherhood."[81] Besides, slave women who deserted their children could depend on their being fed by the master and reared by other women of the slave community. Yet the predominant lesson from the fugitive data is that most slave women formed maternal bonds so strong that they renounced the quest of freedom for the sake of their children.

The writings of Harriet Jacobs give us rare insight into the conflicting emotions that drove the slave mother's deliberations about escaping. Harriet's autobiography, first published in 1861, explains how her feelings for her children initially prevented her from fleeing her master's sexual abuse. Harriet tells how her master deliberately used her children as pawns, thinking their presence on the plantation "would fetter me to the spot."[82] The master's strategy worked for a time:

> I could have made my escape alone; but it was more for my helpless children than for myself that I longed for freedom. Though the boon would have been precious to me, above all price, I would not have taken it at the expense of leaving them in slavery. Every trial I endured, every sacrifice I made for their sakes, drew them closer to my heart, and gave me fresh courage. . . .[83]

Harriet's words reflect the paradox of the slave mother's predicament: her children both bound her to slavery and gave her the courage to resist it. Harriet eventually did escape without her children, spending seven years hiding in closets and crawl spaces. Years later, she bought her children's freedom.

The slave masters' control of Black women's reproduction, dictating when these women gave birth and then usurping their authority over their children, amounted to far more than the physical brutality it entailed. It also reinforced the entire system of slavery in a profound way. Controlling childbearing reproduced slavery both literally and metaphysically. Slave-breeding generated more workers to restock the enslaved labor force. But controlling reproduction and child rearing also reduced slaves to objects created to fulfill the will of their masters. It produced human property without any claims of birth or connection to relatives, past, present, or future. Sociologist Orlando Patterson calls slaves' social isolation "natal alienation," creating "the ultimate human tool, as imprintable and as disposable as the master wished."[84] We often envision the hallmark of slavery's inhumanity as the slave picking cotton under the overseer's lash. As much as slaves' forced labor, whites' control of slave women's wombs perpetrated many of slavery's greatest atrocities.

THE TIGRESS FIGHTS BACK

Despite the absolute power the law granted them, whites failed to crush slave women's spirit. Black women struggled in numerous ways to resist slave masters' efforts to control their reproductive lives. They escaped from plantations, feigned illness, endured severe punishment, and fought back rather than submit to slave masters' sexual domination. Slave women's sexual resistance, note historians Darlene Hine and Kate Wittenstein, "attacked the very assumptions upon which the slave order was constructed and maintained."[85]

A common recollection of former slaves was the sight of a woman, often the reporter's mother, being beaten for defying her master's sexual advances. Clarinda received a terrible whipping when "she hit massa with de hoe 'cause he try to 'fere with her and she try stop him."[86] Minnie Folkes remembered watching her mother being flogged by her overseer when she refused "to be wife to dis man." Decades after her emancipation, Minnie repeated with pride her mother's teaching: "Don't let nobody bother yo principle; 'cause dat wuz all yo' had."[87]

A cook named Sukie Abbott was particularly successful at putting an end to her master's harassment. When Mr. Abbott accosted her in the kitchen while she was making soap, Sukie struck back by pushing him, rear end first, into a pot of boiling lye. "He got up holdin' his hindparts an' ran from de kitchen," another Abbott slave recounted, "nor darin' to yell, 'cause he didn't want Miss Sarah Ann [his wife] to know 'bout it."[88] Mr. Abbott sold Sukie at the slave market a few days later, but he reportedly "never did bother slave gals no mo." No doubt there were, as well, many cases of slave women poisoning their masters in retaliation for sexual molestation.

Playing the Lady

Slave women's procreative ability gave them a unique mode of rebellion. Pregnant slaves could benefit from their masters' interest in a successful pregnancy by "playing the lady"—complaining of some ailment in order to get relief from work. An overseer even accused female slaves on a Georgia plantation of "shamming themselves into the family-way in order to obtain a diminution of their labor."[89] Planters were frequently frustrated by their female slaves' absence from the field on account of feminine illnesses that were difficult to verify. Although many suspected their slaves were up to no good, they feared the cost of an erroneous judgment. A Virginia planter lamented the "liability of women, especially to disorders and irregularities which cannot be detected by exterior symptoms, but which may be easily aggravated into serious complaints."[90] Another complained that he had been tricked by several women on his plantation: in addition to Sarah, who laid up for eleven months before giving birth, "Wilmot, . . . whenever she was with child always pretended to be too heavy to work and it cost me twelve months before I broke her," and "Criss of Mangorike fell into the same scheme and really carried it to a great length for at last she could not be dragged out."[91]

Of course, this criticism of absenteeism exaggerates the latitude slave masters granted pregnant slaves: most expectant mothers received little or no respite from their grueling work load until the final months of pregnancy. Deborah White found it impossible to tell whether slave women who claimed to be ill were actually sick or just fooling their masters. "They certainly had more leverage in the realm of feigning illness than men," she observes, "but they also perhaps had more reason than men to be ill," owing to maladies associated with the menstrual cycle and childbirth.[92] No doubt some slave women took advantage of their masters' dilemma over their productivity and fertility to gain some time away from the fields.

Refusing to Bear Children for the Slave Master

Even more controversial is slave women's rebellion against their role as reproducer. There is evidence that some female slaves refused to bear children by abstaining from sexual intercourse or by using contraceptives and abortives. It is impossible to tell how much of female infertility and miscarriage was self-induced and how much resulted from slaves' harsh living conditions. Healthy pregnancy was hardly possible with the strenuous labor, poor nutrition, and cruel punishment bonded women endured. Still, whites suspected that their slaves took deliberate steps to prevent or terminate pregnancy.

Southern medical journals occasionally documented the abortion practices that planters found so disturbing. Dr. E. M. Pendleton from Hancock County, Georgia, wrote in 1849 that his patients who were slaves had many more abortions and miscarriages than white women.[93] Although he attributed some prenatal deaths to the stress of hard work, he confirmed planters' frequent complaint that "the blacks are possessed of a secret by which they destroy the fetus at an early stage of gestation." John T. Morgan, a physician from Murfreesboro, Tennessee, reported similar findings in a paper read before the Rutherford County Medical Society in 1860. Morgan recorded a number of techniques slave women employed "to effect an abortion or to derange menstruation": they used "medicine," "violent exercise," and "external and internal manipulation"; one stuffed "a roll of rags about two or three inches long and as hard as a stick" into her vagina. But Morgan found that slave women preferred herbal remedies to these "mechanical" means of abortion, including "the infusion or decoction of tansy, rue, roots and seed, of the cotton plant, pennyroyal, cedar gum, and camphor, either in gum or spirits"—techniques slaves probably brought with them from Africa.[94] Midwives conspired with pregnant slaves to induce and cover up abortions.[95] Despite these birth control practices, slave women were less successful at avoiding pregnancy than white women, whose birth rate declined throughout the nineteenth century.[96]

Some male slaves also refused to father children destined to become their masters' property. J. W. Loguen vowed he would never marry until he was free, for "slavery shall never own a wife or child of mine."[97] Henry Bibb similarly declared, "if there was any one act of my life while a slave that I have to lament over, it is that of being a father and a husband of slaves." Bibb tried to flee to freedom with his wife, Malinda, and young daughter, but the party was captured by a patrol. When Bibb later succeeded in escaping without his family, he determined that the daughter he left behind "was the first and shall be the last slave that ever I will father for chains and slavery on this earth."[98] Bibb relinquished his procreative role by eluding the bonds of slavery altogether, a solution far easier for men than women to accomplish.

Infanticide was the most extreme form of slave mothers' resistance. Some enslaved women killed their newborns to keep them from living as chattel. In 1831, a Missouri slave named Jane was convicted of murdering her infant child, Angeline.[99] Jane was charged with "knowingly, willfully, feloniously and of her malice aforethought" preparing a "certain deadly poison" and giving it to Angeline to drink on December 8 and 9. The indictment further alleged that on December 11, so "that she might more speedily kill and murder said Angeline," she wrapped the baby in bedclothes and then "choked, suffocated and smothered" her.

Historian and former federal judge A. Leon Higginbotham, Jr., asks two important questions about this case.[100] First, he questions Missouri's purpose in convicting Jane for murder:

> Did the state prosecute because it cared about the dignity and life of a child born into lifetime slavery with the concomitant disadvantages of Missouri's law? Or did the state prosecute because Jane's master was denied the profit that he would have someday earned from the sale or exploitation of Angeline?

Slavery's dehumanization of Black children leaves little doubt that the courts condemned slave mothers in order to protect whites' financial stake in the children, not out of respect for the children themselves.

Second, Judge Higginbotham questions Jane's purpose in killing her daughter: "Perhaps the mother felt that the taking of her daughter's life was an act of mercy compared to the cruelty she might confront in Missouri's jurisprudence." Jane's motivation may have been to protect her child from slavery's brutality—to spare, rather than harm, her child. Death may have appeared a more humane fate for her baby than the living hell of slavery.

Judge Higginbotham does not ask a more troubling question: What if Jane sacrificed her child as an act of defiance, one small step in bringing about slavery's demise? Although compelled to do so, slave mothers helped to sustain slavery by producing human chattel for their masters. By bearing children, female slaves perpetuated the very system that enslaved them and their offspring. Perhaps Jane killed Angeline because she refused to take any part in that horrible institution. This possibility raises a difficult moral question: When is taking a life justified by a noble social end? But before reaching that issue we are faced with factual questions we cannot answer without more information about slave women's reasoning.

The present state of research leaves too many uncertainties for us to discern a definitive picture of female slave resistance against reproduction.[101] We do not know, for example, whether slave mothers practiced abortion and infanticide selectively, terminating pregnancies or the lives of children that resulted from rape or forced mating. Moreover, while infanticide spared children from the horrors of slavery, it was not a desirable strategy for overthrowing the institution. Slave mothers must have realized that their sporadic practice of infanticide would have little effect and its widespread practice would annihilate the race. The low suicide rate of slaves — only one-third that of whites — suggests that they did not commonly view death as a good way to escape from slavery's horrors.[102] It seems more likely that some slave mothers acted in desperation to protect their children, not to sacrifice them in protest against slavery.

Nor will we ever know for sure how many slave mothers committed infanticide. It appears that female slaves killed their own children more often than white children.[103] But these women were often falsely accused of smothering their babies, either deliberately or carelessly, by rolling over them in bed. Almost 10 percent of infant deaths among slaves in 1850 were attributed to suffocation, compared to only 1.2 percent among whites.[104] Recent investigation has identified the true cause of many of these deaths as poor prenatal care.[105] Black children died at a dramatically higher rate than white children because of the hard physical work, poor nutrition, and abuse that their mothers endured during pregnancy. American slave children had lower birth weights than white American, European, and even Caribbean slave populations.[106]

Whatever her precise motivation, Jane was not alone. Lou Smith recalled what happened when a woman, whose three young children had been sold off, gave birth to a fourth child. When the baby was two months old,

> she just studied all the time about how she would have to give it up, and one day she said, "I just decided I'm not going to let ol' master sell this baby; he just ain't going to do it." She got up and give it something out of a bottle and pretty soon it was dead.[107]

In *Beloved*, Sethe, a former slave who is haunted by the spirit of the daughter she killed as captors approached, explains, "I stopped him. . . . I took and put my babies where they'd be safe."[108]

Keeping the Family Together

Abortion and infanticide were extreme steps taken to maintain some autonomy over the decision to become a mother. But slave women's resistance far more often involved ensuring their children's survival. The growth of the slave population in the face of disease, abuse, and toil is a testament to slave mothers' care of their children. Mothers had to fight not only to keep their children alive but also to keep them close by. When the Virginia planter St. George Tucker planned to move two of his slaves from Missouri to Texas, the women wrote their master a letter suggesting that he sell them locally instead, even providing the names of four potential Missouri buyers. They explained the pain that leaving their home would cause:

> We can't bear to go to Texas with a parcel of strangers—if you were there we should go without saying a word, but to be separated from our husbands forever in this world would make us unhappy for life. . . .
>
> We don't think there will be the least difficulty in getting ourselves sold together with our children from whom we hope you will not separate us. Ersey has six children, the youngest of which is about six weeks old, a fine little Girl. Susan has two Boys, the eldest nearly three years old, and the youngest eight months.[109]

Free Black women with the means to do so purchased freedom for their daughters and sisters. One mother in Augusta, Georgia, remained a slave herself so that she could emancipate her five children with earnings from extra work.[110] In 1893 the former slave Anna Julia Cooper spoke to the World's Congress of Representative Women, held in Chicago and attended by delegates from twenty-seven countries, about the struggle of Black women to safeguard their daughters. Her unforgettable words were:

> Yet all through the darkest period of the colored women's oppression in this country her yet unwritten history is full of heroic struggle, a struggle against fearful and overwhelming odds, that often ended in horrible death, to maintain and protect that which woman holds dearer than life. The painful, patient, and silent toil of mothers to gain a fee simple title to the bodies of their daugh-

ters, the despairing fight, as of an entrapped tigress, to keep hallowed their own persons, would furnish material for epics.[111]

These mothers were forced to deal with whites in the currency of the time. Female slaves had no right to autonomy over their own bodies. Their mothers' only recourse, short of hazarding flight north, was to wrest from slaveholders a "title to the bodies of their daughters."

Some slave women turned to the courts, as well, to win their children's freedom. Polly, a woman wrongfully held in slavery, successfully sued a white man in 1842 for the return of her daughter Lucy.[112] Polly used slave law to prove unlawful possession. She argued that, because she was not in fact a slave at the time of Lucy's birth, she was the rightful owner of her daughter.

Black women, along with Black men, succeeded remarkably often in maintaining the integrity of their family life despite slavery's traumas. Historian Edmund S. Morgan remarked that eighteenth-century Virginia slaves "did manage to live a life of their own within the limits prescribed for them," limits which, although confining, were "not so close as to preclude entirely the possibility of a private life."[113] In his monumental study of Black family life during slavery, Herbert Gutman debunked many of the myths about the destruction of slave families. Contrary to common beliefs about slaves' promiscuity and matriarchal family structure, Gutman found that enslaved men and women often sustained lasting marriages. In the period between 1800 and 1857, for example, most Black adults in Good Hope, South Carolina, eventually settled into permanent marriages and most children grew up within these relationships.[114] Although one in three of the women had children by more than one mate, most had all their children by a single husband. Slaves severed from their original families and thrown together on an unfamiliar plantation developed settled kin networks over time.

In her study of slave family structure in nineteenth-century Louisiana, historian Ann Patton Malone stresses the themes of mutability and constancy that shaped the slave community.[115] The slave community of the old Hercules O'Connor plantation was strong and stable by the 1820s when the widowed owner, Rachel O'Connor, transferred titles for seventeen of her slaves to her half-brother David Weeks, who owned two sugar plantations a hundred miles away. O'Connor hoped to keep her "black family" together until her death, but labor shortages and economic difficulties compelled Weeks to request the "loan" of his O'Connor slaves. Over the next two decades the old community was dismembered as slaves were sent to work on Weeks's plantations, Shadows and Grand Cote. Even this stable and cohesive community, composed almost entirely of descendants of the original workers, was subject to disruption, a fate its members resisted:

> In response to the series of transfers, the O'Connor slave com-
> munity—like a wooden top receiving a glancing blow that inter-
> rupted its steady whir—wobbled and tottered on its fragile axis,
> uncertain about its absent members' return and fearful as to who
> might leave next. The elderly slaves, former allies of the mistress
> with whom they had shared a lifetime, now avoided her or
> served her in stony silence. Friends and relatives of the transfers
> [sic] mourned, and each new departure reopened the wounds of
> severance. On Grand Cote, several of the O'Connor young men
> made a risky effort to find their way back to their home planta-
> tion though they were woefully ignorant of the geography in-
> volved. They reached their destination but were recovered, sent
> back, and punished for absconding.[116]

Malone observes that the story of the O'Connor slave community illustrates the extreme vulnerability of slave families despite their stability and the intense attachments of their members.

Their unions were not sanctioned by law, but slaves devised their own ceremonies and customs to consecrate their domestic relation-ships. Slave spiritual leaders officiated at weddings where the most common ritual was jumping over a broom. As William Davis de-scribed the marital rite in Tennessee, "Dey go in de parlor and each carry de broom. Dey lays de broom on de floor and de woman puts her broom front de man and he puts de broom front de woman. Dey face one 'nother and step 'cross de brooms at de same time to each other and takes hold of their hands and dat marry dem."[117] Whites' recognition of these unofficial marriages depended on each particular owner's production needs at the time; while countless slaveholders recklessly split up married couples, most accommodated or even facil-itated these unions. After all, stable marriages reduced the number of runaways and fostered steady reproduction. Amazingly, despite forced mating, sale of loved ones, and other brutalities of bondage, many slaves lived in settled, intimate families for a good part of their lives. The form of these family relationships depended on the masters' wishes, but they provided a site for slaves to develop their own culture and identities within the confines of servitude.

Yet the enslaved community did not simply replicate whites' nuclear family model. Although the two-parent nuclear family was the societal ideal among slaves as well as their masters, historians may have been tempted to exaggerate its incidence in the slave community in the effort to dispel earlier misconceptions about slave family composition. Elizabeth Fox-Genovese warns that "historians of the slave community have minimized the consequences of enslavement for the relationships between slave women and men, and, in defending the strength and vitality of Afro-American culture, have too easily assumed that the slaves developed their own strong attachment to a 'normal' nuclear family life."[118] Monogamy did not necessarily mean that husbands and wives lived together, since some married "abroad," choosing their partner from another plantation, and since couples were often separated through sale, hiring, inheritance, or flight. Households composed of women and their children were therefore far more prevalent among slaves than among their owners. On George Washington's Virginia plantation in 1799, for example, 66 percent of married slaves were in abroad marriages and only 16.5 percent lived together as husband and wife.[119] One incentive to marry abroad was the slaves' taboo against marrying first cousins, although such marriages were common among whites.

Most significant, slaves created a broad notion of family that incorporated extended kin and non-kin relationships.[120] Although the only recollection Frederick Douglass had of his mother was "a few hasty visits made in the night," he played with his cousins and grew close to his grandmother Betsey until he was hired out at age nine. Because families could be torn asunder at the slave master's whim, slave communities created networks of mutual obligation that reached beyond the nuclear family related by blood and marriage. "A teenager sold from the Upper to the Lower South after 1815 was cut off from his or her immediate Upper South family," for example, "but found many fictive aunts and uncles in the Lower South."[121] Children were expected to address all Black adults as "Uncle" and "Aunt," a practice Gutman suggests "socialized [children] into the enlarged slave community and also invested non-kin slave relationships with symbolic kin meanings and functions."[122] During and following the Civil War, ex-slaves throughout the South took in Black children orphaned by wartime dislocation and death ("motherless children") who were excluded from formal adoption services.[123] Overemphasizing the importance of two-parent units, then, notes Malone, "detracts from the fact that the real strength of the slave community was its multiplicity of forms, its tolerance for a variety of families and households, its adaptability, and its acceptance of all types of families and households as functional and contributing."[124]

The slaves' communal bonds left a legacy that continues to shape the meaning of family in the Black community today. This flexible family structure has proven to be an adaptive strategy for surviving racial injustice. Contemporary studies of the Black family commonly note the practice of informal adoption of children within the extended kinship network.[125] Sociologist Robert Hill estimates that over 15 percent of all Black children have been informally adopted by extended kin.[126] Children whose parents are unable to care for them, because their parents are unmarried, too young, unemployed, or overwhelmed by other children, are often absorbed into a relative's or neighbor's family.[127] It is not uncommon for a Black child's "Mama" to be a woman who did not give birth to her or who is not even related to her by blood. Another scholar of the contemporary Black family, Andrew Billingsley, gives the example of Rev. Otis Moss of Cleveland, Ohio, whose father perished in a car accident a few years after his mother's death: "While young Otis was standing viewing the wreckage, a woman completely unrelated to him took him by the arm and said, 'Come home with me.' He grew up as a member of her family."[128]

Slave Women's Housework—Exploitation or Resistance?

Slave women resourcefully performed a number of domestic tasks for the slave community, spinning thread, sewing clothes, growing crops, and preparing meals to feed and clothe their own people. Women would often return to their quarters in the evening, worn out from picking cotton in the blazing sun, only to weave cloth by firelight for their own kin. We should not romanticize domestic work in the slave quarters: female slaves were disadvantaged by a gendered division of labor that assigned to them the double duty of housework on top of backbreaking toil in the field.[129] (A slave master might humiliate a disobedient male slave by giving him "women's work" such as washing clothes.)

Yet work in the home had a unique dimension born of women's dual service to whites and to their own families. For slave women, work outside the home was an aspect of racial subordination while the family was a site of solace from white oppression.[130] Angela Davis's assertion that slave women performed "the *only* labor of the slave community which could not be directly and immediately claimed by the oppressor" must be couched in the realization that their masters ultimately profited from their care of other slaves.[131] But Davis is right that slave women's devotion to their own households defied the expectation of total service to whites. Black women's housework and nurturing, then, can be seen as a form of resistance, directly benefitting Black people rather than their white masters alone. This feature of slave women's domestic labor complicates the radical feminist interpretation of the family as an institution of violence and subordination. Further, although a slave woman's act of giving birth enhanced the master's workforce, it just as surely ensured the life of the slave community. True, whites had the brute power, through the whip and auction block, to steer the course of their slaves' reproductive lives; but they could not dictate the full value of procreation and mothering for Black women.

∞

Slave women's fight to retain a modicum of reproductive autonomy despite the repressive conditions of bondage indicates the importance of reproduction to our humanity. Slaveholders knew that controlling their slaves' childbearing was critical to the perpetuation of slavery. Slave women had the unique capacity to reproduce the enslaved labor force. Yet despite its profitability, it would be a mistake to view whites' interest in Black women's fertility as entirely financial. Domination of reproduction was the most effective means of subjugating enslaved women, of denying them the power to govern their own bodies and to determine the course of their own destiny. Slave women's resistance against these practices demonstrates even more powerfully that reproductive liberty is vital to our human dignity. Women like Jane, Sukie Abbott, and Anna Julia Cooper viewed reproductive freedom as a liberty worth struggling for—even dying for—because they recognized it as part of what makes us truly human.

THE DARK SIDE OF BIRTH CONTROL

Race completely changes the significance of birth control to the story of women's reproductive freedom. For privileged white women in America, birth control has been an emblem of reproductive liberty. Organizations such as Planned Parenthood have long championed birth control as the key to women's liberation from compulsory motherhood and gender stereotypes. But the movement to expand women's reproductive options was marked by racism from its very inception in the early part of this century. The spread of contraceptives to American women hinged partly on its appeal to eugenicists bent on curtailing the birthrates of the "unfit," including Negroes. For several decades, peaking in the 1970s, government-sponsored family-planning programs not only encouraged Black women to use birth control but coerced them into being sterilized. While slave masters forced Black women to bear children for profit, more recent policies have sought to reduce Black women's fertility. Both share a common theme—that Black women's childbearing should be regulated to achieve social objectives.

This chapter explores how racism helped to create the view of birth control as a means of solving social problems. Birth control policy put into practice an explanation for racial inequality that was rooted in nature rather than power. At the same time, the connection between birth control and racial injustice split the Black community. While some community activists promoted birth control as a means of racial betterment, others denounced abortion and family planning as forms of racial "genocide." Black people's ambivalence about birth control adds an important dimension to the contemporary understanding of reproductive freedom as a woman's right to choose contraception and abortion. We must acknowledge the justice of ensuring equal access to birth control for poor and minority women without denying the injustice of imposing birth control as a means of reducing their fertility.

MARGARET SANGER AND THE BIRTH CONTROL MOVEMENT

In the late nineteenth century, many states enacted statutes prohibiting contraceptives, as well as the distribution of information about them. The Comstock Law, passed by Congress in 1873, classified information about contraceptives as obscene and made its circulation through the mail a crime. Many young Americans would be shocked to discover that the U.S. Supreme Court did not rule laws prohibiting birth control, even if used by married couples, unconstitutional until 1965. *Griswold v. Connecticut* is a major case not only because it held that Connecticut's ban on contraceptives violated the Constitution, but also because it articulated for the first time the right of privacy.[1]

Griswold actually marked the culmination of a movement for access to birth control that began in the early twentieth century. Its chief crusader was Margaret Sanger, who coined the phrase "birth control." Sanger devoted her life to championing women's right to practice contraception, in defiance of prevailing law, social convention, and the Catholic Church.[2] She founded the American Birth Control League in 1921, which joined with other groups in 1939 to form the Birth Control Federation of America (BCFA), eventually becoming America's leading reproductive rights organization, the Planned Parenthood Federation of America. Sanger is still idolized by many reproductive rights activists as the mother of birth control and one of America's most outspoken feminists.

Sanger's original defense of birth control was vehemently feminist. Her advocacy centered on the emancipation of women. She traced her commitment to birth control to the desperate condition of the women she visited as a public health nurse in New York, women saddled with numerous unwanted pregnancies and endangered by self-induced abortions. She saw women's ability to control their own reproduction as essential to their freedom and equal participation in society. Access to birth control would also allow women to freely express their sexuality without fear of pregnancy. She sought to liberate women's sexual pleasure from the confines of maternity, marriage, and Victorian morality. "No woman can call herself free who does not own and control her own body. No woman can call herself free until she can choose consciously whether she will or will not be a mother,"

Sanger declared in her 1920 book, *Woman and the New Race*.[3] Sanger also stressed the importance of contraceptives that women could control themselves, rather than those that depended on men's cooperation, preferring diaphragms to the more common contraceptive methods of condoms and withdrawal.

Women's right to birth control became a subject of national attention when Sanger was arrested twice for violating federal and state anticontraception laws. Her first arrest, in 1914, occurred when the Post Office banned several issues of her magazine, *The Woman Rebel*, and the U.S. Attorney's office charged her with violating the Comstock Law. Facing a possible forty-five-year sentence, Sanger fled to Europe. She returned a year later to publicize the issue of birth control. Under public pressure, the government dropped the charges in 1916. That same year, Sanger opened the first contraceptive clinic in the United States, located in the Brownsville section of Brooklyn, where she distributed diaphragms—known as "pessaries"—to hundreds of women. Ten days later, police raided the clinic, arresting Sanger and her sister, Ethel Byrne, the clinic's nurse. Sanger was convicted of violating the New York criminal law banning distribution of contraceptives and sentenced to thirty days in the workhouse.

Several scholars who have studied the birth control movement in America remark on how its original feminist vision of voluntary motherhood was soon overshadowed by the gender-neutral goal of family planning and population control.[4] What began at the turn of the century as a crusade to free women from the burdens of compulsory and endless childbearing became by World War II a method of sound social policy. The concern for women's right to control their own reproduction was superseded by concern for the nation's fiscal security and ethnic makeup. As Angela Davis puts it, "What was demanded as a 'right' for the privileged came to be interpreted as a 'duty' for the poor."[5]

The career of Margaret Sanger demonstrates how birth control can be used to achieve coercive reproductive policies as well as women's liberation. Of course, Sanger should not be made to shoulder all of the blame for the repressive aspects of the birth control movement. Although its most prominent figure, she did not single-handedly create the political forces that shaped the meaning of birth control.[6] But Sanger's shifting alliances reveal how critical political objectives are to determining the nature of reproductive technologies—whether they will be used for women's emancipation or oppression. As the movement veered from its radical, feminist origins toward a eugenic agenda, birth control became a tool to regulate the poor, immigrants, and Black Americans.

THE EUGENICS MOVEMENT

At the time Sanger began her crusade for birth control, the eugenics movement in America had embraced the theory that intelligence and other personality traits are genetically determined and therefore inherited. This hereditarian belief, coupled with the reform approach of the Progressive Era, fueled a campaign to remedy America's social problems by stemming biological degeneracy. The eugenicists advocated the rational control of reproduction in order to improve society.

I turn to a discussion of eugenics because this way of thinking helped to shape our understanding of reproduction and permeates the promotion of contemporary policies that regulate Black women's childbearing. Racist ideology, in turn, provided fertile soil for eugenic theories to take root and flourish. It bears remembering that in our parents' lifetime states across the country forcibly sterilized thousands of citizens thought to be genetically inferior. America's recent eugenic past should serve as a warning of the dangerous potential inherent in the notion that social problems are caused by reproduction and can be cured by population control.

The eugenics movement has been traced to the writings of Sir Francis Galton, an English scientist, at the turn of the century. Although the idea of improving the quality of humans, as well as plants and animals, through selective breeding had previously been suggested, Galton was the first to popularize an actual eugenics program. Galton became interested in heredity when *The Origin of Species*, written by his distant cousin Charles Darwin, was published in 1859.[7] Galton replaced the Darwinian reliance on the process of natural selection to lead inevitably to the extinction of inferior groups with an argument for affirmative state intervention in the evolutionary process. "What Nature does blindly, slowly, and ruthlessly, man may do providently, quickly, and kindly."[8] In 1883, Galton coined the word "eugenics"—from a Greek root meaning "good in birth"—to "express the science of improving stock" by giving "the more suitable races or strains of blood a better chance of prevailing speedily over the less suitable than they otherwise would have had."[9] Galton's basic premise was that, since intelligence and character were transmitted by descent, society should take steps to encourage the procreation of people of superior stock. "What an extraordinary effect might be produced on our race," Galton declared, "if its object was to unite in marriage those who possessed the finest and most suitable natures, mental, moral, and physical!"[10]

Galton advocated primarily positive eugenics, or improving the race of a nation by increasing the reproduction of the best stock.[11] He suggested that the state should encourage early intermarriage among a select class of men and women and ensure the health of their children. Galton also believed that it was counterproductive to waste public charity on people who produced children with inferior qualities, arguing that "the time may come when such persons would be considered enemies to the state, and to have forfeited all claims to kindness."[12]

Galton's theories were grounded in a belief in the genetic distinctions between races, as well as individuals. Man was divided into different races marked by distinctive features and characters: "The Mongolians, Jews, Negroes, Gipsies, and American Indians severally propagate their kinds; and each kind differs in character and intellect, as well as in colour and shape, from the other four."[13] Galton's disparaging description of the Negro's traits fits the mindset of his time:

> The Negro has strong impulsive passions, and neither patience, reticence, nor dignity. He is warm-hearted, loving towards his master's children, and idolised by the children in return. He is eminently gregarious, for he is always jabbering, quarrelling, tom-tom-ing, or dancing. He is remarkably domestic, and is endowed with such constitutional vigour, and is so prolific, that his race is irrepressible.[14]

Eugenic ideas found fertile ground in America. At the turn of the century white Americans, believing that immigrants were reproducing faster than native Anglo-Saxons, were gripped by a fear of "race suicide." This was just one manifestation of an intense nativism that erupted in vicious race riots across the country. These attacks, primarily of whites against Blacks and natives against immigrants, often ended in dozens of deaths. Thirty-eight people were killed in a race riot in Chicago in the summer of 1919. Meanwhile lynchings terrorized Black citizens in the South. Studies showed that although the overall population was increasing, the birthrate among foreigners was double that among American-born women. "Old stock" Americans were urged to bear more children for the good of the nation. In 1903,

President Theodore Roosevelt made the issue a centerpiece of his national reform agenda, telling Americans in his State of the Union message that "willful sterility is, from the standpoint of the nation, from the standpoint of the human race, the one sin for which there is no atonement."[15]

Racism also provided the theoretical framework for eugenic thinking. White Americans had for over two centuries developed an understanding of the races as biologically distinct groups, marked by inherited attributes of inferiority and superiority. Scientific racism predisposed Americans to accept the theory that social characteristics were heritable and deviant behavior was biologically determined. The use of sterilization as a remedy for social problems was an extension of the brutality enforced against Black Americans. Whites' domination of slave women's wombs to sustain the system of slavery provided an early model of reproductive control. "Eugenic ideas were perfectly suited to the ideological needs of the young monopoly capitalists," Angela Davis points out, as their "[i]mperialist incursions in Latin America and in the Pacific needed to be justified, as did the intensified exploitation of Black workers in the South and immigrant workers in the North and West."[16] It is no wonder that the movement was financed by the nation's wealthiest capitalists, including the Carnegie, Harriman, and Kellogg dynasties.

In *Exterminate All the Brutes*, Swedish author Sven Lindqvist describes a similar process that was occurring across the ocean. He traces the antecedents of the Nazi Holocaust to nineteenth-century European imperialism, which, he says, was also grounded in a brutal racism.[17] The German extermination of Jews mimicked the earlier extermination of Africans by British officers in their quest to dominate the continent. "The step from mass murder to genocide," Lindqvist argues, "was not taken until the anti-Semitic tradition met the tradition of genocide arising during Europe's expansion in America, Australia, Africa, and Asia." Recently translated into English, *Exterminate All the Brutes* has already created intense controversy in Sweden. There is an even stronger link between the American eugenics movement and racist theories developed centuries earlier to justify the enslavement of Africans. Thus, although eugenic policies were directed primarily at whites, they grew out of racist ideology.

The study of eugenics in America mushroomed in the early 1900s, largely due to the efforts of Harvard-trained biologist Charles Davenport. As an associate professor at the University of Chicago, he convinced the Carnegie Institute to establish a center for the experimental investigation of evolution in Cold Spring Harbor, New York, in 1904. With the financial backing of railroad heiress Mrs. E. H. Harriman, Davenport added a Eugenics Record Office to his research station six years later. He and his staff of fieldworkers collected the pedigrees of hundreds of extended families suspected of carrying defective genes. Their monographs, with titles such as *The Hill Folk: Report on a Rural Community of Hereditary Defectives*, described these degenerate families as exhibiting the inherited traits of laziness, mental retardation, and immoral habits, as well as high fecundity.

Davenport reported his early findings in 1911 in his widely read book *Heredity in Relation to Eugenics*.[18] By noting the recurrence of a given character trait, Davenport concluded that heredity determined such diseases as hemophilia, otosclerosis, and Huntington's chorea, as well as behavioral characteristics, including insanity, alcoholism, eroticism, pauperism, criminality, and "feeblemindedness," which could mean anything from mental retardation to low intelligence. Davenport also attributed particular behavioral traits to different races: he observed that Poles were "independent and self-reliant though clannish"; Italians were prone to commit "crimes of personal violence"; and "Hebrews" fell "intermediate between the slovenly Serbians and Greeks and the tidy Swedes, German, and Bohemians."[19] Davenport advocated preventing the reproduction of bad stock through a selective immigration policy, discriminating marriages, and state-enforced sterilization.

Davenport's Cold Spring Harbor project supplied the burgeoning American eugenics movement with adherents and research: it trained and dispersed over 250 field workers, published the *Eugenical News*, and disseminated bulletins and books about the reduction of hereditary degeneracy.[20] As Davenport conducted scientific research, eugenics became the vogue across the country. Ordinary Americans attended lectures and read articles in popular magazines on the subject. Those devoted to studying eugenics joined organizations such as the American Eugenics Society, the American Genetics Association, and the Human Betterment Association. The *Reader's Guide to Periodical Literature* listed 122 articles under "eugenics" between 1910 and 1915, making it one of the most referenced topics in the index.[21] At most American colleges courses on eugenics were well-attended by students eager to learn how to apply biology to human affairs. The American Eugenics Society reached a less erudite audience by sponsoring Better Babies and Fitter Families contests at state fairs across the country.

Paralleling the development of eugenic theory was the acceptance of intelligence as the primary indicator of human value. Eugenicists claimed that the IQ test could quantify innate intellectual ability in a single measurement, despite the objections of its creator, Alfred Binet.[22] Just as damaging, intelligence became a shorthand for moral worth as well as cognitive capacity. The introduction of "mental tests" at the turn of the century to measure intelligence replaced physical measurements, such as cranial capacity, as the means of determining human inferiority and superiority. Measuring intelligence served the eugenics movement particularly well. The mental test was the ideal instrument for eugenics' central task of distinguishing the fitness of stocks because it provided "a seemingly objective, quantifiable measure that could be used to rank genetically transmitted ability."[23]

Psychologist Henry H. Goddard's influential research on the heritability of feeblemindedness revealed that inherited mental deficiency explained the behavior of paupers, prostitutes, and criminals.[24] His popular book, *The Kallikak Family*, compared two family lines descending from a single New Jersey man Martin Kallikak, who had fought in the Revolutionary War. Goddard claimed that the family resulting from Martin's marriage to a Quaker woman was intelligent and successful. The other, resulting from his union with a feebleminded barmaid, was filled with degenerates. Goddard's book was reprinted four times between 1912 and 1919 and had a powerful influence on popular thinking for more than a decade.

Psychologists also used the tests to demonstrate that Blacks and recent immigrants from Southern and Eastern Europe were intellectually inferior to Americans of Anglo-Saxon or Scandinavian descent. During World War I, the army commissioned Robert M. Yerkes, a Harvard eugenicist and president of the American Psychological Association, to administer a massive program to test the intelligence of 1.7 million recruits.[25] Princeton psychology professor Carl C. Brigham analyzed the army data in *A Study of American Intelligence*, published in 1923.[26] He reported that northern Europeans scored higher than Blacks and immigrants from Italy, Poland, Greece, and Russia: "At one extreme we have the distribution of the Nordic group. At the other extreme we have the American negro. Between the Nordic and the negro, but closer to the negro than the Nordic, we find the Alpine and Mediterranean type."[27] Professor Brigham decried the degeneration of the American population through "racial admixture" with Negroes and inferior immigrants and advocated more selective immigration policies that would prevent the influx of the less intelligent groups.

The same year that Brigham's book was published, a new edition of the best-seller *The Passing of the Great Race*, by the New York eugenicist Madison Grant, appeared.[28] Grant, resident anthropologist of the American Museum of Natural History, extolled the superior qualities of the Nordic race, a people of "rulers, organizers, and aristocrats" who were responsible for every great civilization that ever existed. These civilizations had declined, Grant argued, because of the deterioration of the Nordic population through warfare and intermixture with other races of people. In *The Passing of the Great Race*, Grant warned that the Nordic stock in America was similarly threatened by racial intermixture with Blacks and inferior immigrant groups, which inevitably produced children of the "lower" type. Reminiscent of Galton's view of inferior stock as public enemies, he described racial intermarriage as a "social and racial crime of the first magnitude."[29]

Grant's book was accepted as a scientific work and was seriously reviewed in prestigious academic journals.[30] Critical reviews of the book were attributed to "personal resentments from individuals not belonging to the Great Race." Grant was regarded as an important scientist, while his discreditors were labeled as "Bolsheviks and Jews" who were biased against scholarly investigation of racial difference. Like *The Bell Curve*, *The Passing of the Great Race* was a best-seller, with four editions and numerous reprints published between 1916 and 1923. The *Saturday Evening Post* praised its reflection of "recent advances in the study of hereditary and other life sciences," and recommended it as a book that "every American should read."[31] Legislators quoted passages from the book during congressional debates on immigration restrictions, and President Theodore Roosevelt commended it as "the work of an American scholar and gentleman," and stated that "all Americans should be immensely grateful to [Grant] for writing it."[32] The message readers learned from both *The Passing of the Great Race* and *The Bell Curve* is that egalitarian social programs are incapable of improving society. As E. Huntington concluded in his commentary in *Yale Review*, Grant demonstrated a "lesson of biology . . . that America is seriously endangering her future by making fetishes of equality, democracy, and universal education."[33]

IMPLEMENTING EUGENICS

The eugenicists sought to attain their goal of improving the race through a number of means. Many advocated positive eugenics, which encouraged the breeding of superior citizens and voluntary cooperation in forming the most desirable unions. By 1913 twenty-four states and the District of Columbia had enacted laws forbidding marriage by people considered genetically defective, including epileptics, imbeciles, paupers, drunkards, criminals, and the feebleminded. Influenced by testimony of eugenics lobbyists such as Harry Laughlin, Congress passed the National Origins Act of 1924, imposing national quotas that effectively cut off immigration from Southern and Eastern Europe. Others advocated universal intelligence testing in the schools in order to match each child with the type of educational program appropriate for his or her inherited capacities.[34]

Eugenicists opposed social programs designed to improve the living conditions of the poor. They argued that adequate medical care, better working conditions, and minimum wages all harmed society because those measures enabled people with inferior heredity to live longer and produce more children. The Harvard geneticist Edward East, for example, complained that the provision of prenatal care and obstetric services to the poor through clinics and public hospitals was "unsound biologically" because it "nullifie[d] natural elimination of the unfit."[35] The American Eugenics Society lobbied in 1924 against New York legislation providing special educational assistance for retarded children on the ground that "the education of the defective will bolster him or her up to the reproductive period and will make it more possible for him or her to become a parent than would be possible if he or she were less well trained."[36] Some eugenicists also considered democracy an irrational form of government because "an imbecile who knows nothing of civic matters can annul the vote of the most intelligent citizen."[37]

The eugenics movement, however, did not rely on nature to eliminate the unfit. It implemented a more direct means of weeding out undesirable citizens. The movement's most lasting legacy is its coercive enforcement of *negative* eugenics, which aimed to prevent socially undesirable people from procreating. Eugenicists advocated compulsory sterilization to improve society by eliminating its "socially inadequate" members. This was in part a response to the rapid growth in the late nineteenth century of the numbers of poor and mentally ill people housed in state-supported institutions, reported by their physicians to have alarmingly high fertility rates.

Once again, whites' inhumanity to Blacks served as a precedent. The idea of imposing sterilization as a solution for antisocial behavior originated in the castration of Black men as a punishment for crime. In eighteenth-century Virginia, castration was imposed on slaves "convicted of an attempt to ravish a white woman." In 1855, the territorial legislature of Kansas enacted a law making castration the penalty for any Negro or mulatto who was convicted of rape, attempted rape, or kidnapping of any white woman.[38] Other state legislatures considered, but failed to pass, similar legislation. Around that time, a Texas physician, Dr. Gideon Lincecum, disseminated to lawmakers and the press an essay advocating castration as a deterrent to crime. He supported his proposition with an anecdote about a "vicious, disobedient, drunken Negro" who was suspected of raping women of his own race: "After discovering that he had impregnated an idiot white girl, three men went into the field where he worked and castrated him. Less than two years later I heard his mistress say that he had become a model servant."[39] In 1864, a Black man convicted of rape in Belton, Texas, was punished by castration. Castration was also a regular feature of the ritual of lynchings in the South, although not for eugenic purposes.

In 1899, Harry C. Sharp, a physician at the Indiana State Reformatory, pioneered a plan to remedy race degeneration by sterilizing criminals. His paper "The Severing of the Vasa Deferentia and Its Relation to the Neuropsychopathic Constitution," published in 1902, reported the beneficial results of the operations he had performed on prison inmates and called for legislation authorizing state institutions "to render every male sterile who passes its portals, whether it be almshouse, insane asylum, institute for the feebleminded, reformatory, or prison."[40] Over the course of ten years, Dr. Sharp performed vasectomies on 456 inmates.[41] Sharp's proposal sparked a lobbying campaign by physicians across the country advocating mass sterilization of degenerate men. Between 1909 and 1910 alone, medical journals published twenty-three articles promoting compulsory sterilization as a means of stemming social degeneracy.[42] President Theodore Roosevelt, who urged Americans to avert the dangers of "race suicide" by producing large families, also endorsed eugenic sterilization.

Racial prejudice pervaded the pro-sterilization literature. In *Dis-*

eases of Society, Dr. G. Frank Lydston, a University of Illinois professor and one of the leading urologists in the Midwest, traced the causes of vice and crime to inherited tendencies and recommended that "[i]ncurable criminals, epileptics, and the insane should invariably be submitted to the operation."[43] The book's title page displayed a large drawing of a "skull of a Negro murderer."

Sharp's lobbying efforts proved successful. In 1907, Indiana became the first state to pass an involuntary sterilization law, empowering state institutions to sterilize, without consent, criminals and "imbeciles" whose condition was "pronounced unimprovable" by a panel of physicians.[44] Within six years, eleven additional states had enacted involuntary sterilization laws directed at those deemed burdens on society, including the mentally retarded, the mentally ill, epileptics, and criminals. Because most statutes mandated sterilization only for people confined to state institutions, they were imposed primarily against the poor.

In 1914, Harry Hamilton Laughlin, superintendent of the Eugenics Record Office and an active public lobbyist for the movement, prepared a two-volume report that proposed a schedule for sterilizing 15 million people over the next two generations, as well as a model sterilization law to accomplish this plan.[45] The report's explanation of the need for such drastic steps represents a classic statement of the eugenic mission:

> In recent years society has become aroused to the fact that the number of individuals within its defective classes has rapidly increased both absolutely and in proportion to the entire population; that eleemosynary expenditure is growing yearly; that some normal strains are becoming contaminated with anti-social and defective traits; and that the shame, the moral retardation, and the economic burden of the presence of such individuals are more keenly felt than ever before. . . . The word "Eugenics" has for the first time become known to thousands of intelligent people who now seek to understand its full significance and application. Biologists tell us that whether of wholly defective inheritance or because of an insurmountable tendency toward defect, which is innate, members of the following classes must generally be considered as socially unfit and their supply should if possible be eliminated from the human stock if we would maintain or raise the level of quality essential to the progress of the nation and our race.

Laughlin included feebleminded and insane people, criminals, and paupers among the "socially unfit" to be sterilized.[46] This defective "10 percent of our population," Laughlin claimed, "are an economic and moral burden on the 90 percent and a constant source of danger to the national and racial life."

Laughlin's 1922 survey, *Analysis of America's Modern Melting Pot*, studied the ethnic background of the institutional population in order to demonstrate that immigrants made up a disproportionate share of the nation's socially degenerate members. Laughlin's conclusion that "the recent immigrants (largely from Southern and Eastern Europe), as a whole, present a higher percentage of inborn socially inadequate qualities than do the older stocks" helped to propel the passage of the immigration law in 1924.[47] When Laughlin received an honorary degree from the University of Heidelberg in 1936, he wrote to German officials that the award represented "evidence of a common understanding of German and American scientists of the nature of eugenics."[48] Indeed, the Nazis modeled their compulsory sterilization law after one enacted in California.

The eugenicists' legislative victories were stymied by a battle waged in the courts over the constitutionality of compulsory sterilization laws. Opponents argued that the statutes imposed cruel and unusual punishment for sexual crimes, violated the Equal Protection Clause by permitting sterilization of inmates of state institutions, but not of similarly situated noninstitutionalized persons, and denied affected persons due process of law by failing to include necessary procedural safeguards. By 1921, these constitutional challenges succeeded in securing the invalidation of seven eugenics laws. Even the original sterilization law was overturned by the Indiana Supreme Court in 1919.

The sterilization movement renewed its momentum when the U.S. Supreme Court upheld Virginia's compulsory sterilization statute enacted in 1924 to prevent reproduction by "potential parents of socially inadequate offspring." The case arose when, six months after the statute's passage, the Virginia Colony for Epileptics and Feebleminded approved the sterilization of a seventeen-year-old white girl named Carrie Buck. Carrie, the daughter of an allegedly feebleminded woman, was committed to the colony by her adoptive parents when she became pregnant as a result of rape. Carrie's court-appointed guardian, in cooperation with the colony's superintendent, Dr. Albert J. Priddy, appealed the order to create a test case. The case made its way to the U.S. Supreme Court. Harry Laughlin testified in a deposition, based solely on his examination of Carrie's family records, that Carrie suffered from hereditary feeblemindedness. Noting that her sexual depravity was "a typical picture of the low-grade moron," Laughlin concluded that Carrie belonged to the "shiftless, ignorant, and worthless class of anti-social whites of the South."[49] The colony also submitted testimony that Carrie's seven-month-old daughter, Vivian, was mentally below average.

In a 1927 decision, *Buck v. Bell*, the Supreme Court approved the sterilization order.[50] Rejecting arguments that the Virginia sterilization law violated Carrie's equal protection and due process rights, Justice Oliver Wendell Holmes explained the state's interest in preemptively sterilizing people with hereditary defects: "It is better for all the world if, instead of waiting to execute degenerate offspring for crime, or to let them starve for their imbecility, society can prevent those who are manifestly unfit from continuing their kind." Holmes, himself an ardent eugenicist, gave eugenic theory the imprimatur of constitutional law in his infamous declaration: "Three generations of imbeciles are enough."[51]

During the years following the *Buck v. Bell* decision, the number of states with compulsory sterilization laws grew to thirty. Around the time of the decision the focus of sterilization policy shifted to preventing procreation by women who, like Carrie Buck, were deemed unfit to be mothers. There was a corresponding steady increase in the percentage of young women who were sterilized, with many more operations ultimately performed on institutionalized women than men.[52] Young women who were at most mildly retarded were often admitted to facilities for the feebleminded *for the sole purpose of being sterilized*. Several states pursued a program of "admission, prompt sterilization, and speedy discharge" in order to perform the surgery on as many women and as efficiently as possible.[53] Sterilization was viewed as a way of allowing mentally deficient women to be released safely from institutions into society, eliminating the chance that they would bear children who were expected to become wards of the state.

Labeling a young woman feebleminded was often an excuse to punish her sexual immorality. Many women were sent to institutions to be sterilized solely because they were promiscuous or had become pregnant out of wedlock. A review of sterilizations in California found that three out of four of the sterilized women had been judged sexually delinquent prior to their institutional commitment.[54] One sign of the trait was a patient's failure to display "the normal aversions of a white girl to a colored man who was perhaps nice to her."[55]

Walter Fernald, superintendent of the Massachusetts School for Feeble-minded Children, indicated that the trait had more to do with sexuality than with low intelligence. Observing that feebleminded girls were "often bright and attractive," he warned that, if allowed to reproduce, they "bring forth in geometrical ratio a new generation of defectives and dependents, or become irresponsible sources of corruption and debauchery in the communities where they live."[56] Carrie Buck, it turns out, was sterilized because she was poor and had an illegitimate child. There was no reliable evidence that either she or her daughter was mentally deficient. After reviewing the records, Harvard evolutionary biologist Stephen Jay Gould concluded: "Her case never was about mental deficiency; it was always a matter of sexual morality and social deviance. . . . Two generations of bastards are enough."[57] In short, eugenic sterilization enforced social judgments cloaked in scientific terms.

EUGENICISTS' GROWING INTEREST IN BLACKS

The economic crisis of the Depression also increased interest in sterilization as a means of preventing the birth of children who would need public assistance. The location of most sterilizations shifted from the West, where California led in the number of involuntary operations, to the South.[58] Howard Hale recalled in a recent newpaper interview how Virginia sterilization authorities rounded up entire families in the poverty-stricken mountains during the 1930s:

> Everybody who was drawing welfare then was scared they were going to have it done to them. . . . They were hiding all through these mountains, and the sheriff and his men had to go up after them. . . . The sheriff went up there and loaded all of them in a couple cars and ran them down to Staunton [Western State Hospital] so they could sterilize them. . . . People as a whole were very much in favor of what was going on. They couldn't see more people coming into the world to get on the welfare.[59]

The eugenics movement was also energized by issues of race. In the 1930s, it turned its attention from the influx of undesirable immigrants to the Black population in the South. Southern segregationists threatened by Black political advancement borrowed theories from the Northern liberals, who were the chief exponents of eugenics philosophy. It was now clear that the prediction of Social Darwinists that the genetic degeneracy of the Black race doomed it to extinction was wrong. In the decades following Emancipation, poverty had taken its toll on the life prospects of Black sharecroppers in the South. One historian describes the deplorable state of Black health at the turn of the century: "The fertility rates of black women declined by one-third from 1880–1910 as a result of, among other factors, poor nutrition; the life expectancy at birth for black men and women was only thirty-three years; a black mother could expect to see one out of three of her children die before age ten and to die herself before the youngest left home."[60] In *Racial Hygiene*, published in 1929, however, Thurman B. Rice warned that "the colored races are pressing the white race most urgently and this pressure may be expected to increase."[61] The twentieth-century eugenicists were not content to rely on evolutionary forces to eliminate biological inferiors; they proposed instead government programs that would reduce the Black birthrate.

Eugenicists were also worried that intermingling between Blacks and whites would deteriorate the white race. Over half of the papers presented at the Second International Congress of Eugenics in 1921 concerned the biological and social consequences of marriages between people from different ethnic groups.[62] Their titles, including "Some Notes on the Negro Problem," "The Problem of Negro-White Intermixture," and "Intermarriage with the Slave Race," reflect eugenicists' growing interest in the menace of racial intermingling. A textbook published in 1916 informed readers that "many students of heredity feel that there is great hazard in the mongrelizing of distinctly unrelated races. . . . However, it is certain that under existing social conditions in our own country only the most worthless and vicious of the white race will tend in any considerable way to mate with the negro and the result cannot but mean deterioration on the whole for either race."[63] By 1940, thirty states had passed statutes barring interracial marriage. Antimiscegenation laws were a eugenic measure.

A concrete example of the connection between antimiscegenation and eugenics is the correspondence between Walter Ashby Plecker, the Virginia registrar of vital statistics, and the prominent eugenicist Harry Laughlin. Plecker was charged with maintaining racial integrity by zealously enforcing the Virginia antimiscegenation law, which in 1924 was amended to prevent intermarriage between whites and anyone with a trace of Negro ancestry. Plecker sought to enlist eugenicists' support for his plea for better census records to verify the racial history of families. In his last known letter to Laughlin, dated

June 18, 1931, Plecker expressed his fears about the genetic contamination caused by intermarriage: "I would feel somewhat easier about the matter if I thought that these near-whites would not produce children with negroid characteristics. I have never felt justified in believing that in some instances the children of mulattoes are really white under Mendel's Law."[64]

Laughlin, in turn, was eager to learn from Plecker about laws designed to maintain racial purity. Laughlin admonished American-born women to "keep the nation's blood pure by not marrying the colored races (Negroes and Southern Europeans) for if 'men with a small fraction of colored blood could readily find mates among the white women, the gates would be thrown open to a final radical race mixture of the whole population.' "[65] Paul Popenoe, secretary of the Human Betterment Foundation, also crusaded for antimiscegenation laws; interracial mating, he wrote, was "biologically wrong."[66]

Eugenicists found allies in the Ku Klux Klan. Dr. Hiram Wesley Evans, Imperial Wizard of the Ku Klux Klan, relied on the work of Laughlin and other eugenicists.[67] In 1936, *Eugenical News* published a lengthy report written by a Klansman, Earnest Sevier Cox, advocating repatriation of all Negroes of "breeding age" back to Africa.[68] But even more important to the eugenics movement was its alliance with the crusaders for birth control.

SANGER'S ALLIANCE WITH EUGENICISTS

After World War I, Sanger's rhetoric linked birth control less with feminism and more with eugenics. Her insistence on women's right to sexual gratification cost her support from the women's movement, which emphasized maternal virtue and chastity.[69] Feminists of Sanger's time grounded their public activism in the moral superiority of motherhood. Eugenics gave the birth control movement a national mission and the authority of a reputable science.[70] By framing her campaign in eugenic terms, Sanger could demonstrate that birth control served the nation's interests. Birth control not only promoted women's health and freedom, it was also an essential element of America's quest for racial betterment. The language of eugenics, moreover, gave scientific credence to the movement's claim that birth control was an aspect of public health and improved the national welfare. It helped to contest religious objections to birth control as interfering with God's will and to refute inferences that it encouraged sexual promiscuity.

Sanger opposed the Galtonian approach to eugenics, which advocated primarily positive measures to improve the race. She devoted an entire chapter of her 1922 book, *The Pivot of Civilization*, to criticizing the "dangers of cradle competition" and explaining the advantages of birth control to lower the birthrate of the unfit.[71] The study of eugenics, Sanger argued, had demonstrated that "uncontrolled fertility is universally correlated with disease, poverty, overcrowding, and transmission of hereditable traits." Sanger warned that society's failure to curb reckless breeding by the unfit had already launched a devastating degeneration of the population. Sanger painted a stark picture of the resulting social conditions:

> Eugenists demonstrate that two-thirds of our manhood of military age are physically too unfit to shoulder a rifle; that the feeble-minded, the syphilitic, the irresponsible and the defective breed unhindered; that women are driven into factories and shops on day-shift and night-shift; that children, frail carriers of the torch of life, are put to work at an early age; that society at large is breeding an ever-increasing army of under-sized, stunted and dehumanized slaves; that the vicious circle of mental and physical defect, delinquency and beggary is encouraged, by the unseeing and unthinking sentimentality of our age, to populate asylum, hospital and prison.[72]

Sanger predicted that the multiplication of the unfit posed a threat to the political stability of the nation, as well. Reminding the reader that every citizen had the right to vote in a democracy, Sanger warned that "[e]quality of political power has thus been bestowed upon the lowest elements of our population" and that therefore "it is the representatives of this grade of intelligence who may destroy our liberties."[73] Indeed, she blamed the "the spectacle of political scandal and graft, of the notorious and universally ridiculed low level of intelligence and flagrant stupidity exhibited by our legislative bodies" on the political rights of the lower classes.

Sanger argued that a program of positive eugenics would be unable to prevent the dangers posed by reckless breeding because "the most responsible and most intelligent members of society are the less fertile ... [and] the feebleminded are the most fertile." This imbalance, she wrote, constituted "the great biological menace to the future of civilization." The intelligent classes were already using family-planning methods in a deliberate effort to raise their standard of living. Sanger felt that it would be difficult to persuade them to reverse this trend and to participate in a program of "competitive childbearing" for the benefit of the race.

In her autobiography Sanger described her challenge to positive eugenicists at the Sixth International Malthusian and Birth Control Conference:

> A second round table for the eugenists was held at which we took the opportunity to challenge their theories. I said, "Dr. Little, let's begin with you. How many children have you?"
>
> "Three."
>
> "How many more are you going to have?"
>
> "None. I can't afford them."
>
> "Professor East, how many have you, and how many more are you going to have?"
>
> And so the question circled. Not one planned to have another child, though Dr. Little has had two since by a second wife. "There you are," I said, "a super-intelligent group, the very type for whom you advocate more children, yet you yourselves won't practice what you preach. . . . No arguments can make people want children if they think they have enough."[74]

Rather, it was the *negative* side of eugenics that attracted Sanger. Negative eugenics had far greater potential for arousing public concern: "On its negative side it shows us that we are paying for and even submitting to the dictates of an ever-increasing, unceasingly spawning class of human beings who never should have been born at all."[75] Sanger advocated access to birth control as the most practical method for reducing the birthrate of the less desirable classes. "Eugenics without birth control seemed to me a house built upon the sands. It could not stand against the furious winds of economic pressure which had buffeted into partial or total helplessness a tremendous proportion of the human race," Sanger remembered in her autobiography. "The eugenists wanted to shift the birth control emphasis into less children for the poor to more children for the rich. We went back of that and sought first to stop the multiplication of the unfit. This appeared the most important and greatest step towards race betterment."[76] Declaring birth control "the very pivot of civilization,"

Sanger concluded, "As a matter of fact, Birth Control has been accepted by the most clear thinking and far seeing of the Eugenists themselves as the most constructive and necessary of the means to racial health."[77]

Eugenicists at first resisted Sanger's view of birth control as a tool of racial betterment. Many believed that increased access to contraceptives would hinder the cause of improving the race by reducing the birthrate of the superior stocks. As a 1917 article in *Birth Control Review* explained, it was likely that those who "practice birth control most effectively are the prudent, far-sighted, conscientious parents, whose children the race needs; while even possession of a knowledge of contraceptive methods will not affect the reckless and improvident . . . whose children the race would be better off without."[78]

Sanger ultimately convinced some eugenicists of the efficacy of increasing access to birth control. The American Birth Control League turned from legislative lobbying to organizing clinics because clinics could immediately work to reduce the birthrates of their socially inadequate patients.[79] The eugenics movement, in turn, supported Sanger's birth control clinics as a means of reaching groups whose high fertility rates were thought to threaten the nation's racial stock and culture. Sanger complied with the eugenicists' recommendation that her clinics record race and national origin on patient-history cards, providing a source of data on the fertility rates of different racial groups.

The American Birth Control League championed an explicitly eugenic policy of promoting birth control among the socially unfit. The league's "Principles and Aims" opened with the statement: "The complex problems now confronting America as the result of the practice of reckless procreation are fast threatening to grow beyond human control. Everywhere we see poverty and large families going hand in hand. Those least fit to carry on the race are increasing most rapidly."[80] Its first aim was to "enlighten and educate all sections of the American public in the various aspects of the dangers of uncontrolled procreation and the imperative necessity of a world program of Birth Control" and it endorsed "sterilization of the insane and feebleminded and the encouragement of this operation upon those afflicted with inherited or transmissible diseases." Its board of directors included avowed racists such as Lothrop Stoddard, author of *The Rising Tide of Color*, and C. C. Little, president of the Third Race Betterment Conference.

League president Eleanor Jones even proposed merging the organization with the American Eugenics Society to help solve its financial difficulties. Although the merger never occurred, the League maintained close ties with the organization, as well as with the Human Betterment Association, the American Genetics Association, and other eugenic groups, by sharing information about birth control. When financial woes made it difficult to establish independent clinics, the League pressured local public health and welfare agencies to include birth control in their programs. As the nation slumped into economic depression, the League argued that birth control was essential to reducing the number of children on public relief.

The alliance of the eugenics and birth control movements bolstered the contemporaneous struggle for women's emancipation. At a time when white women were largely confined to the domestic realm, eugenics included women as active participants in a crusade of scientific and political importance. Because eugenics concerned the quality of offspring, its prescriptions were often directed at women and women's role in society. The League's "Principles and Aims" declared, for example, "Every mother must realize her basic position in human society. She must be conscious of her responsibility to the race in bringing children into the world." Many eugenicists recognized that women could better promote the interest of improving the race with greater knowledge about maternal health and greater control over their careers and sexuality.[81] According to British socialist Havelock Ellis, "the realization of eugenics in our social life can only be attained with the realization of the woman movement in its latest and completest phase as an enlightened culture of motherhood."[82] But this was a warped conception of women's liberation, for it was an exclusive liberation in the service of racist social ends.

BIRTH CONTROL CLINICS FOR BLACKS

In January 1939, the American Birth Control League and the Clinical Research Bureau joined forces to become the Birth Control Federation of America, with Sanger as honorary chairman of the board. That same year the BCFA established a Division of Negro Service. In her important social history of the birth control movement, *Woman's Body, Woman's Right*, Linda Gordon emphasizes the racist motivation behind the movement's interest in educating Blacks about controlling their fertility. Sanger defended her proposal for a "Negro Project" in 1938 in seemingly racist terms. "The mass of Negroes, particularly in the South," asserted the project proposal, "still breed carelessly and disastrously, with the result that the increase among Negroes, even more than among whites, is from that portion of the population least intelligent and fit, and least able to rear children properly."[83] But analyzing the project's purpose becomes more complicated when we acknowledge that Sanger was quoting verbatim none other than the great civil rights leader W. E. B. Du Bois from an article he wrote for the June 1932 *Birth Control Review*.[84] Gordon notes that the project proposal followed up the statement about the unfit *among* Negroes with a chart comparing the overall increase of the Black population to that of whites, revealing "overt white supremacy."[85]

What Gordon's account leaves out is Blacks' own insistence on expanding birth control services to their communities. Official segregation meant that all birth control facilities established in the South in the early 1930s were for white women only. Prominent Blacks such as Dr. Du Bois had chastised the birth control movement for failing to address the needs of Black people. The BCFA's national advisory council on Negro issues boasted an impressive roster that included Du Bois; Mary McLeod Bethune, founder and head of the National Council of Negro Women; Walter White, executive director of the NAACP; Reverend Adam Clayton Powell, Jr., of the Abyssinian Baptist Church in Harlem; and Professor E. Franklin Frazier.

The birth control movement's alliance with eugenicists and its paternalistic attitude toward Blacks led to a debate about the best method of bringing birth control to Black communities. Sanger succeeded in 1938 in obtaining a $20,000 grant from Albert Lasker to finance an educational campaign among Southern Blacks using primarily Black fieldworkers. Dr. Clarence J. Gamble, an influential member of the board of directors and heir to the Proctor and Gamble fortune, had a different vision. He proposed that the grant be used to set up a demonstration project run by white doctors and aimed at proving to Southern officials that birth control could help reduce the numbers of Blacks on public relief. Sanger and Gamble strategized about using Black workers to most effectively disseminate birth control information among the uneducated Black population. Sanger wrote to Gamble in a 1939 letter:

> It seems to me from my experience . . . in North Carolina, Georgia, Tennessee and Texas, that while the colored Negroes have great respect for white doctors, they can get closer to their own members and more or less lay their cards on the table, which

means their ignorance, superstitions and doubts. They do not do this with the white people, and if we can train the Negro doctor at the Clinic, he can go among them with enthusiasm and with knowledge, which, I believe, will have far-reaching results among the colored people. . . .

The minister's work is also important, and also he should be trained, perhaps by the Federation, as to our ideals and the goal that we hope to reach. We do not want word to go out that we want to exterminate the Negro population, and the minister is the man who can straighten out that idea if it ever occurs to any of their more rebellious members.[86]

This correspondence highlights two important aspects of the provision of birth control to Blacks: Black people were suspicious of white-controlled birth control programs from the very beginning, and white-controlled programs had no intention of allowing Black people to take the reins. Linda Gordon points out as well that Sanger, in her paternalistic reliance on Black doctors and ministers under the supervision of white BCFA officials, did not contemplate "the possibility of popular, grassroots involvement in birth control as a cause."[87] Sanger's view that many Blacks were too ignorant and superstitious to use contraceptives on their own reflected a popular racial stereotype held over from slavery. On the other hand, Sanger had far more confidence than most people of her day in Black women's ability and willingness to take advantage of birth control services. In fact, as I discuss below, most Black people—even in the rural South—already practiced some form of birth control when the BCFA began its missionary work.

In 1939, the Division of Negro Service launched two pilot projects. One project, in Nashville, Tennessee, operated clinics at a Black settlement house called Bethlehem Center and at Fisk University, staffed by Black doctors and nurses. Nine Black public health nurses made home visits to domestics who could not make it to the clinic during the day. The second project operated programs in several rural counties of South Carolina that trained Black nurses to provide contraceptive instruction. But, as Sanger's letter to Gamble showed, BCFA remained firmly in control of the project's policies. Gamble reiterated in a 1939 memo, "There is great danger that we will fail because the Negroes think it a plan for extermination. Hence let's appear to let the colored run it."[88] By 1939, both North and South Carolina had made birth control one of their official public health services—at a time when Massachusetts and Connecticut still had laws making use of contraceptives a crime.[89]

Even if the Negro Project did not intend to exterminate the Black population, it facilitated the goals of eugenicists. Eugenicists considered Southern Blacks to be especially unfit to breed based on a theory of "selective migration," which held that the more intelligent Blacks tended to migrate to the North, leaving the less intelligent ones behind. Selective migration was thought to explain the embarrassing finding that Blacks from Northern cities had scored higher on the army intelligence tests than some groups of Southern whites. In 1935, Otto Klineberg, a psychologist who spent years studying racial differences in intelligence, refuted the selective migration thesis in *Negro Intelligence and Selective Migration*. He concluded, "The superiority of the northern over the southern Negroes, and the tendency of northern Negroes to approximate the scores of Whites, are due to factors in the environment, and not to selective migration."[90] But Klineberg's research did not stop plans to reduce Southern Blacks' birthrate.

WAS MARGARET SANGER A RACIST?

Was Margaret Sanger a racist or a savvy political strategist? Did she advocate birth control for the less fit because she believed they were inferior or did she merely exploit the rhetoric of racial betterment in order to gain support for women's reproductive freedom? These questions help us to examine Sanger's campaign as a case study in the role of political language and objectives in forming our understanding of reproductive liberty. Recent scrutiny of Sanger's collaboration with eugenicists, and especially Linda Gordon's portrayal of her motives as racist, have tarnished her heroic persona. On the other hand, Sanger's strategic alliance with eugenicists has been praised as an effective political move.[91] Historian Carole McCann argues that eugenicists were important to Sanger's crusade "because they provided a sexually neutral language with which to speak publicly about reproduction."[92] Similarly, in *Woman of Valor*, Ellen Chesler describes Sanger's association with scientific eugenicists as a tenuous attempt to counter religious opposition to birth control.[93] Sanger also had to overcome the powerful and respected eugenics movement's resistance to birth control out of concern that it would hasten the already declining birthrate of the upper classes.

But the link between eugenics and the birth control movement is far more significant than this political facilitation. The language of eugenics did more than legitimate birth control. It defined the purpose of birth control, shaping the meaning of reproductive freedom. Birth control became a means of controlling a population rather than a means of increasing women's reproductive autonomy. Birth control in America was defined from the movement's inception in terms of race and could never be properly understood apart from race again.

McCann argues further that although Sanger appropriated the terminology of eugenics, her position on racial betterment differed significantly from that of the eugenics movement. Sanger adopted the eugenicists' view of the dangers of racial deterioration, says McCann, but she rejected their biological explanation for its cause. Charles Valenza, director of public information for Planned Parenthood of New York City, similarly defended Sanger, writing that "charges that Sanger's motives for promoting birth control were eugenic are unfounded."[94] Sanger believed instead that racial degeneration resulted from *social* factors, especially economic pressures, rather than inherent genetic defects. She held uncontrolled fertility responsible for bringing children into conditions of poverty and deprivation: "Children who are underfed, undernourished, crowded into badly ventilated and unsanitary homes, and chronically hungry cannot be expected to attain the mental development of children upon whom every advantage of intelligent and scientific care is bestowed."[95]

McCann and Valenza both point out that three leading historians of this period, James Reed, Linda Gordon, and David Kennedy, all incorrectly attribute to Sanger a quotation reprinted in the May 1919 issue of *Birth Control Review*: "More children from the fit, less from the unfit—that is the chief issue of birth control." "She did not make that statement and, in fact, criticized it," McCann asserts.[96] But this disagreement merely reflected Sanger's objection to the positive eugenics tenet that the rich should have larger families. Besides, why should we consider Sanger's personal motives more important than the eugenic ideas she disseminated in her magazine and propaganda?

Nor was Sanger a racist, argue McCann and Valenza.[97] Sanger had precisely the same interest as Black leaders like Du Bois in educating poor Blacks about family planning in order to improve their health and chances for success in America. "I think it is magnificent that we

are in on the ground floor," Sanger wrote in a private letter to a bene-
factor, "helping Negroes to control their birthrate, to reduce their
high infant and maternal death rate, to maintain better standards of
health and living for those already born, and to create better opportunities to help themselves, and to rise to their own heights through education and the principles of a democracy."[98] Even in her most
eugenical book, *The Pivot of Civilization*, Sanger did not tie fitness for
reproduction to any particular ethnic group.

It appears that Sanger was motivated by a genuine concern to improve the health of the poor mothers she served rather than a desire
to eliminate their stock. Sanger believed that all their afflictions arose
from their unrestrained fertility, not their genes or racial heritage. For
this reason, I agree that Sanger's views were distinct from those of her
eugenicist colleagues. Sanger nevertheless promoted two of the most
perverse tenets of eugenic thinking: that social problems are caused
by reproduction of the socially disadvantaged and that their childbearing should therefore be deterred. In a society marked by racial hierarchy, these principles inevitably produced policies designed to
reduce Black women's fertility. The judgment of who is fit and who is
unfit, of who should reproduce and who should not, incorporated the
racist ideologies of the time.

The Nazi Holocaust provides heinous evidence of this point.
Within three years after the Nazi sterilization law went into effect on
January 1, 1934, the government sterilized 225,000 people. At first,
the Nazi sterilization program was not tied directly to hatred for the
Jews: most of its subjects were sterilized because they were judged
to be feebleminded, not because of their race. But as official anti-
Semitism became more evident, the Nazi eugenic policy easily merged
with the subsequent plan to exterminate the Jews. Jews simply were
made one of the classes, along with the mentally diseased and disabled, subject to the law mandating sterilization and euthanasia. As
Daniel Kevles observed, "a river of blood would eventually run from
the sterilization law of 1933 to Auschwitz and Buchenwald."[99] Eugenic policy may be motivated by many forms of domination. But history shows that it has a particular affinity for racial hatred.

Valenza's contention that "[i]n theory the eugenics movement was
not racist; its message was intended to cross race barriers for the
overall betterment of humanity" misses this point. Eugenic theory did
not transcend the American racial order; it was fed, nurtured, and
sustained by racism.

BLACKS AND THE BIRTH CONTROL MOVEMENT

It would be misleading to paint a picture of the early birth control movement as diametrically opposed to the interests of Black citizens. Contrary to the prevalent interpretation, the birth control movement was not simply "thrust upon an unwilling black population."[100] In fact, Black women were interested in spacing their children and Black leaders understood the importance of family-planning services to the health of the Black community. Blacks in disproportionate numbers enthusiastically used the few birth control clinics across the country that were available to them. Black activists played a critical role both in the national debate about birth control and in the establishment of local family-planning clinics. Their guiding concern for racial justice, however, distinguished their understanding of birth control from the dominant conception linked to eugenic thinking and practice.

Many Black women were already practicing birth control when the birth control movement got under way. After the Civil War, emancipated Black women in the South continued to use folk methods of contraception and abortion.[101] Black women living in Northern cities commonly prevented conception by placing Vaseline and quinine over the mouth of the uterus. *The Women's Era*, a Black women's newsletter, seemed to acknowledge women's right to birth control when it printed in 1894 that "not all women are intended for mothers. Some of us have not the temperament for family life."

During this period, the Black press was the source of an abundance of birth control information for its readers. Historian Jesse Rodrique surveyed a wealth of advertisements and stories in Black newspapers published throughout the 1920s and 1930s that indicate a widespread use of contraception and self-induced abortion. A colorful example comes from the *Pittsburgh Courier*, which

> carried numerous mail order advertisements for douche powder, suppositories, preventive antiseptics, and vaginal jellies that "destroyed foreign germs." A particularly interesting mail order ad was for a product called "Puf," a medicated douche powder and applicator that claimed to be a "new guaranteed method of administering marriage hygiene." It had a sketch of a calendar with the words "End Calendar Worries Now!" written across it and a similar sketch that read "Tear-Up Your Calendar, Do Not

Worry, Use Puf." The instructions for its use indicate euphemistically that Puf should be used "first," meaning before intercourse, and that it was good for hours, leaving little doubt that this product was fully intended to be used as a birth control device.[102]

George S. Schuyler confirmed these practices in a 1932 *Birth Control Review* article, observing, "If anyone should doubt the desire on the part of Negro women and men to limit their families, it is only necessary to note the large scale of 'preventive devices' sold in every drug store in the various Black Belts and the great number of abortions performed by medical men and quacks."[103] Besides douching after intercourse and abortion, Blacks were also relying on condoms, male withdrawal, and abstinence to regulate their fertility.[104]

Between 1880 and 1940 the differential fertility between the races nearly disappeared as a result of plummeting Black fertility rates. For decades the accepted explanation for this decline in fertility was Black people's poor health. Demographers attributed Black women's low pregnancy rates during the 1930s to higher rates of venereal disease, tuberculosis, infections, and rickets. This "health hypothesis" rejected the possibility that Black women's fertility rate declined because they were using contraceptives. Unlike most historians who have downplayed Blacks' voluntary use of birth control, Rodrique attributes the decline in Black fertility rates during this period largely to Black couples' use of a variety of contraceptive methods. Her conclusion is supported by the fact that middle-class Blacks, who had the lowest rates of diseases linked to infertility, also had the fewest children.[105] A study of Black women living in Philadelphia in 1975 found that 40 to 60 percent were practicing birth control by 1940, indicating that most Black people at least knew about and approved of contraceptives at the time of the early birth control movement.[106]

In the years between the two world wars, a distinctive Black discourse on birth control emerged in the Black press, public lectures, and Black women's fiction and poetry.[107] In September 1919, the *Birth Control Review* published a special issue devoted to "The New Emancipation: The Negroes' Need for Birth Control, as Seen by Themselves." It featured a one-act play on Negro life by Mary Burrill and an interview with Chandler Owen, who edited the Negro monthly *The Messenger* with A. Philip Randolph. A 1932 issue of *Birth Control Review* again addressed Black people's need for birth control, with contributions from Dr. Du Bois, Professor Charles S. Johnson of

Fisk University, Dr. W. G. Alexander, general secretary of the National Medical Association, and Elmer A. Carter, editor of *Opportunity*, among others. These writers advocated birth control as a way for Blacks to reduce their dreadful maternal and infant death rates, "preserve their new economic independence," and improve their standard of living.

At the other end of the debate, Marcus Garvey's nationalist organization, the Universal Negro Improvement Association, unanimously passed a resolution at their 1934 annual convention condemning birth control as "attempting to interfere with the course of nature and with the purpose of the God in whom we believe."[108] Philip Francis, "a student of Negro life," endorsed this view in a 1940 guest editorial in the *New York Amsterdam News* that called birth control "race suicide." "It is a move away from the full development of the race and lays the foundation for a weaker minority group in a so-called Nordic civilization," he contended. "The Negro needs more and better babies to overwhelm the white world, in war, in peace and in prosperity." Francis concluded with a call to send "our women back to the home and there breed us the men and women who will really inherit the earth."

Du Bois was one of the first Black leaders to publicly endorse birth control for Blacks. He is best known for his distinguished career as a champion for Black people's civil rights, but he was also an outspoken advocate for women's rights and a passionate defender of Black women in particular.[109] Du Bois often paid homage to Black women, whom he admired for their triumph over adversity. "I have always felt like bowing myself before them in abasement," he wrote in 1920, "searching to bring some tribute to these long-suffering victims, these burdened sisters of mine, whom the world loves to affront and ridicule and wantonly to insult."[110] Du Bois combined in his support for birth control the dual themes of Black people's economic emancipation and women's independence from their traditional childbearing role.

Du Bois devoted much of his 1920 book *Darkwater: Voices from Within the Veil* to exploring the role of Black women, quoting Anna Julia Cooper's now famous passage, "Only the black woman can say 'when and where I enter, in the quiet, undisputed dignity of my womanhood, without violence and without suing or special patronage, then and there the whole Negro race enters with me.' " In the chapter "The Damnation of Women," Du Bois made the feminist assertion that "[t]he future woman must have a life work and economic independence. She must have knowledge. She must have the right of motherhood at her own discretion."[111] In a 1922 article in *The Crisis*, the monthly magazine he edited for two decades, he argued that Black families should adopt birth control, which he called "science and sense applied to the bringing of children into the world," as a means of reducing the high Black infant mortality rate.[112] Both maternal and infant mortality rates in Harlem were double those in other sections of New York City.[113] "We in America are becoming sharply divided into the mass who have endless children and the class who through long postponement of marriage have few or none," Du Bois wrote.

Later Du Bois criticized "the fallacy of numbers," the argument that Blacks should rely on a high birthrate to remedy Blacks' subordinated status, arguing that "quality and not mere quantity really counts."[114] George Schuyler also noted that "the assumption that an increase in births necessarily means an increase in the Negro population" was fallacious: "If 25 percent of the brown children born die at birth or in infancy because of the unhealthful and poverty-stricken condition of the mothers, and 25 percent more die in youth or vegetate in jails and asylums, there is instead of a gain a distinct loss." Oberlin College professor Newell Sims warned in his 1932 article, "Hostages to the White Man," that the strategy of "outbreeding the whites" would likely backfire because "it would probably arouse the white stock like a fire alarm. The 'rising tide of color' bugaboo would be paraded in every quarter of the land till repressive measures would render the Negroes' last state far more difficult than it now is."[115]

Du Bois and other prominent Blacks were not immune from the elitist thinking of their time. As reflected in Du Bois's statement borrowed by Sanger to promote the Negro Project, they sometimes advocated birth control for poorer segments of their own race in terms painfully similar to eugenic rhetoric. In "Eugenics for the Negro," newspaper editor Elmer Carter also bemoaned the fact that his people's practice of birth control was "distinctly dysgenic."[116] "Negroes who by virtue of their education and capacity are best able to rear children shrink from the responsibility," Carter explained, while "the Negro who, in addition to the handicaps of race and color, is shackled by mental and social incompetence serenely goes on his way bringing into the world children whose chances of mere existence are apparently becoming more and more hazardous." A 1932 editorial in the *New York Amsterdam News* praised birth control for offering "one definite means of raising [the Negro] to a higher standard of physical fitness, mental capacity and financial stability."[117] And Professor Sims lamented in *Birth Control Review*, "too many Negro parents have made themselves and their offspring public dependents by having too numerous progeny."

Yet using birth control as a tool for racial betterment had a different meaning for Blacks than it did for most whites. There was a radical distinction in both strategies and goals. For eugenicists and many white birth control advocates, improving the race meant reducing the number of births among people considered genetically or socially defective. But Blacks understood that racial progress was ultimately a question of racial justice: it required a transformation of the unequal economic and political relations between Blacks and whites. Although birth control could aid in this struggle, it could not cure Black people's wretched living conditions by itself. Sanger, writes Donald Pickens, "felt all reform began and ended with birth control."[118] White eugenicists promoted birth control as a way of preserving an oppressive social structure; Blacks promoted birth control as a way of toppling it.

Black supporters of birth control also opposed the eugenic notion that certain races were inherently inferior. The leading Blacks in the birth control movement never presented contraception as a means of eliminating hereditary defects; rather, birth control addressed problems such as high maternal and infant mortality rates that resulted from social and economic barriers. Du Bois and other Blacks active in the birth control movement adamantly opposed sterilization, the chief tool of eugenicists. The *Pittsburgh Courier*'s editorial policy favored birth control but urged Blacks to oppose sterilization programs. Du Bois warned in 1936 in his *Courier* column that these programs "fall upon colored people and it behooves us to watch the law and the courts and stop the spread of the habit."[119]

Community activism was also critical to the spread of birth control clinics in Black neighborhoods throughout the 1930s and 1940s. Black women's clubs worked to educate their less fortunate sisters about birth control as part of their racial uplift campaign. Local maternal welfare groups in Virginia, for example, raised funds to support the birth control clinics at the Medical College of Virginia and the Hampton Institute. The National Association of Colored Graduate Nurses, headed by Mabel Keaton Staupers, collaborated with the BCFA to extend programs to Black neighborhoods. Dr. Lemuel T. Sewell attested in a 1933 article entitled "The Negro Wants Birth Control" that 75 percent of the Black women he treated in Philadelphia "are anxious for birth control information."[120] During this period

Blacks also formed independent birth control organizations that sponsored clinics in Black communities.[121] The Baltimore Urban League along with a sponsoring committee of Black professionals, for example, opened the Northwest Health Center in 1938.

One important clinic was established in Harlem through a joint effort between the National Urban League and Margaret Sanger's Birth Control Clinical Research Bureau. In 1924, James Hubert, executive secretary of the New York chapter of the Urban League, approached Sanger about the possibility of opening a clinic in a Black neighborhood in New York City, where Sanger's organization had been operating a clinic for white women for over a year.[122] Over the next several years Sanger met with Urban League representatives to discuss plans to establish a clinic in Harlem. After $10,000 was raised to fund the clinic, its doors opened in February 1930 on the second floor of a storefront on Seventh Avenue, off 138th Street. The Harlem clinic offered the same services as the Clinic Research Bureau's main branch, providing gynecological examinations, contraceptive information, and diaphragms. Nearly two thousand patient visits were recorded in the first year and several thousand each following year. Until 1933, however, about half of these patients were white women referred from downtown.[123]

The Harlem clinic had a separate advisory board, the Harlem Advisory Council, to help run the clinic and raise funds. In her letter soliciting members for the council, Sanger expressed her goal for the body "to determine the best methods to use for educating the public concerning the aims and purposes of Birth Control," as well as to gain the confidence of Black public health professionals.[124] The council's fifteen distinguished Black members included James Hubert, Mabel Staupers, Louis T. Wright, medical secretary of Harlem Hospital, May Chinn, the only Black female physician in Harlem, and William Lloyd Imes, assistant pastor of the Abyssinian Baptist Church.[125]

Although there was widespread support for its work, the Harlem clinic did not escape the Black community's ambivalence about birth control. Many potential patients suspected that the clinic was really intended to promote race suicide rather than racial betterment. Some Harlem residents believed that Black people's progress in America depended on numerical proliferation and that birth control would hasten racial extinction. Others feared that white doctors would use them as guinea pigs in medical experiments. The placard identifying the clinic as the Clinical *Research* Bureau and its exclusively white staff only helped to fan suspicions. More Black women began to use the clinic after it moved to the Urban League building and hired a Black physician and social worker and two Black nurses.

Although Sanger hoped that the Harlem clinic would demonstrate Blacks' ability to use birth control effectively, she nevertheless resisted giving the Harlem Advisory Council control over the clinic's operation. She felt that her clinic met a need that "the race did not recognize" for itself.[126] She, like other whites in the birth control movement, saw the role of Black leaders and health professionals as facilitating their organizations' efforts among the Black population. They incorporated Blacks in their advocacy to help raise funds and to give legitimacy to the movement's projects in Black communities. But Black members of advisory councils were not invited to participate in national planning, nor were they allowed to manage the clinics that served Black patients.

Despite its limited role, the Harlem Council succeeded in influencing the clinic's approach to issues of race. In addition to the change in the staff's racial composition, the clinic's promotional materials began to respond to the Harlem residents' fears of race suicide and experimentation. For example, the Harlem clinic's pamphlets inserted the word "harmless" in its description of contraceptives and distinguished between birth control and sterilization, emphasizing that birth control is "merely a temporary means of preventing undesired pregnancies." [127]

As the Depression made it increasingly difficult to fund the Harlem clinic, Sanger was forced in 1935 to relinquish the clinic's management to the New York City Committee of Mothers' Health Centers, affiliated with the American Birth Control League. The committee slashed the clinic's services and treated the advisory council with even greater paternalism than Sanger had, prompting council member Mabel Staupers to write, "If the Birth Control Association wishes the cooperation of Negroes . . . I feel that we should be treated with the proper courtesy that is due us and not with the usual childish procedures that are maintained with any work that is being done for Negroes." [128] The League closed the clinic a year later.

∞

By the 1940s, eugenics had been discredited both as bad science and as an excuse for racial hatred. Numerous scholars, such as Franz Boas and Otto Klineberg, had demonstrated scientific errors in the movement's theories about inherited traits. The Carnegie Institute rescinded its support for eugenic studies at Cold Spring Harbor in

1939, and Harry Laughlin resigned as secretary of the Eugenics Record Office, marking the end of eugenics as an official social program in the United States. American eugenicists who had initially supported the German sterilization law were shamed by its eventual connection to the Nazi Holocaust.[129]

Along with this repudiation of eugenic theory, the development of the constitutional doctrine of reproductive autonomy and the changing view of mental retardation have spurred a major reform of sterilization law in the last fifty years. The American Eugenics Society changed its name in 1972 to the less offensive Society for the Study of Social Biology, which still publishes the journal *Social Biology*. But the eugenicists' reign had taken its toll. Between 1929 and 1941, more than 2,000 eugenic sterilizations were performed each year in the United States.[130] It has been estimated that a total of over 70,000 persons were involuntarily sterilized under these statutes.[131] Moreover, the eugenicists' way of thinking about reproduction and social inequality left a lasting imprint on American policy debates.

THE NEW REIGN OF STERILIZATION ABUSE

The last nail was barely in the coffin of eugenic theory before it was revived in the 1960s by genetic explanations of racial differences in intelligence promoted by scientists such as Arthur Jensen and William Shockley. In the early 1970s, Edgar R. Chasteen published *The Case for Compulsory Birth Control* and the well-known biologist Garrett Hardin argued in *Exploring New Ethics for Survival* that supporting children gave the government the right to strip their parents of the capacity to produce more.[132] The civil rights movement had successfully agitated for legal reforms that gave Black Americans greater access to housing, jobs, welfare benefits, and political participation. The white backlash included a new, more subtle form of social engineering. As mandatory sterilization laws were repealed across the country, Black women fell victim to widespread sterilization abuse at the hands of government-paid doctors.

By World War II involuntary sterilizations in the South had increasingly been performed on institutionalized Blacks. The demise of Jim Crow had ironically opened the doors of state institutions to Blacks, who took the place of poor whites as the main target of the eugenicist's scalpel. South Carolina reported in 1955, for example, that all of the twenty-three persons sterilized at the State Hospital over the previous year were Black women.[133] The North Carolina Eugenics Commission sterilized nearly 8,000 "mentally deficient persons" in the 1930s and 1940s, some 5,000 of whom were Black.[134] A study of sterilization in state institutions in North Carolina published in 1950 gives a chilling account of government-sponsored mayhem that continued well into the 1940s.[135] The State Hospital for Negroes in Goldsboro seems to have been in the grisly business of operating on the Black patients confined there for being criminally insane, feebleminded, or epileptic. Before the war, the hospital had a full-time surgeon on staff. Nearly two hundred men were castrated or given vasectomies at a rate far higher than for white men at other institutions. Men convicted of attempted rape or whom hospital authorities considered unruly were castrated to make them "easier to handle." Because they were not considered intelligent enough, none of the patients was asked for consent. All of the doctors and most of the other hospital staff were white.

But most sterilizations of Black women were not performed under the auspices of the eugenic laws. The violence was committed by doctors paid by the government to provide health care for these women. During the 1970s sterilization became the most rapidly growing form of birth control in the United States, rising from 200,000 cases in 1970 to over 700,000 in 1980.[136] It was a common belief among Blacks in the South that Black women were routinely sterilized without their informed consent and for no valid medical reason. Teaching hospitals performed unnecessary hysterectomies on poor Black women as practice for their medical residents. This sort of abuse was so widespread in the South that these operations came to be known as "Mississippi appendectomies." In 1975, a hysterectomy cost $800 compared to $250 for a tubal ligation, giving surgeons, who were reimbursed by Medicaid, a financial incentive to perform the more extensive operation—despite its twenty times greater risk of killing the patient.[137]

Fannie Lou Hamer, the leader of the Mississippi Freedom Democratic Party, informed a Washington, D.C., audience in 1965 that 60 percent of the Black women in Sunflower County, Mississippi, were subjected to postpartum sterilizations at Sunflower City Hospital without their permission.[138] Hamer had suffered this violation herself when she went to the hospital for the removal of a small uterine tumor in 1961. The doctor took the liberty of performing a complete hysterectomy without her knowledge or consent. This practice of sterilizing Southern Black women through trickery or deceit was confirmed by a number of physicians who examined these women after the procedure was performed.

Sterilization abuse was not confined to hospitals in the South. In April 1972, the *Boston Globe* ran a front-page story reporting the complaint by a group of medical students that Boston City Hospital was performing excessive and medically unnecessary hysterectomies on Black patients.[139] Among the charges were: surgeries were performed for "training purposes"; radical and dangerous procedures were used when alternatives were available; medical records did not reflect what had really been done to patients; patients were pressured into signing consent forms without adequate explanation; and doctors treated patients callously, adding to the women's anguish.

In one case, a teenage girl who was twelve weeks pregnant came to the Boston hospital for an abortion. She was told that it was too late for her to have a regular abortion and that a hysterectomy was necessary. When the medical student who observed the operation asked a resident why such drastic action was taken, the resident replied that the doctor "wanted a hysterectomy done for the experience." Another woman was given a tubal ligation without her knowledge following a cesarean section; the doctor falsely listed the procedure as an appendectomy. In response to reporters' questions about the allegations, the chairman of the obstetrics and gynecology department at Boston University Medical School replied that one should not condemn the entire service "because of one bad apple."[140]

The director of obstetrics and gynecology at a New York municipal hospital reported similar outrageous practices: "In most major teaching hospitals in New York City, it is the unwritten policy to do elective hysterectomies on poor black and Puerto Rican women, with minimal indications, to train residents."[141] A study by Dr. Bernard Rosenfeld of Los Angeles County Hospital released in 1973 confirmed that "doctors in some cities are cavalierly subjecting women, most of them poor and Black, to surgical sterilization without explaining either potential hazards or alternate methods of birth control."[142] "The majority of these women signed a medical consent form, not to be sterilized but rather placing their faith in the doctor to discover and rectify the so-called trouble," explained Naomi Gray of Black Women Organized for Action at a 1974 conference on Black women's health.[143] Another tactic was to offer tubal ligations to women while they were in labor.[144] In 1968, a group of Black doctors at the Watts Extended Health and Family Planning Group called for federally financed birth control projects to remain under community control.[145]

How could doctors who had taken the Hippocratic oath treat their patients so brutally? Doctors confided to author Gena Corea during the 1970s that they believed sterilization was the best way to reduce the undesirable population growth of the poor. Dr. C, chief of surgery at a northeastern hospital, for example, gave Corea his opinion that "a girl with lots of kids, on welfare, and not intelligent enough to use birth control, is better off being sterilized."[146] " 'Not intelligent enough to use birth control,' " Corea added, "is often a code phrase for 'black' or 'poor.' " Another doctor explained the justification for violating patients' autonomy: "As physicians we have obligations to our individual patients, but we also have obligations to the society of which we are a part. . . . The welfare mess . . . cries out for solutions, one of which is fertility control."[147]

Another doctor who abided by this philosophy was Dr. Clovis H. Pierce, the only obstetrician in Aiken County, South Carolina, who accepted Medicaid patients. Dr. Pierce demanded a different kind of payment from the indigent Black women who came to him to deliver their babies. Marietta Williams, a twenty-year-old Black woman on welfare, charged Dr. Pierce with refusing to deliver her third child unless she allowed him to sterilize her. He also threatened to take her to court if she did not sign the consent form. When Dorothy Waters balked at the suggestion of sterilization during her last visit before the delivery, Dr. Pierce warned her, "Listen here, young lady, this is my tax money paying for this baby and I'm tired of paying for illegitimate children. If you don't want this sterilization, find another doctor."[148] Dr. Pierce ordered one woman who refused the procedure to be discharged from the hospital, but her mother intervened. (The frightened patient ultimately left the hospital on her own.) Dr. Pierce told the local press that his policy was to require sterilization after delivery of a welfare mother's third baby, a measure he said was to reduce the welfare rolls.[149] The doctor sterilized eighteen welfare mothers at Aiken County Hospital in 1972, of whom sixteen were Black. (Pierce had been paid in the preceding eighteen months hospital fees totaling $60,000 of taxpayers' money.) The Department of Social Services refused to intervene on behalf of these women when they sought government assistance.

Nial Ruth Cox became pregnant in 1964 at age seventeen while living in North Carolina with her eight brothers and sisters and her mother, who were supported by welfare. Ms. Cox reported that, when she turned eighteen, a caseworker told her that because of her "immorality" she would have to be sterilized temporarily or her family would lose their welfare benefits.[150] The doctor told her that the effect of the procedure "would wear off." Cox's mother consented to her daughter's sterilization under a North Carolina law that allowed sterilization of mental defectives under age twenty-one if their parent consented. Cox underwent the operation, which left her permanently infertile, although there was no evidence that she was mentally defective.

Then came the case that exposed the astounding extent of sterilization abuse. Fourteen-year-old Minnie Lee Relf and her twelve-year-old sister Mary Alice Relf were the youngest of six children of a Black couple living in Montgomery, Alabama. The Relf parents were uneducated farmhands, who survived after migrating to the city on relief payments totaling $156 a month. In June 1973, nurses from the federally funded Montgomery Community Action Agency asked the Relfs for permission to admit the youngest Relf sisters to a hospital for injections of the long-acting experimental contraceptive Depo-Provera. Mrs. Relf, unable to read or write, signed the consent form with an "X." Apparently believing that their race and poverty made these young girls candidates for birth control, the nurse had been giving them regular shots. But that spring Washington had ordered an end to the hormonal injections when they were linked to cancer in laboratory animals. Instead, the Relfs later learned, their daughters were sterilized.

In July 1973, the Relfs turned to the Southern Poverty Law Center for help and a class action lawsuit was filed in federal court demanding a ban on the use of federal funds for sterilizations. The lawsuit uncovered the shocking magnitude of sterilization abuse across the South. Judge Gerhard Gesell found that an estimated 100,000 to 150,000 poor women like the Relf teenagers had been sterilized annually under federally funded programs.[151] A study discovered that nearly half of the women sterilized were Black. In *The Legacy of Malthus*, Allan Chase points out that this rate equals that reached by the Nazi sterilization program in the 1930s.[152]

Health care workers used a variety of tactics to trick or pressure these women into "consenting" to the surgery. Like Nial Cox, some women were coerced into agreeing to sterilization under the threat that their welfare benefits would be withdrawn. Doctors forced others, such as Marietta Williams and Dorothy Waters, to submit to the operation before they would deliver their babies or perform an abortion. The court found that "patients receiving Medicaid assistance at childbirth are evidently the most frequent targets of this pressure."

The case eventually led to the passage of federal guidelines governing sterilizations subsidized by the government.[153]

The coercive sterilizations of Black welfare mothers surreptitiously put into effect the proposals of legislators in several states that had failed to become law. During the 1960s state legislatures considered a rash of punitive sterilization bills aimed at the growing number of Blacks receiving Aid to Families with Dependent Children (AFDC).[154] In 1958, Representative David H. Glass introduced a bill in the Mississippi Legislature entitled "An Act to Discourage Immorality of Unmarried Females by Providing for Sterilization of the Unwed Mother under Conditions of this Act," which provided for the chancery court to order the sterilization of single mothers, most of whom were Black. The bill passed the House by a vote of 72 to 37, but was dropped in the Senate after national protest, which included a pamphlet entitled *Genocide in Mississippi* circulated by the Student Nonviolent Coordinating Committee (SNCC).

The Illinois, Iowa, Ohio, Virginia, and Tennessee legislatures considered similar proposals for the compulsory sterilization of welfare mothers who continue to have children out of wedlock. Although none of the sterilization proposals was enacted, Louisiana and Mississippi succeeded in passing laws making it a crime to give birth to two or more illegitimate children. After surveying a number of these sterilization bills, Julius Paul observed in 1968, "The surgeon's knife (sterilization) still seems to have the same magical quality in the minds of some people for 'saving' America from its shame, squalor, and various miseries of human or social instigation (especially poverty) as it did over sixty years ago."[155]

Other women of color were also sterilized at startling rates. For several decades, private agencies, including the International Planned Parenthood Federation, and the Puerto Rican government, with the support of federal funds, waged a crusade to sterilize Puerto Rican women. Women on the island were encouraged to agree to "la operación" by armies of public health workers who offered it at minimal or no cost.[156] Dr. Clarence Gamble, who masterminded the Negro Project in the South, implemented a similar "experiment in population control" in Trujillo Alto, Puerto Rico, from 1950 to 1958.[157] The island-wide sterilization campaign was so successful that by 1968 more than one-third of the women of childbearing age in Puerto Rico had been sterilized, the highest percentage in the world at that time.

A similar effort on Indian reservations during the 1970s left more than 25 percent of Native American women infertile. In four Indian Health Service hospitals alone, doctors performed more than 3,000 sterilizations without adequate consent between 1973 and 1976. For small Indian tribes, this policy was literally genocidal. One physician reported that "[a]ll the pureblood women of the Kaw tribe of Oklahoma have now been sterilized. At the end of the generation the tribe will cease to exist."[158] It is amazing how effective governments—especially our own—are at making sterilization and contraceptives available to women of color, despite their inability to reach these women with prenatal care, drug treatment, and other health services.

Ironically, while Black, Puerto Rican, and Indian women were being pressured into the operation, white middle-class women found it nearly impossible to find a doctor who would sterilize them. Most hospitals followed the "120 formula" prescribed by the American College of Obstetricians and Gynecologists: "if a woman's age multiplied by the number of children she had totaled 120, she was a candidate for sterilization."[159] Even then, she would need the endorsement of two doctors and a psychiatrist. Under this formula, a woman with three children would not become eligible until she reached age forty, and having no children would absolutely bar a woman from being sterilized.

Doctors' reluctance to sterilize middle-class white women continues today. Law professor Ruth Colker tells the story of her law school classmate who decided to be sterilized.[160] The university physician refused to allow her to undergo the procedure unless she agreed to attend several sessions with a psychiatrist, presumably to dissuade her from her decision. Professor Colker recognizes that the "physician's actions reflect the dominant social message—that a healthy (white) woman should want to bear a child." Indeed, the physician seemed to think that a white woman who decides not to have children must be suffering from some mental disorder.

The disparate experiences of women of color and white women led to a clash of agendas concerning sterilization. In the late 1970s, a group of women activists formed the Committee to End Sterilization Abuse and introduced in the New York City Council guidelines designed to prevent coercive sterilization. Their work served as a model for federal sterilization reform. The guidelines had two key provisions: they required informed consent in the preferred language of the patient and a thirty-day waiting period between the signing of the consent form and the sterilization procedure. The group also wanted

rules to prevent the practice of obtaining consent during labor, immediately after childbirth or an abortion, or under the threat of losing
welfare benefits.

In the eyes of birth control advocates seeking to make it *easier* for
white women to obtain voluntary sterilizations, however, these requirements looked like further roadblocks in their path. Representatives of the National Abortion Rights Action League (NARAL) and
Planned Parenthood testified *against* the New York and national
guidelines.[161] In 1970, a pro-sterilization coalition composed of the
Association for Voluntary Sterilization, Zero Population Growth, and
the American Civil Liberties Union (ACLU) launched Operation
Lawsuit to challenge hospitals' refusal to perform elective sterilizations. Within two years, women seeking elective sterilizations brought
twelve lawsuits against hospitals across the country.[162] One plaintiff
was Janet Stein, a twenty-seven-year-old mother of three whose request for voluntary sterilization was refused by a New York hospital.

Some pro-sterilization organizations had their roots in the eugenics
movement. The Association for Voluntary Sterilization, for example,
can be traced back to the Sterilization League of New Jersey,
founded in the 1930s. By 1950, it had become a national organization
known as the Human Betterment Association. When it shifted its political allegiance from the repudiated eugenics movement to the burgeoning birth control movement in the 1960s, it changed its name to
emphasize its support for voluntary rather than compulsory sterilization.[163] Most of the organizations that opposed sterilization reform
had no eugenic motive; they simply failed to understand the concerns
of the poor minority women. Focusing on the obstacle the regulations
would pose to middle-class white women, they ignored the ravages on
minority women's bodies the new law would help to prevent. They
mistakenly believed that protecting women's right to use birth control
meant challenging any restrictions on access to birth control. They
wrongly believed that any criticism of sterilization would give support
to the enemies of women's reproductive choice. But there is nothing
contradictory about advocating women's freedom to use birth control
while opposing coercive birth control practices. The focus on the interests of white privileged women led to a myopic vision of reproductive rights.

In 1978, the Department of Health, Education, and Welfare issued
rules restricting sterilizations performed under programs receiving
federal funds, such as Medicaid and AFDC. The rules adopt the informed consent and thirty-day waiting period requirements advo-

cated by the Committee to End Sterilization Abuse. They also prohibit hysterectomies performed for sterilization purposes, as well as the use of federal funds to sterilize minors and mentally incompetent and institutionalized persons.

The federal regulations, however, have not stopped the sterilization abuse. In the absence of any civil or criminal sanctions or monitoring mechanism, the rules are often ignored. Court cases alleging medical malpractice against the physician provide for only limited damages. Nor do the regulations prevent physicians and other health care workers from urging women of color to consent to sterilization because they think these women have too many children or are incapable of using other methods of birth control. A study conducted by the ACLU shortly after the regulations went into effect discovered that many hospitals were blatantly defying the law.[164]

Although sterilization is the leading method of birth control in the United States, its use is especially widespread among Black women. Data collected from the 1988 National Survey of Family Growth and 1990 Telephone Reinterview, the most recent national estimates of contraceptive use in the United States, show a dramatic racial differential. Between 1982 and 1990, Black women were less likely than white women to use contraception, but those who did were significantly more likely than their white counterparts to be sterilized (41 percent compared with 27 percent).[165] In 1990, some 24 percent of Black women had been sterilized while only 17 percent of white women had undergone the operation.[166] The racial disparity in sterilization cuts across economic and educational lines. One study found that 9.7 percent of college-educated Black women had been sterilized, compared to 5.6 percent of college-educated white women.[167] The frequency of sterilization increased among poor and uneducated Black women. Among women without a high school diploma, 31.6 percent of Black women and 14.5 percent of white women had been sterilized. In an eighteen-year study of low-income Black women in Baltimore who gave birth as teenagers, University of Pennsylvania sociologist Frank Furstenberg and two other researchers discovered that 56 percent had been sterilized at a relatively young age.[168]

Current government funding policy continues to encourage sterilization of poor women. The federal government pays for sterilization services under the Medicaid program, while it does not make available information about and access to certain other contraceptive techniques and abortion. In effect, sterilization was for decades the only publicly funded birth control method readily available to poor women

of color.[169] As I discuss in the next chapter, the government has recently added Norplant, a form of temporary sterilization, to its arse-
nal. The selective funding of birth control options takes place within a
broader context of misdirected government priorities that emphasize
free family planning as a solution to poverty rather than the general
improvement of community health.

BIRTH CONTROL AS RACIAL GENOCIDE

The debate among Blacks over birth control, which began in the
1920s, persisted over the ensuing decades. In an article appearing in
1954 in the popular Black magazine *Jet*, Dr. Julian Lewis, a former
University of Chicago professor, criticized Planned Parenthood's
work in the Black community and warned that the wide-scale practice of birth control would lead to "race suicide."[170] Nearly twenty
years later, in a controversial cover story in *Ebony* magazine entitled
"My Answer to Genocide," Dick Gregory advocated large Black families as insurance against Black extermination. Gregory was especially
wary of white people's motives underlying the promotion of family
planning:

> For years they told us where to sit, where to eat, and where to
> live. Now they want to dictate our bedroom habits. First the
> white man tells me to sit in the back of the bus. Now it looks like
> he wants me to sleep under the bed. Back in the days of slavery,
> black folks couldn't grow kids fast enough for white folks to har-
> vest. Now that we've got a little taste of power, white folks want
> us to call a moratorium on having children.[171]

Gregory's views were not an aberration. A number of articles in both
the white and Black press raised the possibility of a plot to eliminate
Blacks through birth control services. Two studies by William Darity
and Castellano Turner, published in the *American Journal of Public
Health* in 1972 and 1973, showed a widespread worry among Blacks
that family-planning programs were a potential means of racial genocide, especially if the programs provided sterilization and abortion
and were run by whites.[172] One reported that nearly 40 percent of
Blacks surveyed believed that these programs were a scheme to exterminate Blacks. These fears were most prevalent among young, uneducated males in the North.

During the 1960s and 1970s, Black nationalists increasingly adopted the theory that birth control was a form of genocide. The Nation of Islam vehemently opposed birth control as a deliberate white strategy to deplete the Black population. A cartoon in *Muhammad Speaks* depicted a Black woman in an advanced state of pregnancy standing in a jail cell, with the caption: "My Only Crime Was Refusing to Take Birth Control Pills."[173] Another showed a bottle of birth control pills marked with a skull and crossbones. The Black Power conference held in Newark in 1967, organized by Amiri Baraka, passed a resolution denouncing birth control.[174] The May 1969 issue of *The Liberator* admonished readers that "[f]or us to speak in favor of birth control for Afro-Americans would be comparable to speaking in favor of genocide."

Even more mainstream organizations such as the NAACP and the Urban League reversed their earlier support for family planning as a means of racial progress. As head of Operation PUSH, Jesse Jackson in 1972 questioned the timing of the government's interest in family planning for Blacks, noting that its growth "simultaneously with the emergence of blacks and other nonwhites as a meaningful force in the nation and the world appears more than coincidental."[175] Fannie Lou Hamer, who had been sterilized without her consent, also viewed abortion and birth control as a form of racial genocide.[176] Some leaders went further to argue that increasing the Black population was essential for liberation. Marvin Dawes, leader of the Florida NAACP, asserted, "Our women need to produce more babies, not less . . . and until we comprise 30 to 35 percent of the population, we won't really be able to affect the power structure in this country."[177]

Numerous Black women challenged the characterization of birth control as a form of genocide, as well as the "strength in numbers" argument. By the 1940s, Blacks were visibly organizing to increase the availability of birth control in their communities. At its national meeting in 1941 the National Council of Negro Women created a standing committee on family planning and passed a resolution requesting every Black organization to include family planning in its agenda "to aid each family to have all the children it can afford and support but no more—in order to insure better health, security and happiness for all."[178] This was the first time a national women's organization officially endorsed birth control. Black women's groups were also asserting greater independence from the white-dominated mainstream organizations such as Planned Parenthood. In a speech addressed to Planned Parenthood in 1942, Dr. Dorothy Ferebee admonished her audience, "It is well for this organization to realize that the Negro at his present advanced stage of development is increasingly interested more in programs that are worked out with and by him than in those worked out for him."[179]

Many women in the Black liberation movement rejected their brothers' charge to them to bear more children. In her anthology on Black women published in 1970, Toni Cade took up the issue "The Pill: Genocide or Liberation?" "I've been made aware of the national call to Sisters to abandon birth control . . . to picket family-planning centers and abortion-referral groups and to raise revolutionaries," she wrote. "What plans do you have for the care of me and the child?"[180] As head of the Black Women's Liberation Committee of SNCC, Frances Beal wrote, "Black women have the right and the responsibility to determine when it is in *the interest of the struggle to have children or not to have them and this right must not be relinquished to any* . . . to determine when it is in *her own best interests* to have children."[181]

The conflict escalated not only in journals but also in grassroots confrontations. One of the most heated disputes occurred in 1969 between women in the National Welfare Rights Organization and community leaders surrounding the opening of family-planning centers in Pittsburgh.[182] The city's antipoverty board became the first in the country to vote down federal funds to continue Planned Parenthood clinics in six poor neighborhoods. The leader of the militant United Movement for Progress, William "Bouie" Haden, even threatened to firebomb a clinic. (It was discovered that Haden's organization received a $10,000 grant from the Catholic diocese of Pittsburgh.) One mother protested, "Who appointed him our leader anyhow? . . . Why should I allow one loudmouth to tell me about having children?" Black women successfully organized to remove Haden as a delegate from the Homewood-Brushton Citizens Renewal Council and to restore funds to the clinics. In a Black neighborhood in Cleveland, a family-planning center was burned to the ground. The Black Panther Party (BPP) was also split along gender lines on the subject of abortion and birth control. Despite opposition to birth control from some male members, however, the BPP offered contraceptives as part of its free health care program.

Shirley Chisholm, a Black congresswoman from Brooklyn, worked tirelessly in the 1970s to increase the number of family-planning clinics in Black neighborhoods. She flatly rejected the argument equating birth control with genocide:

To label family planning and legal abortion programs "genocide" is male rhetoric, for male ears. It falls flat to female listeners and to thoughtful male ones. Women know, and so do many men, that two or three children who are wanted, prepared for, reared amid love and stability, and educated to the limit of their ability will mean more for the future of the black and brown races from which they come than any number of neglected, hungry, ill-housed and ill-clothed youngsters.[183]

In testimony before a Senate committee, Congresswoman Chisholm attested to her female constituents' pleas for family-planning services. One study published in 1970 found that 80 percent of the Black women in Chicago interviewed approved of birth control and 75 percent were practicing it.[184]

One reason Black women supported family planning was that they were disproportionately victims of unsafe abortions prior to the legalization of abortion in 1973. Half of the maternity-related deaths among Black women in New York City in the 1960s were attributed to illegal abortions. Black women were less likely than white women to be able to afford safe illegal abortions and were generally denied legal therapeutic abortions performed in hospitals. Of all therapeutic abortions performed in New York City at that time, for example, over 90 percent were performed on white women.[185] Black women knew that the *lack* of family planning services was a leading cause of death in their communities. In the 1950s, Dr. Dorothy Brown, the first Black female general surgeon in the United States and a Tennessee state representative, became the first state legislator to introduce a bill to legalize abortion.[186]

Today, with Black women having 24 percent of abortions in the United States, Black women's rights activist Loretta Ross says, "The question is not *if* we support abortion, but *how*, and when, and why."[187] Black feminist critiques of the birth control movement, such as Angela Davis's brilliant chapter "Racism, Birth Control, and Reproductive Rights" in her classic *Women, Race, and Class*, call for abortion rights along with an end to sterilization abuse. Contemporary grassroots organizations, such as the National Black Women's Health Project in Atlanta, take the position that Black women should empower themselves to take control of their reproductive health.

If family-planning programs are a covert attempt to extinguish the Black race, "genocide" is the right word to describe them. Created to describe the Nazi annihilation of the Jews, the term means "the use of deliberate systematic measures (as killing, bodily or mental injury, unlivable conditions, prevention of births) calculated to bring about the extermination of a racial, political, or cultural group or to destroy the language, religion, or culture of a group." [188] The United Nations Convention for the Prevention and Punishment of Genocide includes in its definition of genocide an effort to eradicate a portion of a group. [189] There is ample evidence that some family-planning clinics have been opened in Black communities for the purpose of reducing Black birthrates. But is this racial genocide?

The equation of birth control with racial genocide can also be dangerous. Opposition to all forms of family planning for Blacks leads to an unacceptable restriction of Black women's control over their own procreative decisions. Community activists who call for Black women to avoid birth control altogether in order to produce as many children as possible encroach on women's reproductive autonomy. They also buy into the eugenicist's misguided creed that reproduction determines a group's social status.

This is a minority position among those who oppose birth control as a form of racial domination, however. The predominant concern is not with contraception itself, but with contraception promoted by whites for the purpose of population control. Blacks, it turned out, had good cause to be suspicious of government-sponsored family-planning programs: subsequent investigation proved true nationalists' accusation that these programs were coercing Black women to be sterilized. The critical issue is not whether a program is subsidized by public funds, however, but whether the program is controlled by the Black community it serves and designed to enhance its members' reproductive freedom.

Although some Blacks believe that white-controlled family planning literally threatens Black survival, I take the position that racist birth control policies serve primarily an ideological function. The chief danger of these programs is not the physical annihilation of a race or social class. Family planning policies never reduced the Black birthrate enough to accomplish this result. Rather, the chief danger of these policies is the legitimation of an oppressive social structure. Proposals to solve social problems by curbing Black reproduction make racial inequality appear to be the product of nature rather than power. By identifying procreation as the cause of Black people's condition, they divert attention away from the political, social, and economic forces that maintain America's racial order. This harm to the entire group compounds the harm to individual members who are denied the freedom to have children. Donald MacKenzie observed that eugenic social theory is "a way of reading the structure of social classes onto nature."[190] In the same way, the primary threat to the Black community posed by coercive birth control schemes is not the actual elimination of the Black race; it is the biological justification of white supremacy.

Claims that current government policies that penalize Black reproduction share this legitimating feature of the eugenic rationale are sometimes misinterpreted as an unwarranted fear of racial genocide. John Kramer, dean of Tulane Law School, criticized my argument that reproductive punishments for crime are similar to eugenic laws on the ground that "Black women need not fear that their right to bear children is under serious attack . . . nor do black birthrates suggest that they do."[191] Dean Kramer failed to understand my point about the dangerous message sent by both eugenic laws and policies that penalize Black childbearing. It could as easily be argued that mandatory sterilization laws enforced during the first half of the twentieth century posed no serious danger since they resulted in the sterilization of only 70,000 people. But the impact of these laws went far beyond their reduction of victims' birthrates. They affected the way Americans valued each other and thought about social problems. Eugenic ideology may also facilitate truly genocidal actions. The Nazi compulsory sterilization law of 1933 foreshadowed the Holocaust.[192]

Condemnation of policies that devalue Black reproduction need not arise from a fear of Black extermination. This opposition can arise from the struggle to eradicate white supremacy.

FROM NORPLANT TO THE CONTRACEPTIVE VACCINE
The New Frontier of Population Control

They told us this and they told us that about the Norplant and I'm going through all these changes and I'm trying to have it removed." Yvonne Thomas, a thirty-year-old Baltimore mother, was describing her experience with Norplant, a new, long-acting contraceptive implanted in her arm at a family-planning clinic. When she began suffering from side effects, Thomas returned to have the device removed. But the clinic staff balked at her request. "Then they tell me that it's not putting me in bed, as if they know how I feel on the inside of *my* body. . . . I feel like because I'm a social service mother that's what's keeping me from getting this Norplant out of me. Because I've known other people that has the Norplant that spent money to have it put in and spent money to have it put out with no problems. . . . That's how they make me feel, like *'you got this Norplant you keep it.'*" [1]

Yvonne Thomas is one of thousands of Black women in the United States who have been pressured to try this controversial form of birth control. Like the others, she is a target of a campaign to push the drug on poor Black women in hopes of decreasing their birthrate. Population control policies designed to reduce births of an entire group of people for social ends are usually associated with Third World countries. In the 1990s, legislators and policymakers in the United States seized upon Norplant as a means of domestic population control.

Norplant appears destined to be replaced by injectable contraceptives such as the newly approved Depo-Provera or the experimental "contraceptive vaccine" as the method of choice for reducing Black women's fertility. Unlike that of Norplant, which can be removed (albeit by surgical incision), the contraceptive effect of an injection or vaccine cannot be reversed once the agents are shot into a woman's bloodstream. Injections and vaccines are also easier to administer without a woman's full awareness or consent. Negative publicity generated by women's adverse experiences with Norplant as well as class action lawsuits filed against its distributor may make it impossible to convince enough women to use it. Still, the speedy embrace of Norplant as a means of reproductive regulation and the injuries it has already inflicted are sobering omens of the future of birth control in America. In this chapter, I describe how racial politics created this latest threat to reproductive rights and explain why increasing access to new, highly effective contraceptives does not necessarily enhance reproductive freedom.

THE IDEAL CONTRACEPTIVE?

Norplant consists of six silicone capsules, each about the size of a matchstick, filled with a synthetic hormone called levonorgestral (the same type of progestin used in some birth control pills). The tubes are implanted in a fan-shaped design just under the skin of a woman's upper arm through a small incision. The minor surgical procedure, which takes ten to fifteen minutes, can usually be performed in a clinic or doctor's office under local anesthesia. Norplant prevents pregnancy for up to five years by gradually releasing a low dose of the hormone into the bloodstream. It works mainly by suppressing ovulation, but also keeps sperm from reaching the egg by thickening the cervical mucus. Originally developed by the Population Council, a nonprofit organization that promotes family planning in the Third World, Norplant is now distributed in the United States by the giant pharmaceutical company Wyeth-Ayerst Laboratories, a division of American Home Products.

When the FDA approved Norplant for marketing in December 1990, it was hailed as the first major birth control breakthrough since the pill. The press release from Wyeth-Ayerst proclaimed the "eagerly awaited medical advance" as "the most innovative contraceptive in thirty years."[2] From this perspective, Norplant is the ideal contraceptive—long-acting, effective, convenient. Once the tubes are inserted, a woman is protected against pregnancy for five years without any further hassle. There is no need to remember to take it daily, as with the pill. Women do not have to interrupt sex to use it, as with a diaphragm or contraceptive foam. Nor do women need their partner's cooperation, as with condoms. Norplant's failure rate is only 1 percent over the five-year period; in other words, it is 99 percent effective.[3] Only sterilization has a better record. In fact, Norplant is so foolproof that it is really a form of temporary sterilization. Yet it has the advantage over sterilization of being reversible once the tubes are removed. At first glance, Norplant seems like the answer to women's prayers. It has already been used by more than 1 million women in the United States and 3 million women worldwide.[4]

TESTING THE WATERS—THE *INQUIRER* EDITORIAL

Norplant's potential to enhance women's reproductive freedom was quickly overshadowed by its potential for reproductive abuse. The new contraceptive was instantly embraced by policymakers, legislators, and social pundits as a way of curbing the birthrate of poor Black women. On December 12, 1990, only two days after the FDA's approval, the *Philadelphia Inquirer* published a controversial editorial entitled "Poverty and Norplant: Can Contraception Reduce the Underclass?"[5] Deputy editorial-page editor Donald Kimelman began the piece by linking two recent news items: one announced the approval of Norplant, and the other reported the research finding that half of Black children live in poverty. Kimelman went on to propose Norplant as a solution to inner-city poverty, arguing that "the main reason more black children are living in poverty is that people having the most children are the ones least capable of supporting them."[6] No one should be compelled to have Norplant implanted, Kimelman conceded. But he endorsed giving women on welfare financial incentives to encourage them to use the contraceptive.

The Norplant editorial sent off shock waves across the country. Black leaders were quick to express their outrage at the editorial's racist and eugenic overtones. Norplant's creator, Dr. Sheldon J. Segal, shot off a letter to the *New York Times* unequivocally opposing the use of Norplant for any coercive purpose: "It was developed to improve reproductive freedom, not to restrict it."[7] Black reporters and editors at the *Inquirer* protested the editorial. An emotional meeting brought Black staff members to tears—was their boss implying that those who grew up in large, poor families should never have been born?[8] The *Inquirer*'s Metro columnist, Steve Lopez, issued a stinging rebuttal the following Sunday. "What we have, basically, is the *In-*

quirer brain trust looking down from its ivory tower and wondering if black people should be paid to stop having so many damn kids," Lopez fumed. "By combining contraception and race, the voice of the *Inquirer* calls to mind another David. David Duke."[9] (Lopez was referring to the editorial-page editor, David Boldt, who okayed the editorial.)

The public outcry moved the *Inquirer* to print an apology eleven days later. Admitting that the piece was "misguided and wrong-headed," the paper said it now agreed with critics that the incentives it proposed were tantamount to coercion and that other strategies for eliminating poverty should be explored. As further evidence of America's racial cleavage, David Boldt later wrote that he was astonished by the adverse reaction.[10] He was unaware of Blacks' fear of genocide and had no idea that readers might be angered by the Norplant proposal. A telephone call from Jesse Jackson, he says, cleared things up.

The *Inquirer*'s apology did not put the idea of Norplant incentives to rest. Far from it. Journalists immediately came to the *Inquirer*'s defense. Within days of the apology, *Newsweek* offered careful praise of Kimelman's proposal: "However offensive the editorial, Kimelman was clearly on to something. . . . The old answers have mostly failed. After the shouting stops, the problem will remain. It's too important to become taboo."[11] The *Richmond Times-Dispatch* gave an even stronger endorsement, arguing that Norplant "offers society yet another way to curb the expansion of an underclass most of whose members face futures of disorder and deprivation."[12] A year later Matthew Rees, writing for the *New Republic*, similarly defended Norplant incentives on the ground that "the current threat to children in our inner cities makes it an option that the morally serious can no longer simply dismiss."[13] ("Our inner cities" and "the underclass," of course, are another way of referring to the *Black* urban poor.) Although Rees acknowledged the need to treat poverty's "deeper roots," as well as constitutional objections to interfering with a woman's reproductive decisions, he concluded that "right now, Norplant may be the only practical option we've got."

More ominously, people in positions to steer public policy followed the media's lead. David Frankel, director of population sciences at the Rockefeller Foundation, made light of tensions at the *Inquirer*, writing to the *Washington Post*, "Despite the infantile reaction of some black staffers, . . . birth control incentives would not be genocide. Such incentives would be a humane inducement to social responsibility."[14]

Backers of the Norplant scheme were not uniformly white, as reflected by Washington, D.C., mayor Marion Barry's support of
mandatory Norplant for women on welfare. "You can have as many
babies as you want," Barry stated. "But when you start asking the
government to take care of them, the government now ought to have
some control over you."[15]

MARKETING NORPLANT TO POOR WOMEN

The *Inquirer* episode inaugurated a new wave of birth control politics,
with Norplant at the center. What appeared to be an expensive contraceptive marketed to affluent women through private physicians
soon became the focus of government programs for poor women.
Lawmakers across the country have proposed and implemented
schemes not only to make Norplant available to women on welfare
but to pressure them to use the device as well.

At a time when legislatures nationwide are slashing social programs for the poor, public aid for Norplant became a popular budget
item. Without financial assistance, the cost of Norplant would be pro-
hibitive. The capsules cost $365 and the implantation procedure can
run from $150 to $500. Removal costs another $150 to $500, or more
if there are complications. The government sprang into action. Every
state and the District of Columbia almost immediately made Norplant
available to poor women through Medicaid. Tennessee passed a law
in 1993 requiring that anyone who receives AFDC or other forms of
public assistance be notified in writing about the state's offer of free
Norplant. Women in Washington State who receive maternity care
assistance also get information about Norplant.

By 1994, states had already spent $34 million on Norplant-related
benefits.[16] As a result, at least half of the women in the United States
who have used Norplant are Medicaid recipients. When Planned
Parenthood surveyed its affiliates it discovered that, although only 12
percent of its clients are Medicaid recipients, 95 to 100 percent of
women implanted with Norplant at some of its clinics were on
Medicaid.[17]

There were also efforts to provide Norplant to low-income women
ineligible for Medicaid. California governor Pete Wilson allocated an
extra $5 million to reimburse state-funded clinics for Norplant going
to women without Medicaid or Medi-Cal coverage. North Carolina's

budget similarly set aside a "Women's Health Service Fund" to pay for Norplant for the uninsured. The Norplant Foundation, a non-profit organization established by Norplant's distributor, Wyeth-Ayerst, devotes $2.8 million a year to donate Norplant kits to low-income women.[18]

Simply making Norplant more accessible to indigent women was not enough for some lawmakers. Within two years thirteen state legislatures had proposed some twenty measures to implant poor women with Norplant.[19] A number of these bills would pressure women on welfare to use the device either by offering them a financial bonus or by requiring implantation as a condition of receiving benefits. In February 1991, only a couple of months after Norplant was approved, Kansas Republican state representative Kerry Patrick introduced legislation that would grant welfare recipients a one-time payment of $500 to use Norplant, followed by a $50 bonus each year the implants remained in place. Patrick touted his plan as having "the potential to save the taxpayers millions of their hard-earned dollars" by reducing the number of children on the welfare rolls.[20] He suggested that women needed an extra incentive to get them to take advantage of the state's free supply of Norplant, pointing to a study indicating that only one out of eight women currently used birth control. Republican representative Robert Farr echoed these sentiments when he proposed a similar bill in Connecticut: "It's far cheaper to give you money not to have kids than to give you money if you have kids."[21]

In short order, Louisiana state representative and former Ku Klux Klan Grand Wizard David Duke proposed paying women on welfare $100 a year to use the device. Duke's bill was an attempt to fulfill his campaign promise to enact "concrete proposals to reduce the illegitimate birthrate and break the cycle of poverty that truly enslaves and harms the black race."[22] The scheme also reflected his earlier support for what he called "Nazism," when he claimed in 1985 that "the real answer to the world's problems" was "promoting the best strains, the best individuals."[23] Arizona, Colorado, Ohio, Florida, Tennessee, and Washington have considered similar Norplant bonuses. In addition to these financial incentives, a North Carolina bill would have required that all women who get a state-funded abortion be implanted with Norplant unless it is medically unsafe.

Several states have considered even more coercive means to ensure the infertility of women receiving welfare. In his 1993 State of the State address, Maryland governor William Schaefer suggested that the state should consider making Norplant *mandatory* for women on welfare. Similarly, bills introduced in Mississippi and South Carolina would require women who already have children to get Norplant inserted as a condition for receiving future benefits. Legislation proposed in other states would deny increases in AFDC payments to women who declined the device.

The notion of requiring women on welfare to use birth control had circulated decades earlier. In his 1973 book *Who Should Have Children?* University of Chicago physiologist Dwight J. Ingle advocated selective population control as an alternative to the growing welfare state.[24] Ingle proposed that individuals who could not provide their children with a healthy environment or biological inheritance — including people with genetic defects or low intelligence, welfare recipients, criminals, drug addicts, and alcoholics — should be encouraged, or forced if necessary, to refrain from childbearing. "By this I mean that millions of people are unqualified for parenthood and should remain childless," Ingle explained in the book's foreword. One of Ingle's proposals was the mandatory insertion of pellets containing an "antifertility agent" under the skin of every woman of childbearing age. Women would be required to apply for a license to have the pellet removed; only those who qualified for parenthood would be allowed to become pregnant. William Shockley made a similar proposal in a 1967 letter to the editor of the *Palo Alto Times*.[25] Norplant has the potential to fulfill these eugenicists' fantasies.

WHAT'S RACE GOT TO DO WITH IT?

If these proposals apply to all welfare recipients, what is the relevance of race? Clearly, welfare policy, which concerns how America deals with its poor, is governed by capitalist economics and class politics. Class divisions within the Black community also create differences in Blacks' attitudes toward welfare. Although we should not underestimate this class dimension of programs that regulate welfare mothers, it is crucial to see that race equally determines the programs' features and popularity. Because class distinctions are racialized, race and class are inextricably linked in the development of welfare policy. When Americans debate welfare reform, most have single Black mothers in mind.

Some Norplant proponents — Kimelman and Duke, for example — have explicitly suggested distributing the contraceptive to *Black* women. After the commotion over the *Inquirer* editorial, however, few politicians are likely to link birth control specifically to Black poverty, even if that is their intention. But race lurks behind proposals to induce poor women in general to use Norplant. Not only will these incentives disproportionately affect Black women, but they may be covertly targeted at these women as well.

Part of the reason has to do with numbers. Although most families on welfare are not Black, Blacks disproportionately rely on welfare to support their children. Black women are only 6 percent of the population, but they represent a third of AFDC recipients.[26] The concentration of Black welfare recipients is even greater in the nation's inner cities, where Norplant has primarily been dispensed. For example, in Baltimore, the site of a government campaign to distribute Norplant, 86 percent of women receiving welfare are Black.

It is also true that a larger percentage of Blacks than whites are poor. One-third of all Blacks and half of all Black children live in poverty. Black women are five times more likely to live in poverty, five times more likely to be on welfare, and three times more likely to be unemployed than are white women.[27] Welfare programs, then, have a greater direct impact on the status of Black people as a whole. Any policy directed at women on welfare will disproportionately affect Black women because such a large proportion of Black women rely on public assistance. These policies, in turn, affect all Blacks as a group because such a large proportion of Blacks are poor.

The second reason has to do with perceptions. Although most people on welfare are not Black, many Americans think they are. The American public associates welfare payments to single mothers with the mythical Black "welfare queen," who deliberately becomes pregnant in order to increase the amount of her monthly check. The welfare queen represents laziness, chicanery, and economic burden all wrapped up in one powerful image. For decades, the media and politicians have shown pictures of Black mothers when they discuss public assistance. Now the link between race and welfare is firmly implanted in Americans' minds.

When conservative activist Clint Bolick called Lani Guinier, President Clinton's repudiated Justice Department nominee, a "quota queen," he counted on the public's immediate association of the label with the pejorative "welfare queen."[28] The title automatically linked the Black Guinier to negative stereotypes of Black women on welfare, helping to shut off reasoned debate about her views. Similarly, it is commonplace to observe that "welfare" has become a code word for "race." People can avoid the charge of racism by directing their vitriol at the welfare system instead of explicitly assailing Black people.

In addition, poor Blacks pose a far greater threat to white Americans than do poor whites. The word "underclass" refers not only to its members' poverty but also to a host of social pathologies such as crime, drug addiction, violence, welfare dependency, and illegitimacy. Although poverty may be relatively race-neutral in people's minds, these other depravities are associated with Black culture. Contemporary welfare rhetoric blames Black single mothers for transmitting a deviant lifestyle to their children, a lifestyle marked not only by persistent welfare dependency but also by moral degeneracy and criminality.

White Americans resent the welfare queen who rips off their tax dollars, but even more they fear the Willie Horton she gives birth to. These images are distinctly Black; they have no white counterparts. As I showed in the Introduction, many whites hold deeply embedded beliefs about the dangers of Black reproduction that infect any scheme to solve social problems through birth control. This panic is exacerbated by the predicted end of white numerical supremacy in the United States within decades.[29] Proposals designed to reduce the number of children born to poor parents are an attempt to fend off this threat to white people's welfare, a threat that is specifically Black.

Thus, race and class politics work together to propel coercive birth control policies. The impact of these policies, moreover, crosses the boundaries of race and class. Laws aimed at curbing Black women's fertility restrict poor white women's liberties as well. Programs that apply only to Black women who are poor help to devalue Black people as a whole.

To date, no state legislature has passed a bill offering bonuses for or mandating the use of Norplant. But the numerous proposals for Norplant incentives and the defense of the *Inquirer* editorial show that the idea is alive and well. Commentators and politicians have tested the waters and found growing support for the use of birth control as a solution to the Black underclass. As the social climate becomes increasingly hostile toward welfare mothers and supportive of drastic cuts in welfare spending, there is a good chance that these proposals could become a reality—unless people committed to racial equality, economic justice, and reproductive liberty fight back.

PUSHING NORPLANT ON TEENAGERS

Policymakers have also promoted Norplant as the solution to teenage pregnancy. By preventing pregnancy, they argue, Norplant will allow teenage girls to pursue a career and prevent additional children from being born into poverty and dependence on government aid. "A lot of teenagers needed Norplant. I'm about the only girl in my neighborhood who doesn't have kids," a Black teenager testified on a promotional video about Norplant produced at Emory University. "They need to get some [Norplant] so they can have fun and enjoy life while they be young."[30] Another scene features a conversation between a doctor and another Black girl. "So, what might you tell a young teenage girl?" the doctor asks as he pats the teenager's shoulder. "Get it!" she replies enthusiastically.

The problem of teen pregnancy, too, is intertwined with issues of race and welfare policy. Although most teen mothers are white, the teen birthrate among Blacks is more than double that among whites, and one out of every four Black children is born to a teen mother. Black girls are also more likely to have a child out of wedlock. The gap, however, is rapidly narrowing: the white unwed birthrate has nearly doubled since 1980, while the rate for Black women has risen only 7 percent.[31] Many Americans nevertheless see unwed teen pregnancy as a Black cultural trait that is infiltrating white America. In his editorial "The Coming White Underclass," Charles Murray vividly portrays the burgeoning white illegitimacy rate as an impending crisis, destined to cause the same social catastrophes he attributes to Black single motherhood.[32] He observes that the white illegitimacy rate of 22 percent is dangerously close to the point at which "the trendlines on black crime, dropout from the labor force, and illegitimacy all shifted sharply upward." But for now these problems remain concentrated in the Black community, for, Murray reminds us, "an underclass needs a critical mass, and white America has not had one." Not surprisingly, programs distributing Norplant to teens have been implemented in predominantly Black schools.

In addition, one of the key criticisms of teen pregnancy is that young mothers must often resort to welfare to support their children. According to the Congressional Budget Office, half of all teen mothers go on welfare within five years of giving birth. More than two-thirds eventually receive welfare.[33] Although teen mothers make up only about 7 percent of welfare recipients, they have been a chief target of attacks on the welfare system. A persistent element in the recent federal welfare reform bill's many incarnations was a provision to cut off AFDC to teenagers. "We are the only society . . . that says to a teenage girl, 'We're going to give you a welfare check if you have a baby,' " explained Robert Moffit of the Heritage Foundation. "If you want to reduce the rate of illegitimacy, you have to stop subsidizing it." [34] The link between race and welfare helped to generate support for passing out Norplant to Black teenage girls.

Baltimore was the first city to distribute Norplant aggressively to teenagers. In December 1992, Baltimore's health commissioner, Peter Beilenson, announced a program to encourage the city's inner-city girls to use Norplant at state expense. About 10 percent of girls ages fifteen to seventeen in Baltimore have babies, one of the highest rates in the country, triple the national average. [35] The plan called for doctors, hospitals, and clinics to persuade their "high-risk" teenage patients to have the device implanted. School clinics would also offer Norplant to their female students without the need for parental consent. [36]

Laurence G. Paquin Middle School, a school for pregnant girls and girls who already have babies, became the first Baltimore school to implement a pilot program to provide Norplant in its clinic. All but five of the 350 students at the school are Black. Although other contraceptives are touched on in counseling sessions, the girls are urged to try Norplant. A few other urban high schools, including San Fernando High School in Los Angeles and Crane High School on Chicago's West Side, also include Norplant among the contraceptives distributed from the school clinic. [37]

The distribution of Norplant to teenagers has sparked conflict, even within the Black community. Some Black community leaders have denounced its introduction in high schools for its racism. They are angry that Baltimore's Black community was not consulted about a plan directed at its children. Clergy United for the Renewal of East Baltimore (CURE), a group of ministers representing over two hundred churches, opposed the Baltimore program for "push[ing] the issue of *social* control of an ethnic minority by the majority population whose culture and values may be different." [38] "You know as well as I know that they wouldn't let their twelve-year-old girl get Norplant," the group's leader, Rev. Melvin Tuggle, said of the white officials. "And I know their daughters are just as sexually active as anybody else." [39] Members of the Nation of Islam packed the Baltimore City Council hearing on the issue to express their outrage. Cheers rang out as a representative of Louis Farrakhan shouted, "I'm not going to sit by and let my sisters and my children be destroyed by Norplant."[40] City councilor Carl Stokes, who stormed out of the hearing, charging bias against Norplant opponents, has called the idea of welfare incentives "something I would have thought was unspeakable in America today."[41]

But some of Norplant's most vocal promoters are also Black. Baltimore's Black mayor, Kurt Schmoke, and several other city politicians wholeheartedly endorsed the program. The flamboyant principal of the Paquin School, Rosetta Stith, is a Black woman who has traveled the country espousing the benefits of her Norplant program. She has appeared on national television shows such as *Nightline* and *Crossfire*, arguing that Norplant gives her students "an opportunity to finish high school and go to college."[42] I moderated a program on Norplant at the University of Pennsylvania Law School at which Stith appeared with one of her students, who rose to her feet and upstaged the other panelists with a testimonial about the blessings of Norplant. Ousted surgeon general Joycelyn Elders condemned opponents of Norplant in high schools by likening teenage pregnancy to slavery. "Black people don't want their children born to children," Elders insisted. "They do not want them growing up poor, ignorant slaves. And whoever goes around talking about genocide is someone who likes to see people in slavery."[43]

There is no question that Norplant works as an effective birth control method for teenagers. The low levels of teen contraceptive use are exacerbated by teens' poor compliance with methods that they do use.[44] Contraceptive failure rates are much higher among teenagers than adults because younger women are less conscientious and more fertile than older women.[45] Unlike other birth control methods, Norplant eliminates the need for teenagers to remember to use it daily or at the time of intercourse. Nor do girls have to cope with the embarrassment of getting a boyfriend's cooperation or interrupting sex to use it. It is also appealing to girls that the effects of Norplant are reversible once the implants are removed, so they can have children later in life when they may be better prepared to be mothers. In other words, Norplant seems like the ideal contraceptive for sexually active teenagers. This explains why Republican state senator Shirley Winsley of Washington, who sponsored three Norplant-related bills, stated, "I can hardly believe a fourteen-year-old mother wouldn't want to have Norplant if it was offered to her."[46]

Early research confirmed Norplant's effectiveness for teenage girls.

A study of 100 adolescent mothers comparing Norplant to the pill, reported in the prestigious *New England Journal of Medicine*, concluded that the selection of Norplant "is associated with higher rates of continued use and lower rates of new pregnancy than the selection of oral contraceptives."[47] It found that only 2 percent of adolescents who used Norplant became pregnant within the first year, compared to 38 percent of adolescents who used the pill.[48] In another survey of 280 teens who either delivered a baby or had an abortion at Johns Hopkins Medical Center, nearly half of oral-contraceptive users had discontinued the method a year later, compared to only 16 percent of Norplant users.[49] And while 25 percent of the teens who chose a contraceptive other than Norplant experienced an unplanned pregnancy, none of the Norplant users had become pregnant.[50] University of Texas researchers similarly concluded that Norplant was "especially suitable for young patients."[51]

CAN NORPLANT SOLVE THE "PROBLEM" OF TEEN PREGNANCY?

Does Norplant's effectiveness for birth control mean that it solves the problem of teenage pregnancy? To answer that question requires asking why teenage pregnancy is a problem in the first place. There is no question that there is reason for concern. The United States has the highest teen pregnancy rate in the Western world. Nearly 1 million of the 9 million girls between ages fifteen and nineteen in this country become pregnant each year, with about half giving birth.[52] There are an additional 25,000 pregnancies among girls under age fifteen.[53]

Teenage pregnancy came to be seen as a social crisis only three decades ago. The rate of teen childbirth was actually much higher in the 1950s than in the 1980s, although it started to climb again in 1986. However, very recent data indicate that the adolescent birthrate has even dropped slightly in the 1990s.[54] (Declines in recent decades are attributed more to the increased availability of legal abortion than to greater use of contraceptives.) The public's concern about teenagers having babies has depended much more on the politics of sexuality, abortion, family values, and welfare than on the numbers.[55] When people refer to the "problem" of teenage pregracy they may mean one or a combination of several concerns—teenagers having sex, teenagers getting pregnant, teenagers raising children, teenagers having babies out of wedlock, and teenagers having babies at public expense. Does Norplant solve any of these specific problems?

Teenagers Having Sex

For some people, the problem with teenage pregnancy is that it results from teenagers having sex. Approximately 70 percent of unmarried teenage girls have had sexual intercourse by the age of nineteen; the average age of first intercourse is about sixteen.[56] Adolescent sexual activity, in turn, may be a concern for several reasons: some view it as immoral; others, as hazardous to teenagers' physical health owing to the transmission of diseases, including AIDS. Yet others believe that teenagers, especially very young ones, are not emotionally prepared for sexual activity. Most of the babies born to teen mothers are fathered by adult men, some of whom may be immorally and even illegally coercing these girls to have sex with them.[57] Older men are primarily responsible for the frightening spread of sexually transmitted diseases (STDs) among adolescent girls. Studies show that as many as one in four girls are victims of sexual abuse, and 75 percent of girls in a national survey who had sex before age fourteen reported having coerced sex.[58]

Preventing teenage pregnancy with Norplant is not a solution to the problem viewed this way because it does not guard teenagers from these harms caused by early sexual activity. Indeed, some have argued that the easy availability of Norplant signals tacit approval of teen sex, making the problem worse. For these conservatives, abstinence, not birth control, is the only acceptable answer. There is no hard evidence that Norplant will encourage teenagers to have sex. But Norplant gives no protection against contracting STDs or against coercive sexual experiences. Distributing long-acting contraceptives to young girls unfairly shifts the spotlight away from the adult men who are largely responsible for the problem.

Teenagers Getting Pregnant

For others the problem is not that teenagers are having sexual intercourse, but that sex too often results in unwanted pregnancy. Some 95 percent of all adolescent pregnancies are unintentional.[59] A Johns Hopkins study of 313 sexually active Baltimore girls, for example, found that only 5 percent deliberately set out to have babies.[60] The fact that 40 percent of teen pregnancies end in abortion is further proof of the problem. (A third of all abortions performed each year are done on teenage girls.) Yet teenagers wait on average over a year after they begin having sex before seeking any birth control.[61] Although teenagers in most Western European countries are as sexually active as those in the United States, their pregnancy rate is far lower.[62] Sweden's teen birthrate in 1991, for example, was one-fifth that of the United States. Why is there such a disparity?

One cause appears to be America's ambivalence about teenage sexuality: our culture promotes teen sex on soap operas and music videos while maintaining a puritanical attitude about discussing birth control with teens. The result is the abysmal inadequacy of reproductive health services for teens. Western European governments encourage adolescents' use of birth control by subsidizing contraception education and availability.[63] Congress's policies, on the other hand, have been hampered by political compromises such as the Adolescent Family Life Act of 1988 that focuses on "chastity" and "sexual self-discipline" rather than providing adequate contraceptive services. Although nearly all states require some form of sex education in schools, fewer than 10 percent of American students receive comprehensive information covering topics such as sexual behavior and health, abortion, homosexuality, relationships, and condoms.[64]

Another cause is poverty, the key predictor of adolescent pregnancy. The lower teen pregnancy rates in European countries correspond perfectly with their lower rates of youth poverty.[65] Parts of the United States with less poverty also have less of a problem with pregnant teens. Poverty-striken Louisiana, for example, has a teen birthrate ten times higher than affluent Marin County, California. According to one researcher, this link between pregnancy and poverty "demands that we view early childbearing as a symptom of a much larger problem: the status of disadvantaged youth in this country."[66] Relying on school programs to reduce early pregnancy, then, is being terribly blind to the problem's complex causes.

Dispensing Norplant at school clinics is a radical departure from the typically reticent policy on teen birth control. Norplant will prevent sexually active teens from becoming pregnant; but, as we will see in the next section, it is not the safest way of accomplishing this goal. Moreover, Norplant simply covers up the underlying reasons why so many teenagers are getting pregnant in the first place. June Perry, the director of a social service center in Milwaukee, reports a new trend among the Black teens she serves: girls who have Norplant let their boyfriends cut it out with a razor blade. "The talk is, 'If you love me you will have my baby,' and the girls say, 'I will endure this pain for you,' " Perry recounts.[67] Without addressing the deeper problems of poverty and marginalization, Norplant's effectiveness is fleeting.

Teenagers Raising Children

The concern about teenage pregnancy often focuses specifically on the harm of "children raising children," based on a concern for the young mother, a concern for the child, or both. One line of reasoning is that motherhood is bad for teenagers, ruining their chances for finishing high school and pursuing a career. As a poster from the Children's Defense Fund advises, "Stick with the crowd that has a bright future—don't get pregnant." True, teenagers who have babies are more than twice as likely to be poor, but blaming teen pregnancy for poverty reverses cause and effect. While many policymakers argue that this correlation proves that teenage pregnancy leads to poverty, it is fairer to say that poverty makes pregnancy a more rational option for some teenage girls. High rates of youth poverty *precede* high rates of teen childbearing, not vice versa.[68]

Many adolescent girls have babies not because they eagerly desire motherhood but because they have little incentive to avoid it. As the director of a Cincinnati parenting program explained, "It's not that teenagers want to be pregnant, it's that they don't want not to enough."[69] These teens do not believe that having a baby will ruin their life prospects; and some new, though controversial, evidence indicates that they may be right. Early pregnancy may actually be an adaptive response on the part of some Black teenage girls: it may make sense for many of them to care for infants at the time when they have the fewest employment opportunities, the best health, and the most help from a network of relatives.[70] The leading study, which followed Black teen mothers in Baltimore for nearly two decades, found that early childbearing does not doom women to lifelong destitution.[71] Although they might have achieved more had they postponed childbearing, most of the mothers studied eventually graduated from high school, found full-time jobs, and got off welfare.

Teen mothers who do not finish school typically drop out *before* becoming pregnant; having a baby is a response to poor achievement in school and little hope for a decent job. There is no evidence that delaying childbearing with Norplant will markedly improve these adolescents' chances for success. The myth that inner-city teens would be miraculously lifted out of poverty if they would only stop having babies is one of the cruelest hoaxes of our time.

A related view is that teenage pregnancy is bad for children because adolescents make unfit parents. Studies reveal that the children of teen mothers typically experience a number of disadvantages. Babies born to adolescent mothers, for example, generally have a higher risk of prematurity, low birth weight, and death.[72] While Norplant would avert these problems, it does not solve the socioeconomic causes of a risky pregnancy and deprived childhood. There is evidence that the difficulties experienced by children of teen mothers stem from poverty and not from early childbearing alone. Poverty and shoddy health care lead to high infant mortality rates among Blacks generally. Indeed, the risk of death is *lower* for Black infants born to teen mothers than for those born to older mothers. The often tragic consequences of teen parenting could be alleviated if teen mothers had better social support, including prenatal care, adequate nutrition, and assistance with child care. This does not mean that social policy should *encourage* teenagers to have babies; but it does mean that Norplant will not cure the social problems that have been erroneously attributed to the teen birthrate. Even Rosetta Stith, the Paquin School principal, concedes, "There's not a pill or an implant that's going to solve the teenage pregnancy problem." She adds, "That's going to come when this country decides to be committed to children."[73]

Teenagers Having Babies Out of Wedlock

What distinguishes contemporary teen mothers from those in past decades is that far fewer today get married or put their babies up for adoption. Teenagers make up less than a third of all single mothers; but two out of three teen mothers are not married, compared with only 15 percent in 1960.[74] A whopping 92 percent of Black teen births are out of wedlock.[75]

This worry about teen pregnancy is based on a value judgment that, for moral, social, or economic reasons, only married couples should have children. Those who hold this view believe that unmarried teens should be prevented from having babies because their singleness (rather than their immaturity) disqualifies them for motherhood. As Florida senator Rick Dantzler stated in support of Norplant incentives, "children born to single-parent families, children reared without 'paternal influence,' are tomorrow's criminals."[76]

It follows from this theory that teens may have babies as long as they get married. Although marriage to a financially secure man would improve a young mother's economic situation, marrying may also magnify her problems: for pregnant teens, marriage is correlated with "dropping out of school, having more babies, and ultimately being divorced or separated."[77] The typical indigent teen has little economic incentive to marry her child's father, who probably is also unemployed. She is likely to get more financial support and help with child care if she remains with her immediate family. Finding steady work is a better route off welfare than getting married.

Teenagers Having Babies at Public Expense

Condemnation of teen pregnancy is often couched in complaints about its expense to taxpayers. Because unmarried teen mothers are typically poor, they and their children are likely to be supported by welfare. As Charles Murray explained, cutting off welfare benefits to a young single mother will force her to seek support "from her parents, boyfriend, siblings, neighbors, church, or philanthropies. . . . [A]nywhere, other than the government."[78] Murray's observation reveals another value judgment—that teen mothers' dependency on the government, but not on relatives or private charity, is immoral or unfair. By stopping teens from becoming pregnant in the first place, Norplant prevents the birth of babies who would require government aid. But this justification for Norplant programs fails to scrutinize the underlying judgment that teen mothers do not deserve public assistance as well as the underlying reasons for teen poverty. Moreover, the fear that providing aid to teen mothers will encourage teen childbearing is unfounded. European countries and Canada, which have higher welfare benefits than the United States, also have lower birthrates.

On every count, Norplant falls short of tackling the social roots of the "problem" of teen pregnancy, however defined. Part of the reason is that the problem of teen pregnancy is really, in many cases, a problem of sexual abuse, of poverty, of racism, and of inadequate resources for teen mothers and their children.

Nevertheless, if Norplant increases control over reproduction, what could possibly be wrong with making it more available to poor

Black women and teenagers? The problem with this question is that it assumes that Norplant's efficacy at preventing pregnancy means it promotes women's health and reproductive autonomy. To show why just the opposite is true, I now turn to women's experiences with the new contraceptive. Far from giving poor Black women greater reproductive freedom, it has served as a means for doctors and government officials to dictate their procreative decisions. Once pressured into having Norplant inserted, many have had a tough time getting a doctor to remove it. Meanwhile the tubes remain embedded in their arms, continuing to pump dangerous hormones into their bodies. I once heard a Black health worker aptly describe Norplant as a form of torture.

NORPLANT MAY BE HAZARDOUS TO YOUR HEALTH

Nearly all Norplant users experience at least one of a variety of side effects ranging from annoying inconvenience to potentially serious conditions. The hormone in Norplant can cause the same long list of bodily disruptions as the pill: headaches, depression, nervousness, change in appetite, weight gain, hair loss, nausea, dizziness, acne, breast tenderness, swelling of the ovaries, and ovarian cysts. Norplant has also been linked to rare instances of stroke and heart attack, although a causal connection has not been definitively proven.

Because Norplant does not contain estrogen, it is thought to present less of a risk for heart attack, stroke, and certain cancers than oral contraceptives. But Norplant's continuous release of progestin produces the side effect that is most bothersome to women: it upsets the menstrual cycle. Some women have no period for months at a time; others experience spotting or irregular bleeding; the worst off suffer from prolonged, heavy bleeding that can last for months on end.

Excessive bleeding should not be dismissed as a mere annoyance: it can require costly expenditures for sanitary napkins, it can dramatically interfere with a woman's employment and lifestyle, and it can mask serious gynecological conditions such as ovarian cancer. Anthropologists tell us that menstruation has powerful consequences in many cultures, affecting everything from religious ceremonies to cooking procedures. Some Native American women, for example, have been excluded from certain community functions because of tribal taboos against women's involvement while they are menstruating.[79] Other women have lost their jobs when they were absent too many times owing to constant bleeding. One woman complained that Norplant defeated its own purpose by destroying her sex life: "If they want to know why people don't get pregnant, it's because they are bleeding all the time!" [80] One in four women in a California study said that their sex life worsened with Norplant.

There are yet other dangers peculiar to Norplant's design. Some women have experienced pain and infection at the site where the tubes were inserted. Some claim that the silicone in Norplant capsules caused debilitating immunological reactions similar to those alleged in the silicone breast implant litigation.[81] Two doctors reported in a 1995 issue of *Toxicology and Industrial Health* the case of a twenty-two-year-old patient who suffered severe complications when the Norplant capsules burst in her arm.[82] Not only did her arm swell to three times its normal size, but she was plagued by persistent headaches, gastrointestinal bleeding, asthma, fatigue, muscle aches, and weakness in her arms. The doctors concluded that these ailments were caused by two consequences of the ruptured device—the excessive release of hormones into her bloodstream and a silicone-induced immunological disease. Norplant inserts that are not removed after five years may cause ectopic pregnancy, which could be fatal owing to massive internal hemorrhaging. The possible adverse effects of the lingering hormone on a fetus are unknown.

These are not isolated cases. The severity and prevalence of Norplant's side effects are reflected in the numbers of women who return to get the implants removed. Almost 20 percent of women in test studies had Norplant extracted within one year, most commonly because of bleeding problems. After three years, over half had it taken out.[83]

Women suffering from certain illnesses are at extra risk of harm and should be advised not to use the implant at all. Many of these health conditions disproportionately affect Black women—high blood pressure, heart disease, kidney disease, sickle-cell anemia, and diabetes, for example. Norplant is less effective in women who weigh more than 150 pounds, another concern for Black women, who are more prone to obesity.

Norplant's side effects are especially troubling for poor minority women who rarely see a doctor. Women who do not get regular health care may not know whether or not Norplant is safe for them. There may be delays in treatment of serious side effects or in detection of more dangerous health conditions such as ovarian cancer masked by irregular bleeding.[84] Unlike women who use the pill, Norplant users need not return to the doctor for prescription refills. There is no guarantee, then, that poor patients will return two months after the procedure to discuss any side effects or will maintain regular annual checkups, as recommended. Norplant use requires immediate and regular access to high-quality health care—a privilege most poor Black women do not enjoy.

It is even more likely that physicians will lose track of teenagers once they graduate from the school that dispensed Norplant to them. One study of 136 Baltimore adolescents using Norplant found a high incidence of failure to make routine gynecologic health maintenance visits.[85] The same Texas study that concluded that Norplant was "especially suitable" for teens also found that almost a fifth of the patients did not visit a clinic at all in the six months after Norplant insertion, despite their increased risk of cervical dysplasia and STDs.[86] Other studies of inner-city patients have found similar follow-up rates of only 25 to 40 percent.[87] Rather than making Norplant the perfect teenager contraceptive, teenagers' ignorance and irresponsibility may make Norplant especially dangerous for them.

These are the side effects that women on Norplant have already experienced. But what about Norplant's long-term consequences? Health advocates argue that we do not know enough about the implant's potential for harm because the clinical testing was terribly inadequate. Norplant's developer, the Population Council, points to research collected over fifteen years from 170 clinical trials involving some 55,000 women. Despite the large numbers of women tested, however, there are concerns about the methods the researchers used and the length of time the women were studied.

Most of the testing occurred not in the United States but overseas, in countries such as Brazil, Indonesia, and Egypt. Ethical breaches in administering Norplant to poor, illiterate Third World women place the research findings in question. Researchers in some countries lost track of large numbers of Norplant users (29 percent in Indonesia, for example), jeopardizing both study results and the women's health.[88]

In addition, there has been no research on whether the increases in cholesterol levels experienced by some Norplant users will lead to higher risk of stroke or cardiovascular disease.[89] Nor has research addressed the concern that the long-term administration of the hormone in Norplant may significantly increase women's risk of breast and cervical cancer.[90] Norplant's long-term effects on teenagers are even less certain because all of the clinical trials were conducted on women over the age of eighteen. Some women's health organizations, including the National Women's Health Network and Health Action International (a network of one hundred organizations from thirty-six countries), formally opposed FDA approval of Norplant until its long-term safety could be assured through follow-up studies.

The case of testing in Bangladesh raises serious doubts about both the ethics and the reliability of the Norplant research. An investigation conducted by UBINIG, a Bangladeshi monitoring group, discovered alarming problems with the Norplant clinical trial conducted in Bangladesh between 1985 and 1987 on 600 urban slum women. The organization found that procedures followed by the Bangladesh Fertility Research Program, the national family-planning and biomedical research organization, were marred by gross violations of medical ethics, inadequate methodology, and disregard for the health of the female subjects.[91]

Clinic workers did not give clients a prior medical examination or obtain their informed consent to participate in the testing. Participants were not told about all of Norplant's side effects or that the drug was still in its experimental stage. They did not understand how the device worked or even know its name—nearly everyone referred to the implants as "the five-year needle." Many women were breastfeeding at the time of insertion even though the hormones can travel to a baby through breast milk. The research results were further tainted by giving women monetary incentives for the insertion and then discouraging them from reporting health problems.

Similar methodological errors, ethical lapses, and health complications marked the tryouts in other Third World countries.[92] Under pressure from women's groups, the Brazilian government rescinded its authorization for Norplant testing in 1986. Activist Deepa Dhanraj produced a film entitled *Something Like a War*, which documents abusive testing of Norplant-2, the forerunner of the current version, on thousands of women in India during the 1980s.

Health advocates are also concerned that use of Norplant may increase the risk of STDs. Unlike condoms, Norplant does not provide protection against AIDS and other STDs. Once the implants are in place, women may take fewer precautions against contracting an STD, such as requiring their partner to wear a condom. Studies are already confirming this fear. Although 42 percent of women in a Texas survey used condoms before Norplant, 48 percent of these same women reported that they would rarely or never use them in the future.[93] Therefore, the researchers concluded, "almost one-quarter of the implant acceptors in our sample may be at increased risk of con-

tracting an STD."[94] Of course, the pill and other birth control methods also provide no protection against STDs. But Norplant may be
riskier because its users need not check in with a health care provider
who might remind them about the importance of using condoms. It
also appears that Norplant users are not receiving the necessary
counseling about the importance of continuing protection against
STDs. For women and teens at risk for both unwanted pregnancy
and STDs, the increased potential for contracting AIDS and other
diseases may very well outweigh Norplant's enhanced protection
against pregnancy.

Norplant proponents seem to have ignored this calculation. For example, Douglas Besharov, a scholar at the American Enterprise Institute, believes that the scales easily tip in favor of Norplant. Besharov
acknowledges criticism that Norplant may lead to a marginal increase
in teen sex and to a concomitant increase in STDs, but he is willing to
trade off these disadvantages to teenagers for what Norplant has to
offer society. "Which is worse: the possibility of a marginal increase in
sexual activity," Besharov queries, "or losing the opportunity to reduce abortions and out-of-wedlock births by 10, 20, or even 30 percent? To ask the question is to answer it."[95] The peddlers of Norplant
curiously minimize the serious health risks from the implants themselves, as well as the increased possibility of disease that comes with
them. They also leave out of the equation strategies for improving the
availability and effectiveness of less risky birth control methods.

In many cases prescribing Norplant to teenagers is like using a
bazooka to kill a gnat. Most young teens engage in sex only sporadi-
cally, with sexually active boys reporting no sex at all for an average
of six months each year.[96] Yet Norplant is only appropriate for women
who have sex regularly: it is expensive and intrusive; and it supplies a
constant dose of powerful contraceptive hormones. As one commentator pointed out, "A teenage girl cannot simply stop at the drugstore
on the way to a date to pick up Norplant."[97] Adolescent girls who
have sex a few times a year do not need such drastic pregnancy prevention. The diminished risk of pregnancy for these teens cannot justify Norplant's grave risk to their health. Government officials who
press for mass Norplant distribution to teenagers apparently have not
bothered to engage in this sort of cost-benefit analysis.

Why the rush to forfeit women's health for the good of society?
Perhaps the answer lies in the poverty and race of the women being
sacrificed. Let us think about the hypothetical scheme proposed by
Isabel Sawhill, an economist at the Urban Institute in Washington, to

insert Norplant in the arm of every girl in the country when she reaches puberty. One reason this suggestion sounds so ludicrous is that it would be unthinkable to inflict such a risky device on the daughters of affluent white parents.

THE COMPLICATIONS OF REMOVAL

Removing Norplant can be as dangerous as leaving it in place. The operation required to take out the capsules is more complicated than the insertion procedure, especially if the capsules were implanted improperly in the first place. Because there have initially been far more Norplant insertions than removals, clinicians have not become proficient at the extraction procedure. Some doctors do not even bother to take advantage of the removal training kit Wyeth-Ayerst sends to everyone who orders Norplant, believing the procedure is easier than it really is.[98]

The results of doctors' inexperience have been horrific. Capsules planted too deep force doctors to dig around to locate them in the woman's arm. The rods have sometimes broken up or migrated to other parts of the body. Thick, fibrous scar tissue called keloids often forms around the capsules, making their removal even more treacherous. In very difficult cases, patients have had to return for multiple incisions. They are sometimes left with debilitating nerve damage. It took over an hour for a doctor to remove the implants from a Massachusetts woman's arm. "[My doctor] said that they were stuck in there," the twenty-six-year-old patient recalled. "She was pulling and yanking them, but they weren't going anywhere."[99] Paula Gorman, a day-care provider from Rhode Island, endured a total of six hours of surgery that left noticeable scars on her arm.[100] Again, Black women are at extra risk of injury because they have a higher tendency to develop keloid scarring after a surgical incision.[101]

Norplant's numerous health complications have landed the distributor in massive product-liability litigation. Class action lawsuits consolidating hundreds of cases have been filed in Texas, Illinois, and Florida against Wyeth-Ayerst, claiming health problems connected with Norplant and difficulties in having the implants removed.[102] Thousands of similar lawsuits have been brought in other states. Newspaper, radio, and television advertisements by attorneys recruiting plaintiffs are proliferating, and as many as 50,000 women may ultimately file complaints. The litigation is so huge that in 1995 tort lawyers converged in Houston from around the country to share information about the lawsuits and to coordinate strategies.

The plaintiffs allege that Wyeth-Ayerst designed Norplant negligently, actively promoted the device without adequately warning women about its potentially dangerous consequences, and sold this hazardous product to doctors who were not properly trained at inserting and removing it. Actions filed in Missouri and New Mexico also claim that the company profits by marketing Norplant specifically to minority and low-income women who are unable to "control discontinuation of the product."[103] Besides asking for millions of dollars in damages, the plaintiffs also want an injunction to prevent the company from continuing to sell Norplant to untrained doctors. Wyeth-Ayerst reports that the wave of lawsuits has already caused daily sales to tumble from 800 to 60. *New York Times* reporter Gina Kolata wonders in the title of a recent article, "Will the Lawyers Kill Off Norplant?"[104] On February 24, 1997, however, a federal judge in Texas ruled against the plaintiffs in five cases, finding that Wyeth-Ayerst had adequately notified doctors about Norplant's potential side effects. The fate of the other lawsuits, and of Norplant's widescale distribution, remains uncertain.

To the extent that Norplant should be made available, the medical profession must ensure better information about its short-term and long-term effects on women and adolescents. Health experts should also figure out ways to minimize the risk of STDs through use of condoms and to ensure access to regular gynecologic checkups and counseling. But if we could accomplish all this, I question whether any additional benefits of Norplant would outweigh its potential hazard to women's health and reproductive autonomy. Of course, nearly all contraceptives carry some degree of health risk, as do pregnancy and childbirth. The fact that Norplant has side effects is not enough to prevent women who are aware of these potential problems from willingly using it. But health risks are cause to prohibit or restrict distribution of a product that has not been adequately tested, that has not been fully explained to users, and that is being foisted on certain groups to achieve social objectives.

NORPLANT'S COERCIVE DESIGN

Norplant's health risks are only the tip of the iceberg. Its hazard for poor Black women is compounded by the coercion that has marked its distribution to this group. The relative permanence and accessibility of Norplant has proven to be a double-edged sword. The very features that enhance Norplant's convenience for women also allow for its coercive deployment. Unlike every other method of birth control except the IUD, a woman cannot simply stop using it when she wants to. As Judy Norsigian of the National Women's Health Network puts it, "It's a contraceptive that's controlled by the provider, not the woman."[105] Because its use, once it is implanted, does not depend on a woman's compliance and is easy to monitor, it works well as a means for regulating women's reproduction.

Women's inability to remove the inserts without medical assistance facilitates abuse in several ways. It currently gives doctors and other health care workers the opportunity to impose their own judgments upon poor minority patients by refusing to remove the device. If in the future the government offers incentives for Norplant or mandates its use, officials will be able to ensure that the implants remain in place. Even aside from these deliberate abuses, Norplant is designed to deprive women of control over their reproductive health. By relieving women of the day-to-day management of birth control, it places poor women at the mercy of a health care system that remains insensitive to their needs.

A study of young, low-income women in South Carolina who requested early removal discovered some disturbing aspects of the counseling they received. A majority reported that the information they had been given "emphasized the positive aspects and minimized the possibility of adverse side effects," giving them the false impression that side effects were uncommon and less severe than they later experienced.[106] Others who were offered Norplant in the hospital after giving birth felt that medical staff took advantage of the situation to pressure them into consenting to use it. As one woman explained,

> I really did not want it but after I had my baby, they came in my room and asked me to look at the educational movie. . . . They put mine in the day I had my little girl. . . . [T]hey just kept hassling me.

Another echoed this experience:

> They were telling me, "What you gonna do for birth control? Are you gonna get a Norplant? It's good. . . . Medicaid will pay

for that to go in, you know." I had a week to figure out what I was gonna do . . . so I just jumped on that.[107]

Judith Scully, an attorney and gynecological health care worker at a Chicago clinic, confirms that young Black women are being steered toward long-acting contraceptives. "Doctors are saying, 'I've got the answer for you,' and then telling them to choose between Norplant and Depo-Provera," Scully told me.[108] Women who are not given other contraceptive options may believe that Norplant is the only appropriate method of birth control available to them.

TRYING TO GET NORPLANT OUT

Being able to get Norplant removed quickly and easily is critical to a user's control over reproductive decisionmaking. Yet poor and low-income women often find themselves in a predicament when they seek to have the capsules extracted. Their experience with Norplant is a telling example of how a woman's social circumstances affect her reproductive "choices." A woman whose insertion procedure was covered by Medicaid or private insurance may be uninsured at the time she decides to have the tubes removed. A woman who had the money to pay for implantation may be too broke to afford extraction. Some women have complained that they learned of the cost of removal—from $150 to $500—only after returning to a physician to have the implants taken out.

The scarcity of doctors willing and able to remove Norplant poses another set of problems. The doctors in the clinic who inserted the device may not be trained at removing it. A small clinic may not have enough doctors on staff to perform time-consuming, complicated removal procedures. Many centers have a long backlog of patients in line for Norplant extractions. These obstacles force women with limited resources to search around for another doctor who can perform the operation. A new doctor may be hard to find, however, for the threat of legal liability makes some practitioners wary of removing Norplant improperly inserted by someone else.

Imagine the panic of bleeding for weeks on end, witnessing your hair fall out, or gaining fifty extra pounds only to be turned away from every clinic you approach to remove the source of your affliction. An indication of users' desperation: an Ohio woman trapped in this bind tried to slice the implants out herself with a razor blade, but was not able to cut deep enough.[109] A teenager on Medicaid in Chicago who used a sharpened pencil to dig out the capsules only succeeded in pushing them deeper into her arm.[110] Is it an exaggeration to call this experience a form of torture?

The suffering visited on these Norplant users is not just an accident of their own financial problems. State funding structures and health professionals' private biases have worked together to pressure poor women to keep the device in place.

Some state legislatures impose Medicaid reimbursement requirements with the deliberate aim of making it difficult for recipients to have the implants removed. These states implant Norplant for free, but will cover the cost of early removal only in cases of "documented medical necessity." This means that poor women must scrape together the funds themselves, even if they are suffering from side effects or decide that they want to have a child. Those who cannot find the money must wait out the five years until the state will pay for the procedure. Many private insurance companies mimic this policy, and doctors in states that do pay for removal have misinformed their patients about Medicaid coverage.

A physician's directive issued by the state of Oklahoma discloses the government's purpose of coercing poor women to keep the implants in place for as long as possible:

> It is not the intent of the Department to cover removal of the Norplant system prior to the expiration of five years unless there is documented medical necessity. Payment is not intended to be made for the removal of the contraceptive for the convenience of the patient, minor menstrual irregularities, or for the purpose of conception.[111]

By enticing poor women to use Norplant with the offer of free implantation and then refusing to pay for removal, the state has achieved the same end as more controversial financial bonuses.

There are reports that poor women routinely have trouble getting doctors to remove Norplant. Investigators from the International Reproductive Rights Research Action Group tracked thirty-eight poor Black women in Soperton, a rural community in Georgia, who had been implanted with the device. Some claimed that doctors refused outright to remove the Norplant despite their complaints of side effects.[112] One woman was told that since Medicaid did not pay for the cost of removal, she would have to cover the cost herself, *as well as re-*

imburse Medicaid for the cost of the insertion procedure. "If you didn't know where Soperton was, you'd think it was a Third World country," a researcher for the National Black Women's Health Project observed.[113]

The case of a Native American woman in South Dakota is reminiscent of the forced sterilization practices of the 1970s. When she requested that her doctor remove the implants after she had gained sixty-five pounds, she was told the operation would be contingent upon her consenting to a tubal ligation.[114] The Department of Human Services in Tippah County, Mississippi, tried to force Rose Sexton, a poor twenty-year-old white woman, to keep Norplant in her arm against her will and against the wishes of her husband and mother. The agency argued that Rose, who as a minor had already given up three children for adoption, was unable to care for children due to her limited intellectual ability. When Rose went to the public clinic to have the device removed because of the side effects, the Department of Human Services petitioned the juvenile court for an order restraining her from taking the implants out. A lawyer from North Mississippi Rural Legal Services eventually persuaded the agency to drop the motion.[115]

The South Carolina study mentioned above discovered similar obstacles. A majority of participants recalled that the medical staff reacted with reluctance to their request to remove the implants.[116] Doctors and nurses expressed skepticism about patients' experience of side effects and urged the women to "wait it out." As one woman reported:

> I was still having heavy bleeding . . . and they said, well, it takes a little while, so I went for a year. . . . It didn't get no better. I mean, who wants to go 19 days' worth of bleeding? They don't jump to take it out but they sure do want to put it in.[117]

The women generally felt that their difficulty getting the implants removed stemmed from their doctors' belief that young unmarried women on Medicaid should not be having children. The doctors were enforcing their conclusion that Norplant was good for their patients, regardless of their patients' thoughts on the matter. Some women suspected that they had been used as guinea pigs to test the drug's safety; they believed doctors were reluctant to extract the rods precisely because they wanted to observe the side effects their patients were experiencing. There is some basis for their suspicions: Blacks have been the unwitting subjects of cruel medical experimentation for centuries, most notably the Tuskegee syphilis experiment that lasted from 1932 to 1972.[118]

Publicly funded programs are also under financial pressure to dissuade clients from removing Norplant before its five-year expiration. A clinic that has just invested $500 in the insertion procedure will be reluctant to spend another $500 of its budget for early removal. Clinic workers in Los Angeles, for example, admit that women who come in to have Norplant removed are encouraged to try it a little longer for just this reason. "We don't want her to have it [out] after spending all that money," explains Pam Garcia of Planned Parenthood of Pasadena.[119] Although Garcia says Planned Parenthood will remove the device if the patient insists, it is clear that financial concerns compete with attention to their patients' wishes.

The Los Angeles Regional Family Planning Council recognizes that Norplant counseling is especially susceptible to workers' biases. Its counselors receive a training notebook that requires them to write down their honest reactions to statements such as "All drug-abusing women should have Norplant" and "All sexually active teens should have Norplant."[120] The council hopes that pushing counselors to recognize their biases ahead of time will prevent abuse of patients' rights. But what about the counselor who thinks that his or her biases are well-founded? This training technique is unlikely to deter a health care worker who firmly believes that all women on welfare should use Norplant from imposing this view on poor minority clients.

Whatever the precise reason, Black women around the country report a sense that health care workers do not respect their personal decision to remove the contraceptive. We would expect clinic staff to help patients understand the physiological aspects of their symptoms and to allay any unwarranted fears about Norplant's consequences for their health. But many workers are going beyond informing their patients and attempting to manipulate their decisions about using Norplant. They have already decided what "choice" they want poor Black women to make—keep Norplant in at all costs.

NORPLANT INCENTIVES: ACCESS OR EXCESS?

Government aid to purchase Norplant and proposals for financial incentives to use it raise another set of concerns. Do these programs *benefit* poor and low-income women by making an expensive contraceptive available to them or do they *coerce* these women into using this

form of birth control? Because most of the Norplant proposals are offers to provide a bonus rather than threats to take away aid, their proponents argue that they do not coerce poor women to use the implant.
Indeed, Norplant incentives are promoted as a way of *expanding* the
reproductive options of women on welfare.

There is evidence that public funding of Norplant does influence
women's decision to use this particular contraceptive. A study of
Black inner-city patients at a Planned Parenthood clinic in Baltimore
sought to find out how women who select Norplant differ from
women who choose the pill. The researchers discovered that the
strongest predictor of that decision was the method of payment:
"Ninety-five percent of women who selected the implant were Medicaid recipients, compared with only 32 percent of those who selected
the pill."[121] The Alan Guttmacher Institute similarly found that patients at family-planning clinics who received Medicaid were twelve
times more likely to get the implant than clinic patients who were ineligible for Medicaid.[122]

This evidence could easily suggest that, by paying for Norplant, the
government benefitted these patients by enabling them to pick their
contraceptive of choice. Without government assistance, few of these
poor and low-income patients would be able to afford the $550 the
clinic charged for the implant kit, insertion fee, counseling, and follow-up visits. The same patients studied could have chosen Medicaid
reimbursement for the pill if they wanted to.

Dr. David Grimes, former chairman of the National Medical Committee of Planned Parenthood, dismisses charges of coercion by
pointing out, "If we put at the disposal of poor people the same contraceptive that is available to persons who are more affluent, that is a
social equalizer."[123] Planned Parenthood views even financial incentives to use Norplant as an enhancement of reproductive choice. As
Tina Proctor of the Aurora, Colorado, branch argued, "Our agency
believes that if a woman chooses to accept extra welfare payments for
using Norplant, it's a choice that the woman makes and if she can get
something extra for using birth control, that's positive."[124] Kansas
representative Kerry Patrick similarly defended his Norplant incentive bill on *60 Minutes* as increasing poor women's freedoms: "Why not
try a program with an incentive? Why not give the welfare woman a
choice? Why not empower her to make a decision as to whether or
not she should use Norplant?"[125] To take another example, reproductive rights advocates do not see government funding of abortion services as pernicious government encouragement of abortion; rather,

a major part of the pro-choice agenda is to push for passage of abortion-funding legislation at the state and federal levels.

A Voluntary "Choice"?

True, no one has suggested passing a law that mandates that certain women have Norplant embedded in their arms. As Samuel Parrish, head of adolescent medicine at the Medical College of Pennsylvania, points out, "I don't know of a single clinic in town that would say, 'Your mom wants you on this, so therefore, hold still.'"[126] The Constitution would not tolerate hauling women and girls into clinics to be forcibly injected with Norplant. But lesser forms of pressure can make a decision unacceptably involuntary. A woman who has no money to feed her children faces greater pressure to accept a financial bonus to use Norplant than does an affluent woman. We can easily recognize that the poor woman's decision is less voluntary and that the government's financial enticement wields a strong influence over her judgment.

Indeed, Congress recognized as much when it passed the Family Planning Services and Population Research Act in 1970 that prohibits programs receiving federal funds from coercing women to undergo an abortion or sterilization procedure "by threatening . . . the loss of . . . any benefit."[127] The American Medical Association opposes Norplant incentives on the ground that government benefits should never be "made contingent on the acceptance of a health risk."[128]

These offers not only place pressure on poor women to forfeit their ability to have children and to overlook the potential danger Norplant poses to their health; they also place on these women a pressure to use the contraceptive that wealthier women (and most white women) do not experience. Even if we would not call a financial benefit "coercive," we can still recognize that the government is exploiting poor women's economic desperation to get them to make a decision they otherwise would not make.[129] We still must decide, however, whether or not the poor woman's decision to use Norplant is sufficiently voluntary to be her "choice."

The central question in cases of government incentives is whether the form of pressure the state uses is acceptable. This is true about consent to any deal. A person's consent does not necessarily enhance her autonomy since she may agree to a transaction out of submission to a more powerful authority or to adverse circumstances outside her control. Has a woman "consented" to sex, for example, if she agreed only after the man threatened to hit her? What if he threatened to fire her or leave her? Legal determinations about whether a decision was freely made are never simply conclusions about what the actors did. They are value-laden judgments about what should be considered choice.[130] This determination, in turn, depends on whether we think consent resulted from an acceptable inducement. We might decide that threatening to end a relationship is an acceptable inducement to engage in sex while threatening to smash someone's face is not.

Moreover, a woman's freedom to choose among reproductive options does not mean she has reproductive freedom. We should also be concerned about the quality of options available to her. It is possible that all of the alternatives decrease her control over her reproductive health. As a German health activist put it, "more choice has no meaning in itself; what is important is the question: more choice of what?"[131] It makes a mockery of the concept of reproductive liberty to say that telling young Black women to pick between Depo-Provera and Norplant, for example, increases their "choice."

The issue, then, is more complicated than asking whether providing Norplant expands poor women's choices. We must question whether the government's inducements are acceptable within an understanding of why reproductive choice is important in the first place. Does the government's distribution of Norplant enhance Black women's control over their reproductive health?

Norplant is promoted on the assumption that poor Black women are incapable of taking responsibility for their own sexuality and reproduction. As conservative Richard Neuhaus bluntly observed in *National Review*, often underlying whites' promotion of Norplant for teens is "the unsavory assumption that inner-city black kids are little more than rutting animals incapable of the discipline we expect from our own kind—an assumption accurately described as racist."[132] Norplant is a way of giving that function over to government programs for a period of five years at a time.

Moreover, the government pushes this birth control method on all women receiving public assistance regardless of its suitability for each woman—it disregards whether Norplant would cause intolerable or dangerous side effects, whether she has access to removal, and whether she wishes to have a child. Certainly bribing women to implant a potentially harmful device they cannot remove on their own is not what reproductive liberty is about. These programs use contraception as a means of social control over individual misbehavior rather than as a means of women's control over their own reproduction. Norplant may be an infallible way of preventing pregnancy, but it is a miserable means of promoting reproductive autonomy.

Does the End Justify the Means?

Others contend that criticism of Norplant has undermined the contraceptive's potential for good. A report issued by the Hastings Center, an ethics think-tank, argues that focusing on the coercive potential of long-acting contraceptives like Norplant ignores the equally important risk that women will be improperly influenced *not* to use them. Thus, the authors conclude, "In these instances it can be appropriate and responsible to use different techniques to influence a woman to consider long-term contraceptive use, even if she is not immediately inclined to do so."[133] Unlike the previous argument that sees acceptance of Norplant incentives as entirely voluntary, this position holds that incentives may be ethical even if they exert some degree of pressure.

The state has more reason to influence teenagers' sexuality and reproduction than that of adults, for example. Teenagers have less right to make autonomous decisions because they are not always mature enough to judge what is in their own best interest. The state is allowed to override teenagers' wishes in many contexts—marriage, alcohol consumption, voting, to name a few. Directed counseling may be required to counteract the negative influences of peer pressure, poor judgment, and misinformation bombarding teens. In addition is the strong argument that delaying pregnancy benefits most teenagers rather than devalues them. Norplant incentives directed to adolescent girls attempt to put off motherhood, not deny it altogether.

Proponents of Norplant bonuses also point out that the government often attempts to influence citizens' behavior through financial incentives. It offers income tax deductions to wealthy people, for example, to get them to make charitable contributions. Why are incentive programs that prod poor women into acting in socially responsible ways any different?

This argument correctly raises the possibility that we might want the government to influence people to act in the public interest. A basic premise of this book is that the single-minded focus on individual liberty as the full meaning of reproductive freedom disregards the social context in which we make procreative decisions. We cannot determine whether Norplant incentives are coercive, for example, without looking at the social constraints facing poor women offered monetary bonuses. But recognizing that there may be countervailing reasons to encourage Norplant use does not end the inquiry; it brings us to scrutinize the reasons why certain teenagers and women are encouraged to use long-acting contraceptives.

Do these Norplant policies address the state's legitimate concerns? George Will asks, "What is more dangerous to the flourishing of black America, Norplant for teenagers or a growing number of black adolescents headed for a life of poverty because they were born into poverty to a single mother whose life chances were blighted by a pregnancy at age 15?"[134] His question implies that Norplant incentives are acceptable, even if coercive, because they will reverse the course of "black adolescents headed for a life of poverty." This line of reasoning is based on the faulty premise that Black people's poverty is caused by their reproduction—the belief that, as the *Inquirer* editorial asserted, Black poverty persists because "the people having the most children are the ones least capable of supporting them."

Blaming the birthrate for poverty ignores the structural reasons for people being poor. The public funding of Norplant at a time of drastic cuts in welfare spending is particularly significant. This willingness to pay for poor women's birth control but not for their basic needs is strong evidence that the government is more interested in population reduction than in furthering poor women's welfare. Perhaps this is the greatest danger of Norplant incentives: they reinforce the belief that the solution to Black poverty is to curb Black reproduction.

I find the very terms of the Norplant debate offensive. The fighting over Norplant assumes that Black women's reproduction is a proper arena for social regulation. The only question asked is what are the appropriate means to regulate it—mandates or bonuses, for example. While politicians squabble over the most effective means to reduce Black fertility, the notion of Black women's control over their own reproduction escapes discussion. Why have government programs that distribute Norplant been promoted so heavily in the Black community? Why is Norplant dispensed at Black inner-city high schools and not white suburban ones? The coercive nature of the device itself, as well as the incentives used to promote it, treats Black women's bodies as objects of social supervision.

NORPLANT AND INTERNATIONAL POPULATION CONTROL

The history of Norplant's introduction underscores this point. Norplant was originally developed by the Population Council, working through its international research branch, as a tool of population control in Third World countries. Its research was financed by nearly $15 million in U.S. foreign aid. The scientists designed the contraceptive specifically for distribution to poor, uneducated women of color. Norplant is ideal for this aim: it is more socially acceptable than sterilization, the method used for decades to reduce Third World birthrates, yet its effectiveness does not depend on the continuing cooperation of women thought to be too ignorant or backward to use other contraceptive methods.

Indonesia, the country with the fourth largest population in the world, was one of the first sites of Norplant use. Under pressure to decrease population growth, the Indonesian government dispenses two-thirds of the world's supply of the contraceptive.[135] This high rate of Norplant implantation comes at the expense of citizens' rights. In the city of Bogor, only government employees who use Norplant or sterilization for birth control receive their paychecks on time.[136] Some jobs, such as work on Indonesia's tea plantations, require proof of Norplant use. Teams of government agents and military personnel scour villages in so-called safaris recruiting women to have the device implanted.[137] In order to meet strict quotas, the safaris seldom ensure that women give fully informed consent to the procedure. Women even report being threatened at gunpoint. A USAID program located in Peru in the late 1980s used a less blatant tactic: it offered clients a choice between only Norplant and sterilization.[138]

Additionally, there is every indication that the Indonesian government intends for women to retain the implants, regardless of the consequences for their health. A 1990 Population Council report found that Indonesian doctors trained to insert the device were completely unprepared to remove the inserts after the expiration of five years.[139] Even apart from the flagrant government abuses, it is unconscionable to market Norplant to women in areas that lack the basic health systems necessary for even minimally safe use of the device. Yet Indonesia is held up by U.S. foreign aid officials as a birth control success story.

The Norplant experience in Bangladesh offers another example of abuse. Before its clinical trials were under way, the Bangladesh Fertility Research Program (BFRP) promoted Norplant as "particularly suitable for our semi-literate population" because it does not require day-to-day use.[140] "The effectivity question is mentioned and is specially targetted towards . . . the poorer section of the population," the BFRP explained, "so that population control can be ensured." From the beginning, the objective of Norplant research in Bangladesh was "to create the conditions for *mass promotion*," not to test its safety for Bangladeshi women.[141]

In a 1987 article, BFRP's director, Dr. Halida Hanum Akhter, further praised the advantages of the implants:

> It has been found by researchers that contraceptive pills containing progestin and more commonly used other reversible methods necessitate continuous motivational involvement by the user. In a country like Bangladesh this fact is more true than in the developed world. It is, therefore, necessary to introduce methods in Bangladesh which can continue to be effective for long periods without continuous motivation by Family Planning Workers. Norplant is perhaps the most effective method which is likely to prove successful here.

Part of Norplant's "success" in Bangladesh was due to women's difficulty in getting the implants removed. A researcher there found that only 25 percent of women who wanted Norplant removed were successful at getting doctors to take it out on their first request.[142] On average, it took three requests to persuade a doctor to extract the implants, with women waiting seven weeks for the operation. Some were told that it was medically impossible to remove the device before the five-year duration expired. One distraught woman reported that she could not get anyone to listen to her until she lied by saying her two children had drowned in the river and her husband wanted another child.[143]

These views on Norplant reflect a widespread attitude among population control advocates: to them, the "effectiveness" of a contraceptive means its ability to guarantee widespread birth control, period. This preoccupation with reducing fertility allows little concern for either the safety of the device or women's ability to control its operation. Unlike the concept of reproductive freedom that focuses on women's liberty and equality, population control centers on decreasing births of an entire group with the objective of changing economic, political, or ecological conditions.[144]

A host of private foundations, consulting firms, academic centers, and government agencies have combined their efforts in a powerful political establishment that promotes family planning in the Third World. The Population Council, the developer of Norplant, is one of the major players in this arena. For several decades, these Western population control agencies have shipped birth control programs overseas based on the philosophy that overpopulation is the primary cause of poverty and instability in developing countries. Flowing from this premise is the belief that native women must be persuaded or forced to have fewer children, with efficacy in preventing pregnancy taking precedence over their health and autonomy.[145] Given this history abroad, it is not surprising that, once transplanted to the United States, Norplant has been used for similarly coercive ends.

The Population Council's contribution to repressive family-planning agendas raises doubts about its professed commitment to informed consent and freedom of choice. According to Betsy Hartmann, director of the Population and Development Program at Hampshire College, "the Council has actively promoted the mass introduction of easily abusable contraceptive technologies into already abusive population control programs."[146] The council defends its research by calling for safeguards to ensure women's voluntary acceptance of new types of birth control. Recall, for example, Dr. Sheldon Segal's letter to the *New York Times* objecting to the coercive use of Norplant. But why does the council insist on developing long-acting technologies that are inherently susceptible to abuse, rather than safer, user-controlled methods? In fact, the council's liberal veneer lends legitimacy to population control programs whose abuses would otherwise be more glaring.[147]

Moreover, the Population Council's origins are closely linked to the American eugenics movement. Frederick Osborn, one of America's key eugenics strategists and a long-time officer of the American Eugenics Society, helped John D. Rockefeller III establish the Population Council in 1952. As the council's first president and a member of its board of trustees, Osborn promoted his eugenic philosophy through the organization's birth control research. On March 5, 1969, Osborn wrote to Rockefeller, "The best hope of improving genetic qualities of the race lies in the universal extension of effective and easy means of birth control."[148] Osborn believed that this work could be accomplished more effectively "in the name of the Population Council than in the name of eugenics" and described the council's development of new birth control techniques as "the most important practical eugenic measure ever taken."

The development of Norplant, then, is tightly linked both to the eugenics movement in America and to population control efforts abroad. No doubt Wyeth-Ayerst's decision to market Norplant in the United States was based on estimates of a growing demand for long-term contraceptives in this country. But contrary to the hype accompanying its U.S. introduction, Norplant was not created to increase the choices of liberated American women. It was designed to limit the reproductive control of Third World women to better accomplish the aim of population policy—producing fewer people in developing countries.

LESSONS FROM THIRD WORLD INCENTIVE PROGRAMS

Employing incentives to induce sterilization or contraceptive use is a familiar aspect of international population control policy. Incentive programs have been implemented in Third World countries for decades, causing controversy within both overseas communities and the international population establishment. Women in Bangladesh receive food aid only if they show a card confirming that they have been sterilized. Sterilization gets Korean couples a priority for business and housing loans and medical care for their children.[149] The much criticized one-baby policy in China is also enforced through a system of government benefits. The most common system makes a one-time payment to "acceptors" who agree to use birth control, to "motivators" who persuade others to use birth control, or to doctors who provide the birth control. Supporters of incentives argue that these programs help to educate people about contraceptives and to overcome cultural resistance to using them.

By paying a fee for each sterilization performed or IUD inserted, however, incentive schemes have permitted unscrupulous villagers to use women's bodies for profit. "Once the procedure is finished, so is the patient," writes Dr. Zafrullah Chowdhury of the People's Health Center in Bangladesh. "No one cares about them post-operatively, if they have complications, if further problems arise later. They have served their usefulness."[150] One of the most appalling examples of profiteering was the "IUD factory" in Pakistan, where doctors, motivators, and women collaborated to have IUDs repeatedly inserted, removed, and reinserted for multiple bonuses.

Hartmann points out as well that incentive advocates sidestep the fundamental question of why people need to be pushed into having fewer children in the first place. "Isn't it because of the very absence of the most powerful incentive of all: the economic and social security of having fair access to the fruits of development?" she asks.[151] Incentive programs have tried to substitute mass sterilization for the equitable distribution of wealth in Third World countries, sacrificing the health and dignity of poor women of color in the process. Feminists in these countries argue that family-planning programs must be motivated instead by the aim of giving women the social power needed to control their own reproduction.

The *Inquirer*'s infamous editorial tried to distance Norplant incentives from these deplorable programs overseas. "This is not Indira Gandhi offering portable radios to women who agree to be sterilized," Kimelman maintained. Presumably what distinguishes the acceptable U.S. proposals from the intolerable Indian program is that Norplant is only temporary while sterilization is permanent.

But the problem with Third World sterilization programs has as much to do with the government's objective as with the precise method of birth control. The coercion involved in paying poor women to implant Norplant in their bodies and then refusing to pay for its removal—even when they are suffering from medical side effects—is also deplorable. It is often easier to recognize atrocities when they are committed by foreign governments. Like their Third World counterparts, however, this domestic policy violates women's bodily integrity as well as their reproductive self-determination. We can only grasp the full weight of Norplant schemes in the United States when we situate them within the massive worldwide effort to reduce dark-skinned populations.

THE NEW FRONTIER: INJECTABLE AND IMMUNOLOGICAL CONTRACEPTIVES

There are already signs that policymakers determined to curtail Black birthrates will soon discard Norplant as the contraceptive of choice. Negative publicity arising from the class action lawsuits, as well as word of mouth concerning Norplant's side effects and removal problems, has dampened interest in the device in targeted communities. Some attribute Norplant's fall from grace to allegations about Black genocide.

Clinics across the country have seen a dramatic decline in Norplant use. The Johns Hopkins family-planning center in Baltimore reported doing less than twenty Norplant inserts in three months in 1995. "That's what we used to do in the course of a couple weeks," its director commented.[152] Planned Parenthood clinics in Washington, D.C., have stopped supplying the implants altogether because of their patients' reluctance to use them.[153] A Detroit gynecologist says he has removed three-fourths of the capsules he had inserted and does not expect to implant any more.[154] And while thirty-six out of fifty girls offered Norplant at the Paquin School complied in the program's first semester, the number who agreed to use it dropped to four the following semester.[155]

Medicaid records confirm that in twelve large states the number of removals skyrocketed after a couple of years, as the number of insertions plummeted.[156] Taxpayers will soon become fed up with the cost of removing the device; Ohio alone spent $1.9 million for Norplant extractions by July 1994. Without more draconian methods, the effort to pressure poor Black women to use Norplant en masse appears destined for failure.

The leading candidate for Norplant's immediate replacement is the injectable contraceptive Depo-Provera. Depo-Provera, the trade name for medroxyprogesterone acetate, is manufactured by the Upjohn Company and used by 15 million women in over ninety countries. Depo-Provera also delivers progestin into the bloodstream, making it the contraceptive most similar to Norplant. Depo-Provera, however, shoots an intense concentration of the hormone into the system, rather than releasing it gradually as does Norplant. Its effect lasts from three to six months.

Many women on Depo-Provera suffer from the same side effects caused by Norplant and other hormonal contraceptives, including heavy bleeding, although most have no periods at all after a year. Upjohn is also studying long-term users' risk of bone loss and osteoporosis. The FDA banned the marketing of Depo-Provera as a contraceptive until recently, based on studies showing that beagles formerly used in contraception testing developed breast cancer when given high doses of the drug.

Depo-Provera has some advantages over Norplant: at a cost of $45 every three months, it is more affordable than Norplant's exorbitant lump-sum expense. Depo-Provera can be used in secret, whereas Norplant leaves telltale ridges where the implants are embedded. In addition, some Third World women are more receptive to an in-

jectable contraceptive owing to their association of shots with inocu-
lations against disease. The hormone shot also avoids the problems
Norplant users have experienced with insertion and removal procedures. On the other hand, Depo-Provera gives women suffering from
side effects no recourse until the drug wears off. An injection is also
closer to temporary sterilization because its effects are irreversible
once the hormones are shot into a woman's bloodstream.

The FDA approved Depo-Provera for use in the United States
only in 1992, after decades of heated debate about the drug. Depo-
Provera's distribution here has renewed interest in injectable contraceptives. Some clinics report that most of their patients prefer
Depo-Provera to Norplant.[157] While Norplant has received the most
attention, the Maryland contraceptive program initiated in 1993 also
offered Depo-Provera to low-income women. Over 360 women received injections in the program's first three months.[158] State legislative proposals to distribute long-acting contraceptives are beginning
to include funding for Depo-Provera, along with Norplant. In 1994,
Indiana approved a $175,000 contract with Upjohn that allows the
state to offer Depo-Provera free at family-planning clinics, more than
the amount allocated for Norplant.[159]

Depo-Provera has an alarming track record for abuse both in the
United States and in developing countries. American doctors, who
had access to the drug as a cancer therapy even before its approval for
contraceptive use, regularly administered it to Southern Black and
Native American women for birth control.[160] A 1978 FDA audit of a
Depo-Provera trial at Emory University in Atlanta discovered reckless disregard for the health of the 4,700 Black subjects. The drug has
been administered to women in Third World countries such as Thai-
land, Mexico, and India without adequate patient counseling or medical supervision. The South African government under apartheid
pressured Black women to use Depo-Provera by distributing free injections at factories and farms, sometimes threatening women with
the loss of their jobs if they did not consent.[161] In France, 20 percent
of immigrants from sub-Saharan Africa on contraceptives use the
drug, compared to only 4 percent of French-born women.[162]

This history suggests that lawmakers will soon seize upon Depo-
Provera to replace or supplement Norplant in programs designed to
discourage women on welfare from having children. Doctors are already offering a choice between Norplant and Depo-Provera to
young Black women who walk into their clinics.

Now population control research is heading on a radical course.

"Contraceptive vaccines" promise to regulate fertility by manipulating the body's immune responses. They work by stimulating the immune system to shut down some body functions necessary for pregnancy, analogous to the way vaccines given to infants cause the body to fight childhood diseases such as smallpox, mumps, and measles.[163] Different vaccines attack the development of reproductive hormones, eggs, sperm, or the early embryo. Of course, pregnancy is not a disease, says health activist Judith Richter, who wants to reject the term "vaccine" in favor of "immunocontraceptive."[164] Under investigation for two decades, the best-studied immunological approach uses antibodies to a hormone called human chorionic gonadotrophin (hCG) that is essential for the implantation and development of the embryo.[165] The effect of the anti-hCG vaccine would last six to twelve months. It has already undergone clinical testing for safety on women in India and Australia.

Researchers are also developing an oral contraceptive vaccine that will prevent pregnancy for years in a single dose. The possibility of using recombinant DNA technology in a vaccine has unfurled yet another range of research in this field. One project seeks to create a vaccine from genetically altered salmonella bacteria that would be marketed as a powder. But the complexity of immunological research makes it hard to predict when an antifertility vaccine will actually hit the market. It is difficult to identify antigens that will produce an immune response as well as to develop and test safe delivery systems.

Nevertheless, the population control establishment is devoting a huge effort to this investigation. It is estimated that 10 percent of worldwide spending on contraceptive research is currently devoted to developing immunizations.[166] Banking on the venture's eventual success, billionaire Ross Perot has invested $2.8 million in a Texas biotechnology company called Zonagen, Inc., which is developing an antipregnancy vaccine.[167] The fledgling company has teamed with Germany's Schering AG, the world's largest manufacturer of oral contraceptives, which has agreed to finance clinical testing of the vaccine.

Immunological contraceptives pose a novel, and more alarming, set of risks than existing methods. Their antibodies may trigger dangerous immune responses, such as allergies and autoimmune disorders. They may also exacerbate existing infectious diseases and immune disturbances, perhaps hastening the onset of AIDS. In addition, the risks to a developing fetus, if pregnancy occurs despite the vaccination, are unknown. Like Depo-Provera's, a vaccine's effects are irreversible. While a Norplant user may be able to get the inserts removed from her arm, women who are vaccinated will have no choice but to wait several months—or years—for the immune response to wear off.

Activists fear that vaccines are even more susceptible to government abuse than is Norplant because women can be inoculated without their consent or even their knowledge. An especially unscrupulous or incompetent program could add the contraceptive antibody to another vaccine and administer the combination without the patient's awareness. Rumors have already circulated in Tanzania, Indonesia, the Philippines, and other countries that a laced tetanus vaccine given to schoolgirls causes abortions and sterility. Whether these rumors are true or not, they have decreased participation in immunization programs. The development of immunological contraceptives has begun to poison Third World women's acceptance of vaccines—an acceptance that, ironically, helped to market contraceptive injections.

Because vaccines can be delivered in pills, food, or liquids, the potential for abuse on a mass scale is chilling. Already, biologists have proposed slipping antisperm antigens into bait as a way of reducing burgeoning wildlife populations. The scheme's potential for human population control was not lost upon a *New York Times* journalist:

> Biologists say that new vaccines under development . . . will provide a humane method for drastically reducing populations of rabbits in Australia, rats in Indonesia, white-tailed deer in the United States, and other rapidly multiplying species that threaten the environment. . . . Genetically engineered vaccines are being developed in several countries for controlling populations of animal pests. Since the vaccines work by immunizing a female against the male's sperm, the same principle should be effective as a contraceptive in humans. . . . [T]he method could make contraception far more accessible to residents of poor countries.[168]

In a 1969 *Science* article, the Population Council's then president, Bernard Berelson, seriously considered a similar proposal of mass use of a "fertility control agent" that would be available in five to fifteen years and "would be included in the water supply in the urban areas."[169] Berelson seemed more worried about the plan's "administrative feasibility" than ethical concerns, asking, "How are 'fertility control agents' or 'sterilants' to be administered on an involuntary mass basis in the absence of a central water supply or a food-processing system?"

Harmed by contraceptive research in the past, women around the world are protesting the development of antifertility vaccines.[170] In 1987, Brazilian feminists, who had run the Norplant trials out of the country a year earlier, put a stop to the Population Council's proposed testing of the anti-hCG vaccine. Ten thousand citizens, including three hundred scientists, signed a petition opposing the immunological research in Brazil. An international lobby against contraceptive vaccines, coordinated by the Women's Global Network for Reproductive Rights, began organizing in 1993.

By 1995, a coalition of over four hundred organizations from thirty-nine countries was demanding an immediate halt to the research. Their petition, "Call for a Stop to Research on Antifertility 'Vaccines' (Immunological Contraceptives)," declared that this technology had an unprecedented potential for abuse and that the health risks inherent in manipulating the immune system for contraceptive purposes outweighed any possible advantage to women. It also called for a radical reorientation of contraceptive research "to enable people—particularly women—to exert greater control over their fertility without sacrificing their integrity, health, and well being."[171]

Most of the institutions conducting this research responded to the petition, arguing that providing new contraceptive methods only increases women's choice, that abuse could be prevented through proper monitoring, and that predicting the worst creates "a fortress mentality and a paranoid society."[172] People who question the direction of medical research are often accused of being antiscience. It is assumed that developing novel reproductive technologies necessarily constitutes progress, that technological innovation necessarily betters humankind. But it is not true that every new form of birth control will ultimately benefit women just because it is more effective at preventing pregnancy. Indeed, Norplant's brief history on the American market demonstrates that long-acting contraceptives that are not user-controlled and not adequately tested pose grave dangers to women's health and liberty. Why should these concerns not steer the course of medical research? The developers of the contraceptive vaccine have not justified creating a birth control method likely to *increase* abuse that we know already exists.

∞

Despite all the commotion over the *Inquirer* editorial, lawmakers managed to install programs that distributed a powerful contraceptive highly susceptible to abuse to thousands of poor Black women. This is only the first step. As the climate grows increasingly hostile toward welfare mothers, especially those who are Black, we can expect increasingly coercive measures to pass. The population control researchers are poised to supply the technologies needed to meet policymakers' objectives—technologies that sacrifice women's health and autonomy for the sake of "effective" birth control. Underlying these measures are the twin assumptions that the problem of Black poverty can be cured by lowering Black birthrates and that Black women's bodies are an appropriate site for this social experiment. Once again the notion of Black women's reproductive liberty has dropped out of the picture.

4

MAKING REPRODUCTION A CRIME

On February 2, 1992, twenty-eight-year-old Cornelia Whitner gave birth to a healthy baby boy named Kevin at Easely Baptist Medical Center in Pickens County, South Carolina. When the hospital staff discovered traces of cocaine in the baby's urine, they notified child welfare authorities. Two months later, Whitner was arrested for "endangering the life of her unborn child" by smoking crack while pregnant.

On the day of her hearing, Whitner met briefly in the hallway with her court-appointed attorney, Cheryl Aaron, for the first time. Aaron advised Whitner to plead guilty to the child neglect charges, promising to get her into a drug treatment program so that she could be reunited with her children. Aaron, who had previously prosecuted pregnant addicts herself as a Pickens County prosecutor, did not think to challenge the application of the child neglect statute to a fetus or the constitutionality of the charges brought against her client. In fact, scores of women across the country arrested for smoking crack while pregnant had similarly pled guilty to charges of child abuse, distribution of drugs to a minor, or lesser offenses. They were typically placed on probation and required to get drug treatment.

In this case, the lawyer's advice turned out to be terribly mistaken. The April 20 hearing before Judge Frank Eppes started abruptly. "Is this a crack baby?" the judge asked Whitner gruffly. "Why wouldn't you just take a pistol and put it in your mouth and blow your head off?"[1] Whitner replied by pleading for help with her drug problem. Aaron went on to explain that her client was in counseling and had stayed off drugs since Kevin's birth. The baby was in good health. All Whitner wanted was to be placed in a residential treatment facility. Turning a deaf ear, Judge Eppes simply responded, "I think I'll just let her go to jail." He then sentenced Whitner to a startling eight-year prison term.

On the other side of the country, Darlene Johnson, a twenty-seven-year-old mother of four, stood before California Superior Court judge Howard Broadman for sentencing.[2] She was eight months pregnant at the time. Johnson had already pled guilty to three counts of felony child abuse for whipping her six- and four-year-old daughters with a belt for smoking cigarettes and poking a hanger in an electrical socket. A child welfare report mentioned scars and bruises on the girls' bodies. Because Johnson had a prior criminal record for petty theft and credit card forgery, she faced serving time in state prison. At first Judge Broadman indicated he would grant Johnson's request for probation, which was also the recommendation of the probation officer assigned to the case. Then, noting that Johnson might become pregnant again while receiving welfare, he made an unexpected proposition: he gave Johnson a choice between a seven-year prison sentence or only one year in prison and three years on probation, with the condition that she be implanted with Norplant.

Johnson, whose appointed attorney was not present at the time, questioned the implant's safety. Judge Broadman assured her that Norplant was not experimental (the FDA had approved the contraceptive less than a month before) and that its effects could be reversed by "just tak[ing] the thing out." "It's a thing that you put into your arm and it lasts for five years. . . . It's like birth control pills, except you don't have to take them every day," was the judge's only description of the device.[3] Caught off guard and fearing the prospect of spending the next seven years in prison, Johnson agreed.

Johnson returned to Judge Broadman eight days later when she learned from the public defender that her diabetes, high blood pressure, and other health problems made it dangerous for her to use Norplant and that the order might violate her constitutional rights. Broadman refused to rescind the order on grounds that Johnson had voluntarily agreed to its terms and that "[i]t is in the defendant's best interest and certainly in any unconceived child's interest that she not have any more children until she is mentally and emotionally prepared to do so."[4] Broadman was not even moved by an expert's declaration that Norplant was contraindicated for someone with Johnson's health condition or statement that it would be "medically irresponsible" for any doctor to insert Norplant in a woman's arm under such coercive circumstances.

The ACLU joined Johnson's appeal of Broadman's order, arguing that state-coerced birth control violated the fundamental right to pro-create. The California attorney general filed a five-page brief agreeing that Johnson's acceptance of the Norplant condition was not know-ing or voluntary. The case caused a national stir — not the least of which occurred in Broadman's own courtroom when an antiabortion activist fired a shot that narrowly missed the the judge's head, mut-tering "Norplant kills babies." Ultimately, an appellate court dis-missed Johnson's appeal as moot after Johnson violated the terms of her probation by testing positive for drugs and was remanded to prison.[5]

∞

States have recently turned their attention to reproduction as a focus for criminal punishment. The cases of Cornelia Whitner and Darlene Johnson represent two controversial ways in which the criminal jus-tice system is penalizing pregnancy — the prosecution of women for exposing their babies to drugs in the womb and the imposition of birth control as a condition of probation. These criminal cases, which have multiplied over the past decade, have two things in common: both punish women, in effect, for having babies and both unduly in-volve poor Black women.

In what way do these cases punish pregnancy? When a pregnant woman is arrested for harming the fetus by smoking crack, her crime hinges on her decision to have a baby. She can avoid prosecution if she has an abortion. If she chooses instead to give birth, she risks going to prison. Similarly, when a judge gives a defendant the choice between Norplant or jail, incarceration becomes the penalty for the defendant's decision to remain fertile. If she violates probation by be-coming pregnant, she will be sent to prison. Prosecutors and judges see poor Black women as suitable subjects for these reproductive penalties because society does not view these women as suitable mothers in the first place.

Previous chapters have described how birth control policy has at-tempted to curtail the numbers of Black children based on the premise that Black fertility is the cause of social problems. In criminal cases, the government more directly punishes Black mothers for their children's difficulties. In this chapter, I explain why this combination of crime, race, and reproduction gravely threatens Black people's wel-fare as well as our concept of procreative liberty.

PUNISHING CRACK ADDICTS FOR HAVING BABIES

A growing number of women across the country have been indicted for criminal offenses after giving birth to babies who test positive for drugs.[6] The majority of these women, like Cornelia Whitner, are poor and Black. Most are addicted to crack cocaine. Charges of "prenatal crime" used to occur twice a decade. Then, in the mid-1980s, prosecutors decided to tackle the panic over an alleged explosion of "crack babies" by prosecuting their mothers. Between 1985 and 1995, at least two hundred women in thirty states were charged with maternal drug use. Creative statutory interpretations that once seemed little more than the outlandish concoctions of conservative pundits were used to punish women. The charges have included distributing drugs to a minor, child abuse and neglect, reckless endangerment, manslaughter, and assault with a deadly weapon.

At the same time, state legislators seized upon the issue as a hot political item. Eighty-two percent of Americans questioned in a 1989 ABC poll agreed that "a pregnant woman who uses crack cocaine and addicts her unborn child should be put in jail for child abuse."[7] In 1990, lawmakers in thirty-four states debated bills concerning prenatal substance abuse.[8] In California alone, some twenty different bills relating to the problem of drug use during pregnancy were pending before the legislature at one time.[9] Melanie Green, a Black woman, was arrested in Rockford, Illinois, when her baby died of oxygen deprivation two days after birth. She was charged with involuntary manslaughter on the ground that the baby's death was "linked to cocaine exposure late in the pregnancy." When the grand jury failed to indict Green, the Illinois state legislature adopted the Infant Neglect and Controlled Substances Act of 1989, making the state's civil child abuse and reporting statutes apply to newborns who test positive for drugs.[10] A proposed bill making drug use during pregnancy a felony failed to pass.

The prosecution of drug-addicted mothers is part of an alarming trend toward greater state intervention into the lives of pregnant women under the rationale of protecting the fetus from harm. Increasingly, the interests of the fetus are pitted against those of the mother. Courts have allowed children to bring tort suits against their mothers for prenatal negligence. Pregnant women have been compelled to undergo cesarean sections, blood transfusions, and other medical interventions for the sake of the fetus. Employers have excluded fertile women from certain jobs to prevent fetal exposure to workplace hazards. In addition, the U.S. Supreme Court has approved greater restrictions on abortion. As the antiabortion movement portrayed the fetus as a separate person and the medical profession treated the fetus as an independent patient, the fetus acquired more and more legal rights of its own, often against the pregnant woman carrying it.

The protracted battle between those who favor protecting the rights of the fetus and those who favor protecting the rights of the mother has been waged in the media, the courtroom, and the streets. Legal scholars often approach the issue by weighing the state's interest in protecting the fetus against the mother's interest in her own bodily autonomy. But can we determine whether the prosecutions are fair simply by deciding upon the duties a pregnant woman owes to her fetus and then assessing whether the defendant has met them? Both sides of the debate have largely overlooked a critical aspect of government prosecution of drug-addicted mothers.

Just as important to this controversy as the politics of fetal rights is the politics of race. Race entered the debate in the form of the crack epidemic and the frightening image of the "crack baby" that helped to define it. Race also provided the backdrop of hostility toward Black mothers that made prosecuting pregnant women permissible. A leading advocate for women charged with prenatal crimes recently stated that "for the first time in American history . . . what a pregnant woman does to her own body becomes a matter for the juries and the court."[11] But, as we saw in Chapter 1, a pregnant slave woman's body was subject to legal fiat centuries ago because the fetus she was carrying already belonged to her master. The criminal regulation of pregnancy that occurs today is in some ways unprecedented. Yet it belongs to the continuing legacy of the degradation of Black motherhood traced in previous chapters. The prosecutions are better understood as a way of punishing Black women for having babies rather than as a way of protecting Black fetuses.

CREATING THE CRACK EPIDEMIC

Crack cocaine exploded on the American scene in the early 1980s, and its abuse quickly rose to epidemic proportions.[12] A 1985 *New York Times* story about a local drug treatment program identified crack for the first time in print media, referring to teenagers' "cocaine dependence resulting from a new form of the drug called 'crack,' or rock-like pieces of prepared 'freebase' (concentrated) cocaine."[13] Crack (named for the crackling sound it makes as it burns) immediately became popular in the inner cities. Because crack was smoked rather than snorted, it produced an instantaneous high. It was also cheap. While a gram of powdered cocaine cost over $50, individual "rocks" of crack could be purchased for a tenth that amount.

Crack's apparent confinement to inner-city neighborhoods made it the perfect target for Reagan's ferocious War on Drugs and the media's disparagement of Black Americans. The media soon imbued crack with phenomenal qualities: it was instantly addicting, it intensified the sex drive, and it turned users into violent maniacs. While powdered cocaine was glamorized as a thrilling amusement of the rich and famous, crack was vilified for stripping its underclass users of every shred of human dignity.[14] By June 1986, *Newsweek* had declared crack to be "The Plague Among Us," which its editor in chief vowed to cover "as a crisis, reporting it as aggressively and returning to it as regularly as we did the struggle for civil rights, the war in Vietnam, and the fall of the Nixon presidency."[15] (*Newsweek* and *Time* each ran five cover stories on the crack crisis in that year alone.) Federal spending on the nation's drug problem skyrocketed from $200 million in the 1970s to $13 billion in 1992, most devoted to law enforcement.

One of crack's peculiar qualities appeared to be the drug's appeal to women.[16] Approximately half of the nation's crack smokers are female. The concern about women's crack use was no doubt exaggerated by gender stereotypes that make female drug addicts more disturbing than male drug addicts. (Women are actually more likely to be addicted to alcohol or pills.) Still, most crack-addicted women are of childbearing age, and many are pregnant, which contributed to the huge increase in the number of newborns testing positive for drugs observed in hospitals during the late 1980s. In many urban hospitals, the number of drug-exposed infants quadrupled between 1985 and 1990. But crack was by no means the only drug involved.

News of this surge in maternal drug use broke in 1988 when the National Association for Perinatal Addiction Research and Education (NAPARE) published the results of a study of babies in hospitals across the country. NAPARE found that 11 percent of newborns in thirty-six hospitals surveyed were affected by their mothers' illegal drug use during pregnancy.[17] In several hospitals, the proportion of drug-exposed infants was as high as 15 and 25 percent. Extrapolating these statistics to the population at large, it was estimated that as many as 375,000 drug-exposed infants are born every year.[18] This figure covered all drug exposure nationwide and did not break down the numbers based on the extent of drug use or its effects on the newborn.

The media parlayed the NAPARE report into a horrific tale of damage to hundreds of thousands of babies. A review of newspaper accounts of the drug exposure data reveals a stunning instance of journalistic excess. Even the most careful reporters felt free to make wildly exaggerated claims about the effects of prenatal drug use. Although NAPARE's figures referred to numbers of infants *exposed* to, not *harmed* by, maternal drug use, the *Los Angeles Times* wrote about 375,000 babies "tainted by potentially fatal narcotics in the womb each year."[19] Some articles attributed all 375,000 cases to crack, although experts estimate that 50,000 to 100,000 newborns at most are exposed specifically to cocaine (both powdered and crack) each year.[20] (In one editorial the figure ballooned to 550,000 babies having "their fragile brains bombarded with the drug."[21]) "Crack was even responsible for the creation of an entirely new, and now leading, category of child abuse: exposure of babies to drugs during pregnancy," the *Los Angeles Times* claimed in a front-page story—as if crack were the *only* drug used by pregnant women.[22] The press often gave medically inaccurate descriptions of crack's impact on children. The *New York Times*, for example, stated that pregnant women were "producing a new generation of innocent addicts," erroneously implying that babies exposed prenatally to crack are all born automatically hooked on the drug.[23]

Having whipped up a panic over crack exposure, the media next created the drama's leading characters—the pregnant addict and the crack baby, both irredeemable, both Black. The pregnant crack addict was portrayed as an irresponsible and selfish woman who put her love for crack above her love for her children. In news stories she was often represented by a prostitute, who sometimes traded sex for crack, in violation of every conceivable quality of a good mother. The chemical properties of crack were said to destroy the natural impulse to mother. "The most remarkable and hideous aspect of crack cocaine seems to be the undermining of the maternal instinct," a nurse was quoted as observing about her patients.[24] The pregnant crack addict, then, was the exact opposite of a mother: she was promiscuous, uncaring, and self-indulgent.

She was also Black. In the focus on maternal crack use, which is stereotypically associated with Blacks, the media left the impression that the pregnant addict is typically a Black woman. Even more than a "metaphor for women's alienation from instinctual motherhood,"[25] the pregnant crack addict was the latest embodiment of the bad *Black* mother. The monstrous crack-smoking mother was added to the iconography of depraved Black maternity, alongside the matriarch and the welfare queen. Crack gave society one more reason to curb Black women's fertility.

The crack baby was equally hopeless. Always pictured trembling and shrieking in an overcrowded hospital ward, the crack baby suffered from multiple ailments that often killed him. But these images that induced pity for the helpless victim were eclipsed by predictions of the tremendous burdens that crack babies were destined to impose on law-abiding taxpayers. Permanently damaged and abandoned by their mothers, they would require costly hospital care, inundate the foster care system, overwhelm the public schools with special needs, and ultimately prey on the rest of society as criminals and welfare dependents. It was estimated that Americans were already spending an additional $200 million a year "to keep up with the crack onslaught," leading to the startling prediction that crack babies "will cost this nation $100 billion in remedial medical and developmental costs over the next decade."[26]

The crack baby's emotional impairment set this casualty of maternal drug use apart from all others. In addition to medical complications, crack babies were supposed to suffer from irreversible neurological damage that warped their very character. Nurses reported that these infants stiffened when they were cuddled, displaying "emotional detachment" and "impaired human interaction."[27] Teachers described the school-age children alternatively as expressionless zombies or uncontrollable demons prone to sudden temper tantrums.[28] The crack baby, then, was as unnatural as his mother: just as the pregnant crack addict had no maternal instinct, the crack baby lacked an innate social consciousness.

This frightening portrait of damaged crack babies may have caused as much harm as the mothers' crack use itself. The data on the extent and severity of crack's impact on babies are highly controversial, to say the least. At the inception of the crisis numerous medical journals reported that babies born to crack-addicted mothers suffered a variety of medical, developmental, and behavioral problems.[29] But more recent research reveals that these early studies were seriously flawed.[30] The initial results were made unreliable by the lack of controls and the selection of poor, inner-city subjects at high risk for unhealthy pregnancies. Maternal crack use often contributes to underweight and premature births. This alone is reason for concern. But many of the problems seen in crack-exposed babies are just as likely to have been caused by other risk factors associated with their mothers' crack use, rather than the crack itself.

Women who smoke crack are often poor, homeless, malnourished, sick, and physically abused. They may smoke, drink, and use other illegal drugs besides crack. They are also likely to receive little or no prenatal care. Researchers cannot tell us which of this array of hazards actually caused the terrible outcomes they originally attributed to crack. Babies born under these wretched conditions are likely to be unhealthy whether or not their mothers smoke crack. Nor can researchers authoritatively determine the percentage of infants exposed to crack in the womb who actually experience these consequences.[31] It is impossible to predict, for example, if a child whose mother smoked crack will suffer any adverse medical effects at all. Some findings of earlier studies, such as a high incidence of sudden infant death syndrome and stroke, were not replicated in subsequent, more careful research.

Moreover, some researchers have found that the harmful effects of prenatal crack exposure may be temporary and treatable.[32] A Northwestern University study of pregnant cocaine addicts found that comprehensive prenatal care may improve the outcome of pregnancies complicated by cocaine abuse.[33] Research has also discovered dramatic differences in the effects of maternal alcohol abuse depending on the mother's socioeconomic status. Although all women in a study drank at the same rate, the children born to low-income women had a 70.9 percent rate of fetal alcohol syndrome, compared to a 4.5 percent rate for those of upper-income women.[34] The main reason for this disparity was the pregnant women's nutrition. While the wealthier women ate a regular, balanced diet, the poorer women had sporadic, unhealthy meals. Crack is not good for anyone. But these studies suggest that its potentially harmful consequences for babies can be minimized, or even prevented, by ensuring proper health care and nutrition for drug-dependent mothers.

The medical community's one-sided attention to studies showing detrimental results from cocaine exposure added to the public's distorted perception of the risks of maternal crack use.[35] For a long time, journals tended to accept for publication only studies that supported the dominant view of fetal harm. Research that reported no adverse effects was ignored, even though it was often more reliable. The number of articles concerning crack's impact was also unprecedented. Medical journals published four times as many papers concerning prenatal cocaine exposure as had been published concerning the prenatal effects of the heroin epidemic a decade earlier.[36] Now experts are denouncing the earlier rush to judgment. Reviewing the literature of the past decade, two researchers conclude: "We think it is clear now, from a multitude of studies, that the effect of prenatal cocaine exposure is minimal at birth and is probably limited to minor growth deficits."[37]

My point is not that crack use during pregnancy is safe, but that the media exaggerated the extent and nature of the harm it causes. News reports erroneously suggested, moreover, that the problem of maternal drug use was confined to the Black community. A public health crisis that cuts across racial and economic lines was transformed into an example of *Black* mothers' depravity that warranted harsh punishment.

It is doubtful that the medical profession's about-face on crack exposure will have much impact on the public's perception of the "epidemic." The image of the crack baby—trembling in a tiny hospital bed, permanently brain-damaged, and on his way to becoming a parasitic criminal—is indelibly etched in the American psyche. It will be hard to convince most Americans that the caricature of the crack baby rests on flimsy, exaggerated data. Unfortunately, many will refuse to believe that it is not primarily crack that is destroying the health of poor Black children.

THE STATE'S PUNITIVE RESPONSE

The crisis of drug-exposed babies cried out for action. State prosecutors, legislators, and judges around the nation responded, and their response was punitive. They have punished women who use drugs while pregnant by jailing them during their pregnancy, by seizing custody of their babies at birth, and by prosecuting them for crimes.

The most common penalty for a mother's prenatal drug use is the permanent or temporary removal of her baby.[38] Thousands of low-income Black mothers have lost custody of their babies on the basis of a solitary drug test. About a dozen states have enacted statutes that require the reporting of positive newborn toxicologies to child welfare authorities, and many hospitals interpret child abuse reporting laws, passed thirty years ago in all fifty states, to require them to report positive results. In some states, a positive drug screening automatically triggers neglect proceedings to obtain custody of the baby. As a result, child abuse and neglect petitions containing allegations of the mother's drug use quadrupled in New York City between 1986 and 1989, paralleling the onset of the crack epidemic.[39] Crack exposure is now the leading grounds for newborn foster placement in that city.[40]

In cities across the country, policymakers are debating whether newborns whose mothers smoke crack should be taken to foster care right away.[41] More and more agencies snatch drug-exposed babies from their mothers immediately after birth, pending an investigation. In the subsequent custody determination, a positive neonatal toxicology often raises a strong presumption of parental unfitness. Several states have facilitated this process by expanding the statutory definition of neglected children to include infants who test positive for controlled substances at birth. But a positive toxicology (which may be false) reveals only that the mother ingested drugs shortly before the delivery. It tells us nothing about the extent of the mother's drug use, any harm to the baby, or the mother's parenting abilities. Equating evidence of maternal drug use with child neglect circumvents the inquiry into the mother's competence to care for her child that is customarily necessary to deprive a parent of custody. This could mean separating a mother from her newborn based on occasional—or even a single instance of—drug use. Some mothers have lost custody of their older children as well.

Of course, the state should remove babies from drug-addicted mothers when they are at risk of harm. But it is also harmful to children to be wrongfully taken from their mothers on insufficient evidence of unfitness, often to be cast into a more perilous foster care system. A recent class action lawsuit against the Illinois child welfare service alleged that children in foster care "frequently have been shuffled among six or more temporary living arrangements for two or more years and hundreds of them have been victims of neglect or abuse at an increasing rate."[42]

When foster homes run out, children are "warehoused" in overcrowded and dangerous shelters and newborns are "boarded" in hospital wards. The "crack babies" who are being removed from their mothers in droves are, of course, the most difficult to place with families. Lawsuits filed in Illinois, New Jersey, and New York charged that state child welfare agencies were needlessly confining crack-exposed newborns to hospitals for months at a time rather than placing them in foster care or residential centers.[43] The shortage of drug treatment services and other support for drug-dependent mothers makes it difficult for them to regain custody of their children. By the time competent mothers are ultimately reunited with their children, the severing of their bond in the first moments of life has already inflicted tremendous damage. Commentators such as Abe Rosenthal of the *New York Times*, who call for the immediate, permanent seizure of "poisoned babies," seem oblivious to these painful consequences, as well as to the wide-scale disruption these removals have unleashed on the Black community.[44]

Another penalty is the "protective" incarceration of pregnant drug addicts charged with unrelated crimes. In 1988, a Washington, D.C., judge sentenced a thirty-year-old Black woman named Brenda Vaughn, who pleaded guilty to forging $700 worth of checks, to jail for the duration of her pregnancy.[45] The prosecutor had agreed to probation, the typical penalty for such a minor offense. Instead Judge Peter H. Wolf stated at sentencing that he wanted to ensure that the baby would be born in jail to protect it from its mother's drug abuse: "I'm going to keep her locked up until the baby is born because she'd tested positive for cocaine when she came before me. . . . She's apparently an addictive personality, and I'll be darned if I'm going to have a baby born that way."

Although the Vaughn case was picked up by the press, defendants' drug use during pregnancy often affects judges' sentencing decisions in unnoticed cases. It does not matter to these judges that the conditions in America's jails are hazardous to fetal health. Women in prison often live in filthy and overcrowded spaces, eat poorly, are exposed to contagious diseases and violence, get little or no prenatal care, and have easy access to drugs—hardly a protective environment for a developing fetus.

Civil commitment offers another avenue for judges to mandate treatment for pregnant substance abusers. Minnesota is the only state so far to pass a law specifically authorizing civil commitment of pregnant women who engage in the "habitual and excessive use" of drugs. Physicians in Minnesota who suspect their pregnant patients of drug use must test them and report positive results to government authorities. The law also encourages anyone who has reason to believe a pregnant woman is using drugs to turn her in. Pregnant women who fail to get treatment on their own have been detained in the hospital against their will after court proceedings. In other states, pregnant women have been involuntarily confined under ordinary state civil commitment laws that apply to drug-dependent or mentally ill persons.

Taking a more innovative route, some judges have taken custody of the *fetus* through the juvenile court system to protect it from the mother's drug use. An Illinois judge compelled a pregnant heroin user to enter drug rehabilitation by making her fetus a ward of the state, ruling that the woman was abusing it.[46] In Waukesha County, Wisconsin, Children's Court judge Kathryn Foster ruled that a viable fetus was a child entitled to protection under the state's child welfare laws and detained the crack-addicted mother in an inpatient treatment center. (The Wisconsin Supreme Court reversed the detention order on April 22, 1997.)[47] A juvenile court judge in Ohio similarly ordered a pregnant woman to be placed in a "secure drug facility" to guard the fetus from the woman's cocaine use.[48]

Finally, district attorneys across the country grabbed the opportunity to become front-line champions in the assault on drug use during pregnancy. In the late 1980s, criminal cases brought against women for prenatal drug exposure began to hit the headlines.

THE FIRST CONVICTION

When Judge O. H. Eaton, Jr., issued a verdict in a Florida courtroom on July 13, 1989, it may have seemed like a run-of-the-mill drug-trafficking conviction. But it was a landmark decision. It was this country's first criminal conviction of a mother for exposing her baby to drugs while she was pregnant.[49] Jennifer Clarise Johnson, a twenty-three-year-old Black woman, gave birth to her son, Carl, in 1987, and to her daughter, Jessica, in 1989. Both babies appeared healthy and normal at birth. Because Johnson had admitted to her doctors that she smoked crack shortly before the deliveries, the babies were tested. Both tested positive for metabolites of cocaine. The Florida state attorney's office, which had recently embarked on a policy of prosecuting women for prenatal drug use, decided to press for a conviction. Next to South Carolina, Florida has initiated the most prosecutions for drug use during pregnancy in the country.

The state charged Johnson with two crimes: two counts of delivering a controlled substance to Carl and Jessica, a crime carrying a potential thirty-year sentence, and one count of felonious child abuse against Jessica. (Judge Eaton later threw out the child abuse charge because there was insufficient evidence that Jessica was actually harmed by her mother's drug use.) Because the relevant Florida drug law did not apply to fetuses, the prosecution had to prove that Johnson had delivered cocaine to her children *after* they were born. The prosecutor overcame this roadblock by inventing a novel interpretation of the statute.

Assistant state attorney Jeff Deen built his case of drug delivery through the testimony of the obstetricians who attended the births, Drs. Randy Tompkins and Mitchell Perlstein. Dr. Tompkins, who delivered Jessica, testified that even after delivery "maternally altered" blood circulates between the placenta and the baby through the still-attached umbilical cord. He estimated that from forty-five to sixty seconds elapsed from the time the baby had completely emerged to the clamping of the umbilical cord. Tompkins added that once Jessica was delivered from the birth canal she was a person and no longer a fetus, even though the umbilical cord was still attached.[50] Perlstein, who delivered Carl, testified to similar facts with respect to Carl's birth.[51] Deen also put the county medical examiner on the stand, who testified that a nearly unpronounceable cocaine derivative called benzoylecgonine remains in the bloodstream in decreasing amounts for forty-eight to seventy-two hours after cocaine is ingested.[52]

Deen patched together this testimony, along with Johnson's admission that she smoked crack within hours of both deliveries, to establish an unprecedented application of the drug law. He argued that Johnson had passed the cocaine metabolite to her babies *through their umbilical cords* after they were born, in the sixty seconds before the cords were cut.

Deen's case was built on shaky ground. First, his statutory argument posed serious due-process problems. True, Deen succeeded in presenting a theory that could be stretched to fit the words of the statute. But the plain reading of the drug delivery law did not give Johnson fair warning that it prohibited her conduct during pregnancy.

There was also a gaping hole in the circumstantial evidence against Johnson. The state's entire case hung on proving the presence of the cocaine metabolite in the umbilical cord blood during the critical sixty-second window. Even Deen's own witness conceded that the best way to be sure of what substances were flowing through the umbilical cord would have been to test a blood sample from the cord itself. But there was no record of such a test being performed. How then could the doctors tell whether the cocaine found in the babies' urine after they were born had been passed from Johnson after their birth or before? In fact, Dr. Stephen Kandall, a neonatologist at Beth Israel Medical Center in New York and president of the New York Pediatric Society, testified for the defense that it was impossible to tell from a newborn's urine sample precisely when drugs entered the body. Although it was theoretically possible that a tiny amount of cocaine metabolite traveled through the baby's umbilical cord after delivery, it was also possible that none was transferred during those crucial seconds.

Judge Eaton disregarded both problems with the state's case against Johnson. After a brief three-hour recess, he found Johnson guilty of delivering cocaine to her children. She was sentenced to one year of residential drug treatment and fourteen years probation. Although he spared Johnson jail time, Judge Eaton imposed a number of conditions to monitor her personal life. She had to submit to random drug testing, remain employed, and notify officials if she became pregnant. She was barred from frequenting any bar or restaurant that served alcohol. Johnson's conviction also carried the threat of incarceration should she fail to meet any of the probation conditions.

THE SOUTH CAROLINA EXPERIMENT

The State of South Carolina bears the dubious distinction of prosecuting the largest number of women for maternal drug use. Many of these cases arose from the collaboration of Charleston law enforcement officials and the Medical University of South Carolina (MUSC), a state hospital serving an indigent minority population. In August 1989, nurse Shirley Brown approached the local solicitor, Charles Condon, about the increase in crack use she perceived among her pregnant patients. That very month, the solicitor of Greenville County, in another part of the state, had announced a policy of prosecuting mothers whose babies tested positive for drugs, a story important enough to make front-page news.[53]

Condon immediately held a series of meetings that brought in additional MUSC staff, the police department, child protective services, and the Charleston County Substance Abuse Commission to develop a strategy for addressing the problem. The MUSC clinicians may have had intentions of helping their patients, but their input was soon overshadowed by law enforcement objectives. The approach turned toward pressuring pregnant patients who used drugs to get treatment by threatening them with criminal charges. As Condon expressed it, "We all agreed on one principle: We needed a program that used not only a carrot, but a real and very firm stick." Condon also pressed the position that neither the physician-patient privilege nor the Fourth Amendment to the U.S. Constitution, which prohibits warrantless searches and seizures, prevented hospital staff from reporting positive drug tests to the police.

Within two months MUSC had instituted the Interagency Policy on Cocaine Abuse in Pregnancy (Interagency Policy), a series of internal memos that provided for nonconsensual drug testing of pregnant patients, reporting results to the police, and the use of arrest for drug and child abuse charges as punishment or intimidation.[54] Although the program claimed "to ensure the appropriate management of patients abusing illegal drugs during pregnancy,"[55] its origin suggests that it was designed to supply Condon with defendants for his new prosecutorial crusade. The arrests had already begun by the time the hospital's board of directors officially approved the new policy. Hospital bioethicists later criticized the hasty process orchestrated by Condon for neglecting the careful internal deliberation one would expect of a program affecting patient care.[56] Condon personally broadcast the new policy in televised public service announcements that advised pregnant women, "not only will you live with guilt, you could be arrested."[57]

During the first several months, women who tested positive for crack at the time they gave birth were immediately arrested. Then Condon added an "amnesty" program to the Interagency Policy: patients testing positive for drugs were offered a chance to get treatment; if they refused or failed, they would be arrested. Patients who tested positive were handed two letters, usually by Nurse Brown: one notified them of their appointment with the substance abuse clinic; the other, from the solicitor, warned them, "If you fail to complete substance abuse counseling, fail to cooperate with the Department of Social Services in the placement of your child and services to protect your child, or if you fail to maintain clean urine specimens during your substance abuse rehabilitation, you *will* be arrested by the police and prosecuted by the Office of the Solicitor."[58]

The policy offered no second chances. Women who tested positive for drugs a second time or who delivered a baby who tested positive were arrested and imprisoned. Depending on the stage of pregnancy, the mother was charged with drug possession, child neglect, or distribution of drugs to a minor. Uncooperative women who declined treatment were arrested based on a single positive result. Crystal Ferguson, for example, requested an outpatient referral because she had no one to care for her two sons at home; she was arrested for failing to comply with Nurse Brown's order to enter a two-week residential program with no child care.

The Interagency Policy resulted in the arrests of forty-two patients, all but one of whom were Black. (Nurse Brown noted on the chart of the sole white woman arrested that her boyfriend was Black.) The arrests were scenes one might imagine in some totalitarian regime, not the sanctity of a maternity ward. Police arrested some patients within days or even hours of giving birth and hauled them off to jail in handcuffs and leg shackles.[59] The handcuffs were attached to a three-inch wide leather belt that was wrapped around their stomachs. Some women were still bleeding from the delivery. One new mother who complained was told to sit on a towel when she arrived at the jail. Another reported that she was grabbed in a chokehold and shoved into detention.

The day after giving birth, Ellen Laverne Knight was handed papers to sign instead of her baby. "Nurse Brown was a bitch," Knight recalled. "She came and said I had to go into a room to talk to someone. It was the police. They said I have a right to remain silent. I found out I was going to jail. They brought me my clothes, they handcuffed me, they put a sheet over my hands, they pushed me out in a wheelchair. I spent the night in city jail without a sanitary napkin."[60] Needless to say, these arrests meant tearing newborn infants away from their mothers at a crucial time for bonding and nurturance.

Women who were pregnant at the time of their arrest sat in jail cells waiting to give birth. When they went into labor, they were rushed by ambulance to the hospital, where they continued to be treated like prisoners. Lori Griffin was transported weekly from the jail to the hospital in handcuffs and leg irons for prenatal care. Three weeks after her arrest, she went into labor and was taken, still in handcuffs and shackles, to MUSC. Once at the hospital, she was kept handcuffed to her bed *during the entire delivery*.[61]

This ruthless desecration of maternity signifies the depths to which poor Black mothers have sunk in society's estimation. The sight of a pregnant Black woman bound in shackles is a modern-day reincarnation of the horrors of slave masters' control of slave women's wombs. Of course, the women's circumstances are different, as are the regulators' precise interests in guarding the fetus. But there is an eerie link between these degraded Black mothers of Charleston, South Car-

olina, and their foremothers who were forced to breed for slaveholders less than two centuries ago. Thinking about an expectant Black
mother chained to a belt around her swollen belly to protect her unborn child, I cannot help but recall how whites forced their pregnant
slaves to lie face down in a hole to protect the fetus while they
whipped the mother's back. Once again, Black women give birth in
chains!

THE COUNTERASSAULT

Most women charged with prenatal crimes are pressured into accepting plea bargains to avoid jail time. These cases quietly slip away
without appellate scrutiny. When women have appealed, however,
they have almost always been victorious. With one exception, every
appellate court to consider the issue, including the highest court in
several states, has invalidated criminal charges for drug use during
pregnancy.

Most decisions center on the court's interpretation of the criminal
statute cited in the indictment. Courts have held that the state's child
abuse, homicide, or drug distribution law was not meant to cover a
fetus or to punish prenatal drug exposure. The Florida Supreme
Court, for example, threw out Jennifer Johnson's conviction in 1992
on the ground that the state legislature had not intended "to use the
word 'delivery' in the context of criminally prosecuting mothers for
delivery of a controlled substance to a minor by way of the umbilical
cord."[62] A few courts have held that prosecuting a woman for conduct
during pregnancy violates her constitutional right to privacy.

State legislatures have also rejected the punitive bills that prolifer-
ated in the late 1980s. While some states have included prenatal drug
exposure in their civil child neglect laws, none has explicitly made it a
crime. Some states have enacted instead laws designed to increase
women's access to drug treatment. For example, in 1991 Missouri
adopted legislation that mandates treatment and education for pregnant addicts while expressly prohibiting the use of information about
their drug use as a basis for criminal prosecution. This legislative
trend, however, has not deterred prosecutors from bringing charges
under statutes that are already on the books. By operating on their
own, rather than by legislative mandate, renegade prosecutors can
more easily avoid the scrutiny entailed in passing a law and impose
their personal notions of criminal justice in a discriminatory fashion.

After winning a number of state court victories, Lynn Paltrow, director of special litigation for the Center for Reproductive Law and Policy in New York, decided to take the offensive. In October 1993, Paltrow filed in federal district court a class action lawsuit against the City of Charleston and MUSC on behalf of Crystal Ferguson and another Black woman who had been jailed under the Interagency Policy.[63] The plaintiffs demanded $3 million for violations of a number of constitutional guarantees, including the right to privacy in medical information, the right to refuse medical treatment, the right to procreate, and the right to equal protection of the law regardless of race.

The complaint was supported by declarations from an impressive array of national and local experts, among them Dr. Barry Zuckerman, chairman of the Department of Pediatrics at Boston University School of Medicine and one of the most prolific writers on the subject of prenatal substance abuse; Jay Katz, professor emeritus of Law, Medicine, and Psychiatry at Yale Law School, who authored the influential book on medical ethics, *The Silent World of Doctor and Patient*; and Louise Haynes, the former director of the Office of Women's Services at the South Carolina Commission on Alcohol and Drug Abuse. Federal Judge C. Weston Houck nevertheless refused to halt the program pending trial, stating, "I think the public is concerned about children who, through no fault of their own . . . are born addicted." On January 8, 1997, the federal jury in *Ferguson* rejected the plaintiffs' claims that the hospital had violated their Fourth Amendment and equal protection rights.

The federal government became involved several months after the federal lawsuit was filed. The National Institutes of Health found that the Interagency Policy constituted research on human subjects, which MUSC had been conducting without federally mandated review and approval.[64] The hospital had embarked on an experiment designed to test the hypothesis that threats of incarceration would stop pregnant women from taking drugs and improve fetal health. Yet it had never taken the required precautions to ensure that patients were adequately protected; indeed, it had surreptitiously collected confidential information about them and given it to the police.

The Civil Rights Division of the Department of Health and Human Services (HHS) also began investigating whether MUSC had violated the civil rights of its Black patients by discriminating against them in referring patients to the solicitor for arrest and prosecution. In October 1994—five years after the policy's inception—MUSC dropped the program as part of a settlement agreement with HHS.

Under threat of losing millions of dollars in federal funding, the hospital dismantled its joint venture with the solicitor's office and the police.

Despite the federal reprimand, MUSC's collaboration with prosecutors retains enthusiastic support in South Carolina. Condon's crusade against pregnant addicts as a circuit solicitor helped him win a landslide victory for state attorney general in November 1994. Newly elected, Condon, a Republican, launched a blistering attack on the Clinton administration in the pages of *Policy Review*, the journal of the conservative Heritage Foundation.[65] In "Clinton's Cocaine Babies—Why Won't the Administration Let Us Save Our Children?" he accused the HHS investigation of shutting down "one of the first 'crack baby' prevention programs in the nation" in order to cater to politically correct liberals and feminists. "Unfortunately, the policy of the Clinton administration is to protect, not the children, but the 'rights' of the mothers to escape the consequences of their actions," he wrote. Condon claimed that the program's success at getting "scores" of women off drugs made it a model that other states sought to emulate. But the lack of reliable documentation makes it impossible to verify his claims. It is just as likely that any decline in positive test results was caused by drug-dependent women avoiding MUSC's clinic out of fear of arrest. And if the policy was motivated by concern for the children, why mention that most of the patients are on welfare and that "a single cocaine baby can run up a lifetime tab of $1 million in medical and educational costs"?

In the summer of 1996 the South Carolina Supreme Court delivered to Condon the boost he needed to revive his assault on pregnant crack users.

THE WHITNER SETBACK

Cornelia Whitner, the South Carolina woman sentenced to eight years in prison for child abuse, did not initially appeal her conviction. She had been locked up for nineteen months in Leath Correctional Institution before a lawyer from the local ACLU contacted her through Cheryl Aaron about challenging her conviction. Lynn Paltrow, the lawyer who filed the federal class action lawsuit, flew to South Carolina to help represent Whitner. Whitner's lawyers filed a petition for postconviction relief claiming that the trial court lacked jurisdiction to accept a guilty plea to a nonexistent offense. The relevant criminal statute punished the unlawful neglect of a *child*, not a fetus, they argued.

The judge who heard the petition was persuaded. On November 22, 1993, Judge Larry Patterson threw out the conviction and released Whitner from prison. Attorney General Condon filed a notice of appeal that day. On the other side, major medical, public health, and women's organizations, including the American Medical Association and its South Carolina affiliate, the American Public Health Association, the National Council on Alcoholism and Drug Dependence, and NOW Legal Defense and Education Fund, joined in amicus briefs opposing prosecution of women for prenatal drug use.

On July 15, 1996, the South Carolina Supreme Court dealt a disastrous blow to the antiprosecution effort. In a 3 to 2 decision, the court reinstated Whitner's conviction, holding that a viable fetus is covered by the child abuse statute.[66] The court based its conclusion on prior case law that recognized a viable fetus as a person. South Carolina courts, for example, allowed civil actions for the wrongful death of a fetus. The key criminal law precedent was *State v. Horne*, decided in 1984, concerning South Carolina's homicide law. The defendant Horne had repeatedly stabbed his wife, who was nine months pregnant, in the neck, arms, and abdomen. The woman survived, but the fetus had died by the time doctors performed an emergency cesarean section. The court upheld Horne's conviction for voluntary manslaughter, extending liability for killing a fetus from the civil to the criminal context.

According to the *Whitner* court, these precedents dictated its interpretation of the child abuse statute: "[I]t would be absurd to recognize the viable fetus as a person for purposes of homicide laws and wrongful death statutes but not for purposes of statutes proscribing child abuse." Moreover, punishing fetal abuse would further the statute's aim of preventing harm to children. "The consequences of abuse or neglect that take place after birth," the court reasoned, "often pale in comparison to those resulting from abuse suffered by the viable fetus before birth."

The two dissenting judges noted that the majority's ruling was inconsistent with a 1995 decision that construed "child" in another provision of the Children's Code concerning adoption to mean "a child in being and not a fetus." They argued that other parts of the child neglect law, such as the list of acts that constitute harm, seemed to contemplate an already-born child. The majority's mistake, according to the dissenters, was to look for guidance in the common law of tort and feticide rather than in the relevant statutory language itself. Besides, the South Carolina legislature's failure to pass several proposed bills to punish drug use during pregnancy proved that lawmakers did not intend the child neglect statute to cover such conduct.

There was yet another inconsistency: the state abortion statute — the only law that specifically regulates a pregnant woman's conduct toward the fetus — also treats a viable fetus differently from a child in being. "A pregnant woman, under the majority opinion, now faces up to ten years in prison for ingesting drugs during pregnancy," the dissenting opinion pointed out, "but can have an illegal abortion and receive only a two-year sentence for killing her viable fetus." On the other hand, the decision apparently allows a woman to use drugs until the twenty-fourth week of pregnancy without risking arrest — even though harm can occur during the first two trimesters as well.

The decision meant that Cornelia Whitner was returned to jail to serve out the remaining six years of her sentence. It also meant abandoning her son, now a healthy four-year-old living with her aunt. Four other women indicted on similar charges also faced being sentenced to prison terms. But *Whitner*'s ramifications are far more devastating. The holding opens the door for a new wave of prosecutions in South Carolina, as well as in other states that wish to follow its lead. Paul Logli, the Illinois prosecutor who tried to charge Melanie Green with manslaughter, publicly applauded the decision. "This is a landmark, precedent-setting decision," Attorney General Condon exclaimed. "This decision is a triumph for all those who want to protect the children of South Carolina." As the state's chief law enforcement officer, Condon has visions of replicating his Charleston experiment in other hospitals across South Carolina.

The ruling also opens up a Pandora's box. If harm to a viable fetus constitutes child abuse, then an endless panoply of activities could make pregnant women guilty of a crime. "There are not enough jail cells in South Carolina to hold the pregnant women who have a drug problem, drink a glass of wine with dinner, smoke cigarettes . . . or decide to go to work despite their doctor's advice that they should stay in bed," Paltrow pointed out. "Thousands of women are now child neglecters."

Of course, the state of South Carolina will not go after thousands of pregnant women on child neglect charges. It will not even prosecute all the pregnant women who abuse drugs and alcohol. Instead, it will escalate its crusade against the women it has prosecuted in the past—poor Black women who smoke crack. I now turn to the reasons behind this blatant racial discrimination.

THE PROSECUTIONS' RACIAL BIAS

Poor Black women nationwide bear the brunt of prosecutors' punitive approach. According to a 1990 memorandum prepared by the ACLU Reproductive Freedom Project, 70 percent of the fifty-two cases documented at that time involved Black defendants.[67] The disproportionate prosecution of Black women could be seen most clearly in the states that had initiated the most cases. In Florida, ten out of eleven criminal cases had been brought against Black women. Similarly, of eighteen women in South Carolina charged with either criminal neglect of a child or distribution of drugs to a minor, seventeen were Black. The racial disparity has not diminished in subsequent years.[68]

The reason Black women are the primary targets of prosecutors is not because they are more guilty of fetal abuse. A study of twenty-four hospitals conducted by the South Carolina State Council on Maternal, Infant, and Child Health in 1991 found that high percentages of pregnant women were abusing marijuana, barbiturates, and opiates—drugs used primarily by white women.[69] MUSC's own record showed that drug use among pregnant patients was evenly distributed among white and Black women. Yet nearly all of the women the hospital reported to the solicitor were Black. These local surveys showing little difference in rates of substance abuse among Black and white women during pregnancy parallel national statistics.

Rather, this discriminatory enforcement is a result of a combination of racism and poverty. Poor women, who are disproportionately Black, are in closer contact with government agencies, and their drug use is therefore more likely to be detected. Black women are also more likely to be reported to government authorities, in part because of the racist attitudes of health care professionals. In the end, it is these women's failure to meet society's image of the ideal mother that makes their prosecution acceptable.

Who Gets Reported

To charge drug-dependent mothers with crimes, the state must be able to identify those who use drugs during pregnancy. Because indigent Black women are generally under greater government supervision—through their associations with public hospitals, welfare agencies, and probation officers—their drug use is more likely to be detected and reported.[70] These women are already enmeshed in a social welfare structure that makes them vulnerable to state monitoring of every aspect of their lives. Hospital screening practices are particularly to blame. The government's main source of information about prenatal drug use is hospitals' reporting of positive infant toxicologies to child welfare or law enforcement authorities. This testing is performed almost exclusively by public hospitals that serve poor minority communities.

Charleston's Interagency Policy, for example, was developed specifically for the only hospital in the area accessible to indigent Black patients. In addition, the policy applied only to the Medicaid patients attending the obstetrics clinic; it was not enforced against the hospital's private patients. Everyone on the hospital staff knew that only Black women were subject to the policy.[71] Condon tried to explain away the program's blatant racial targeting as the innocent result of demographics. "It is true that most of the women treated were black," he conceded. "The hospital serves a primarily indigent population, and most of the patient population is black."[72] But why had Condon singled out MUSC as the lone site for the punitive program? Surely hospitals with a white clientele also had pregnant patients who abused drugs. One of the women arrested in Greenville County noted the unfairness: "The only patients in the hospital who this is happening to are on Medicaid. There are private patients who are doing drugs and nothing is done about that. If the idea is to protect the babies, they should be protecting all babies."[73]

Private physicians who treat more affluent women tend to refrain from testing their patients for drug use, and certainly would not report them to the police. Officials of private hospitals told federal investigators in a nationwide survey that they did not consider the problem serious enough to warrant implementing a drug screening protocol.[74] These doctors have a financial stake in securing their patients' business and referrals. It is also more likely that their patients are their friends, neighbors, and business associates or come from the same social circle.[75] Physicians who practice in fancy offices, therefore, identify and empathize with their patients. They may find it hard to suspect their patients of drug use. Even if they do, they see their patients' addiction as a disease requiring treatment, not a criminal act deserving punishment. They would be appalled at the notion of handing each patient a warning that the office was collaborating with the police and that she might be arrested based on test results.

Moreover, hospitals decide whom to screen for drug use by applying criteria that are more likely to select Black women. One factor that commonly triggers an infant toxicology screen is the mother's failure to obtain prenatal care, a factor that correlates strongly with race and income.[76] Black women are twice as likely as white women to begin prenatal care late in their pregnancies or receive none at all, owing to financial and other barriers.

Worse still, many hospitals have no formal screening procedures, relying solely on the suspicions of health care professionals. The protocol used at Greenville Memorial Hospital, for example, lists as risk factors that trigger testing no or limited prenatal care and "behavior strongly suspect of recent drug abuse during prenatal visits and/or delivery." The Florida reporting statute does not require documentation of maternal drug use but only "reasonable cause to suspect it." This discretion allows doctors and hospital staff to perform tests based on their stereotyped assumptions about the identity of drug addicts.[77]

Women who smoke crack report being abused and degraded by hospital staff during the delivery. Their experiences suggest that staff often harbor a deep contempt for these women born at least partly of racial prejudice. The indigent Black patients in Greenville, for example, held a common belief that the hospital nurses intentionally ignored them during labor and withheld pain medication despite their cries for help, as if to punish them for using drugs. "You're supposed to hurt" was often the nurses' response.[78] "K," a twenty-four-year-old woman from Brooklyn, recounted a similar experience:

> Bad . . . they treat you bad. . . . That was like I had my daughter, when the nurse came, and I was having the stomach pain and my stomach was killing me. I kept callin and callin and callin. She just said you smokin that crack, you smoke that crack, you suffer.[79]

According to court documents in the *Ferguson* case, Nurse Brown, the chief enforcer of the Charleston Interagency Policy, frequently expressed negative views about her Black patients to drug counselors and social workers, including her belief that most Black women should have their tubes tied and that birth control should be put in the water in Black communities.[80] (The federal jury nevertheless rejected the patients' equal protection claim.) It is not surprising that these nurses would turn their Black patients in to the police.

Evidence of Racial Bias

In fact, health care professionals report Black women who use drugs during pregnancy more readily than they report their white patients. This racial bias was demonstrated in a study of pregnant women in Pinellas County, Florida, published in the prestigious *New England Journal of Medicine*.[81] Researchers studied the results of toxicologic tests on pregnant women who received prenatal care in public health clinics and in private obstetrical offices in Pinellas. Florida had adopted a policy requiring hospitals to report to local health departments evidence of drug and alcohol use during pregnancy.

The study found that there was little difference in the prevalence of substance abuse by pregnant women along either racial or economic lines, nor was there any significant difference found between public clinics and private offices.[82] If anything, the rate of positive results for white women (15.4 percent) was slightly higher than that for Black women (14.1 percent). Despite similar rates of substance abuse, however, Black women were *ten times* more likely than whites to be reported to government authorities. Both public health facilities and private doctors were more inclined to turn in Black women than white women for using drugs while pregnant.

Perhaps some of the disparity was due to the severity of symptoms displayed by Black infants or the signs of crack intoxication displayed by Black women. But the striking difference in the reporting rates suggests that racial prejudice and stereotyping must be a factor. Studies in other states have uncovered a similar racial disparity in the testing and reporting of prenatal drug use despite equal rates of substance abuse.[83]

This willingness to turn in pregnant Black drug users corresponds to a long history of disregard for Black female patients' autonomy.[84] In past centuries, doctors experimented on slave women before practicing new surgical procedures on white women. Marion Sims, for example, developed gynecological surgery in the nineteenth century by performing countless operations, without anesthesia, on female slaves purchased expressly for his experiments. In the 1970s, it was revealed that doctors had coerced hundreds of thousands of Black women into agreeing to sterilization by conditioning medical services on consent to the operation. More recently, a survey published in 1984 found that 13,000 Black women in Maryland were screened for sickle-cell anemia without their consent or the benefit of adequate counseling. We can add MUSC's unethical research on its pregnant Black patients to this legacy of medical experimentation on the bodies of Black women without their consent.

Doctors have also been more willing to override Black patients' autonomy by performing forced medical treatment to benefit the fetus. Doctors and hospital administrators have petitioned courts on numerous occasions to order procedures, such as cesarean sections and blood transfusions, against the patient's will. Many commentators have argued that judicial decisions that allow doctors to operate without consent equate women with inert vessels, valuing them solely for their capacity to nurture the fetus.[85] But closer examination reveals that part of the reason pregnant patients' wishes are so easily subordinated has to do with race and class.

A national survey published in 1987 in the *New England Journal of Medicine* discovered twenty-one cases in which court orders were sought, in eighteen of which petitions were granted.[86] Eighty-one percent of the women involved were women of color; all were treated in a teaching-hospital clinic or were receiving public assistance. Judges and doctors dismiss these women's reasons for refusing medical treatment by calling them angry, irrational, fearful, stubborn, selfish, and uncooperative. Just as doctors more readily breach the confidentiality of pregnant Black patients by reporting their test results, they more readily violate the autonomy of pregnant Black patients by forcing them to undergo unwanted medical procedures.

Why Crack?

Added to this biased reporting is the type of substance abuse that brings pregnant women under scrutiny. It is telling that, out of the universe of maternal conduct that can injure a fetus, prosecutors have chosen to focus on crack use. The singling out of pregnant women's crack addiction for punishment cannot be justified by either its prevalence or the degree of harm to the fetus.

Numerous maternal activities are potentially harmful to the developing fetus, including drinking alcohol and coffee, taking prescription and nonprescription drugs, smoking cigarettes, failing to eat properly and being obese, playing certain sports, and residing at high altitudes for prolonged periods.[87] Conduct by people other than the pregnant woman can also threaten fetal health. A pregnant woman's exposure to secondary cigarette smoke, sexually transmitted and other infectious diseases, environmental hazards such as toxic chemicals, radiation, and lead, and physical abuse can harm the fetus.

The injury to a fetus from excessive alcohol far exceeds the harm from crack exposure. Heavy drinking during pregnancy can cause fetal alcohol sydrome, characterized by serious physical malformations and mental deficiencies. In fact, prenatal alcohol exposure is the most common known cause of mental retardation in this country.[88] Crack does not cause anything near this pattern of severe defects. The incidence of fetal exposure to drugs other than crack is high as well. A survey of 2,200 women who gave birth at the University of Washington Hospital in Seattle from March 1989 to March 1990 and who used drugs during or immediately before pregnancy revealed that 20 percent smoked marijuana (associated with impaired fetal development and reduced gestational length),[89] 16 percent used cocaine (powdered and crack), and 9 percent used heroin, methadone, or amphetamines.[90] The National Institute on Drug Abuse's 1990 Household Survey suggests that about 73 percent of women drank alcohol during pregnancy and 17.4 percent smoked marijuana, whereas only 4.5 percent used cocaine. A 1989 study of 2,278 highly educated women found that 30 percent consumed more than one drink a week while pregnant.[91]

In fact, the state could make a far more solid case for prosecuting pregnant women who smoke cigarettes. Cigarette smoking has been more firmly linked than crack to spontaneous abortions and sudden infant death. In addition, researchers have held cigarettes responsible for a greater reduction in infant birth weight than crack, as well as for a larger number of affected children.[92] If prosecutors did charge women with this crime, we should find a disproportionate number of *white* defendants: 18 percent of white mothers smoke cigarettes during pregnancy, compared with 14 percent of Black mothers.[93]

The *New York Times* recently ran a story about the growing popularity of methamphetamines—also known as crank, speed, or meth—among rural and suburban women in the West and Midwest.[94] "The biggest difference between crack and crank," the *Times* reporter noted, "is the constituency: crank users are mainly white." At a conference held in San Francisco to discuss the drug, researchers from the National Institute of Justice reported that crank users arrested in eight Western cities were more likely to be women than men. The effects of female crank addiction have been seen in maternity wards. Senator Dianne Feinstein of California told the conference participants that more babies born at one Sacramento hospital have been exposed to methamphetamines than to crack. An outreach worker in Spokane, Washington, found that about 40 percent of the 335 pregnant women she placed in drug treatment programs in the last few years were addicted to crank.

I cite these statistics not to suggest that pregnant women who smoke, drink, or get high on crank should join crack-addicted mothers behind bars. Rather, these statistics show that targeting crack use during pregnancy unfairly singles out Black women for punishment. Drug use can be found among pregnant women of all socioeconomic, racial, and ethnic backgrounds, but inner-city Black communities have the highest concentrations of crack users.[95] The Pinellas County study, for example, found that Black women tested positive more frequently for cocaine use during pregnancy, whereas white women tested positive more frequently for marijuana. Although there are white crack smokers, the public's image of the pregnant crack addict is distinctively Black. Selecting crack abuse as the primary fetal harm to be punished, then, has a discriminatory impact that cannot be medically justified. With 375,000 drug-exposed babies born every year, the prosecution of a few hundred women must be more symbolic than a real attempt to solve the problem. Could it be that blaming Black mothers who smoke crack serves other societal purposes?

First, choosing these particular mothers makes the prosecution of pregnant women more palatable to the public. Prosecutors have selected women whom society views as undeserving to be mothers in the first place. If prosecutors had brought charges instead against wealthy white women addicted to alcohol or pills, the policy of criminalizing prenatal conduct would have suffered a hasty demise. The Charleston solicitor recognized as much when he confessed, "there's not enough political will to move after pregnant women who use alcohol or cigarettes. There is, though, a political basis for this interagency program. Leaders can take a position against crack."[96] Can you imagine a white woman dragged in leg shackles from a suburban hospital hours after giving birth? Society is much more willing to condone the punishment of poor Black women who fail to meet the middle-class ideal of motherhood.

Americans view white mothers who use drugs in a completely different light. The lovable Meg Ryan played an alcoholic mother, Alice Green, in the 1994 movie *When a Man Loves a Woman*. Alice's addiction makes her a dreadful mother: she forgets the kids' appointments, leaves most of the parenting to her husband and nanny, and smacks her daughter across the face when the eight-year-old catches her guzzling vodka from a bottle. No doubt Alice drank while she was pregnant. At one point, Alice arrives home drunk after running errands only to realize that she has misplaced the younger daughter somewhere along the way. What struck me most about the movie was that the mother remains the sympathetic heroine throughout the movie, despite her atrocious care for her children. While audiences knew Alice desperately needed treatment for her drinking problem, it probably never occurred to them that she should be arrested or that her daughters should be taken away from her. The ending is what we would expect for a white, middle-class mother: she overcomes her addiction at a pastoral rehabilitation clinic and is reunited with her children.

In addition to legitimizing fetal rights enforcement, prosecuting crack-addicted mothers shifts public attention from poverty, racism, and a deficient health care system, implying instead that poor infant health results from the depraved behavior of individual mothers. Poverty—not maternal drug use—is the major threat to the health of Black children in America. When *Newsweek* charged that "[d]rug addiction among pregnant women is driving up the U.S. infant mortality rate," it blamed Black mothers for a trend that predated the crack epidemic.[97] Poor Black mothers are thus made the scapegoats for the causes of the Black community's ill health. Punishing them assuages the nation's guilt for an underclass of people whose babies die at rates higher than those in some Third World countries. Making Black mothers criminals appears far easier than creating a health care system that ensures healthy babies for all our citizens.

The prosecution of Black mothers addicted to crack complements the distribution of Norplant and other long-acting contraceptives to women on welfare. Both policies lay the blame for Black children's problems on Black women having babies. While charging crack users with crimes punishes them for Black children's poor health, pressuring Black women to use Norplant restrains them as a way of curtailing Black children's poverty. Portraying Black mothers as irredeemable drug addicts who are their children's worst enemy supports the view that population control is the only answer to Black people's plight.

PUNISHMENT FOR HAVING A BABY

Recognizing this backdrop of biased reporting and historical devaluation of Black motherhood, we can better understand prosecutors' reasons for punishing drug-dependent mothers. I view these prosecutions as punishing these women, in essence, for having babies. Judges such as the ones who convicted Cornelia Whitner and Jennifer Johnson are pronouncing not so much "I care about your baby" as "You don't deserve to be a mother."

It is important to recognize at the outset that the prosecutions are premised on a woman's pregnancy and not on her illegal drug use alone. Prosecutors charge these defendants, not with drug use, but with child abuse or drug distribution through the umbilical cord — crimes that only *pregnant* drug users can commit. At Jennifer Johnson's sentencing, the prosecutor made clear the nature of the charges against her: "About the end of December 1988, our office undertook a policy to begin to deal with mothers like Jennifer Johnson . . . as in the status of a child abuse case, Your Honor. . . . *We have never viewed this as a drug case.*"[98]

Moreover, pregnant women receive harsher sentences than drug-addicted men or women who are not pregnant. The drug user's pregnancy not only greatly increases the likelihood that she will be prosecuted, but also greatly enhances the penalty she faces upon conviction. In most states, drug use is a misdemeanor, while distribution of drugs or child abuse is a felony.[99]

The unlawful nature of drug use should not be allowed to obscure the basis of the crimes at issue. The legal rationale underlying the prosecutions does not depend on the illegality of drug use. Harm to the fetus is the crux of the government's legal theory. Criminal charges have been brought against women for conduct that is legal but was alleged to have injured the fetus. For example, Pamela Rae Stewart, a white woman in San Diego, was charged with criminal neglect in part because she failed to follow her doctor's orders to stay off her feet and refrain from sexual intercourse while she was pregnant.[100]

When a drug-addicted woman becomes pregnant, she has only one realistic avenue to escape criminal charges: abortion. Seeking drug treatment is usually not a viable alternative. It is unlikely that the pregnant addict will be able to find a drug treatment program that will accept her. Even if she does, she may not be able to overcome her addiction in time. Even if she successfully completes drug counseling before the birth, she may still be charged for drug use that occurred before she was able to kick her habit. The threat of prosecution may coerce some women to terminate the pregnancy rather than risk imprisonment. In February 1992, Martina Greywind was charged with reckless endangerment for sniffing paint fumes while she was pregnant.[101] Twelve days after her arrest she had an abortion and the charges were dropped.

A woman who has an abortion will probably avoid criminal liability altogether. Even an illegal third-trimester abortion carries a lower penalty than crimes of prenatal misconduct. In South Carolina, for example, a drug-using woman who aborts a viable fetus faces a jail term of two years, compared to a possible ten-year penalty for child abuse if she gives birth to the baby.

Women who are punished for drug use during pregnancy, then, are penalized for choosing to have the baby rather than having an abortion. It is *the choice of carrying a pregnancy to term* that is being penalized. Looked at this way, we can see that when the state convicts pregnant Black women for smoking crack it is punishing them for having babies.

IDENTIFYING THE CONSTITUTIONAL ISSUE

Seeing the prosecutions as punishment for reproduction changes the interests at stake. In the *Johnson* case, the prosecutor framed the constitutional issue as follows: "What constitutionally protected freedom did Jennifer engage in when she smoked cocaine?"[102] That was the wrong question. Johnson was not convicted of using drugs. Her "constitutional right" to smoke cocaine was never at issue. Johnson was prosecuted because she chose to have a baby while she was smoking crack. Had she smoked crack during her pregnancy and then had an abortion, she would not have been charged with a crime.

The correct question, then, is "What constitutionally protected freedom did Jennifer engage in when she decided to have a baby, even though she was using drugs?"

Understanding the prosecution of drug-dependent mothers as punishment for having babies clarifies the constitutional right at stake. The woman's right at issue is not the right to abuse drugs or to cause the fetus to be born with defects. It is the right to choose to be a mother that is burdened by criminalizing conduct during pregnancy. This view of the constitutional issue reveals the relevance of race to the resolution of the competing interests. Race has historically determined the value society places on a woman's right to choose motherhood. The devaluation of Black motherhood gives the right to decide to bear a child unique significance.

Prosecutions of drug-addicted mothers infringe on two aspects of the right to reproductive liberty. First, they infringe on the right to choose to bear a child, which is essential to an individual's personhood and autonomy. This freedom implies that state control of the decision to carry a pregnancy to term can be as pernicious as state control of the decision to terminate a pregnancy. The constitutional right of privacy has been interpreted to protect intimate or personal affairs that are fundamental to an individual's identity and moral personhood from unjustified government intrusion.[103] At the forefront of the development of the right of privacy has been the freedom of personal choice in matters of marriage and family life.[104] Once an interest is included in the right of privacy, the government needs a compelling reason to infringe it.

Although the right of privacy is at the center of an intense jurisprudential debate, it is universally recognized to include the decision to bear a child. As the Supreme Court stated in *Eisenstadt v. Baird*, "If the right of privacy means anything, it is the right of the individual, married or single, to be free from unwarranted governmental intrusion into matters so fundamentally affecting a person as the decision whether to bear or beget a child."[105] The right of privacy protects both the choice to bear children and the choice to refrain from bearing them. The historical experiences of Black women illustrate that the dual nature of this right goes beyond the logical implications of making a choice. Punishing a woman for having a baby as well as forced maternity at the behest of the state violates her autonomy over the self-defining decision of whether to bring another being into the world.

Even under the Court's current analysis, which distinguishes between direct and indirect governmental interference in reproductive decisionmaking, government intrusion as extreme as criminal prosecution would unduly infringe on protected autonomy. Criminal prosecutions of drug-addicted mothers do more than discourage a choice; they impose a severe penalty on the drug user for choosing to complete her pregnancy.

Second, the prosecutions infringe on reproductive liberty by imposing an invidious government standard for procreation. Government standards for childbearing are one way that society denies the humanity of subordinated groups. The first approach emphasizes a woman's right to autonomy over her reproductive life; the second highlights a woman's right to be valued equally as a human being. In other words, the prosecution of crack-addicted mothers infringes upon both a mother's right to make decisions that determine her individual identity and her right to equal respect as a human being by recognizing the value of her motherhood. In the last chapter, I will elaborate these violations of traditional liberal notions of liberty and offer a redefinition of reproductive liberty informed by concern for racial equality.

PROTECTING BLACK FETUSES?

Finding that the prosecutions infringe upon women's constitutionally guaranteed freedom to bear a child shifts the burden onto the government to justify its punitive actions. There is good reason to question the government's justification for the prosecutions—the concern for the welfare of unborn children. I have already discussed the selectivity of the prosecutions with respect to poor Black women. This focus on the conduct of one group of women weakens the state's asserted rationale for the prosecutions.

There is more reason to be suspicious. The history of state neglect of Black infants casts further doubt on the professed concern for the welfare of the fetus. When a nation has always closed its eyes to the circumstances of pregnant Black women, its current expression of interest in the health of unborn Black children must be viewed with distrust. The most telling evidence of the state's disregard of Black children is the high rate of infant death in the Black community. In 1989, the mortality rate of infants born to Black mothers was 18.6 deaths per thousand births—more than twice that for infants born to white mothers (8.1). Although the national rate has declined in the 1990s, the racial gap is widening: in 1992, the rate was 16.8 for Black infants, compared to 6.9 for whites.[106] That is higher than the infant death rate in Costa Rica, Cuba, and Singapore, as well as in some twenty other industrialized countries. In New York City, while infant mortality rates in upper- and middle-income areas were generally less than 9 per thousand in the late 1980s, the rates exceeded 19 in the poor Black communities of the South Bronx and Bedford-Stuyvesant and reached a staggering 27.6 in Central Harlem.[107] Black babies in the nation's capital die at a rate *triple* that of the country as a whole.[108]

The main reasons for these high mortality rates are poverty and inadequate health care, including health care for pregnant women.[109] Granted maternal crack use contributes to low birth weight, a leading cause of infant death. But crack is a small and recent addition to an old story. The conditions of poverty—poor nutrition, shoddy housing, vulnerability to disease, and stress—threaten the healthy development of a fetus. Babies born into poverty (half of Black children) are also more susceptible to deadly illnesses such as influenza and pneumonia. Most Black women who are pregnant face financial and other barriers to receiving proper health care.[110] Only half of all Black mothers in America receive adequate prenatal care; and they are twice as likely as white women to get deficient prenatal care or none.[111]

The inability to pay for health care services is the major stumbling block.[112] Most poor women depend on overextended public hospitals for prenatal care because of the scarcity of neighborhood physicians who accept Medicaid. The number of obstetricians and gynecologists willing to accept Medicaid or uninsured patients is decreasing. In fact, obstetricians and gynecologists are less likely than most primary and secondary care physicians to accept Medicaid patients.[113] A quarter of Black Americans fall between the cracks, earning just enough to make them ineligible for Medicaid but working at low-paying jobs that do not offer health insurance.[114]

Women falling into these categories delay commencing prenatal care until later in pregnancy and make fewer visits to the doctor than women with private insurance. Institutional, cultural, and educational barriers also deter poor minority women from using the few available services. Black women's access to prenatal care actually *declined* during the 1980s due to funding cuts, at the very time prosecutors initiated their crackdown on pregnant addicts.[115]

The number of Black infant deaths could be reduced dramatically by a national commitment to ensuring that all pregnant women receive high-quality prenatal care. Programs specifically designed to provide prenatal care to low-income, high-risk women have succeeded in substantially reducing the rates of low birth weight and high infant mortality. In 1990, a White House Task Force on Infant Mortality recommended eighteen specific measures costing a total of $480 million a year to reduce infant mortality. It proposed expanding Medicaid to cover 120,000 additional pregnant women and children in low-income families, increasing federal spending on prenatal care, and requiring states to provide a uniform set of Medicaid benefits to pregnant women.[116] More widespread health care services are also needed: prenatal care alone cannot reverse the effects of a woman's lifetime of poor health or ensure that children will remain healthy after they are born. Instead, welfare cuts threaten to rip this safety net from under an even greater number of low-income families.

Harvard law professor Randall Kennedy, who is Black, disagrees. Kennedy believes that the prosecutions are an example of the criminal justice system protecting Black citizens, something, he argues, Black communities need more of. Acknowledging that Black women are charged in disproportionately high numbers, Kennedy asks: "If, however, the racial demographics of the offending statistics were reversed—if upwards of 80 percent of the women prosecuted were white—would that not raise the disturbing possibility that law enforcement authorities were demonstrating more empathy for the sufferings of white infant victims than black infant victims of criminality?" The problem concerning law enforcement in Black neighborhoods, Kennedy says, is not excessive policing and invidious punishment; it is "a failure of the state to provide black communities with the equal *protection* of the laws."[117]

Charleston police chief Reuben Greenberg, also Black, contends that opponents of the Interagency Policy "don't care about the race issue." Like Kennedy, he sees prosecuting crack-addicted mothers as a benefit to Black children: "I was glad that somebody was finally doing something to help kids in the black community. It was giving kids a chance who otherwise would not have anything close to an equal playing field. At least at the point of birth, that child ought to be given the best opportunity for a full and productive life."[118]

As might be expected, Attorney General Condon is fond of holding up Greenberg's endorsement of his punitive program to discredit charges of racial discrimination. But the fact that repressive policies find support among Blacks does not make them any less racist. Supreme Court justice Clarence Thomas, for example, has consistently voted with the Court's most conservative members to reach decisions that, according to most civil rights activists, thwart the cause of racial justice. White people also disagree about which policies best advance their interests.

What matters is that the weight of medical research, public health expertise, and sheer common sense demonstrates that Professor Kennedy, Police Chief Greenberg, and others who believe that incarcerating pregnant women benefits Blacks are simply wrong. I will address the prosecutions' negative health consequences in a moment. But first these supporters must answer a simple question: If a policy of putting pregnant women in jail really led to healthier children, wouldn't we see at least an equal number of white mothers behind bars? Is it really credible that conservative Southern prosecutors are *more* interested in saving Black babies than white babies? Just as we should be skeptical of the spread of Norplant to Black women and teens on the pretext of enhancing their reproductive freedom, we should be skeptical of prosecutions of Black women on the pretext of protecting unborn Black children from harm.

The belief that putting pregnant addicts in jail will help their children is grounded in a naive faith in the neutrality of the criminal justice system. Professor Kennedy's premise that Blacks benefit from greater law enforcement overlooks America's history of using criminal laws to subjugate Blacks. Slave codes created a separate set of crimes for slaves that were sanctioned by public punishment not applicable to whites and included behavior that was legal for whites. The law defined as criminal any conduct performed by Blacks that threatened white supremacy, such as learning how to read and write.

After Emancipation, white lawmakers soon realized that they could return their former chattel to the condition of slaves by imprisoning them for criminal offenses. The Thirteenth Amendment's prohibition of involuntary servitude included an exception for citizens convicted of a crime. Prison officials in Louisiana "wondered aloud whether the real reason for sending blacks to prison 'upon the most trivial charges' was not 'the low, mean motive of depriving them of the right[s] of citizenship.'"[119] Reconstruction legislatures sought to maintain their control of freed slaves by passing criminal laws directed at Blacks that made petty larceny a serious offense. As a result, Southern prison populations swelled and became for the first time predominantly Black. The prison population in Georgia, for example, tripled from 432 to 1,441 within two years after a hog-stealing law was enacted.[120]

Many critics of national drug policy argue that the "War on Drugs" serves a similar purpose today. By selecting petty drug offenses as the target for a massive law enforcement effort, the government facilitates the incarceration of millions of inner-city Blacks. The threat of draconian penalties even for mere possession forces most defendants — guilty or innocent — to plead guilty. Although Blacks account for only 12 percent of the nation's drug users, between 80 and 90 percent of those arrested for drug offenses are young Black males.[121] The United States has achieved the highest incarceration rate in the world by imprisoning Black men for nonviolent drug-related crimes.

The prosecutions of poor Black mothers are an even more egregious instance of government manipulating the criminal law on the basis of race. This is not a case of extending to the Black community the benefit of a criminal law that already protects whites. Prosecutors invented the crime of prenatal drug use in the 1980s in order to castigate poor Black mothers who smoke crack. Kennedy's hypothetical positing of 80 percent of the women prosecuted as white instead of Black does not work because it is unimaginable. There are few white "infant victims of criminality" because their mothers are not perceived as criminals. This is not a neutral offense that just happens to be applied more often to one group rather than the other. This criminal law is virtually "for Blacks only."

FINDING DRUG TREATMENT

Many Americans support the prosecution of pregnant addicts based on the mistaken belief that it is easy for these women to find treatment for their problem. These mothers deserve to be punished for hurting their children, it is thought, because they have irresponsibly kept smoking crack when help was available to them. The Charleston solicitor, for example, justified bringing criminal charges against MUSC patients on the grounds that they had refused the hospital's offer of drug treatment. Prosecution, he contended, was the last resort after a rehabilitative approach failed.

But had Charleston officials really done everything they could to treat patients' addiction? Women caught using drugs were simply handed a piece of paper announcing their drug treatment appointment. No provision was made for transportation to the treatment center or for child care. In fact, there was not a single residential treatment center for pregnant addicts in the entire state at the time the Interagency Policy was instituted.[122] For a long time Charleston residents, including Police Chief Greenberg, fought to keep a residential treatment center supported by a federal grant from locating in the city.

Patients faced similar circumstances in Greenville. It was two years *after* the Greenville solicitor started prosecuting women that the county opened a residential treatment facility for pregnant, Medicaid-eligible women—a facility with only ten beds to deal with an estimated 1,500 drug-affected births a year.[123] There was no attempt to get women into treatment until after they gave birth to a baby who tested positive and were charged with a crime—*after* their drug use may have had its harmful effects. The situation in Florida was no different. There were only 135 spaces available for over 4,000 substance-abusing women in the state at the time of Jennifer Johnson's conviction.

Protecting the welfare of drug addicts' children requires adequate facilities for the mothers' drug treatment. Yet a drug addict's pregnancy serves as an *obstacle* to obtaining this help. Most treatment centers either refuse to treat pregnant women or are effectively closed to them because the centers are ill-equipped to meet the needs of pregnant addicts. Most hospitals and programs that treat addiction exclude pregnant women on the grounds that their babies are more likely to be born with health problems requiring specialized prenatal care. Program directors feel that treating pregnant addicts is worth neither the increased cost nor the risk of tort liability should a woman sue the clinic for harm to the baby.[124] This blanket preclusion of an entire class of people, however, is contrary to the way health care facilities typically evaluate prospective patients. Drug treatment programs could address the special needs of pregnant women by seeking expert advice on their management and arranging for prenatal care rather than excluding them.

The experience in South Carolina and Florida is typical of the nationwide scarcity of drug treatment services for pregnant drug addicts.[125] Developed at a time when drug addiction was seen as a male problem, the drug treatment system has historically ignored women's needs. Eighty percent of the nation's treatment resources are spent on men.[126] There are far fewer slots available to women in general than to men in publicly funded centers. A 1979 national survey by the National Institute on Drug Abuse found only twenty-five drug treatment programs that described themselves as specifically geared to female addicts.[127] A decade later, the situation had barely improved—

especially for pregnant women. A congressional survey of hospitals in large metropolitan areas showed that two-thirds had no place to refer pregnant women for drug treatment.[128]

Pregnant women have trouble finding treatment even in the nation's largest cities. A 1989 survey of seventy-eight drug treatment programs in New York City discovered that 54 percent denied treatment to pregnant women, 67 percent refused to treat pregnant addicts on Medicaid, and 87 percent excluded pregnant women on Medicaid addicted specifically to crack. Fewer than half of those programs that did accept pregnant addicts provided prenatal care, and only two provided child care.[129] A similar search among twenty-seven facilities in Chicago came up with only seven inpatient programs that accepted pregnant women.[130] Even these were inaccessible to indigent addicts: the minimum cost was $12,000 a month and none accepted Medicaid. Increased federal and state spending on programs for pregnant substance abusers in the 1990s still falls short of meeting the need.

The exclusion of pregnant women from drug treatment has recently been contested as a violation of women's civil rights. The Philadelphia Human Relations Commission has looked into alleged pregnancy discrimination by twenty city drug and alcohol treatment centers. In 1993, the New York Court of Appeals invalidated a hospital policy barring all pregnant women from drug detoxification services without a showing of medical necessity for violating the New York Human Rights Law.[131] While these challenges have improved pregnant women's access to treatment in a few cities, they have not created the nationwide availability needed to address the problem.

In addition, there are formidable barriers facing pregnant women who seek to use centers that will accept them.[132] Most drug treatment programs are based on male-oriented models, which are not geared to the needs of women. The lack of accommodations for children is perhaps the most imposing obstacle to treatment. Most outpatient clinics do not provide child care, and many residential treatment programs do not admit children. Furthermore, treatment programs have traditionally failed to provide the comprehensive services that women need, including prenatal and gynecologic care, contraceptive counseling, appropriate job training, and counseling for sexual and physical abuse. Predominantly male staff and clients are often hostile to female clients and employ a confrontational style of therapy that makes many women uncomfortable. Women who cannot hack it are simply written off as failing the program. The typical focus on individual pathology tends to exclude social forces that are critical to understanding minority women's drug use. In addition to these barriers, long waiting lists often make it impossible for a pregnant woman to get treatment before her due date. Further, because Medicaid rarely covers the entire course of a typical treatment program, poor women may not be able to afford full treatment even at centers that will accept them.

The experience of one Black pregnant crack addict, whom I will call Mary, exemplifies these barriers to care. Mary needed to find a residential drug treatment program that provided prenatal care and accommodations for her two children, ages three and eight. She tried to get into HUG (Hope, Unity, and Growth), the sole residential treatment program for women with children in Detroit, but there was no vacancy. Mary's only source of public prenatal care was Eleanor Hutzel Hospital, which has a clinic for high-risk pregnancies. She was also able to receive drug counseling on an outpatient basis from the adjacent Eleanor Hutzel Recovery Center. But Mary encountered an eight-week waiting list at the hospital, and inadequate public transportation made it extremely difficult for her to get there. In the end, she received deficient care for both her addiction and her pregnancy.[133]

Until treatment is available, it is unfair to punish pregnant addicts who cannot kick their habits in time. But making this point plays into the prosecutors' misdirected approach to the problem. Providing treatment should not be seen as a way of justifying punishment. Waiting until a pregnant woman seeks prenatal care or delivers a baby is already too late to offer her help. Rather, devoting attention to ending the problem of women's substance abuse would preclude the need for drastic measures once a woman becomes pregnant.

THE REAL HARM TO UNBORN CHILDREN

Finally, and perhaps most important, overwhelming evidence shows that prosecuting addicted mothers will not achieve the government's asserted goal of healthier pregnancies. Indeed, the prosecutions will have just the opposite effect. Pregnant addicts who seek help from public hospitals and clinics are the ones most often reported to government authorities. The threat of criminal sanctions based on this reporting has already driven some pregnant drug users away from treatment and prenatal care.

Every leading medical and public health organization in the country has come out in opposition to the prosecutions because of these concerns. In 1990, the American Medical Association issued a detailed report on legal interventions during pregnancy stating its concern that "a physician's knowledge of substance abuse . . . could result in a jail sentence rather than proper medical treatment."[134] According to the American Academy of Pediatrics, "Punitive measures taken toward pregnant women, such as criminal prosecution and incarceration, have no proven benefits for infant health."[135] The American College of Obstetricians and Gynecologists, the March of Dimes, and the National Council on Alcoholism and Drug Dependence, among others, have also issued policy statements denouncing the criminalization of maternal drug use.

Despite these official pronouncements, many public hospitals routinely divulge confidential patient information to prosecutors and child welfare agencies. Jennifer Johnson's trial offers a chilling display of what happens when doctors become law enforcement agents. Patients have historically shared a confidential relationship with their doctors. One of the cardinal rules of medical ethics is that physicians must be loyal to their patients; with rare exceptions, they must not act as agents for other conflicting interests. Yet Johnson's own obstetricians provided the most damning evidence against her. Dr. Randy Tompkins testified that Johnson told him that she had used cocaine the morning she went into labor. Dr. Riaz Arifuddin, the pediatrician who attended Carl after his birth, also testified that Johnson had disclosed her crack use the night before. It was her trust in her doctors that prompted the hospital to test Johnson and her babies for drugs. Johnson's obstetricians also provided testimony about blood traveling through the babies' umbilical cords that built the prosecutor's case of drug delivery.

Other people in whom Johnson confided testified against her. Sandra Gomez, a child-protection investigator with the Department of Health and Rehabilitative Services, divulged what Johnson had said about her crack habit.[136] Johnson's mother was declared a hostile witness in order to elicit testimony against her daughter.

Even worse, Johnson's trial sent the message that an addict's very efforts to seek treatment would be used against her in a criminal case. The state's entire proof of Johnson's criminal intent was based on her attempts to get help. The prosecutor argued that Johnson's concern showed that she knew that her crack use harmed the fetus. An ambulance driver testified that, a month before Jessica's birth, Johnson had summoned an ambulance after a crack binge because she was worried about its effect on her unborn child.[137] Dr. Tompkins also testified that Johnson disclosed her crack use because she was concerned about its impact on Jessica's health. The prosecutor made a list of everyone Johnson turned to for help and subpoenaed them to trial.

One wonders whether Johnson would have spoken honestly with her doctors if she had known she would hear her words echoed from the stand. Would she have cooperated so freely in Gomez's investigation of her children? Would she have discussed her drug problem with her mother? Would she have called an ambulance for help? Clearly, the threat of prosecution will make pregnant women who use drugs wary of giving health care professionals information critical to their and their children's health.

The threat of criminal charges also deters pregnant women from seeking any prenatal care or drug treatment at all. The South Carolina policy is predicated on the assumption that a crack addict who reads the warning handed out at the clinic will be scared into getting treatment. But how can a pregnant addict who wants a healthy baby guarantee she will be able to make all of the appointments? How can she be sure she will be able to overcome her habit before the fetus becomes viable? In the end, she may decide not to risk being turned in by the people she would otherwise turn to for help.

Health care workers in San Diego noticed that their pregnant clients became distrustful after Pamela Rae Stewart's 1987 arrest for taking barbiturates while pregnant. Some failed to return for prenatal care altogether.[138] The director of a center in Chicago that houses drug-exposed babies suspects that their mothers do not come to visit for fear they will be arrested.[139] In its report to a House of Representatives subcommittee investigating drug treatment for pregnant women, the General Accounting Office (GAO) concluded that "[t]he threat of prosecution poses yet another barrier to treatment for pregnant women and mothers with young children."[140] Another GAO study found that "some women are now delivering their infants at home in order to prevent the state from discovering their drug use."[141] Women in Detroit told a team of researchers that they would go underground to avoid detection for fear of going to jail or losing their children; the researchers were unable to replicate the study in Tampa because women there were afraid to incriminate themselves.[142]

These women's desperation has been compounded by the new welfare reform law. An amendment to the 1996 legislation introduced by Texas senator Phil Gramm denies all federally funded means-tested entitlements, including welfare, Medicaid, and food stamps, to anyone convicted of a drug-related felony.[143] This provision puts women like Cornelia Whitner and Jennifer Johnson in an impossible Catch-22. If they are reported and convicted of prenatal drug use, they may be cut off from drug treatment, prenatal care, and the means to care for their children. The stakes are just too high: a pregnant woman who cannot overcome her addiction has little choice but to avoid detection.

Pregnancy is a time when women are most motivated to seek treatment for drug addiction and make positive lifestyle changes. Contrary to their depiction in the media, most are desperate to kick their habits and provide the best they can for their babies. What these women dread most about criminal charges is the possibility of losing their children. The government should capitalize on this opportunity by encouraging substance-abusing women to seek help and by providing them with comprehensive treatment. Most experts agree that the "carrot" works far better than the "stick." Community programs that implement a comprehensive approach to treatment and creative outreach efforts have been successful in reaching drug-using women and their families.[144] While improving access to these short-term remedies, we must also address the reasons why these women turn to drugs.

Punishing pregnant women who use drugs only makes their children worse off. It deprives infants of their mothers' care, while abandoning them to the hardships of poverty that will prove far more destructive than prenatal crack exposure. More devastating, the prosecutions create an adversarial health care system that threatens the welfare of countless babies to be born in the future. They drive further away poor Black women who are already marginal to the health-care system and who already view health care providers with suspicion. A punitive approach also banishes these women further from the public's concern and compassion. It fortifies the view that poor Black mothers do not deserve our respect. The government's decision to punish crack-abusing mothers, then, is irreconcilable with the goal of helping them.

A policy that attempts to protect fetuses by denying the humanity of their mothers will inevitably fail. I hear this false dichotomy in the words of Muskegon, Michigan, narcotics officer Al Van Hemert: "'If the mother wants to smoke crack and kill herself, I don't care.' . . . 'Let her die, but don't take that poor baby with her.'"[145] We must question such a policy's true concern for the dignity of the fetus, just as we question the motives of the slaveowner who protected the unborn slave child while whipping his pregnant mother. Although the master attempted to separate the mother and fetus for his commercial ends, their fates were inextricably intertwined. The tragedy of crack babies is initially a tragedy of crack-addicted mothers. Both are part of a larger tragedy of a community that is suffering a host of indignities, including the denial of equal respect for its members' reproductive decisions. A commitment to guaranteeing the reproductive freedom of Black women, rather than punishing them, is the true solution to the problem of unhealthy babies.

THE NORPLANT CONDITION

We saw in Chapter 3 that the long-acting contraceptive Norplant was immediately embraced by commentators and politicians as a means of curtailing the numbers of children born into poverty. The new contraceptive just as quickly became the subject of proposals for punishing women convicted of child abuse or of drug use during pregnancy. Norplant had been approved less than a month when Judge Howard Broadman ordered Darlene Johnson to submit to its implantation as a condition of probation. The qualities that make Norplant ideal for welfare incentives also make it ideal for mandated birth control in criminal cases. Once the device is inserted, a defendant cannot remove it on her own, and it is easy for a probation officer or other official to check whether the capsules remain in place just by looking at the woman's arm.

Several states considered legislation requiring Norplant implantation in women who give birth to drug-exposed babies. A bill introduced in Ohio, similar to proposals made in numerous states, sought to amend the definition of criminal child neglect to include drug use during pregnancy. In addition, the Ohio measure would have required women convicted of "prenatal child neglect" for the first time to choose between completing a drug treatment program or undergoing Norplant insertion. Norplant implantation would be mandatory for repeat offenders. This bill replaced a previous proposal to require sterilization for women convicted more than once of prenatal child neglect.

Even without the legislature's imprimatur, judges have used Norplant as a convenient mechanism for imposing contraception as a condition of probation. Although Darlene Johnson's case was the first involving Norplant, judges have placed restrictions on procreation as a probation requirement on numerous occasions in the past. Trial judges in at least twenty reported cases since 1966 covering ten states have ordered probationers or plea bargainers to be sterilized, to use contraceptives, to refrain from sexual intercourse, or to avoid getting pregnant while under court supervision or until they were married.[146] It is impossible to tell, however, the total number of women who have submitted to Norplant or some other form of contraception in order to avoid going to jail. A defendant who has accepted this offer is unlikely to appeal her sentence and judges are unlikely to report their decision.

Like most prosecutions for prenatal drug exposure, these probation orders have not survived appeal. No appellate court has ever upheld the imposition of any form of birth control as a condition of probation.[147] In 1993, Illinois passed an amendment to the Unified Code of Corrections banning any forced contraception in sentencing or probation after Bloomington judge Ronald Dozier ordered a woman who fractured her baby's skull to submit to Norplant implantation before placing her on probation.

There is nothing unusual about a judge placing restrictions on a defendant's conduct as a condition of probation. A judge might prohibit the probationer from drinking alcohol or from associating with certain friends, for example. These restrictions are designed to help the offender resist the temptation to commit another crime and to increase the chances for rehabilitation. Probation usually benefits the offender because, even with these constraints, it is less confining than prison and makes it easier to participate productively in society.

Appellate courts have routinely upheld restrictive conditions that are reasonably related to the two goals of probation—rehabilitation of the defendant and protection of the public safety. Even conditions that would ordinarily violate defendants' constitutional rights (requiring submission to random drug tests or an electronic monitor, for example) are lawful because they serve these aims without the need for incarceration. Judge Broadman had previously imposed such innovative probation terms as "ordering convicts to learn to read, donate their cars to charity, or wear T-shirts proclaiming their guilt."[148] He ordered Darlene Johnson to take parenting classes and to refrain from smoking and drinking alcohol while pregnant, along with the Norplant condition.

But does requiring a defendant to use contraceptives serve these rehabilitative and protective functions? Proponents argue that keeping certain convicts from becoming pregnant benefits them and society by ensuring that they will not repeat their crimes while they are taking steps to transform their behavior. Norplant will prevent a child abuser like Darlene Johnson from hurting any future children she might have until she learns to be a better parent. The same reasoning would apply to potential harm to a fetus, as in the case of a woman convicted of using drugs during pregnancy. This condition is no different, they point out, from forbidding a man convicted of assaulting his wife from contacting her during the term of his probation.[149]

Although this argument works best when the crime involves harm to children, it is not necessarily limited to these cases. A judge might conclude that barring a woman from having children would bolster her attempt to turn her life around, regardless of the crime she committed. A reprieve from the stresses and strains of parenting gives the probationer a better opportunity to finish school, complete a counseling or drug treatment program, find employment, or whatever other activities aid in her rehabilitation.[150] The argument that the Norplant condition was not reasonably related to Johnson's crime because birth control cannot prevent child abuse is based on a misunderstanding of this rationale. Judge Broadman required Johnson to use Norplant as a supplement to the other probation conditions designed more directly to train her to be a better parent and to protect her children from harm.

If birth control conditions do further the goals of probation, are they not necessarily better than putting a woman in jail? Not if they are imposed for discriminatory reasons. Judges tend to order these conditions in cases where the defendants, like Johnson, are poor or low-income women of color. Of four defendants ordered to use Norplant within its first year on the U.S. market, all were on welfare and three were nonwhite.[151] Stephen Trombley notes that all of the cases during the 1960s in which judges ordered contraception as a condition of probation involved Blacks or Latinas.[152] But how can any probation condition be discriminatory if it *benefits* the defendant by increasing her liberty? After all, the judges in these cases could have simply sent these women to prison for the maximum term.

Understanding the harm in these conditions requires demolishing the assumption that probation requirements necessarily benefit the defendant. In fact, birth control conditions do not benefit the minority women forced to choose them. Instead, they attach an additional penalty to the sentence, related more to the women's economic status and race than to the crime they committed. In short, they punish these women for having babies.

First, even proponents of contraceptive conditions concede that imposing Norplant would be both coercive and discriminatory if judges threatened certain women with longer jail terms for the very purpose of pressuring them to use birth control.[153] This was precisely Judge Broadman's tactic in a case similar to Darlene Johnson's. When Norma Duran Garza was convicted by a jury of felony child abuse, a long prison sentence was not even in the cards. The probation department recommended that Garza serve only one year in a local jail followed by probation. But when Garza rejected Norplant as a condition of probation because birth control violated her religious beliefs, Judge Broadman sentenced her to four years in prison. (Garza is challenging the decision for violating her First Amendment right to free exercise of religion.) [154] Garza went to prison not only for child abuse, but also for refusing to stop having children.

Second, even where judges have not raised the stakes of incarceration, they have increased the burdens attached to probation. To be sure, the defendant herself chose the probation condition because she considered it preferable to going to jail. But the problem in these cases lies not in the difference between probation and incarceration but in the difference between the type of condition that judges impose on minority welfare recipients and those imposed on white middle-class women. It is the difference, that is, between probation with Norplant and probation without it. Women like Darlene Johnson must choose between birth control and jail because that is the choice that judges give them. While some would prefer to use Norplant over going to prison, they would prefer even more a better set of alternatives, the alternatives that wealthier, white defendants get to choose from.

Because the Norplant condition infringes on such a significant liberty, it should be imposed only if absolutely necessary to protect future victims or ensure the defendant's rehabilitation. I have already described how critical the freedom to make reproductive decisions is to human dignity, reflected in its protection under the right to privacy. Sacrificed as well is the defendant's interest in bodily integrity, which is violated by any state-compelled surgical procedure. As we saw in the previous chapter, Norplant remains in the woman's body after insertion and can pose a continuing risk to her health. Judges can satisfy their concern for the defendants' future children with less intrusive probation terms, such as requiring the probationer to attend parenting training, submit to the supervision of physicians and social workers, and refrain from striking her children.

Indeed, Broadman seemed satisfied at first with imposing these requirements on Johnson, but added Norplant to the list at the last moment. Judge Dozier conceded that "[f]or reasons unrelated to the Norplant condition, the court rejected the state's recommendation for a seven-year prison term and would have imposed the probation term regardless of whether or not Norplant was a condition."[155] Requiring these women to use Norplant, then, does not *increase their freedom* by allowing them to avoid prison. To the contrary, it appears that Norplant and other birth control conditions unnecessarily *increase the penalty* exacted against minority women.

Of course, preventing the birth of children will guarantee that they are not abused, just as cutting off a thief's hands might guarantee that he no longer picks locks. But the price of effectiveness is sometimes too high. Courts have struck down conditions that sweep too broadly even though they might help to prevent future criminality. Prohibiting a gay defendant convicted of lewd acts from "frequenting places where homosexuals congregate," or barring a convicted prostitute from entering a particular section of town and speaking to men in public may reduce the temptation to do wrong but they encroach too drastically on defendants' liberties to be reasonable.[156] Besides, closer inspection reveals that these restrictions do not really address the reasons the defendants engaged in crime and are therefore unlikely to keep them from repeating the same conduct in the future. We might even suspect that the judges who ordered these excessive conditions believed that gay men and prostitutes needed extra regulation because of their deviance from gender norms.

Similarly, judges who exact birth control conditions seem more concerned with preventing certain female defendants from having children than with deterring them from repeating their offenses. It is no answer to say that these defendants either waived or forfeited their constitutional right to procreative liberty when they were convicted of a crime. My question is, why do judges deem these particular women to have forfeited their right to be mothers? The crimes they committed place these women at the judge's mercy, but it is their race and poverty that subject them to the judge's reproductive regulation. Presiding over a criminal case gives judges the power to do what legislatures have proposed but failed to accomplish: they can require Black women on welfare to curb their fertility with Norplant on pain of going to prison.

When Judge Broadman offered Norplant to Darlene Johnson as an alternative to jail, his motivation was not primarily Johnson's rehabilitation. Nor did he seem concerned with the safety of the two daughters she had confessed to abusing. He was worried that Johnson, who was eight months pregnant, might have another child while receiving welfare:

> THE COURT: Are you on welfare?
> THE DEFENDANT: I was.
> THE COURT: Okay. And you will be again, right?
> THE DEFENDANT: Yeah.
> THE COURT: Do you want to get pregnant again?
> THE DEFENDANT: No.
> THE COURT: Okay. As a condition of probation, you know, this new thing that's going to be available next month, you probably haven't heard about it. It's called Norplant.[157]

A year earlier, Judge Broadman ordered Linda Zaring, a woman who had pled guilty to heroin use, to "not get pregnant" during the five-year term of her probation. Broadman told Zaring, "I want to make it clear that one of the reasons I am making this order is you've got five children. You're thirty years old. None of your children are in your custody or control. Two of them are on AFDC. And I'm afraid that if you get pregnant we're going to get a cocaine or heroin addicted baby."[158] (Judge Broadman revoked Zaring's probation and sent her to prison two months later when she arrived in court twenty minutes late.) The California appellate court that struck down Broadman's order chastised him for his "apparent imposition of personal social values in the sentencing decision." According to attorneys who have appeared before him, Broadman believes he is improving the world through his own brand of social engineering. "Howard really wants to be a social worker," a local attorney explained, "but he's not, he's a judge."[159]

This reproductive penalty has been imposed for offenses, such as stealing, where there is not even an arguable connection between the punishment and the crime. A Los Angeles judge sentenced Mercedes Dominguez, a Latina woman with two children who was pregnant and receiving public assistance, to probation for second-degree robbery on the condition that she refrain from becoming pregnant again until after she was married.[160] At the probation sentence hearing, the judge explained to Dominguez the consequences of her becoming pregnant again: "You are going to prison unless you are married first. You already have too many of those [children]. . . . If you insist on this kind of conduct you can at least consider the other people in society who are taking care of your children. You have had too many that some others are taking care of other than you and the father." The judge imposed the birth control condition not to deter Dominguez from committing future robberies but to prevent her from adding more of her children to the welfare rolls.

In the 1920s and 1930s American courts approved sterilization as a condition of probation based on the prevailing eugenic philosophy that explained criminality as an inherited trait.[161] In her 1907 article *Hereditary Crime*, Gertrude C. Davenport contended that, despite society's efforts to repress crime, "there would still remain those committed by habitual criminals—criminals who are bred as race horses are bred, by the process of assortive mating. Such are outside the pale of beneficent environment. They can no more help committing crime than race horses can help going."[162] Legislatures implemented the biological explanation for crime in eugenic sterilization laws that mandated sterilization or castration of habitual criminals.

Eugenic approaches to law enforcement still have adherents. Colorado representative Bill Jerke recently floated the idea of offering prisoners sterilization in return for deducting ten days from their sentences, explaining "we're talking about reducing the crime rate down the road."[163] His bill authorizing prison directors to provide family-planning services (except abortion) that they determined to be appropriate failed to pass.

The modern-day reproductive punishments I have examined, however, are not eugenic because they are not based on the belief that criminality is inherited. Their aim is not to prevent the passing down of crime-marked genes. They are based, however, on the same premise underlying the eugenic sterilization laws—that social problems can be cured by keeping certain people from having babies and that certain groups therefore do not deserve to procreate. In either case, reproductive penalties turn offenders into objects rather than human beings, objects that can be manipulated for the dominant society's good.

I do fear, though, that punishing women for becoming pregnant prepares our society to accept a truly eugenic program. If the public grows accustomed to Black women being implanted with Norplant under the threat of imprisonment or jailed because they gave birth to a child who tested positive for drugs, will people be less quick to question a government program that uses these same techniques because it is believed that their children are genetically predisposed to crime and poverty?

I am not so sure that the precise ground used to justify punishing Black women for having babies matters—whether Black children's intrinsic problems are traced to genetics, or to crack, or to a cycle of welfare dependency, or to ghetto culture. There were more Black women coercively sterilized under government welfare programs by the 1970s than feebleminded people compelled to be sterilized under the 1920s eugenic laws. These women were no less branded inferior and undeserving of motherhood than the "poor white trash" subjected to mandatory sterilization. Whether it is Justice Holmes pronouncing "three generations of imbeciles are enough" or Judge Broadman declaring "three generations of welfare recipients are enough," the degrading effect is the same.

5

THE WELFARE DEBATE
Who Pays for Procreation?

On August 22, 1996, President Bill Clinton signed into law the most dramatic reform of his administration, perhaps of the last several decades. The sweeping welfare reform law ended the New Deal federal guarantee of cash assistance for American children living in poverty.[1] For sixty years, since the passage of the Social Security Act of 1935, all applicants who met federal eligibility criteria were entitled to receive benefits under a relief system jointly funded by the states and the federal government. The new law gives states vastly increased authority to run AFDC, the major assistance program serving poor families, with lump-sum federal grants. It also establishes a lifetime limit of five years for payments to any family and requires family heads to find a job within two years. In this way, Clinton fulfilled his campaign pledge to "end welfare as we know it" in time for the 1996 presidential election.

During the preceding debate it quickly became clear that control of welfare would be shifted to the states and that welfare funding would be drastically cut—the question was, how much? When Senator Daniel Patrick Moynihan stood up to attack the proposals, he found himself alone, commenting, "the Senate floor is all but empty."[2] The exclusion from the mainstream debate of any consideration of *enhancing* public assistance to the poor signifies the resounding defeat of the progressive ideal of a universal and dignified welfare system. Worse yet, welfare has taken on a new social role: it is no longer seen as charity but as a means of modifying poor people's behavior. Chief among the pathologies to be curtailed by new regulations is the birthrate of welfare mothers—mothers who are perceived to be Black. Welfare reform has become the main arena for current schemes to restrict Black female fertility, raising broader questions about state funding of reproduction.

THE RACIST ORIGINS OF THE WELFARE SYSTEM

It is important to remember that the system that Congress dismantled was never intended to end poverty, let alone provide adequate subsistence for the poor. The fight to salvage pieces of the existing welfare system tended to overlook its serious flaws. It was easy to forget that America's welfare system already stood out among Western nations for its stinginess and limited social programs. (Take, for example, the defeat of Clinton's proposal for universal health care insurance, a program that has been enacted as a matter of course in every other industrialized country.) The system of poor relief liberals sought to save was also designed to subordinate Blacks, devalue women's work, and mollify demands for economic justice.[3]

Although Americans now view welfare dependency as a Black cultural trait, the welfare system systematically excluded Black people for most of its history. Historian Linda Gordon traces the origins of welfare's stratified structure to women's advocacy for maternalist legislation during the Progressive Era.[4] "Mothers' pensions," initially provided through state and local programs, laid the groundwork for the modern federal welfare system and shaped the terms of the debate about single motherhood that still govern welfare policy discussions today. Through a crusade that identified exclusively with women and children, the women reformers in the early part of this century convinced the public that single motherhood was an urgent social problem that should be addressed through social welfare. The resulting maternalist welfare policy provided government aid so that the female victims of misfortune and male irresponsibility would not have to relinquish their maternal duties in the home in order to join the work force. Other progressive critics, such as Mimi Abramovitz, Frances Fox Piven, and Richard Cloward, emphasize that while the government has subsidized certain "deserving" mothers to enable them to stay at home, its welfare policy has also ensured the availability of less privileged women to do low-wage work.

While recognizing the reformers' monumental accomplishment, Gordon criticizes the programs' gross inadequacy in meeting the needs of female-headed families. Why did welfare programs designed by feminists end up failing women so miserably? Gordon's answer to this paradox is the reformers' adherence to a patriarchal family norm that fostered a misguided faith in the "family wage." The women crusaders believed in the prevailing sexual division of labor that "prescribes earnings as the sole responsibility of husbands and unpaid domestic labor as the only proper long-term occupation for women."[5] Mothers were supposed to be economically dependent on men. They therefore advocated a living wage for each family that enabled the husband to support a dependent, service-providing wife, rather than programs that would facilitate female independence. The reformers also limited the programs' generosity because they were afraid that welfare might provide an incentive for dependency on public assistance, accompanied by moral degeneracy and family breakdown.

Besides its misguided faith in the family wage, the Progressive welfare movement was flawed by the elitism of the privileged, white activist network that led it. A defining aspect of its welfare vision was the social control of poor immigrant families and the neglect of Black women. Worried about urban immigrants' threat to social order, the reformers treated welfare as a means of supervising and disciplining recipients as much as a means of providing charity. According to this social work perspective, the cure for single mothers' poverty lay in socializing foreign relief recipients to conform to "American" family standards. Aid generally was conditioned on compliance with morality provisions and was often administered by juvenile court judges who specialized in punitive and rehabilitative judgments.

Black mothers, on the other hand, were simply excluded. The first maternalist welfare legislation was intended for white mothers only. Administrators either failed to establish welfare programs in locations with large Black populations or distributed benefits according to standards that disqualified Black mothers.[6] The racial exclusivity of mothers' aid programs coincided with the passage of Jim Crow laws, official disenfranchisement of Blacks, and the entrenchment of formal racial segregation—also Progressive reforms intended to strengthen social order. As legal scholar Michael McConnell has noted, "The progressive reform movement in the South, with few exceptions, was also the white supremacist movement."[7] It must be remembered that the first decades of this century also witnessed the virulent campaign to stem immigration of "inferior races" and imposition of eugenic sterilization laws.

Even in the North, Blacks were excluded from cultural reform efforts designed to assimilate European immigrants. To these liberal white do-gooders, Blacks simply seemed unassimilable. "For the white northern reformers early in the century," Gordon explains, "the primary fact was that they did not notice these minorities—did not imagine them as indicated objects of reform. For the southerners, the immigrants appeared reformable and integratable as blacks did not."[8] Their maternalist legislation was intended to assimilate women who had the potential of becoming citizens, but Blacks stood entirely outside the elite white women's paternalistic concept of the national community. As a result, in 1931 the first national survey of mothers' pensions broken down by race found that only *3 percent* of recipients were Black.

Black women were also left out of the feminist welfare activist network. Gordon demonstrates the welfare movement's resulting ideological anemia by contrasting the elite white reformers' programs with the welfare vision of Black women activists of the era.[9] Although Black women reformers also relied on motherhood as a political platform, their approach to women's economic role differed dramatically from that of their privileged white counterparts. Black women eschewed the viability of the family wage and women's economic dependence on men. Instead, they accepted married women's employment as a necessity, advocating assistance for working mothers.

Moreover, while white reformers relied largely on the romantic rhetoric of moral motherhood, Black women's organizations stressed the value of mothers' work in the home. According to historian Eileen Boris, "black suffragists were redefining the political and demanding votes for women on the basis of their *work* as—rather than their merely being—mothers."[10] Black activist women showed their respect for housewives, for example, by making them eligible for membership in the National Association of Wage Earners.

The New Deal incorporated the local mothers' pension programs into a federal system of welfare. It also solidified welfare's stratification along racial as well as gender lines. The fate of mothers' aid was sealed when it was assigned to a program separate from the government's provision for men. Social insurance (Social Security and unemployment insurance) provided a dignified entitlement to primarily white, male wage earners and their wives; Aid to Dependent Children (ADC) doled out humiliating relief to poor single mothers. While Social Security laws obligated the federal government to pay beneficiaries a fixed amount, "ADC clients faced caseworkers, supervisors, and administrators with discretion regarding who got aid and how much they got."[11] These government bureaucrats required recipients to meet not only means standards but also degrading morals, or "suitable home," tests that typically probed clients' sexual behavior.

ADC's inferiority was enhanced by its provision of aid exclusively to the child, defeating the position that mothers' aid compensated women's service to society as a principle of entitlement.[12] While rejecting this positive aspect of feminist reformers' view of mothers' aid, the male-dominated New Deal regime incorporated the most limiting aspects of the earlier reformers' view—the reliance on male wages to meet the needs of families and the moral supervision of recipients of poor relief.

As the New Dealers set up the federal welfare system's stratified structure, they also ensured that Blacks would be left out altogether. Northern Democrats struck a deal with their Southern brethren that systematically denied Blacks eligibility for social insurance benefits. Core programs allowed states to define eligibility standards and excluded agricultural workers and domestic servants in a deliberate effort to maintain a Black menial labor caste in the South.[13] Whites feared that Social Security would make both recipients and those freed from the burden of supporting dependents less willing to accept low wages. In addition, New Deal public works programs blatantly discriminated against Blacks, offering them the most menial jobs and paying them sometimes half of what white workers earned.

Even ADC was created primarily for white mothers, who were not expected to work. Black mothers, who had always been in the paid labor force in far higher numbers than white mothers, were considered inappropriate clients of a system geared to unemployable women. One Southern public assistance field supervisor reported that

> [t]he number of Negro cases is few due to the unanimous feeling on the part of the staff and the board that there are more work opportunities for Negro women and to their intense desire not to interfere with local labor conditions. The attitude that they have always gotten along, and that "all they do is have more children," is definite.[14]

The relatively few Black recipients received smaller stipends on the ground that "blacks needed less to live on than whites."[15]

The civil rights movement finally opened the welfare system to Black citizens. It forced states for the first time to relax the welfare eligibility requirements that had excluded Blacks for decades. During the 1960s, the National Welfare Rights Organization (NWRO), a grassroots movement composed of welfare mothers, joined forces with neighborhood welfare rights centers and legal services lawyers to agitate for major changes in the welfare system's eligibility and procedural rules. This welfare rights movement secured entitlements to benefits, raised benefit levels, and increased availability of benefits to families headed by women. As a result, says historian Gwendolyn Mink, "by 1967, a welfare caseload that had once been 86 percent white had become 46 percent nonwhite."[16] The majority of Black women nevertheless continued to work at paid jobs and the majority of welfare recipients remained white.

This expansion of federal welfare entitlements was bolstered by President Lyndon Johnson's War on Poverty, which attempted to eliminate further the racial bias incorporated in the New Deal programs.[17] Under pressure from civil rights protests and international scrutiny, the federal government set up a number of programs designed to integrate more Blacks into the national political economy. The Office of Economic Opportunity used federal funds to empower community action groups run by local Black activists; federal affirmative action and job-training programs broke long-standing racial barriers to union jobs; the Department of Housing and Urban Development gave housing subsidies to the poor.

But Black welfare activists had won a Pyrrhic victory. As Gordon notes, they got themselves included "not in social insurance but mainly in public assistance programs, which by then had become even stingier and more dishonorable than they had been originally."[18] As AFDC became increasingly associated with Black mothers already stereotyped as lazy, irresponsible, and overly fertile, it became increasingly burdened with behavior modification rules, work requirements, and reduced effective benefit levels.[19] Social Security, on the other hand, effectively transferred income from Blacks to whites because Blacks have a lower life expectancy and pay a disproportionate share of taxes on earnings.

Black mothers' inclusion in welfare programs once reserved for white women soon became stigmatized as dependency and proof of Black people's lack of work ethic and social depravity. The image of the welfare mother quickly changed from the worthy white widow to the immoral Black welfare queen. The rhetoric of motherhood has lost all of the persuasive force it wielded during the Progressive Era. When in 1967 Black members of the NWRO demanded the same benefits white mothers were receiving, Senate Finance Committee chairman Russell Long called them "Black Brood Mares, Inc.," sneering that "if they can find the time to march in the streets, picket, and sit all day in committee hearing rooms, they can find the time to do some useful work."[20] Part of the reason that maternalist rhetoric can no longer justify public financial support is that the public views this support as benefitting primarily Black mothers.

Meanwhile, a white backlash decimated the War on Poverty programs within a decade. In *The Color of Welfare*, sociologist Jill Quadagno demonstrates that it was precisely the War on Poverty's link to Black civil rights that doomed it: whites opposed its programs as an infringement of their economic right to discriminate against Blacks and a threat to white political power. President Richard Nixon abolished the Office of Economic Opportunity in 1973, nine years after its creation, when its expansion of Blacks' political participation appeared to foment rebellion in cities such as Detroit and Newark. At a time when European trade unions were fighting for full-employment policies and more comprehensive welfare provisions, the AFL-CIO defended its "property right" to exclude Blacks from its ranks and opposed the civil rights campaign for an open labor market. Peaking in 1968, federal housing subsidies underwent a precipitous decline when white homeowners backed by the powerful real estate lobby adamantly resisted residential integration. The NWRO charged that Congress was being "vindictive" when it enacted a series of welfare limits following urban riots in the summer of 1967.[21] For Quadagno, our deficient welfare system is "the price the nation still pays for failing to fully incorporate African Americans into the national community."[22]

THE END OF WELFARE AS WE KNEW IT

The new federal law threatens to roll back the meager gains won by the 1960s welfare rights movement, once again placing poor Black mothers and their children at the mercy of state legislatures and local bureaucrats. Under the Social Security Act of 1935, the federal government reimbursed states for part of the AFDC benefits they disbursed as long as the state plans comported with federal requirements. Among the most critical federal standards were criteria for eligibility, ensuring that all applicants who met a standard of need were entitled to benefits. Federal entitlements also represented a national commitment to providing a safety net for poor families. Although states remained free to determine a maximum assistance payment, even one that left families below the poverty level, they nevertheless could not exclude eligible applicants.

The demise of federal eligibility standards began several years ago as states secured federal waivers allowing them to implement experimental welfare programs. Even before the federal law went into effect in 1996, more than half of the nation's welfare recipients were covered by state rules that, without the waivers, would have violated federal law.[23] Without a federally enforceable right to benefits, most states are likely to cut back eligibility standards and procedural safeguards. Not only will behavior modification rules proliferate, but fiscal pressures will drive reductions in benefit levels, job training, child care, and other service programs.

The new law represents a disastrous turn in the way we think about welfare. Numerous critics have noted that American welfare policy, by differentiating between welfare and social insurance programs, has long branded AFDC recipients as immoral freeloaders who are responsible for their own fate.[24] Mainstream politicians never fully acknowledged that recipients' poverty resulted from economic and social forces that prevented them from finding work. The welfare system never included a serious effort at aggressive job-creation or eradication of social barriers to employment. Yet until recently welfare policy minimally sought to reduce poverty and improve the living conditions of recipients. Welfare was stingy and humiliating, but at least it responded to the needs of poor children. In the new era of welfare, government assistance has become a tool of social control, a means of improving the behavior of poor families. Under the new scheme, even the neediest children are cast deeper into poverty if their mothers do not conform.

STOPPING WELFARE MOTHERS FROM HAVING BABIES

The major goal of some welfare reformers is to reduce the number of children born to women receiving public assistance. A variety of avenues have been proposed to achieve this goal. We already saw in Chapter 3 several suggestions involving long-acting contraceptives. The most benign is to make Norplant and other long-acting contraceptives available to poor women through Medicaid. Some measures combine this approach with the added incentive of offering a cash bonus to women on welfare for using Norplant. The most coercive proposal is to mandate Norplant insertion as a condition for receiving welfare benefits.

Another option is to deny additional payments for children born to women who are already receiving AFDC. A number of states already have enacted so-called welfare family caps, and others are considering this type of legislation. Typically the birth of a new baby to a family on welfare will increase the total payment the family receives by a prescribed increment. Family cap provisions generally deny this new birth benefit increase for children born or conceived while the mother is receiving AFDC. New Jersey, Georgia, Arkansas, and Wisconsin were the first states to enact family caps, between 1992 and 1994. In the next two years, they were followed by sixteen others across the country, including Arizona, Illinois, Maryland, Massachusetts, and Texas. Republican Speaker of the House Newt Gingrich proposed legislation eliminating welfare payments for children born to welfare mothers and unwed teens and diverting the money to programs that would put their babies up for adoption or place them in orphanages.[25]

While some of these birth-deterring provisions have been too controversial to pass, family caps are a bipartisan favorite. The Clinton administration routinely approved state requests for federal waivers of AFDC eligibility requirements to put family cap programs in place. Department of Health and Human Services secretary Donna Shalala told reporters, "We're sending a clear message that we will pay for your first kid for a short time while you get ready for the work force. But we will not pay for the second kid."[26] At a congressional hearing on welfare reform, however, Shalala conceded that there was no evidence that family caps would reduce welfare rolls: "We have no evidence that a family cap will deter the behavior of an individual who chooses to have a second child."[27]

"Family cap" is really a misnomer since the laws do not put an absolute ceiling on the number of children who receive benefits. "Child exclusion" more accurately describes the denial of benefits for certain children born to welfare families. Ordinarily, the state determines a standard of family need according to the number of family members, sources of income, and other factors. Under the family cap, a family's standard of need is not adjusted upward to accommodate the new child. These laws are premised on the assumption that the promise of benefits entices women to have additional children. So the penalty applies only to children born or conceived after the mother began receiving public assistance. Families receive benefits for children they already have when they enter the welfare rolls. This means that a mother receiving assistance for one child who has a second child cannot count the new baby for computing benefit levels, but a mother with two children signing up for welfare for the first time can count both. In New Jersey at the time its exclusion went into effect, for example, the first mother would continue to receive $322 per month; the second mother would get $424.

THE FIRST FAMILY CAP LAW

New Jersey was the first state to get a federal waiver for a child exclusion law. The provision is part of a package of welfare reform bills called the Family Development Act adopted in January 1992. The act's goal, according to the state of New Jersey, is "to attack head-on the nation's urgent problems of long-term and intergenerational welfare dependency." Among its provisions is Bill 4703, which eliminated "the increment in benefits under the program for which that family would otherwise be eligible as a result of the birth of a child during the period in which the family is eligible for AFDC benefits." In New Jersey, the eliminated increment amounts on average to $64 a month for a child born to a woman who already has two children.

Implementation of the New Jersey family cap required federal approval because the exclusion conflicted with federal AFDC eligibility standards. The Social Security Act authorized the secretary of HHS to waive compliance with federal guidelines for experimental or demonstration projects that promote the act's objectives to care for needy children and to strengthen their families. New Jersey filed a lengthy proposal describing the family cap provision as a five-year experimental project designed to test whether the harsh measure could break the cycle of poverty that ensnared welfare recipients. On July 20, 1992, then secretary of HHS, Louis Sullivan, granted the necessary waiver. The family cap was implemented statewide the following October.

The act softens the blow by allowing a working mother to keep her earnings until they reach one-quarter of her monthly grant. New Jersey argues that this financial incentive for parents to work has the potential to offset the cash increment they would have received before the exclusion. But Nina Perales of the Puerto Rican Legal Defense and Education Fund believes "it is unrealistic to think that women will benefit from this provision unless they begin work in the month the baby is born and they have no child care costs."[28] Of course, even that assumes that the mother will be able to find a job. Senator Moynihan accused New Jersey lawmakers of effectively ordering six-week-old babies "to shape up or starve."[29]

The child exclusion makes no exceptions for births that could not have been deterred, such as births resulting from rape, incest, or failed contraception. Nor does it make an exception for multiple births. What happens if a mother receiving AFDC for one child gives birth to triplets? Under the family cap, this family of five must now survive on a grant calculated to meet the needs of a family of two.

Had there been any doubt about the purpose to deter childbirth, the law's primary sponsor, Assemblyman Wayne Bryant, made it explicit. Bryant, the Black Democratic representative of New Jersey's poorest city, Camden, was the Assembly's majority leader until Republicans took control of the state legislature in 1992. In an introductory statement, he said, "This bill is intended to discourage AFDC recipients from having additional children during the period of their welfare dependence."[30] For some women this would mean using fail-safe forms of birth control such as Norplant and sterilization. For those who got pregnant, it might mean getting an abortion. New Jersey's right-to-life groups opposed the family cap on the ground that it would increase the number of abortions in the state. The New Jersey Human Services Commission reports that in the eight months after the family cap's adoption, abortions increased by about 300 over the preceding year while the national abortion rate decreased slightly.[31] Women say that the child exclusion has induced them to get an abortion they did not want.[32] There have been conflicting reports about the lasting effect of the New Jersey family cap.[33] New Jersey is evaluating the success of the Family Development Act by measuring its impact on the fertility rate of affected welfare mothers, compared to birthrates in a control group. In its first report, the team of Rutgers University researchers concluded there was "no reduction in the birthrate of welfare mothers attributable" to the family cap.

Bryant, himself a wealthy attorney, claimed to be helping his poorer brothers and sisters achieve self-sufficiency. Eliminating the increment, argues Bryant, is not a denial of benefits but "another way that folks could be responsible like the rest of us." Since working people's salaries are not increased when they have a baby, neither should people on welfare receive an increase in AFDC benefits. He explained:

I don't understand why we believe that we should set up some sheltered kind of existence that makes them live in an unreal world. . . . Why would we want to insulate, and to bring a group of people into a false existence like that, for some reason, if you're in this spot, you have no obligations? Everything is going to be free, and good for you. . . . They can't think for themselves [and] we have to worry about everything that happens in their life.[34]

To call the life of a mother struggling to take care of a baby on an extra $64 a month "sheltered" displayed an incredible blindness to the facts of poverty. Bryant forgot that AFDC, unlike working people's salaries, is geared toward a family's need. Families receiving AFDC are already living in poverty; all the new birth increment does is allow them and the additional baby to survive. People who have a job will have to adjust their budget to cover the expenses of a new baby, but most will not be rendered penniless by the birth.

Bryant also forgot that working families receive government benefits, in the form of earned income tax credits, tax exemptions, and child care credit, that subsidize the cost of an additional child. For a single mother with two dependent children in New Jersey earning $20,000 a year, these tax benefits could amount to $2,873 (compared to only $778 for a welfare mother).[35] The working mother does not need the tax deduction as much as the welfare mother needs the increase in her grant. In no way does the child exclusion *equalize* the situation of middle-class citizens and those on welfare. In fact, it sends their worlds spiraling even farther apart.

RACE AND FAMILY CAPS

In the past, legislators have felt no compunction about asserting the racial motivation behind their proposals to limit the fertility of women on welfare. In 1958, Mississippi state representative David H. Glass introduced a bill mandating sterilization for any unmarried mother who gave birth to another illegitimate child. Glass explained that his objective was to reduce the number of Black children on welfare:

During the calendar year 1957, there were born out-of-wedlock in Mississippi more than 7,000 negro children, and about 200 white children. The negro woman, because of child welfare assistance, [is] making it a business, in some cases of giving birth to illegitimate children. . . . The purpose of my bill was to try to stop, or slow down, such traffic at its source.[36]

With an increasingly mechanized economy, Mississippi found that Blacks were no longer as useful a source of cheap, unskilled labor. Instead, to many whites, Blacks had become an unwanted welfare burden. The bill answered the question posed by the state welfare commissioner: "how much longer will the white population of Mississippi consent to be taxed and drained of its substance for the benefit of a race, and a nation, which shows no appreciation for their sacrifice?"[37] Glass's proposal was also viewed as a way of forcing Blacks to migrate from Mississippi to the North. In a pamphlet entitled *Genocide in Mississippi*, the Student Nonviolent Coordinating Committee quoted Representative Stone Barefield as saying during floor debate on the bill, "When the cutting starts, they'll head for Chicago."[38] According to Hodding Carter, editor of the *Delta Democrat-Times*, "the measure was tabled but there is widespread sentiment for some sort of means for coping with the fantastically high number of illegitimate Negro births."[39] Bills denying additional AFDC benefits to women who had more than two children or conditioning future welfare payments on their sterilization were introduced in several states during the 1970s. Although these failed to pass, Mississippi and Louisiana did enact laws making it a crime to bear a child out of wedlock, punishable by thirty to ninety days in jail.

Contemporary politicians decry welfare mothers' irresponsible reproduction, using rhetoric identical to that of Mississippi lawmakers three decades ago, except they have cleansed it of its express racial terms. Perhaps because he is Black himself, Wayne Bryant did not hide the fact that his law was aimed at New Jersey's Black communities. Half of AFDC recipients in New Jersey are Black. Bryant favored himself as a great savior of his people. In public hearings on the legislation, as well as in interviews with the media, he boldly declared that he intended the family cap to transform Black people's lifestyle. At an October 1991 hearing, for example, Bryant stated: "I am saying, as an African American, I will not tolerate anyone having my people disproportionately in a system that is going to keep them permanently in poverty, without having some responsibility."[40] Explaining the impetus for his proposal, he told the *Washington Post*, "We cannot survive if we have too many of our people locked in poverty."[41] He often referred to the New Jersey welfare law as "a modern form of slavery."

Bryant's outspoken support for the family cap proved to be very convenient for white legislators, who were only too happy to let the Black assemblyman play "front man" for the bill. As one white New Jersey senator confessed, "It would be very difficult for a white to raise [the subject of welfare dependency]. . . . [Wayne Bryant] is doing us all a favor by focusing the debate."[42]

Congress also indicated that its welfare reform efforts specifically addressed problems in the Black community. The House Republicans' proposed Personal Responsibility Act of 1995—a key provision of the Contract with America—explicitly cited statistics of Black behavior to explain the need for its measures. The act referred to the rising illegitimacy rate for Black Americans and stated that "the likelihood that a young black man will engage in criminal activities doubles if he is raised without a father and triples if he lives in a neighborhood with a high concentration of single parent families."[43] In promoting his Contract with America, House Speaker Newt Gingrich attributed Black people's poverty to their laziness.[44]

As we have seen in previous chapters, race fuels the welfare debate even when it is not mentioned. Although most families who receive AFDC are not Black, Black women disproportionately rely on this form of government aid to support their children.[45] Moreover, the American public associates AFDC with the image of the mythical Black welfare queen or teenage girl who deliberately becomes pregnant to receive public assistance. It is fair to say, then, that welfare policies designed to discourage childbearing will disproportionately affect Black women and have these very women in mind.

Like birth control programs and reproductive punishments, contemporary welfare policies share features of eugenic thinking. Eugenicists framed their arguments not only in terms of improving the race, but also in terms of reducing the cost of subsidizing the unfit. In his celebrated study of a degenerate family, *The Jukes*, Richard L. Dugdale included detailed calculations of the amounts the Jukes had cost New York State by 1877. He estimated the family's financial burden to society at "over a million and a quarter dollars of loss in seventy-five years, caused by a single family 1,200 strong, without reckoning the cash paid for whiskey, or taking into account the entailments of pauperism and crime of the survivors in succeeding generations, and the incurable disease, idiocy, and insanity growing out of this debauchery, and reaching further than we can calculate."[46] Later Charles Davenport asserted, "It is a reproach to our intelligence that we as a people, proud in other respects of our control of nature, should have to support about half a million insane, feebleminded, epileptic, blind and deaf, 80,000 prisoners and 100,000 paupers at a cost of over 100 million dollars per year."[47]

In 1935, Dr. J. N. Baker, Alabama's health officer, praised the Nazi sterilization law before the state legislature for its economic efficiency: "With bated breath, the entire civilized world is watching the bold experiment with mass sterilization recently launched by Germany. It is estimated that some 400,000 of the population will come within the scope of this law. . . . It is estimated that, after several decades, hundreds of millions of marks will be saved each year as a result of the diminution of expenditures for patients with hereditary diseases."[48]

During the 1930s some eugenicists proposed tying government payments to family size in order to encourage the breeding of "better stock." We must recall that one of their greatest worries was that the least fit appeared to have increased fertility while the socially desirable classes experienced a decline in their birthrate. British eugenicist Ronald A. Fisher, author of the 1930 classic *The Genetical Theory of Natural Selection*, proposed a plan to reverse this trend "by which the eugenically valuable qualities of the nation are being destroyed."[49] Fisher advocated a comprehensive scheme of family allowances from the government. Fisher's plan was exactly the opposite of a welfare program, such as AFDC, that provides benefits to poor families with children. Rather, "The government would provide an allowance for each child proportional not to the family's absolute need but to its earned income; high-income families would receive more per child than low-income families."[50] The American Eugenics Society apparently concurred in Fisher's idea, publishing in 1935 a pamphlet declaring: "It is hard to see how a perfect eugenic system can prevail until every intelligent married couple is able to have as many children as it wishes without lowering its economic status."[51] For these eugenicists, government welfare was not aimed at helping the needy participate fully as citizens; its purpose was to exclude them as members of society.

Of course, the current welfare family caps are not premised on notions of recipients' genetic inferiority. But, like eugenic programs of the past, they are seen as a way of ridding America of the burden poor people impose. Once again, curbing reproduction is touted as a solution to social injustice.

REFUTING THE MYTHS ABOUT WELFARE AND REPRODUCTION

Policies that discourage women on welfare from having children are justified by a set of myths about the connections between family structure, welfare, race, and poverty. These myths hold that the promise of benefits induces childbirth, that welfare dependency causes poverty, and that marriage can solve the problem of children's poverty. The contemporary perception of procreation by the poor as costly and pathological was most notably promoted by Charles Murray, who, in 1984, argued that welfare induces poor women to have babies;[52] in 1993, declared that "illegitimacy is the single most important social problem of our time";[53] and in 1994, claimed that the higher fertility rates of groups with lower average intelligence, who fall at the bottom of the economic ladder, help to perpetuate welfare dependency.[54] The solution, Murray proposed, was to eliminate welfare benefits for all working-age adults. This thinking leads to the conclusion that, since reproduction by the poor perpetuates poverty and other social ills, policies designed to reduce their fertility are an efficient means of at once reducing poverty and cutting welfare costs.

The myths about welfare and reproduction have broad-based support, as evidenced by the bipartisan passage of the 1996 federal welfare reform law. While his views were once considered on the political fringe, Murray now "has a platform in respectable publications and is welcomed as a savant by Republicans in Congress."[55] These themes run throughout the House Republicans' Personal Responsibility Act, some of which survived in the new federal law. For ease of reference, I will attribute the myths to a conservative political philosophy while acknowledging their growing acceptance by the general public.

Myth No. 1: Welfare Induces Childbirth

Welfare reform measures designed to discourage reproduction are based on the belief that welfare encourages poor women to bear children, combined with taxpayer resentment for having to pay to support them. Poor people violate the middle-class norm of childbearing that holds it is irresponsible to have children when one cannot afford to support them. Senator Lauch Faircloth explained this reasoning during recent hearings on welfare reform:

> [M]iddle-class American families who want to have children have to plan, prepare, and save money because they understand the serious responsibility involved in bringing children into the world. But welfare recipients do not have to prepare or save money before having children because they know they will get money from the Federal Government, and that the taxpayers of the country will take care of their children.[56]

Does this mean that procreation is a privilege of the middle and upper classes alone? Sidestepping the question of whether the poor should have children at all, conservatives rail against the burden that it imposes on hardworking taxpayers. As Representative Marge Roukema asked during the congressional debate on the Family Support Act, "How much longer do you think the two-worker couple will tolerate the welfare state and its cost to them in taxes to support that welfare mother? . . . The answer is that they should not have to."[57]

A number of conservative writers have argued that the promise of increased AFDC payments creates a financial incentive for welfare recipients to have more children.[58] This claim is refuted by empirical research and plain common sense. Many studies have found no significant causal relationship between welfare benefits and childbearing.[59] The vast majority of welfare mothers have only one or two children; in fact, the average number of children in a family receiving welfare is somewhat smaller than in families that do not. According to Marian Wright Edelman of the Children's Defense Fund, the average number of children in a family receiving AFDC is just 1.9.[60] Furthermore, AFDC family size has declined in the last twenty years: while 32.5 percent of AFDC families had four or more children in 1969, only 9.9 percent had that many in 1990.[61]

Moreover, fertility rates do not correspond to the level of welfare benefits provided by the states. The state with the highest percentage of AFDC families with four or more children (Mississippi) pays the lowest amounts—only $24 monthly for an additional child. The claim that welfare induces childbearing ignores the social and emotional reasons for having a baby. In any case, it would be irrational for a woman on welfare to assume the tremendous costs and burdens of caring for an additional child given the meager increase in AFDC payments that results. In fact, the benefit structure already deters childbirth since "[t]he average per capita amount of a welfare grant *decreases* as the number of persons in the household increases."[62] As it is, welfare mothers suffer a net financial loss every time a child is added to the family. Child exclusion laws only push these families deeper into poverty.

A more plausible claim is that, although poor women do not become pregnant deliberately in order to receive AFDC benefits, they are more likely to become pregnant with the security of AFDC benefits to rely on than without them. The availability of welfare lessens the financial burden poor women would otherwise have to bear in having children and therefore reduces their incentive to take every possible precaution against pregnancy. As conservative writer Mickey Kaus explained, "With AFDC in place, young girls look around them and recognize, perhaps unconsciously, that other girls in their neighborhood who have had babies on their own are surviving, however uncomfortably."[63] In short, Kaus asserts, "Welfare may not have been the main cause of the underclass, but it *enabled* the underclass to form." Welfare may not induce childbearing by indigent women, but refusing to provide welfare might discourage it. Basing public policy on this claim still assumes a clientele that is prone to dependence and sloth, and that needs state incentives to reproduce responsibly.

Myth No. 2: Welfare Causes Dependency

Conservatives also advocate AFDC cutbacks on the grounds that long-term reliance on welfare is immoral and that the provision of welfare itself causes welfare dependency. Welfare reform rhetoric describes childbearing by the poor as fueling a cycle of poverty by producing children who will inevitably depend on the government for sustenance. Conservatives claim that the reliance of the poor on welfare (rather than poverty itself) causes social problems, including the perpetuation of welfare dependency into the next generation. Mothers who receive welfare are thought to teach their children a life of dependency by undermining their children's motivation to support themselves.

This worry about the intergenerational transmission of welfare dependency was reflected by Justice Clarence Thomas's condemnation of his sister's reliance on welfare: "She gets mad when the mailman is late with her welfare check. That's how dependent she is. What's worse is that now her kids feel entitled to the check too. They have no motivation for doing better or getting out of that situation."[64] In fact, Thomas's sister, Emma Mae Martin, "worked two minimum-wage jobs while her brother attended law school, but stopped working [for four or five years] to take care of an elderly aunt who had suffered a stroke."[65] Both she and her eldest child were employed at the time of Thomas's appointment to the Supreme Court.

Yet conservatives assert no similar condemnation of long-term dependency on inherited wealth, life insurance proceeds, government agricultural subsidies, and Social Security benefits. Indeed, we do not view this type of reliance on financial assistance as dependency at all. A welfare rights activist and former recipient, Theresa Funiciello, explains the unfairness of the distinction made between children supported by Social Security and those supported by AFDC:

> No one has suggested the mother on Social Security suffers from "dependency," yet everyone seems concerned about dependency when it comes to welfare. There is no rational public policy basis for treating families in essentially identical circumstances in such radically different ways. . . . The only real difference between "survivor" and "welfare" families . . . is the imprimatur of the father. The message: the needs and rights of women and children are determined not by universal standards but by the nature of their prior relationship to a man.[66]

Another difference between "survivor" families, who depend on Social Security, and "welfare" families, who depend on AFDC is that white children are more likely to belong to "survivor" families, while Black children are more likely to be part of "welfare" families.

According to feminist scholars Nancy Fraser and Linda Gordon, "[∂]ependency . . . is an ideological term" which "carries strong emotive and visual associations and a powerful pejorative charge."[67] As a result, what is considered dependency has changed along with the major social and economic transformations. It was only with the rise of industrial capitalism that the meaning of economic independence was expanded to include the white workingman's wage labor in addition to property ownership and self-employment. Paupers, slaves, and housewives, who were excluded from wage labor, constituted the underside of the workingman's independence and were kept economically and politically dependent. As major forms of dependency deemed proper in industrial usage became objectionable, "dependency" became an increasingly negative term and was attributed with greater frequency to the fault of the individual rather than the social structure.

This distinction in the moral outrage directed at different types of dependency parallels the stratification of the American welfare system into two basic categories: Social Security and what is commonly called welfare (mainly AFDC). Social Security retains its political popularity because it is perceived as an insurance program despite its strong redistributive effects and its dependent clients.[68] Yet Social Security itself encourages some dependencies while discouraging others. It "subvert[s] adults' sense of responsibility for their parents" while promoting wives' dependence on their husbands' wages.[69]

Because Social Security's beneficiaries are thought to recoup what they contributed to the program, they are neither stigmatized nor supervised. So taxpayers complain about supporting poor mothers on AFDC through their income taxes, but not about the transfer of their Social Security payments to the widows and children of deceased workers, who may even be more affluent than the taxpayers who support them. In 1992, nearly four million children and caretaker parents received Social Security benefits totaling about $14 billion.[70] The budget for AFDC was only 50 percent greater, even though its caseload was three times larger.

The stratification of the American welfare system becomes even more suspect if we consider an even broader meaning of welfare that extends beyond AFDC and Social Security. Linda Gordon suggests that welfare "could . . . accurately refer to all of a government's contributions to its citizens' well-being."[71] This interpretation would include home mortgage deductions, the provision of public schools, and corporate tax breaks, and would reveal that most welfare helps Americans who are not in fact poor. Of the $711 billion in federal entitlement spending in 1992, AFDC accounted for less than $20 billion.[72] Less visible public income transfers structured through the income tax system benefit higher-income groups the most. "At less than 4 percent of total federal social welfare spending, AFDC is fiscally an insubstantial part of the American welfare state," conclude the authors of *America's Misunderstood Welfare State.*[73]

The myth of welfare dependency also includes the view that the public would not have to support poor children if their parents would go to work. Congress, at least formally, has required mothers receiving AFDC to enroll in work programs since 1971. Several states also implemented their own programs that attempt to force welfare recipients to work by cutting off benefits after two years. A key element of the 1996 federal reform law similarly requires adult welfare recipients to find work within two years.

The underlying belief that people rely on welfare because they lack incentive to work (a condition to be cured by forcing them to get jobs) is also a myth. It is refuted by the fact that most welfare recipients work while on welfare, either continuously or intermittently, when they are able to get jobs.[74] Many women who work full time still live in poverty. Any work disincentive that exists is not caused by overly generous welfare benefits, but by the miserable conditions of available full-time jobs: poverty wages, loss of welfare benefits, and inadequate child care and health insurance. As an officer in a California work program explained: "[A] single woman with three children, who has to pay for child care, can't live off $6 an hour. That is an economic reality that goes beyond the welfare cycle we want to break."[75]

Besides, there are simply not enough full-time jobs around to absorb the millions of current welfare recipients who will be forced to find work.[76] Sociologist William Julius Wilson has warned time and time again, "The disappearance of work in the ghetto cannot be ignored, isolated or played down."[77] Reducing the need for AFDC will require dramatic economic and social changes, including aggressive job creation, a higher minimum wage (or a guaranteed minimum income), lower marginal tax rates on welfare recipients' earnings, better schools and effective job training, subsidized child and health care, and elimination of inequalities in the labor market—changes that conservatives are apparently unwilling to pursue.

Myth No. 3: Marriage Can End Children's Poverty

According to the conservative vision, single motherhood is especially immoral and harmful, in part because conservatives believe out-of-wedlock childbearing causes poverty. Contemporary welfare reform rhetoric resurrects the early reformers' anxiety about single motherhood. The House Republicans' proposed Personal Responsibility Act declared that "marriage is the foundation of a successful society" and "an essential social institution which promotes the interests of children and society at large." A list of "negative consequences of an out-of-wedlock birth on the child, the mother, and society" followed. The act would have imposed a number of measures designed to penalize unwed mothers and their children. It prohibited, for example, mothers under the age of eighteen from receiving AFDC benefits for any child born out of wedlock, regardless of when aid is sought for the child, unless the mother marries the child's father or someone who adopts the child.

It is true that families headed by single females are disproportionately poorer than families with an adult male present. The U.S. Census Bureau reported that the 1991 poverty rate was 12.1 percent among married-couple households with children, compared to 59.0 percent in single-mother households.[78] But this correlation does not prove that single motherhood *causes* poverty. Nor can it predict that marriage or paternal child support will ensure children's financial well-being. Even researchers who find some causal connection between child poverty and family structure attribute only 10 to 20 percent of poverty to the rise of female-headed households.[79] Rather, children's poverty results from inadequate family income, due to the declining ability of one parent—especially the mother—to earn enough to stay above the poverty line. This problem is exacerbated by working conditions that make it virtually impossible for mothers to combine low-wage jobs with child-raising.

There is no sound evidence that welfare is an incentive for women to create single-mother households. A 1984 study concluded that "[t]he attractiveness of welfare and welfare dependency exhibits no effects on black female family heads."[80] Indeed, efforts to discourage single motherhood by cutting welfare benefits have failed, with the proportion of families headed by unmarried women rising even with benefits falling.[81] True, AFDC gives some women who might otherwise be forced to depend on a husband's income the financial ability to establish their own households. Battered women's advocates are worried, for example, that welfare cuts will compel victims to remain in violent homes out of economic desperation.[82]

The judgment that this type of independence is bad, however, is not based on evidence that welfare causes poverty. Rather, this is a normative decision which prefers encouraging women's economic dependence on husbands over providing aid for child care directly to women or improving women's own economic opportunities in combination with state subsidies.[83] This judgment falls especially hard on Black mothers: since the 1980s, over half of all Black families with children have been headed by women who have never married.[84] Penalizing single mothers will disproportionately harm Black children.

It is especially unlikely that marriage or child support will eradicate the poverty of most Black children. Research suggests that there are racial differences in paths to poverty for women. Whereas many white women are left impoverished by divorce, Black single mothers are more likely to be the victims of "reshuffled poverty," caused by the dissolution of a poor two-parent household. While about half of poor white single mothers became poor at the time they established a single-mother household, only a quarter of Black women did—the Black mothers were poor already.[85] A study of children's poverty concluded that "[f]amily structure patterns are more powerful determinants of the economic fates of white than black children."[86] Moreover, Black children living with two parents are still more likely to be poor than white children in female-headed households. Just as marital breakdown is unlikely to be the cause of Black mothers' poverty, so marriage is unlikely to be the solution.

Collecting child support from fathers will be no more successful than marriage at ending children's poverty. Since 1975 Congress has enacted increasingly tough measures designed to recoup welfare costs by collecting child-support.[87] Yet intensified state and federal campaigns to improve child support collection have failed either to lower the poverty rate for children or to reduce significantly the number of children on welfare. HHS projects that higher child-support payments would enable less than 10 percent of families on welfare to rise above the poverty level.[88]

Of course, there are many affluent fathers whose financial support could lift their children out of poverty. But, to use a well-worn expression, it is impossible to squeeze blood from a stone. No matter how vigorously enforced, a child-support order cannot raise the earnings of a low-income or unemployed father. Again, relying on paternal child-support penalizes Black children. Black mothers are less likely to be poor because of separation from the father and Black fathers are less likely to earn the wages necessary to ensure adequate support for their children. The incarceration rate for young Black men is also many times higher than for whites. Policies that replace welfare with child-support collection, therefore, tend to benefit white children and disadvantage Black children. Researchers calculated, for example, that under Wisconsin's percentage-of-income child-support formula, white families obtained a $481 million annual gain whereas Black and Hispanic families suffered more than a $200 million loss.[89] In short, while the state should help mothers to go after child support from fathers with decent incomes, it is ludicrous to believe that child support can relieve Black children's poverty.

Even if marriage would improve poor mothers' financial well-being, this result would not justify affirmatively linking their economic options to marriage. But this is precisely the effect of "bridefare" programs that give mothers monetary rewards for marrying. The New Jersey Family Development Act, for example, allows families to earn income up to 150 percent of the poverty-line income and still keep their AFDC benefits, Medicaid, and emergency housing assistance if, and only if, the mother marries.[90] This means that a woman with two children who marries can keep her children's AFDC benefits as well as up to $21,000 of earned income a year.[91] Its primary sponsor, Assemblyman Wayne Bryant, hoped to entice welfare mothers into replicating a middle-class family structure. "We want to do . . . away with what I call the 'invisible man,' [where welfare allows] men and women [to] conjugate [*sic*] together and yet not encourage the family like we do in middle-class families," Bryant explained.

Mothers can get the best bridefare package only if they marry a man other than the natural father of their children. New Jersey legislators apparently had in mind women who deliberately get pregnant out of wedlock, apply for welfare, and then marry the father—all to take advantage of the bridefare boon. But is that possibility any more unsavory than the prospect of desperate mothers bribing neighborhood men to marry them in order to maximize their monthly grants?

The bridefare provision, however, denies this "income disregard" to an unmarried woman who lives with the working father of her children, to a working mother who does not have a husband, and to two mothers who decide to pool their resources to support their children in a single household. Although Bryant claimed the law was designed to teach welfare mothers "to become successful, responsible, and self-sufficient in our society," he clearly was more interested in women's marital status than their financial independence. In fact, bridefare favors nonworking welfare mothers who rely on a husband's salary over independent, wage-earning mothers on welfare. Measures like the one in New Jersey do not tie welfare to marriage in order to end children's poverty. They tie welfare to marriage in order to penalize single, rebellious Black mothers.

WELFARE AS A WAIVER OF PRIVACY

The regulation of welfare mothers' fertility is bolstered not only by these myths but also by a legacy of disrespect for the privacy of welfare recipients. Public relief for single mothers is structured to permit bureaucratic supervision of clients in order to determine their eligibility based on both means- and morals-testing. Middle-class Americans avoid these impositions because they receive their benefits in the form of entitlements and tax breaks that are not subject to the discretion of caseworkers, supervisors, or administrators. While poor single mothers must endure government surveillance for their paltry benefits, "self-sufficient" traditional families receive huge public subsidies— Social Security, tax breaks, and government-backed mortgages, for example—without any loss of privacy.[92]

By regarding welfare benefits as an undeserved subsidy, the law allows states to treat recipients as subjects whose behavior may be modified to fit current social policy. The notion that receipt of welfare benefits should be conditioned on prescribed improvements in recipients' lifestyle has recently gained favor across the country. Over the last several years, the federal government has granted waivers to more than thirty states allowing them to change their welfare programs to incorporate a form of behavior modification.[93] States are experimenting with schemes that cut off benefits if recipients fail to go to work, stay on welfare past a set period of time, have babies out of wedlock, or cannot stop their children from dropping out of school. These new programs are based on the twin premises that paying welfare benefits entitles the government to regulate mothers' behavior and that only mothers who conform to middle-class values deserve government support.[94] Journalist Rosemary Bray, a former welfare recipient herself, calls the social supervision of welfare clients "a control many Americans feel they have bought and paid for every April 15."[95] The new federal law sets states free to experiment even more with these behaviorial conditions on welfare benefits.

Means- and morals-testing allows welfare bureaucrats to place recipients under surveillance to check for cheating or lapses in eligibility. This probing forces recipients to assume a submissive stance lest offended caseworkers throw them off the rolls. With the power to cut a client's lifeline, bureaucrats often berate and degrade the mothers who pack the welfare office, adding to the humiliation of begging for public assistance. "Think of the worst experience you've ever had with a clerk in some government service job—motor vehicles, hospital, whatever—and add the life-threatening condition of impending starvation or homelessness to the waiting line, multiply the anxiety by an exponent of ten," writes Theresa Funiciello, "and you have some idea of what it's like in a welfare center."[96] Clients are made to wait in long lines, shuttled back and forth, and told to return another day. Noncompliant recipients are sometimes arrested or beaten up by security guards.

The indignity does not end at the welfare office. Welfare mothers must also allow caseworkers to search their homes. A Black domestic's experience with poor relief in the 1930s remains typical of that of welfare recipients today:

> The investigators, they were like detectives, like I had committed a crime. . . . I had to tell them about my life, more than if I was on trial . . . the investigator searched my icebox. . . . I was ashamed of my life . . . that's how you're made to feel when you're down and out like you're nothing better than a criminal.[97]

A contemporary mother similarly described her experience with welfare workers: "I know they be wanting to *know* everything. They are so nosy. They control your life. I don't like it."[98] Plans to weed out fraudulent claims by welfare cheats, like one instituted in 1995 by New York City mayor Rudolph Giuliani, have intensified harassment of welfare recipients and thrown legitimate clients off the rolls.[99] Although we never hear about them, there are far more people entitled to benefits who do not receive them than welfare cheats.

Why do constitutional guarantees such as the right of privacy and the right against unlawful searches and seizures not prevent these government intrusions into citizens' personal lives? Privacy doctrine does not shield people who receive welfare benefits. An individual's acceptance of government benefits is deemed to constitute a waiver of privacy. The Supreme Court has routinely allowed states to regulate poor families by conditioning benefits on conformance to various mandates. Because these families are not entitled to government support, the Supreme Court has reasoned, the government may force them to open up for inspection, shrink, rearrange, or break up in order to qualify for benefits. Although the Court sometimes finds an egregious invasion of poor families' privacy to be unconstitutional, most of the day-to-day decisions of family life remain vulnerable to state regulation.

Over and over again, the Court has upheld welfare regulations that determine eligibility for benefits based on household composition despite their negative effects on families' chosen living arrangements.[100] In 1995, the Court held that states could group into a single "assistance unit" all needy children living in the same household under the care of one relative even though this rule results in a decrease in AFDC benefits for each child.[101] All the government needs is a "rational" reason for its regulation, which can include the goal of decreasing welfare expenditures. One of Americans' most cherished freedoms is the right to keep government agents out of our homes. The police must obtain a search warrant to inspect even the homes of suspected criminals. Yet the Court has ruled that welfare workers can demand home entry as a condition of welfare eligibility; there is no need to get judicial approval even when an applicant protests the home inspection.[102]

This loss of privacy often entails state intrusion in welfare recipients' reproductive decisionmaking. Since welfare's inception, states have conditioned payments on mothers' compliance with standards of sexual and reproductive morality, such as "suitable home" or "man in the house" rules. The ADC law passed in 1935 provided that the state may "impose such other eligibility requirements—as to means, moral character, etc.—as it sees fit." More recently, welfare mothers have been required to undergo mandatory paternity proceedings involving state scrutiny of their intimate lives. Under the Family Support Act of 1988, the states are required to meet federal standards to establish the paternity of children born out of wedlock as a means of procuring child support from absent fathers. The Supreme Court has approved the federal requirement that welfare mothers cooperate in establishing the paternity of their children and tracking down the father.[103] Mothers must submit to investigation that often delves into their sexual activities, or else lose their benefits. In one case, a woman was denied public assistance for refusing to turn over a calendar on which she had allegedly written the names of her sexual partners.[104]

Some family cap laws open up another area for government prying. Arkansas allows recipients to avoid the exclusion if they prove that the child was conceived by rape or that they were using a "reliable" method of contraception. Although this exception relieves some of the hardship of undeterrable births, it also means having to reveal intimate details of your sex life to government workers in order to get benefits. In addition, the exception pressures women to use the most invasive means of birth control. Because the contraceptive must be 96 percent reliable or better to qualify, welfare mothers have to use Norplant or IUDs to qualify for the exception. We have already seen the problems associated with long-lasting, provider-controlled devices.

GOVERNMENT FUNDING OF ABORTIONS

Why does the constitutional right to privacy, which protects a woman's decision to terminate a pregnancy, not protect a welfare mother's decision to have a baby? To explore this question, we must begin with Supreme Court cases deciding whether or not poor women have a right to government funding of an abortion. *Roe v. Wade* and subsequent cases guaranteed women's freedom from government interference in their private reproductive decisions. But what about women too poor to pay for private health care? If the facilities needed to effectuate a reproductive decision cost money, poor and low-income women—who are disproportionately Black—may not be able to afford to take advantage of them. Prenatal care, abortion services, reproduction-assisting technologies, fetal surgery, contraceptives, and family-planning counseling are some examples of the means to realize reproductive choices that may be financially out of reach.[105] Institutional, cultural, language, and educational barriers also deter poor women of color from using the limited services that are available.[106]

Poor women's inadequate access to reproductive health services is bolstered by traditional constitutional jurisprudence. Current legal doctrine fails to recognize these barriers as a constitutional issue at all for two principal reasons. First, the prevailing view holds that the Constitution protects only an individual's "negative" right to be free from unjustified intrusion, rather than the "positive" right to actually lead a free life. Second, this view restricts constitutional protection to interference by the state. The Constitution, then, does not obligate the government to ensure the social conditions and resources necessary for individual liberty or to protect the individual from degradation inflicted by social forces other than the state. This means that citizens have no constitutional right to government benefits, even benefits needed to subsist.

The ability to deny benefits, however, can give the government intolerable power over citizens' exercise of their constitutional rights. That power expands the more we live on "government largess";[107] but it is mightiest against those who depend on benefits for their very survival. The government could grant benefits only on the condition that recipients relinquish their protected liberties. It could attach strings to receiving a welfare check that would violate the Constitution if commanded directly. Could a state, for example, deny unemployment compensation to a Seventh-Day Adventist who was fired for refusing to work on her Sabbath? In a 1963 decision, the U.S. Supreme Court held that this was unconstitutional.[108] The state could not force the woman to choose between her religious practices and receiving government assistance.

This reasoning is encompassed in the unconstitutional conditions doctrine. This principle holds that the government may not condition the conferral of a benefit on the beneficiary's surrender of a constitutional right, although the government may choose not to provide the benefit altogether. An unconstitutional condition exists when the government penalizes individuals for exercising their constitutional rights by denying benefits that would otherwise be available to them.

Only four years after *Roe v. Wade* ensured women's constitutional right to abortion, the Court had to decide whether the Constitution also required the government to pay for the cost of abortions for poor women. Although nothing in the Constitution obligated the government to provide this benefit, without government support many indigent women who wanted to terminate a pregnancy would be unable to exercise their newly established right. Laws denying government support for abortion services raise an unconstitutional conditions problem. The Medicaid funding scheme explicitly excludes payment for a constitutionally protected activity. The government's refusal to pay for abortion places a condition on the receipt of Medicaid funds: pregnant women may receive medical benefits as long as they do not use them to exercise their right to obtain an abortion.

Welfare recipients do not fare well under the unconstitutional conditions doctrine, however. In *Maher v. Roe*, the Court upheld a Connecticut statute that denied public funding of abortions that were not medically necessary, even though the state paid for the expenses incidental to childbirth.[109] How could Connecticut justify its allocation of resources to one constitutionally protected activity and not the other? This was certainly not a cost-saving measure, since paying for abortions would save the state the cost of prenatal care and delivery. Recognizing first that "[t]he Constitution imposes no obligation on the states to pay the pregnancy-related medical expenses of indigent women, or indeed to pay any of the medical expenses of indigents," the majority reasoned further that states may make "a value judgment favoring childbirth over abortion and . . . implement that judgment by the allocation of public funds."[110] Rather than impermissibly burdening the decision to have an abortion, the Court said, the funding scheme simply made it more attractive for indigent women to choose to have the baby. It was perfectly permissible for Connecticut to allocate benefits so as to encourage women to have babies and to discourage them from having abortions, even though this was their constitutional right.

The passage in 1977 of the Hyde Amendment, a yearly Medicaid rider, ended most federal involvement in subsidizing abortion services and relegated that role to the states. The provision prohibited federal reimbursement of Medicaid funds even for most therapeutic abortions. Under the current version of the Hyde Amendment, Medicaid pays for abortions only when the woman's life is endangered by pregnancy or if the pregnancy is the result of rape or incest, an exemption that draws a perpetual battle in Congress. The number of federally funded abortions dropped from nearly 300,000 in 1977 to under 300 in 1992 as a result of the amendment. Most states have restrictive policies similar to that of the federal government and pay for very few abortions. Consequently, state abortion funding has been the major subject of litigation brought by pro-choice groups. As of 1994, only seventeen states used their own funds to subsidize abortions for poor women under most circumstances, owing either to legislation or court order.

Three years after the *Maher* decision, the Court narrowly upheld the Hyde Amendment in *Harris v. McRae*.[111] The Court again distinguished between the government's affirmative interference with abortions and its failure to pay for them. "Although government may not place obstacles in the path of a woman's choice, it need not remove those not of its own creation," the Court reiterated. "It simply does not follow that a woman's freedom of choice carries with it a constitutional entitlement to the financial resources to avail herself of the full range of protected choices."

The Court thus avoided the unconstitutional conditions problem by distinguishing between direct state interference with a protected activity and the state's mere refusal to subsidize a protected activity. It is one thing for the government affirmatively to interfere with women's access to abortions and another to fail to pay for them. The former, the Court concedes, raises a constitutional issue because it involves state action, whereas it characterizes the latter as a constitutionally insignificant failure to act. Under this reasoning, a condition on benefits becomes a constitutional nonsubsidy rather than an unconstitutional penalty.

But the Court could only characterize the denial of abortion funding as a nonaction by taking as the baseline the lack of funds for any medical decisions. If, on the other hand, one takes as the baseline the government's subsidy for all other medical care *except* abortion, it looks as if "the state is singling out abortion for unfavorable treatment."[112] More broadly, the Court measured government action and inaction against a baseline of the current arrangements of wealth and privilege. The refusal to pay for abortions did not disturb the prevailing conditions of poverty and therefore seemed like no action at all. The fact that many indigent woman could not exercise their reproductive rights and the harm that resulted from this inability seemed irrelevant to the Court's analysis.

SILENCING POOR WOMEN'S DOCTORS

The Supreme Court's decision in *Rust v. Sullivan*,[113] upholding a ban on abortion counseling in federally funded clinics, illustrates the particular perils of this approach for Black women. Congress enacted Title X of the Public Health Service Act in 1970 to give millions of poor and low-income women access to reproductive health services that they otherwise could not afford. In 1988, the HHS (under the Reagan administration) issued regulations that prohibited family-planning clinics receiving Title X funds from informing their patients about abortion. The regulations, which were soon dubbed "the Gag Rule," banned clinics from counseling their pregnant patients about abortion, from referring them to an abortion provider, and even from telling them where this information could be obtained. The regulations also required the clinics to give their pregnant patients a referral list of health care providers that promoted "the welfare of mother and unborn child," but which did not include any health care providers that offered abortion as their principal business. Newly elected President Clinton repealed the regulations on January 22, 1993—the twentieth anniversary of the *Roe v. Wade* decision. But the damage inflicted by the Supreme Court's endorsement could not be erased.

This stifling of medical information endangered the health and lives of low-income women. Under the Hyde Amendment, the federal government already refused to pay the cost of abortion for these women.

Now it was commanding their doctors to hide information about abortion, as well. Doctors could neither tell patients of the availability of abortion, nor discuss the possible risks and benefits. The government's policy was plainly designed to discourage clinic patients from even considering abortion as an alternative. The mandated silence on abortion and referral only to providers not offering abortion threatened to mislead women who had already decided to terminate a pregnancy about the legality and availability of a safe abortion. The limitation on referrals typically left on the list only hospitals and private physicians that were financially and geographically out of patients' reach.

Many women are unaware of their right to an abortion or where to obtain a safe, inexpensive one. They often turn to newspaper ads that steer them in a dangerous direction. Recent newpaper stories reveal horrible accounts of poor women who have suffered botched abortions at the hands of unlicensed doctors practicing in unsafe abortion mills. A clinic operating under the regulations would encourage some pregnant women to believe that abortion was not legal, available, and safe. This obfuscation of services could also mean dangerous delays in the already difficult process of obtaining an abortion.

Moreover, the regulations posed a special threat to women suffering from certain serious medical conditions, such as heart disease, hypertension, diabetes, sickle-cell anemia, and cancer, whose progression might be accelerated by pregnancy. For example, a woman with diabetic retinopathy who becomes pregnant may go blind.[114] The regulations prevented doctors from advising these women that abortion might reduce the long-term risks to their health. The required support of the pregnancy and recommendation of prenatal care would give the false impression that pregnancy did not jeopardize their health. Patients could not possibly have made an informed assessment of the risk that pregnancy posed to their health without information about abortion as well as prenatal care. Indeed, the doctors' ethical obligation of truth-telling required disclosure of this information.

The regulations' impact would have been most dramatic for Black patients. These women are more likely than white women to rely on publicly funded clinics because they are less likely to have private health insurance, sufficient income to pay a private physician, or a continuing doctor-patient relationship.[115] Fewer than half of Black patients visit private doctors; they rely much more than white patients on hospital emergency rooms for health care.[116] Of the nearly 4 million women in 1988 who used a Title X clinic for their last family-planning visit during the previous year, 28 percent were Black.[117] This number represented over half of Black women, compared to less than a third of white women. These figures show not only that a large number of Black women would be denied information, but also that the Black community as a whole would feel the deprivation of health services the most.

The lack of a continuing relationship with a personal physician has a profound impact on Black women's encounters with the medical system. While most middle-class white women can negotiate health services with the help of a personal physician who is socially like them, most Black women must face complicated and impersonal medical institutions on their own. A Haitian woman's explanation of why she discontinued prenatal care at a public hospital illustrates how health care's structure repels many poor Black women:

> My friend say go to doctor and get checked. . . . My friend be on phone much time before they make appointment. They no have space for 30 days. When I go to hospital, it confusing. . . . I go early, and see doctor late in the afternoon. . . . I wait on many long lines and take lots of tests. I no understand why so many tests every time. No one explain nothing. No one talk my language. I be tired, feel sick from hospital. I go three times, but no more. Too much trouble for nothing.[118]

Black women are less likely to be aware of controversies surrounding informed consent, sterilization, and the side effects of contraceptives such as Norplant reported in the newspaper, consumer reports, and health publications.[119] But they know, as their rejection of Norplant shows, when they are being abused.

At the same time, the regulations' medical consequences would be gravest for Black women. Black women more often suffer from the medical conditions aggravated by pregnancy. Black women have higher rates of diabetes, cardiovascular disease, high blood pressure, and cervical cancer. They are also three times more likely to die from complications of pregnancy and childbirth. Although I have emphasized the harm in policies that discourage poor Black women from having babies, these women are also entitled to information about abortion to make a considered decision about whether to carry the pregnancy to term. In addition, Black women are more likely than white women to face barriers to obtaining abortion services such as inability to afford an abortion or to locate a safe abortion provider in their neighborhood. Delays in learning the whereabouts of available abortion services, therefore, can be especially devastating.

Why would lawmakers bent on reducing the birthrate of poor Black women deny these women funding for abortions? Would the legislators enacting family caps not be eager to provide welfare mothers with information about abortions? In fact, why does *my* support for government subsidies for abortion services not contradict my opposition to state-induced birth control? On a theoretical level, family caps and the denial of funding for abortion are not contradictory: both limit indigent women's control over their own bodies by making it more difficult to realize their reproductive decisions. More concretely, these policies work together to achieve a common end that is against the interests of Black women. Faced with the untenable position of having no money either to get an abortion or to raise a child, poor Black women will be pressured into taking drastic steps to avoid childbirth. More and more will turn to long-acting contraceptives and sterilization as a way out. *This* reproductive decision, it is important to note, is fully funded by the government.

Despite these serious risks to patient health and autonomy, a divided Supreme Court concluded that "[t]here is no question but that the statutory prohibition . . . is constitutional."[120] The Court's opinion did not even mention the pain and confusion that women would experience because of the regulations. How did the Court make their suffering invisible? And how could it countenance the purposeful withholding of critical medical information from patients? The Court declined to give special protection to the medical communications at issue because it concluded that the doctor-patient relationship in Title X clinics was not worthy of protection: "[T]he doctor-patient relationship established by the Title X program [is not] sufficiently all-encompassing so as to justify an expectation on the part of the patient of comprehensive medical advice."[121]

In fact, patients should be able to expect their physicians to provide comprehensive advice in the patient's best interests. Disagreeing with the majority's assumption, Justice Harry Blackmun stated that "[a] woman seeking the services of a Title X clinic has every reason to expect, as do we all, that her physician will not withhold relevant information regarding the very purpose of her visit."[122] In addition, the Court wrongly assumed that Title X patients have the ability to seek other medical advice. In fact, these women may encounter numerous obstacles in attempting to obtain reproductive health services elsewhere. Title X clinics are often the only provider of medical services and health information that their patients can afford. This, in turn, is the unfortunate result of a federal policy more interested in making birth control appropriations for poor women than providing them with high-quality health care services.

But more significant is the way the Court minimized the importance of open medical communication in physicians' encounters with these particular patients. Relying on its earlier abortion-funding decisions, the Court reasoned that the regulations were merely a government refusal to subsidize the delivery of abortion information. Because the claimants depended on government aid, their claims became constitutionally irrelevant. Were the regulations a government omission or an affirmative interference in the rights of indigent patients? The patients' lawyers argued that the regulations did constitute government action: "Lured into Title X clinics by the apparent promise of reliable health care, indigent women leave the clinic not merely unenlightened but affirmatively misled."[123] More broadly, the government actively protects the rights of private patients through laws that require medical information, while deliberately promoting ignorance of this same information among poor women.

The Court's distinction between government action and inaction allowed it unabashedly to impose separate standards of justice for the rich and the poor. The Court probably would have applied far stricter scrutiny had the regulations banned abortion advice given in a *private* doctor's office. In upholding the regulations, one federal appellate court explicitly acknowledged this distinction between public and private patients, finding a potential problem with restricting abortion advice given to private patients who used Title X clinics.[124] The Supreme Court thus approved a system of truth-telling for patients who can pay for their care and deception for those who cannot. Just as the Court interpreted reliance on welfare as a waiver of privacy rights, so it interpreted reliance on publicly funded health care as a forfeiture of patient autonomy. The Court did not recognize any injury in violating the autonomy of patients who rely on public clinics, patients who are disproportionately Black women.

WHO SHOULD PAY FOR PROCREATION?

For decades the debate about government funding of reproductive decisionmaking centered on abortion. Now new welfare laws raise the question whether the government is obligated to support the decision to have a child. As Florida Republican Rick Dantzler put it, "Does a man have the right to impregnate a woman, and does that woman have the right to bear a child knowing Uncle Sam will pick up all the responsibility? Do they have the constitutional right to do that and make us pay for it?"[125] A New Jersey federal judge has answered No.

In 1994, several New Jersey welfare recipients filed a federal class action lawsuit against HHS, challenging its waiver to New Jersey authorizing implementation of the Family Development Act.[126] Although it was the Bush administration that granted the waiver, the Clinton administration had replaced its Republican predecessor as the courtroom adversary of the reproductive rights movement. The plaintiffs claimed that the waiver violated several federal regulations governing the administrative process and experiments involving human subjects. The HHS action also infringed their constitutional rights to equal protection and due process, the plaintiffs contended. Two of the plaintiffs had become pregnant as a result of rape and decided to have the baby anyway. One was a mother of two when she gave birth to triplets, and was now trying to raise five children on the same monthly check. Another, a Roman Catholic, felt the family cap pressured her to have an abortion in violation of her religious beliefs.

The plaintiffs were represented by a coterie of public interest organizations—New Jersey Legal Services, NOW Legal Defense and Education Fund, the New Jersey ACLU—as well as a prestigious Newark law firm known for its pro bono assistance. Dozens of other women's and civil rights groups joined the cause as *amici curiae*. On the other side of the political spectrum, several right-to-life groups also opposed the child exclusion out of concern that it would pressure women on welfare to get abortions. The Clinton administration responded that its waiver grant reflected a reasoned judgment that the New Jersey reforms were likely to promote the objective of AFDC—"breaking the cycle of poverty for AFDC recipients, enhancing their individual responsibility, and strengthening their family structure."[127]

Judge Nicholas H. Politan was very receptive to New Jersey's experiment at reforming the state's welfare system. In a May 1995 decision, *C.K. v. Shalala*, he dismissed the plaintiffs' complaint that the HHS waiver process was too hasty, worrying that adding "another layer of bureaucracy" would "prolong further the stranglehold of welfare dependency" and "dissuade states from even attempting innovative welfare reform." The judge was willing to sacrifice devotion to administrative protections of welfare recipients for the sake of encouraging welfare reform. "The court will not impose a burden upon the secretary to expend her department's finite resources simply to dot every 'i' and cross every 't' with respect to good-faith efforts at reform, especially when the nation is crying out for welfare alternatives which genuinely promote economic self-sufficiency," Politan stated.[128]

Politan also rejected the plaintiffs' contention that the family cap violated the Social Security Act by denying benefits to eligible children. Politan found that additional children were not *excluded* from receiving benefits; they simply had to *share* in the cash grant allotted to their households. Since AFDC eligibility has always been premised on the household as the basic unit of assistance and since there is no set minimum benefit required per household, the New Jersey law did not run afoul of federal mandates.

Judge Politan was no more solicitous of the plaintiffs' constitutional challenges. The court turned to Supreme Court precedent, which had dealt with a different sort of family cap on welfare benefits in a 1970 case. *Dandridge v. Williams* involved a Maryland regulation that placed an absolute ceiling of $250 monthly on each family, regardless of the family's size or financial need.[129] Familes with six children received the same amount as families with only three children. Recipients argued that this scheme violated the equal protection rights of younger children, who received less of the pie than older children, and the rights of children in larger families, who received lower per capita payments than children in smaller families.

Because Maryland had no duty to provide public assistance, let alone a particular level of welfare payments, the Court held that its plan was an economic regulation subject to minimal judicial scrutiny. All that the state was required to show was a rational basis for the benefits cap. The Court found that the state's interest in encouraging employment was a sufficiently rational reason to defeat recipients' equal protection challenge. The Court rejected the objection that some families had no employable member on the grounds that "the Equal Protection Clause does not require that a state must choose between attacking every aspect of a problem or not attacking the problem at all."[130] The Court did not consider whether the Maryland law violated recipients' right to reproductive liberty, and, because its decision came before *Roe v. Wade*, it is hard to tell how it might have ruled on this issue.

The New Jersey plaintiffs argued, however, that no legitimate state interest supported the family cap, because it "penalizes vulnerable and needy children for their parents' behavior over which they have no control: the circumstances of their birth." In a number of cases, the

Supreme Court had held that blameless children could not be denied public education and other benefits because of their parents' misconduct, such as being illegal immigrants or having children out of wedlock.[131] Judge Politan failed to see how the family cap punished children for their parents' behavior, however. Instead, he reiterated that the New Jersey provision "merely imposes a ceiling on the benefits accorded an AFDC household." But Politan was plainly wrong: the provision denies the new birth increase on the basis of the mother's AFDC status alone; it does not impose a maximum grant level on families. This distinction separates the New Jersey child exclusion from the Maryland family cap at issue in *Dandridge*.

Politan went on to find that the "ceiling" was justified by the state's legitimate interest in promoting individual responsibility and stabilizing family structure. He bought the argument that, far from imposing any unfairness on welfare recipients, the family cap simply "puts the welfare household in the same situation as that of a working family, which does not automatically receive a wage increase every time it produces another child."[132]

Because Politan did not see the cap as a penalty, he did not follow the plaintiffs' argument that it violated recipients' procreative rights. Quoting *Harris v. McCrae* and *Rust v. Sullivan*, the court pointed out that New Jersey was under no obligation to fund its citizens' reproductive decisions. Besides, the plaintiffs were better off with the family cap than they would be if New Jersey decided to eliminate its AFDC program altogether (which it was constitutionally permitted to do). He therefore dismissed the recipients' lawsuit with prejudice.

Was Judge Politan correct that the abortion-funding decisions validate family caps?

Family caps certainly raise an unconstitutional conditions problem. Suppose New Jersey passed a law providing that women receiving welfare would be fined $500 or sentenced to six months in jail for each additional child that they had. Few would dispute that this law would be unconstitutional. Yet child exclusion laws achieve the same effect by denying the standard new birth benefits to families on welfare. As a result, welfare mothers who have another child receive less aid per child than before the child was born. Family caps reduce welfare benefits needed for survival to penalize protected reproductive decisions the government disapproves. By discouraging childbirth through welfare benefits schemes, then, the government is doing indirectly what it could not do directly.

Additionally, family caps only inflict this penalty for childbearing on welfare recipients. These laws only exclude children born or conceived while their families are on welfare; families get full benefits for children they already have when they join the welfare rolls. What is more, child exclusions impose an absolute restriction no matter how few children a welfare mother has. So, a welfare mother who already has one child will be denied benefits for a sole additional child, while a family with five children newly entering welfare will get benefits for all of them. What is discouraged, then, is not having too many children, but having any children at all while on welfare.

The Supreme Court rejected the unconstitutional conditions approach to the government's refusal to pay for abortions. Can child exclusion laws be distinguished from the government's failure to fund abortions? They can on several grounds. Because I believe that the abortion-funding cases were wrongly decided, I am reluctant to lay out this argument. It entails the danger of minimizing the harm inflicted by the denial of abortion subsidies to make the harm of family caps seem greater. I take the position that the denial of abortion funding and family caps are *both* impermissible government manipulations of poor women's reproductive decisionmaking. But distinguishing the two might be necessary to convince the Supreme Court that family caps are unconstitutional. It is important to give the Court a hook on which to hang its decision should it be moved by the suffering that family caps are sure to inflict on poor children.

First, the government's professed interests supporting the two laws are entirely different; indeed, they are contradictory. While the Court approved the government's denial of abortion funding designed to *encourage* childbirth, it has never agreed that the government has an interest in *discouraging* childbirth. In its most recent abortion-rights decision, *Planned Parenthood v. Casey*, the Court stated that a state may not "restrict a woman's right . . . to carry a pregnancy to term . . . to further state interests in population control."[133] Abortion politics weakens support for family caps. As shown by right-to-life groups' participation in the litigation opposing the New Jersey law, family caps do not have the support of many people who favor denial of abortion funding.[134] Of course, there are many more conservatives, like Newt Gingrich and Phil Gramm, who oppose government assistance for both reproductive decisions.

Second, it is harder to characterize the government's denial of the new birth benefit as inaction.[135] While the government stays out of the business of subsidizing abortions so that it may encourage childbirth, states continue to pay AFDC benefits to millions of families. Given this baseline of welfare funding, the refusal to pay the increment for disfavored births alone looks much more like government action. Seeing family caps as an affirmative intrusion in a welfare mother's decision to have children triggers heightened judicial scrutiny of these laws, dramatically increasing the chances that they will be struck down.

Washington University law professor Susan Frelich Appleton predicts, however, that the Court is unlikely to reach this conclusion, given its reluctance to apply strict scrutiny to anything less than reproductive restrictions enforced by criminal punishment or civil sanctions.[136] She proposes a middle ground in the undue-burden test, formulated in *Casey*, that asks whether the law's purpose or effect "places a substantial obstacle in the path" of reproductive choice. This is not hard to prove: lawmakers freely boast that family caps are designed to reduce the birthrate of welfare mothers.

Finally, the penalty imposed by family caps for the exercise of reproductive rights is arguably more burdensome than that imposed by abortion funding laws. *Maher* and *McRae* upheld the government's refusal to pay the medical costs of a single act of abortion. Family caps, on the other hand, disqualify a child from subsistence benefits needed indefinitely for food, clothing, and shelter. This is not to say that compelling a woman to carry an unwanted pregnancy to term is not oppressive. This is a life-changing experience that often has devastating consequences. It restricts women's abilities to control their own bodies and their life prospects. Nevertheless, it is easier for an indigent woman to come up with the money for an abortion than for an indigent family to support a child for years. The penalty is more burdensome in another respect: while the denial of abortion funding hurts the women whose reproductive decisions are at stake, family caps harm not only women but their children as well.

Judge Politan was completely oblivious to these consequences for poor families. He blithely dismissed the struggle welfare mothers would face trying to care for a new child on the same meager grant, stating that the cap "simply requires her to find a way to pay for her progeny's care." And he seemed to think this feat would be no more difficult for a family living in poverty than for middle-class households. "This is not discrimination," Politan asserted. "Rather this is the reality known to so many working families who provide for their children without any expectation of outside assistance."[137]

Like Judge Politan, many legislators and their constituents will have a hard time seeing family caps and other laws discouraging pro-

creation as penalizing women on welfare for exercising their reproductive rights. In their minds the proposals do not charge poor
women for having children; they simply decline to subsidize the activity. Although these measures impose a deterrent to childbearing that
wealthier people do not face, their proponents see them as replacing
the constraints on poor women's reproductive decisions that would
exist but for the state's generosity.

The response to an unconstitutional conditions argument is likely
to be, "Sure, poor women have a right to make reproductive decisions, but why should government have to pay for them?" Roland
Corning, the author of the South Carolina bill mandating Norplant
insertion, expressed this sentiment on national television when he declared, "They can have all the children they want. They just have to
pay for them."[138] He added that his bill, if enacted, would save taxpayers in his state $36 million in welfare and medical costs in the first
year. Never mind that an indigent or even low-paid woman cannot
support her children. That is the point: she should take steps to guarantee that she does not become pregnant. And bills like Corning's
would provide the means.

Welfare rights advocates, then, will find it difficult to explain why,
if the state has no affirmative obligation to subsidize citizens' activities
at all, taxpayers are nevertheless required to support a poor woman's
decision to have a baby. This predicament arises from the unchal-
lenged assumption that the ability to exercise our constitutional rights
should depend on our wealth. Although welfare reformers avoid saying it, their policies effectively impose a rule that poor people should
not have children. If the government were required to subsidize citizens' reproductive decisions, and if reliance on public assistance
therefore did not constitute a waiver of privacy, there would be no
place for a special doctrine to prohibit government conditions that
pressure these constitutionally protected decisions. An affirmative
claim to public assistance for reproductive decisions is, of course, in-
comprehensible under current constitutional doctrine because of the
barrier it has erected between government action and inaction. Claiming government assistance, then, requires challenging this wall of constitutional thinking.

It also requires confronting Americans' particular resentment at
paying for poor women's reproductive decisions. The government already confiscates citizens' property in the form of taxes for a variety
of purposes. Tax money even goes to many redistributive programs,
such as Social Security, farm subsidies, and corporate bailouts. But

taxpayers reserve a special condemnation for welfare that redistributes income to the poor—especially to support their children.

RACE AND THE LIMITS OF SOCIAL REFORM

Why do Americans cling to the myths that welfare breeds irresponsible childbirth, perpetuates poverty, and encourages dependency? Why have Americans disdained basic protections, such as national health insurance, family allowances, and paid parental leave, that citizens of other industrialized nations take for granted? Why do Americans prefer a stingy welfare system that leaves millions of children living in wretched conditions below the poverty line? The common explanation traces the American rejection of social legislation to liberal culture that values individualism, reveres private property, and distrusts government power. Gaston Rimlinger, for example, argued that support for national welfare programs was weaker in America than in Europe because "in the United States the commitment to individualism—to individual achievement and self-help—was much stronger. . . . The survival of the liberal tradition, therefore, was . . . stronger and the resistance to social protection more tenacious."[139]

Pointing to liberal culture is too easy an explanation, however. Jill Quadagno questions this prevailing theory of Americans' hostility to welfare:

> The problem with explaining welfare state development in terms of liberal values is that Americans have tolerated major exceptions to that antigovernment ethos—notably an extensive Civil War pension system in the nineteenth century, numerous state-level welfare programs in the "Progressive Era" and the 1920s, and the persistent and ardent efforts by voluntary associations to win both public and private benefits. If Americans are ideologically opposed to state intervention, then why have so many worked so steadfastly toward this end?[140]

America's inadequate welfare system stems less from noble liberal ideals than from a racist unwillingness to include Blacks as full citizens. White Americans have been perfectly willing to adopt "universal" social insurance programs as long as Blacks were formally or effectively excluded from participation. New Deal reformers could promote Social Security as a universal program designed to benefit all classes only by first disqualifying Black workers. Today welfare programs such as AFDC that have increasingly become associated with Black mothers and their children are vilified and being dismantled. White Americans have resisted paying for subsidies perceived to benefit primarily Blacks.

Privileged racial identity gives whites a powerful incentive to leave the existing social order intact. Many white Americans remain uninterested in advancing the welfare of Black Americans; many others see helping everyone as contrary to their self-interest because they perceive Black people's social position in opposition to their own. Under American racist ideology, welfare programs that benefit Blacks are antithetical to white interests because Blacks' social advancement diminishes white superiority. White Americans therefore have been unwilling to create social programs that will facilitate Blacks' full citizenship and economic well-being, *even when those programs would benefit whites*.

Race has proven to be a barrier to social reform in America. As economist Robert Heilbroner noted, the "merging of the racial issue with that of [social] neglect serves as a rationalization for the policies of inaction that have characterized so much of the American response to need."[141] Even white workers' and feminist movements have compromised their most radical dreams in order to strike political bargains that sacrifice the rights of Blacks. W. E. B. Du Bois explained white resistance to labor and education reform during Reconstruction by the fact that poor and laboring whites preferred to be compensated by the "public and psychological wage" of racial superiority.[142] Legal scholar Derrick Bell has similarly argued that whites in America— even those who lack wealth and power—believe that they gain from continued economic disparities that leave Blacks at the bottom. In his most recent exposition of this thesis, Bell dismally concludes, "Black people will never gain full equality in this country."[143]

The constraining impact of racism was brought home in a *New York Times* photograph of a poor white woman in Louisiana taken shortly after the former KKK Grand Wizard David Duke lost the election for governor.[144] Duke had campaigned on a pledge to reduce the numbers of Blacks on welfare by cutting benefits and by offering female recipients a monetary bonus to use Norplant. In the caption beneath the photograph the woman explained that, although she relied on welfare herself, she voted for Duke because Blacks "just have those babies and go on welfare." This woman was willing to decimate programs that benefitted her in order to ensure that Black people could not benefit from them.

This is the dilemma Black citizenship poses for radical welfare reform: While a strong welfare state is required to make Blacks full participants in the political economy, whites' refusal to extend full citizenship rights to Blacks persistently blocks efforts to establish an inclusive welfare system. On the one hand, racial justice demands aggressive government programs to relieve poverty and redress longstanding barriers to housing, jobs, and political participation. Yet white Americans have resisted the expansion of welfare precisely because of its benefits to Blacks. Harold Cruse's words in 1968 still ring true today: "White America has inherited a racial crisis that it cannot handle and is unable to create a solution for it that does not do violence to the collective white American racial ego." [145] Black citizenship is at once America's chief reason for and impediment to a strong welfare state.

With the passage of the new welfare law, America has once again sacrificed Black people as its way out of the dilemma. But this renunciation is even more insidious than those of the past. For this brand of welfare reform does not simply exclude Black women; it penalizes their reproduction. The law not only cuts off Black children from benefits needed to survive but it blames their very birth for their disadvantaged status.

Racial injustice, then, has had a profound impact on our conception of welfare: beyond denying Blacks benefits to which whites were entitled, it limited the meaning of liberty for all Americans. Racism has created a welfare system in America that throws poor children of all races deeper into poverty and ultimately worsens the living conditions of all Americans. Racism has created a notion of social accountability that leaves poor people to fend for themselves and conditions any government charity on forfeiture of personal liberties. Part of this constrained meaning of liberty is the view that reproductive freedom depends on wealth and social status. As I discuss in my concluding chapter, just as racism has impaired our understanding of reproductive liberty, attention to race can also help us to redefine reproductive liberty in a way that accounts for its importance to human dignity and equality.

6

RACE AND THE NEW REPRODUCTION

A friend of mine recently questioned my interest in a custody battle covered on the evening news. A surrogate mother who had agreed to gestate a fetus for a fee decided she wanted to keep the baby. "Why are you always so fascinated by those stories?" he asked. "They have nothing to do with Black people." By "those stories" he meant the growing number of controversies occupying the headlines that involve children created by new methods of reproduction. More and more Americans are using a variety of technologies to facilitate conception, ranging from simple artificial insemination to expensive, advanced procedures such as *in vitro* fertilization (IVF) and egg donation.[1]

In one sense my friend is right: the images that mark these controversies appear to have little to do with Black people and issues of race. Think about the snapshots that promote the new reproduction. They always show white people. And the baby produced often has blond hair and blue eyes—as if to emphasize her racial purity. The infertile suburban housewife's agonizing attempts to become pregnant via IVF; the rosy-cheeked baby held up to television cameras as the precious product of a surrogacy arrangement; the complaint that there are not enough babies for all the middle-class couples who desperately want to adopt; the fate of orphaned frozen embryos whose wealthy progenitors died in an airplane crash: all seem far removed from most Black people's lives. Yet it is precisely their racial subtext that gives these images much of their emotional appeal.

Ultimately, my attraction to these stories stems from my interest in the devaluation of *Black* reproduction. As I have charted the proliferation of rhetoric and policies that degrade Black women's procreative decisions, I have also noticed that America is obsessed with creating and preserving genetic ties between white parents and their children.

This chapter explores the reasons for the racial disparity that marks the new reproduction, as well as the impact of race on the right to create children by technological means.

LIBERATING TECHNOLOGY OR PATRIARCHAL TOOL?

New means of procreating are often heralded by legal scholars and social commentators as inherently progressive and liberating. In this view, reproduction-assisting technologies expand the procreative options open to individuals and therefore enhance human freedom. These innovations give new hope to infertile couples previously resigned to the painful fate of childlessness. In addition, the new reproduction creates novel family arrangements that break the mold of the traditional nuclear family. A child may now have five parents: a genetic mother and father who contribute egg and sperm, a gestational mother who carries the implanted embryo, and a contracting mother and father who intend to raise the child.[2] One of the new reproduction's most influential proponents, John Robertson, opens his book *Children of Choice* by proclaiming that these "powerful new technologies" free us from the ancient subjugation to "the luck of the natural lottery" and "are challenging basic notions about procreation, parenthood, family, and children."[3]

New reproductive technologies promise to fulfill couples' yearning to have genetically related children. They also make it possible to use new genetic knowledge to create children with superior traits. Pregnant women may choose to abort a fetus determined, through amniocentesis, ultrasonography, or other diagnostic techniques, to have a genetic defect. Sperm and egg donation allows parents to select gametes from donors who possess favored qualities. With IVF (fertilization of the egg in a petri dish followed by transfer to the uterus), parents can screen test-tube embryos for defects before implantation—"nipping it in the embryo," as a newspaper headline proclaimed. In the future, doctors will be able to tinker with genes contained in the embryo to enhance their encoded messages or remedy genetic disorders.[4]

My impression of these technologies, however, is that they are more conforming than liberating: they more often reinforce the status quo than challenge it. True, these technologies often free unconventional parents from the constraints of social custom and legal stipulations. They have helped single women, lesbians, and gay men whom society regards as unqualified to raise children to circumvent legal barriers to parenthood.[5] Informal surrogacy arrangements between women, for example, may provide a means of self-help for women who wish to have children independently of men; and they require no government approval, medical intervention, or even sexual intercourse.[6] Under this arrangement, a fertile woman would informally promise an infertile woman who wants a child to impregnate herself with a donor's sperm and to give the baby to the infertile woman for adoption.

But these technologies rarely achieve their subversive potential. Most often they complete a traditional nuclear family by providing a married couple with a child.[7] Instead of disrupting the stereotypical family, they enable infertile couples to create one. Most IVF clinics accept only heterosexual married couples as clients, and most physicians have been unwilling to assist in the insemination of women who depart from this norm.[8] They routinely deny their services to single women, lesbians, welfare recipients, and other women who are not considered good mothers.[9]

The new reproduction's conservative function is often imposed by courts and legislatures. Laws regulating artificial insemination contemplate use by a married woman and recognition of her husband as the child's father, and recent state statutes requiring insurance coverage of IVF procedures apply only when a wife's eggs are fertilized using her husband's sperm. On the other hand, courts have been willing to grant parental rights to sperm donors against the mother's wishes "when no other man is playing the role of father for the child," such as when the mother is a lesbian or unmarried.[10]

Radical feminists have powerfully demonstrated that the new reproduction enforces traditional patriarchal roles that privilege men's genetic desires and objectify women's procreative capacity.[11] They make a convincing case that new reproductive technologies serve more to help married men produce genetic offspring than to give women greater reproductive freedom. High-tech procedures resolve the male anxiety over ascertaining paternity: by uniting the egg and sperm outside the uterus, they "[allow] men, for the first time in history, to be absolutely certain that they are the genetic fathers of their future children."[12] Some feminists have questioned the forces that drive so many women to endure the physical and emotional trauma entailed in IVF.[13] The arduous process involves stimulating ovulation with daily hormone injections, retrieving the eggs from the ovaries, and inserting the fertilized embryos into the uterus, usually followed by heartbreaking disappointment. In extreme cases, IVF has caused long-term, and even lethal, harm to women's reproductive organs, such as the growth of ovarian cysts.

The desire to bear children is influenced by the stigma of infertility and the expectation that all women will become mothers. Added to this is the desire to produce a genetically related child. Despite very low rates of live births resulting from IVF (on average, only about 20 percent),[14] some women feel a "duty" to undergo the ordeal before they give up on the possibility of genetic parenthood.[15] But many women who undergo IVF are themselves physiologically *fertile*, although their husbands are not.[16] These women could therefore become pregnant using a much safer and cheaper process—artificial insemination, for example. Underlying women's desire to undergo IVF, then, is often their husbands' insistence on having a genetic inheritance. Because this technology inflicts so much distress on women's bodies for the benefit of men, feminist author Janice Raymond calls it a form of "medical violence" against women.[17]

Surrogacy also fulfills the father's desire to pass his own genes on to a child. In the typical arrangement, a man whose wife is infertile hires a fertile woman, or surrogate, to bear a child for the couple. The surrogate is impregnated with the husband's sperm and carries the fetus to term. She agrees to relinquish parental rights to the child, whom the wife subsequently adopts. The surrogate's service, then, allows the husband to have a child who is genetically related to him, despite his wife's infertility. William Stern, the contracting father in the well-publicized *Baby M* case, explained that, as the only survivor of a family that had been annihilated in the Holocaust, he wanted a genetically related child in order to perpetuate his family's bloodline.[18] "The desirability of having his own biological offspring became compelling to William Stern, thus making adoption a less desirable alternative," the New Jersey trial judge acknowledged in upholding the surrogacy contract.[19]

Surrogacy arrangements devalue the mother's biological relationship to the child in order to exalt the father's. Harvard law professor Martha Field points out that the very term "surrogate" emphasizes the arrangement's purpose—allowing a man to be a genetic father rather than enabling a woman to become a mother: "The woman is a 'surrogate'—a surrogate uterus or a surrogate wife—to carry his genes."[20] Most surrogate mothers intentionally donate their genetic material, as well as their wombs, to bear a child who will not be legally theirs. Not surprisingly, then, most of the money the surrogate

receives pays for the surrender of her parental rights—her legal claim
to the child arising from their biological bond. The contract Baby M's
mother signed provided: "$10,000 shall be paid to MARY BETH
WHITEHEAD, Surrogate, *upon surrender of custody* to WILLIAM STERN,
the natural and biological father of the child born pursuant to the provisions of this agreement. . . ."[21] Whitehead would have received only
$1,000 for her services if she had delivered a stillborn child.

In custody disputes that arise when the surrogate mother refuses to
relinquish the baby, enforcing the contract would mean denying her
genetic claim to legal maternity. Yet surrogacy advocates contend that
holding surrogates to their bargain is necessary to protect contracting
couples' interests and to ensure the viability of the practice. John
Robertson even argues that procreative liberty includes a constitutional right to state enforcement of surrogacy agreements.[22] Even
judges who refuse to enforce surrogacy contracts, and base custody
instead on the best interests of the child, tend to grant custody to the
contracting couple in part because of their class advantages.[23] The
high court in the *Baby M* case, for example, awarded the Sterns joint
custody of Melissa largely because of the couple's financial security
and ability to provide the child with such luxuries as piano lessons.
Meanwhile a parade of expert witnesses disparaged Whitehead's fitness as a mother based on her "myopic" and "narcissistic" efforts to
get Melissa back.

The law should favor gestational mothers who decide they want to
keep the baby, not because the mother's genetic tie is more important
than the father's but because the mother has already established a relationship with the baby. Instead, surrogate mothers are valued for
their service to the biological father—facilitating his more important
genetic connection to the child.

HOW RACE SHAPES THE NEW REPRODUCTION

While acknowledging that poor women of color are the most vulnerable to reproductive control, the feminist critique identifies male
domination as the central source of the oppressive use of reproduction-assisting technologies. But these technologies reflect and reinforce a racist standard for procreation, as well. Similar to technologies
that *prevent* births, the politics of technologies that *assist* births is
shaped by race.

One of the most striking features of the new reproduction is that it is used almost exclusively by white people. Of course, the busiest fertility clinics can point to some Black middle-class patients; but they stand out as rare exceptions. Only about one-third of all couples experiencing infertility seek medical treatment at all; and only 10 to 15 percent of infertile couples seeking treatment use advanced techniques like IVF.[24] Blacks make up a disproportionate number of infertile people *avoiding* reproductive technologies. White women seeking treatment for fertility problems are twice as likely to use high-tech treatments as Black women.[25] Only 12.8 percent of Black women in the latest national survey used specialized infertility services such as fertility drugs, artificial insemination, tubal surgery, or IVF, compared with 27.2 percent of white women.

As my story that opened this chapter reflects, media images of the new reproduction mirror this racial disparity. Most of the news stories proclaiming the benefits of the technology involve infertile white couples. When the 1986 *Baby M* trial propelled the issue of surrogacy to national attention, major magazines and newspapers were plastered with photos of the parties (all white) battling for custody of Melissa.

Ten years later, in January 1996, the *New York Times* launched a prominent four-article series called "The Fertility Market." The front page displayed a photograph of the director of a fertility clinic surrounded by seven white children conceived there. The continuing page contained a picture of a set of beaming IVF triplets, also white.[26]

The following June, *Newsweek* ran a cover story entitled "The Biology of Beauty" reporting scientific confirmation of human beings' inherent obsession with beauty.[27] The article featured a striking full-page color spread of a woman with blond hair and blue eyes. The caption asked rhetorically: "Reproductive fitness: Would you want your children to carry this person's genes?" The answer, presumably, was supposed to be a resounding, universal "Yes!"

When we do read news accounts involving Black children created by these technologies, they are usually sensational stories intended to evoke revulsion precisely because of the children's race. Several years ago a white woman brought a highly publicized lawsuit against a fertility clinic she claimed had mistakenly inseminated her with a Black man's sperm, instead of her husband's, resulting in the birth of a Black child.[28] The woman, who was the child's biological mother, demanded monetary damages for her injury, which she explained was due to the unbearable racial taunting her daughter suffered. Two reporters covering the story speculated that "[i]f the suit goes to trial, a

jury could be faced with the difficult task of deciding damages involved in raising an interracial child."[29] Although receiving the wrong
sperm was an injury in itself, the fact that it came from someone of the
wrong race added a unique dimension of harm to the error. This second harm to the mother was the fertility clinic's failure to deliver a
crucial part of its service—a white child.

In a similar, but more bizarre, incident in The Netherlands in 1995,
a woman who gave birth to twin boys as a result of IVF realized when
the babies were two months old that one was white and one was
Black.[30] The Dutch fertility clinic mistakenly fertilized her eggs with
sperm from both her husband and a Black man. A *Newsweek* article
subtitled "A Fertility Clinic's Startling Error" reported that "while
one boy was as blond as his parents, the other's skin was darkening
and his brown hair was fuzzy."[31] A large color photograph displayed
the two infant twins, one white and one Black, sitting side by side—a
racial intermingling that would not occur in nature. The image presented a new-age freak show, created by modern technology gone
berserk.

The stories exhibiting blond-haired blue-eyed babies born to white
parents portray the positive potential of the new reproduction. The
stories involving the mixed-race children reveal its potential horror.

REASONS FOR THE DISPARITY

These images, along with the predominant use of fertility services by
white couples, indisputably show that race affects the popularity of
reproductive technologies in America. What are the reasons underlying this connection between race and the new reproduction?

First, it has nothing to do with rates of infertility. Blacks have an
infertility rate one and one-half times *higher* than that of whites.[32] (The
racial disparity may actually be greater due to underreporting of infertility by married Black women.) While the overall infertility rate in
America was declining, the infertility rate of young Black women
tripled between 1965 and 1982.[33] The reasons for the high incidence
of infertility among Black women include untreated chlamydia and
gonorrhea, STDs that can lead to pelvic inflammatory disease; nutri-
tional deficiencies; complications of childbirth and abortion; and environmental and workplace hazards.

In fact, the profile of people most likely to use IVF is precisely the
opposite of those most likely to be infertile. The people in the United

States most likely to be infertile are poor, Black, and poorly educated.[34] Most couples who use IVF and other high-tech procedures are white, highly educated, and affluent.

Besides, the new reproduction has far more to do with enabling people to have children who are genetically related to them than with helping infertile people to have children.[35] *Baby M* and other well-known surrogacy cases involved fertile white men with an infertile wife who hired a surrogate so they could pass on their own genes to a child. Moreover, as many as half of the women who undergo IVF are themselves fertile, although their husbands are not. Both scenarios involve *fertile* people who use new reproductive technologies to create genetic offspring. In short, use of high-tech fertility treatment does not depend on the physical incapacity to produce a child.

Instead, the racial disparity appears to stem from a complex interplay of financial barriers, cultural preferences, and more deliberate professional manipulation.

Economic Barriers

The high cost of high-tech procedures places them out of most Black people's reach. The median cost of one IVF cycle is about $8,000; and, owing to low success rates, many patients try several times before having a baby or giving up. Using donor eggs makes the procedure even more expensive — $10,000 to $20,000 for each attempt. (Ironically, eggs from Black donors may be the most costly because they are so scarce.) Most medical insurance plans do not cover IVF, nor is it included in Medicaid benefits. Medicaid, moreover, will not reimburse the full cost of covered infertility services, making most private physicians unwilling to serve Medicaid recipients. Half of the specialized fertility centers surveyed by the Alan Guttmacher Institute refused patients on Medicaid.[36]

Between 1985 and 1991, ten states passed laws requiring insurance coverage of infertility services, eight of which included IVF.[37] But the trend toward mandatory inclusion seems to have come to a halt. Of course, these provisions do not assist the millions of uninsured Americans whose incomes fall barely above the Medicaid level, a group that is disproportionately Black. Without some form of subsidy, only a tiny minority of Black Americans have the means to pay for these expensive procedures.

The government could increase Black people's access to new reproductive technologies by expanding public funding. "Although black couples are *twice* as likely as white couples to be infertile," bioethicist George Annas has noted, IVF is "not promoted for black couples, nor has anyone openly advocated covering the procedure by Medicaid for poor infertile couples."[38] To the contrary, state lawmakers have recently begun eliminating state subsidies for any fertility service in an effort to lower costs and keep poor women from having more children. In the last few years, at least eight states have prohibited Medicaid coverage for fertility drugs and therapies in response to taxpayer protest against paying these costs.[39] A bill introduced in New York in 1994 also proposed excluding reimbursement for the reversal of a tubal ligation.

Treating infertility at public expense, critics assert, conflicts with the ongoing campaign to reduce the numbers of children born on welfare. They are right: it does not make sense for a state to provide a poor woman fertility treatment only to deny her benefits to care for the child. Even liberal senator Ted Kennedy (the ninth child of the Kennedy family, columnist Ellen Goodman reminds us) voted to rescind government aid for fertility drugs.[40] "Our goal in using tax dollars wisely is to reduce welfare dependency, not create more of it," he asserted. Under present constitutional doctrine, the government has no obligation to provide fertility services to those who cannot afford them.

High-tech approaches such as IVF require not only huge sums of money, but also a privileged lifestyle that permits devotion to the rigorous process of daily hormone shots, ultrasound examinations, blood tests, egg extraction and implantation, travel to and from a fertility clinic, and often multiple attempts—a luxury that few Black people enjoy. As Dr. O'Delle Owens, a Black fertility specialist in Cincinnati, explained, "For White couples, infertility is often the first roadblock they've faced—while Blacks are distracted by such primary roadblocks as food, shelter, and clothing."[41] Black people's lack of access to fertility services is also an extension of their more general marginalization from the health care system.

Racial Steering

There is some evidence that fertility doctors and clinics deliberately steer Black patients away from reproductive technologies. Physicians import their social views into the clinical setting and may feel that fertility treatment is inappropriate for Black women who they think are unable to care for their children. As a genetic counselor confessed to anthropologist Rayna Rapp, "It is often hard for a counselor to be value-free. Oh, I know I'm supposed to be value-free, but when I see a welfare mother having a third baby with a man who is not gonna support her, and the fetus has sickle-cell anemia, it's hard not to steer her toward an abortion. What does she need this added problem for, I'm thinking."[42] Georgetown law professor Patricia King similarly concludes that the racial disparity in the use of clinical genetic services may be related to physician referrals.[43]

But racial steering is more likely to occur on a less conscious level. It is frequently dressed up in medical garb. The very diagnosis of infertility depends on social factors. To begin with, the definition of infertility—the inability of a couple to conceive after twelve months of unprotected intercourse—is a social determination as much as a physiological condition. In some cultures, the meaning of infertility involves a woman's failure to bear sons. Courts are split on the issue of whether infertility qualifies as an illness and disability for purposes of coverage under insurance policies and the Americans with Disabilities Act of 1990.

Second, doctors' diagnoses of the cause of infertility often depend on race. Doctors characterize endometriosis, the abnormal growth of uterine tissue outside the uterus, which can cause infertility, as a white, "career woman's disease." Endometriosis is commonly treated as part of infertility therapies. Although epidemiologists find no higher incidence of the ailment in this group of women, many gynecologists insist on associating endometriosis with a middle-class, professional lifestyle. Niels Lauersen, a New York Medical College obstetrics professor, seemed to blame the victim when he claimed the disease strikes women who are "intelligent, living with stress [and] determined to succeed at a role other than 'mother' early in life."[44]

The flip side of this attribution is doctors' view that Black women are unlikely to suffer from endometriosis. According to Dr. Donald Chatman, "most textbooks of gynecology are in agreement that endometriosis is rare in the indigent, nonprivate patient and, therefore, by inference . . . uncommon in the black woman."[45] Instead, gynecologists are more likely to diagnose Black women as having pelvic inflammatory disease, which they often treat with sterilization. In 1976, Dr. Chatman found that over 20 percent of his Black patients who had been diagnosed as having pelvic inflammatory disease actually suffered from endometriosis.[46] Calling endometriosis the "career woman's disease" has a dual effect. It stigmatizes white women's careerism for causing infertility (that can be treated with new reproductive technologies) and it excludes Black women, who are less likely to be professionals, from the class of women whose infertility is treatable.

Socioeconomic screening criteria not based specifically on race exclude Black women, as well. Prospective IVF patients must pass eligibility tests that include such nonmedical factors as "a 'stable' marriage, sufficient education to comply with treatment regimens, and the financial resources to provide 'adequately' for a child."[47] All of these criteria tend to eliminate Blacks.

For example, since most Black children in America today are born to single mothers, a rule requiring clients to be married works disproportionately against Black women desiring to become mothers. One IVF clinic addresses the high cost of treatment by offering an egg donor program that waives the fee for patients willing to share half of their eggs with another woman.[48] The egg recipient in the program also pays less by forgoing the $2,000 to $3,000 cost for an egg donor. I cannot imagine that this program would help many Black patients, since it is unlikely that the predominantly white clientele would be interested in donations of *their* eggs.

The Sickle-Cell Screening Disaster

In fact, where new reproductive technologies have been directed toward Blacks, they have been used to restrict procreative freedom, not increase it. The history of sickle-cell screening and reproductive counseling for Blacks is a telling example. Sickle-cell anemia, a painful and disabling blood disease, is a recessive inherited condition that disproportionately affects Blacks, as well as several other ethnic groups. Only children who receive copies of the affected gene from both parents will have sickle-cell *disease*; carriers of only one copy of the gene (called sickle-cell *trait*) exhibit no symptoms at all. Having sickle-cell trait confers resistance to malaria, a notable benefit to people native to equatorial Africa, where the gene is most prevalent. While 1 in 10 Black Americans is a carrier for sickle-cell trait, only 1 in 500,000 has two copies of the sickle-cell gene and is therefore likely to develop symptoms of sickle-cell anemia.[49] A blood test that can detect sickle hemoglobin has been used since the 1960s. A more reliable test that can detect the sickle-cell gene itself became available in the early 1980s.

Around 1970, proposals for sickle-cell screening programs gained support in both the medical establishment and the Black community. Like others at risk for genetic disorders, Black people deserve available information about their risks, the disease, and treatment so that they can make informed decisions about their procreative future. Initially, the influential *Journal of the American Medical Association* called for a program to screen Blacks of marriageable age so that couples who discovered that both carried the sickle-cell trait could consider the one-in-four risk that their children would suffer from the disease. President Nixon pledged to reverse the nation's "sad and shameful" neglect of sickle-cell anemia. Seventeen states instituted wide-scale screening programs, and in 1972 Congress passed the National Sickle-Cell Anemia Control Act, which provided for research, screening, counseling, and education. By 1975, there were more than 250 screening programs around the country, which tested almost half a million Blacks.

What began as a strategy to improve the health of Blacks soon turned into an instrument of medical abuse. Because screening programs often provided no counseling, there was rampant confusion between carriers of the trait and those who had the disease. Many people who had only sickle-cell trait were mistakenly convinced that their health was in jeopardy. Even the preamble of the federal law stated erroneously that 2 million Americans had sickle-cell *disease*, rather than the *trait*.

Instead of offering the tests as a voluntary source of information, fourteen states made them mandatory for Blacks enrolling in school, obtaining a marriage license, or confined in mental institutions and prisons.[50] Of course, five-year-olds had no need for test results designed to help couples make reproductive decisions. Nor were the tests helpful to adults in the absence of accurate information about the disorder and acceptable options for avoiding the disease in their children.

Hysteria over the sickle-cell trait also led to widespread discrimination. Autopsies of four Black army recruits who died during basic training revealed severe sickling of the red blood cells. The possibility that carriers' blood might sickle at high altitudes was used to justify denying Blacks entrance to the Air Force Academy. Almost all of the major commercial airlines fired or grounded Black pilots and flight attendants with sickle-cell trait.[51] Major corporations also screened Blacks applying for jobs. Sickle-cell carriers were charged higher premiums by some insurance companies or denied insurance altogether.

Sickle-cell screening was also the basis for proposals to restrict Black women's procreative liberty. Carriers were often counseled simply not to have children. In an article about counseling patients with sickle-cell disease published in a major medical journal in 1971, white members of the Department of Obstetrics and Gynecology at the Tennessee College of Medicine advocated sterilization for women with the illness.[52] The article concluded that "the expected rate of reproductive success, when considered in conjunction with the negative attributes concerning motherhood, does not justify a young woman with sickle-cell disease being exposed to the risk of pregnancy. We advocate primary sterilization, abortion if conception occurs, and sterilization for those that have completed pregnancies."[53]

Henry Foster, chairman of the Department of Obstetrics and Gynecology at Meharry Medical College in Nashville, whose nomination for surgeon-general was derailed in 1995, sharply disputed the recommendation of sterilization. Foster argued that the high maternal mortality rate the authors reported resulted from inadequate prenatal care. He believed that if Black patients were provided accurate screening, informed counseling, and proper clinical management, they would have alternatives to sterilization. Foster stressed how race affected the type of reproductive counseling that doctors give pregnant women regarding the implications of sickle-cell disease. Advice provided to Black patients, Foster wrote, often "is highly inadequate, misleading, and, on occasion, dangerous."[54] He pointed out that certain complicating risks, such as premature rupture of the membranes, experienced by women with sickle-cell disease in other hospitals had not occurred at Meharry, under the care of Black physicians.

Dr. Foster was clearly correct that race influences medical judgments concerning new reproductive technologies. Sickle-cell carriers are not the only identifiable carriers of genetic disease and Blacks are not the only ethnic group associated with a genetic disorder. In fact, carriers of at least fifty genetic disorders could be identified at the time of the sickle-cell testing programs. Yet none experienced the degree of institutionalized abuse visited upon Black carriers of the sickle-cell trait. Once again, racism worked to convert technology into a means of denying rather than promoting reproductive liberty.

Black Culture and the New Reproduction

The racial disparity in the use of reproductive technologies may be partly self-imposed. Although economics plays a major role, it does not provide the complete explanation for Black people's avoidance of these means of procreation. Even Black couples who can afford a nice home, car, and other amenities of a middle-class lifestyle are not turning to high-tech fertility services in the same proportions as their white cohorts. It would also be possible for Black women to enter into informal surrogacy arrangements with Black men without demanding huge fees.

One reason may be the extent to which Blacks have bought into stereotypes about their own reproductive capacities. The myth that Black people are overly fertile may make infertility especially embarrassing for Black couples.[55] One Black woman who eventually sought IVF treatment explained, "Being African-American, I felt that we're a fruitful people and it was shameful to have this problem. That made it even harder."[56] Blacks may find it more traumatic to discuss their problem with a physician, especially considering the paucity of Black specialists in this field.

In addition, Black people may be less likely to seek a technological fix for natural circumstances beyond their control. Infertile couples' reliance on advanced technologies reflects a confidence in medical science to solve life's predicaments. According to Elaine Tyler May, author of *Barren in the Promised Land*, a history of childlessness in America, America's obsession with reproduction began after World War II when "a heightened faith in science and medicine gave rise to the belief that everyone should be able to control his or her private destiny with the help of professional experts."[57] The contemporary white women May quotes frequently express an expectation of controlling their reproductive lives through medical intervention. One explained, "There is a tremendous amount of medical help available and I feel guilty not doing everything in my power to achieve pregnancy."[58] Sociologist Arthur Greil similarly observes that the affluent white couples he interviewed "embraced the pursuit of medical/technical solutions as the most plausible approach to dealing with the problem of infertility."[59]

Some researchers have linked the contrasting response of infertile Black women to their spiritual or psychological outlook on adversity.

"If infertility is one in a series of negative, seemingly irreversible events in a woman's life," sums up public health expert Elizabeth Heitman, "she may be more likely to attribute it to fate or God's will than seek to address it in science."[60] There may be a more rational explanation for this reluctance, as well. Considering the history of sickle-cell screening, the Tuskegee syphilis experiment, and other medical abuses, many Blacks harbor a well-founded distrust of technological interference with their bodies and genetic material at the hands of white physicians. Rayna Rapp interviewed a Black secretary, for example, who rejected prenatal genetic testing because the laboratory form included a release to use discarded amniotic fluid for experimentation.[61] Her husband worried that the amniocentesis might make the family vulnerable to abusive medical research.

This theory would explain why Blacks are likely to request high-tech life-sustaining treatment for a hospitalized family member even though they tend to refrain from high-tech fertility services.[62] In the former case, Blacks may rely on technological intervention even in the face of a physician's recommendation to discontinue treatment because of a distrust of the doctors' appreciation of their loved one's life. Both responses, then, are consistent with a suspicion of the medical profession born out of a history of disrespect and abuse.

While stories about infertility have begun to appear in magazines with a Black middle-class readership, such as *Ebony* and *Essence*, these articles conclude by suggesting that childless Black couples seriously consider adoption.[63] The ethic of dealing with infertility differs drastically between Blacks and whites. Infertile white couples are expected to turn to adoption only as a last resort, after exhausting every available means of producing a genetically related child. The Black community, on the other hand, expects its financially secure members to reach out to the thousands of Black children in need of a home.

Blacks' Rejection of Genetic Marketing

Blacks may also have an aversion to the genetic marketing aspect of the new reproduction. When infertile couples pay for the services of surrogate mothers and egg or sperm donors, they are purchasing the genetic material of their future children. When they undergo IVF, they are buying the assurance that their offspring will receive the parents' own genetic components. Black folks are skeptical about any obsession with genes. They know that their genes have been considered undesirable and that their alleged genetic inferiority has been used for centuries to justify their exclusion from the economic, political, and social mainstream. Only recently *The Bell Curve* was a national bestseller, reopening the public debate about racial differences in intelligence and the role genetics should play in social policy.[64] In a society in which Black traits are consistently devalued, a focus on genetics will more likely be used to justify limiting Black reproduction rather than encouraging it.

Blacks have understandably resisted defining personal identity in biological terms. In America, whites have historically valued genetic linkages and controlled their official meaning. As the powerful class, they are the guardians of the privileges accorded to biology and they have a greater stake in maintaining the importance of genetics. The legal regulation of racial boundary lines during the slavery era, for example, concerned *whites*, not Blacks: "The statutes punishing voluntary interracial sex and marriage were directed only at whites; they alone were charged with the responsibility for maintaining racial purity."[65]

Blacks by and large are more interested in escaping the constraints of racist ideology by defining themselves apart from inherited traits. They tend to see group membership as a political and cultural affiliation. Whites defined enslaved Africans as a biological race. Blacks in America have historically resisted this racial ideology by defining themselves as a political group. By the turn of the twentieth century, Black Americans had developed a race consciousness rooted in a sense of peoplehood that laid the foundation for later civil rights struggles.[66] With the exception of an extreme version of Afrocentrism that links Africans' intellectual and cultural contributions to the genetic trait of melanin (the pigment in dark skin),[67] "blackness" is gauged by one's commitment to Black people.

Black family ties have traditionally reached beyond the bounds of the nuclear family to include extended kin and non-kin relationships. Terms that connote genetic relationships — "brother," "sister," and "blood" — are used to refer to people linked together by racial solidarity. Black people's search for their ancestral roots has focused on cultural rather than genetic preservation. Their "ancestors" are not necessarily connected to them by a bloodline; they are all African people of a bygone era.

Most Blacks downplay their white genetic heritage to identify socially with other Blacks. Even children of interracial couples (having one Black and one white parent) tend to identify themselves as Black, often as a political choice.[68] Others refuse to identify with one race or the other, preferring to define themselves as both Black and white, mixed, or simply human. This identification, too, is often a refusal to base identity on biological inheritance. For most Blacks, ethnic identity is a conscious decision based primarily on considerations other than biological heritage. "The choice is partly cultural, partly social, and partly political, but it is mostly affectional," writes Yale law professor Stephen Carter.[69]

This distinction between cultural and genetic unity is reflected in Black opposition to transracial adoptions.[70] Some Blacks take the position that Black adoptive children should be placed only with Black families to ensure the transmission of Black cultural traits. The National Association of Black Social Workers (NABSW), for example, has long opposed transracial placements because "Black children belong, physically, psychologically, and culturally in Black families in order that they receive the total sense of themselves and develop a sound projection of their future."[71] These children are not genetically linked to their new families, but, according to this view, they should be tied to the Black community. When the NABSW condemned placements with white families as a "form of genocide," it was speaking of a cultural, not a biological, annihilation.

A Black parent's essential contribution to his or her children is not passing down genetic information but sharing lessons needed to survive in a racist society. Black parents transmit to their children their own cultural identity and teach them to defy racist stereotypes and practices, training their children to live in two cultures, both Black and white.[72] Some feel they must cultivate in their children what W. E. B. Du Bois described as a double consciousness; others see their task as preparing their children "to live among white people without *becoming* white people."[73] Some Black sociologists have opposed transracial adoption on the ground that only Black parents are capable of teaching Black children these necessary "survival skills."[74]

This aspect of blackness is contradicted by the fact that some Blacks have valued particular genetic traits, such as light skin color and straight hair, because of their desire to look whiter. In some Black bourgeois communities, whiter features signified higher social standing.[75] The Black elite of Washington, D.C., at the turn of the century, for example, was well known for requiring a white appearance for entry into its circle. Despite Black people's sorry history of color consciousness, however, sharing genetic traits seems less critical to Black identity than to white identity.

The notion of racial purity is foreign to Black folks. Our communities, neighborhoods, and families are a rich mixture of languages, accents, and traditions, as well as features, colors, and textures. Black life has a personal and cultural hybrid character.[76] There is often a melange of physical features — skin and eye color, hair texture, sizes, and shapes — within a single family. We are used to "throwbacks" — a pale, blond child born into a dark-skinned family, who inherited stray genes from a distant white ancestor. My children play with a set of twins who look very different from each other. The boy has light skin, green eyes, and "kinky" sandy-colored hair; the girl has dark skin, brown eyes, and long black wavy hair. Of course, there are physical differences among white siblings as well, but those differences do not have the same social import. We cannot expect our children to look just like us.

Blacks' view of genetic relatedness is tempered as well by the importance of self-definition, which escapes the constraints of inherited traits. If personal identity is not dependent on one's biological "race," then it must be deliberately chosen. In fact, the image of the individual shackled to his genetic destiny conflicts with the basic tenets of liberalism; it contradicts a definition of personhood centered on the autonomous, self-determining individual and denies the possibility of individual choice. As constitutional scholar Laurence Tribe observed, "one's sense of 'selfhood' or 'personhood,' and the related experience of one's autonomous individuality, may depend, at least in some cultural settings, on the ability to think of oneself as neither fabricated genetically nor programmed neurologically."[77] Blacks have defied the inferior status of blackness that whites attached to their biology by inventing their own individual identities.

The quest for self-definition in a racist society is the preeminent focus of Black intellectual thought. In the 1960s, Lerone Bennett, Jr., declared,

> Identified as a Negro, treated as Negro, provided with Negro interests, forced, whether he wills or no, to live in Negro communities, to think, love, buy and breathe as a Negro, the Negro comes in time to see himself as a Negro. . . . He comes, in time, to invent himself.[78]

Bennett's words are reminiscent of Du Bois's classic description of Black Americans' striving for a self-created identity:

> It is a peculiar sensation, this double-consciousness, this sense of always looking at one's self through the eyes of others, of measuring one's soul by the tape of a world that looks on in amused contempt and pity. One ever feels his twoness, an American, a Negro; two souls, two thoughts, two unreconciled strivings; two warring ideals in one dark body, whose dogged strength alone keeps it from being torn asunder.
>
> The history of the American Negro is the history of this strife, this longing to attain self-conscious manhood, to merge his double self into a better and truer self.[79]

The theme of willful self-creation is especially strong in the writings of Black women.[80] The fiction of authors such as Zora Neale Hurston, Toni Morrison, and Alice Walker revolves around Black female characters who learn to invent themselves after breaking out of the confines of racist and sexist expectations. Black women's autobiographical accounts also describe the process of self-creation, exemplified by Patricia Williams's statement, "I am brown by my own invention. . . . One day I will give birth to myself, lonely but possessed."[81] Denied self-ownership and rejected from the dominant norm of womanhood, Black women have defined themselves apart from the physical aspects of race.

THE IMPORTANCE OF THE GENETIC TIE

I have suggested that the suspicion of genetic marketing and the appreciation of self-definition in Black culture may help to explain Blacks' aversion to high-tech reproduction. Conversely, race may also influence the importance whites place on IVF's central aim—producing genetically related children. Using technology to create genetic ties focuses attention on the value placed on this particular form of connection.

Of course sharing a genetic tie with children is important to people of different races and in cultures that have no racial divisions. It seems natural for people to want to pass down their genes to their children. We perceive a special relationship created by a shared genetic identity. When a new baby enters a family, one of the first responses is to figure out whom she resembles. Most parents feel great satisfaction in having children who "take after" them. Bringing into the world children who bear their likeness gives many people both the joy of creating another life and the comfort of achieving a form of immortality passed down through the generations. Joe Saul, the protagonist of John Steinbeck's play *Burning Bright*, expressed his tormenting desire to have a child in terms of an eternal charge:

> A man can't scrap his blood line, can't snip the thread of his immortality. There's more than just my memory. More than my training and the remembered stories of glory and the forgotten shame of failure. There's a trust imposed to hand my line over to another, to place it tenderly like a thrush's egg in my child's hand.[82]

In our society, people often see the inability to produce one's own children as one of nature's most tragic curses. Infertile people often suffer horribly, and even people who have voluntarily decided to remain childless often refuse to cut off the possibility of creating children through sterilization. The desire to have children of one's own is so intense that it is commonly attributed to nature. Thus, the opening paragraph of a popular guide to infertility treatment declares: "Call it a cosmic spark or spiritual fulfillment, biological need or human destiny—the desire for a family rises unbidden from our genetic souls."[83] Some legal scholars have argued that an individual's interest in having offspring of his own genes is so great that it amounts to a constitutionally protected procreative liberty.[84]

Many also believe that certainty about one's genetic heritage benefits children. According to this view, genetic derivation is a critical determinant of self-identity, as well as biological makeup. Adopted children may struggle not only with the question, "Who are my real mother and father?" but also with the more profound inquiry, "Is genetic relatedness necessary for an authentic sense of self?" Taken to its extreme, this perspective defines personhood according to genetic attributes.

This conception of identity rooted in genetic heritage underlies the most extreme rhetoric of advocates who support adoptees' searches for their birth parents.[85] Critics of adoption claim that adopted children suffer from "genealogical bewilderment"—a condition stemming from ignorance of their genetic orgins. Adoptee Betty Jean Lifton writes of feeling "extruded from . . . her own biological clan, forced out of the natural flow of generational continuity, . . . forced out of nature itself."[86]

This insecurity may also trouble children whose genetic fathers are anonymous sperm donors. Margaret Brown, the nineteen-year-old product of artificial insemination, lamented, "I feel anger and confusion, and I'm filled with questions. Whose eyes do I have? Why the big secret? Who gave my family the idea that my biological roots are not important? To deny someone the knowledge of his or her biological origins is dreadfully wrong."[87] Some scientists also see identity as defined by genetics. One Harvard biologist, for example, declared that understanding human genetic composition is "the ultimate answer to the commandment, 'Know thyself.' "[88]

Recent years have witnessed a resurgence of public interest in genetics that has intensified the genetic tie's social importance. A 1994 issue of the *New York Times Book Review*, for example, reviewed five books concerning the link between genetics and human behavior. Its cover displayed a face woven into a model of DNA and the question "How Much of Us Is in the Genes?"[89] Numerous scholars have noted a trend in science, law, and popular culture toward "genetic essentialism," "geneticism," "geneticization," and a "prism of heritability" that erroneously reduces human beings to their genes.[90] Contemporary society increasingly looks to genetics for explanations of human behavior, accepting the view that "personal traits are predictable and permanent, determined at conception, 'hard-wired' into the human constitution."[91]

The Human Genome Initiative, an ongoing government-sponsored project to map the complete set of human genetic instructions, is the largest biology venture in the history of science. The U.S. Department of Energy projects costs of $200 million a year for about fifteen years.[92] Scientists are attempting to detect genetic markers that indicate a predisposition to complex conditions and behaviors, as well as single-gene disorders. They anticipate creating genetic tests that will be able to predict a person's susceptibility to hemophilia, mental illness, heart disease, and alcoholism. This possibility was dramatized by Jonathan Tolins's 1993 play, *The Twilight of the Golds*, which portrayed the catastrophic fallout when a family learns through genetic testing that the daughter's unborn child will be gay.

More disturbing, researchers claim to have discovered not only the genetic origins of *medical* conditions, but also biological explanations for *social* conditions. Even happiness, a recent *New York Times* story tells us, is dictated by our genes.[93] Our ability to tinker with the genes children inherit, as well as the belief that these genes determine human nature, exaggerates the importance of genes in defining personal identity and, consequently, the importance of genetic connections.

Yet we also know that the desire to have genetically related children is a cultural artifact. The legal meaning of the genetic tie offers telling insight into its indeterminacy. For example, the institution of slavery made the genetic tie to a slave mother critical in determining a child's social status, yet legally insignificant in the relationship between male slaveowners and their mulatto children. Although today we generally assume that genetic connection creates an enduring bond between parents and their children, the law often disregards it in the cases of surrogate mothers, sperm donors, and unwed fathers. The importance of genetic connection, then, is determined by social convention, not biological edict.

A number of feminists have advocated abandoning the genetic model of parenthood altogether because of its origins in patriarchy and its "preoccupation with male seed."[94] The norm of fatherhood grounded in genetic transmission sees mothers as fungible receptacles of male gametes and devalues the importance of social bonds. Men seem to be more invested than women in the quest for a genetic connection with their children. The man who entered in the first formal surrogacy contract made this distinction: "I guess for some women, as long as they have a child, it's fine. But . . . I need to know that he's really mine."[95]

Most scholarship on the new reproduction, however, fails to consider the tremendous impact that the inheritability of race has had on the meaning of genetic relatedness in American culture. Although race is really a social construct, it has been treated as an inherited status for centuries. In this society, perhaps the most significant genetic trait passed from parent to child is race. How important is race to the desire to create genetically related children? It is impossible to tell: the decision to have children is influenced by a multitude of social, cultural, and biological factors. But surely the inheritability of race plays some role in the degree of importance whites invest in genetic ties with their children.

The social and legal meaning of the genetic tie helped to maintain a racial caste system that preserved white supremacy through a rule of racial purity. The colonists maintained a clear demarcation between Black slaves and white masters by a violently enforced legal system of racial classification and sexual taboos. The genetic tie to a slave mother not only made the child a slave and subject to white domination; it was also supposed to pass down a whole set of inferior traits.

For several centuries a paramount objective of American law and social convention was keeping the white bloodline free from Black contamination. Before high-tech procedures were available, husbands guaranteed a genetic relationship to children by enforcing their wives' fidelity. Under a racial caste system, female marital fidelity was doubly important: it ensured not only paternity but also racial purity. Since only white women could produce white children, they were responsible for maintaining the purity of the white race. While white men impregnated Black women with impunity, the law ensured that white women had children only with their husbands so that their children would be pure white. William Smith, a professor at Tulane University, explained in 1905 that fornication with a Negro was a greater crime for a white woman than for a white man because "he does not impair, in any wise, the dignity or integrity of his race; he may sin against himself and others, and even against his God, but not against the germ-plasm of his kind."[96] The first laws against interracial fornication arose from legislators' "particular distaste that white women, who could be producing white children, were producing mulattoes."[97] As early as 1662, Virginia amended its law prohibiting fornication to impose heavier penalties if the guilty parties were from different races. By being faithful to their husbands, white women were also faithful to their race.

The law punished with extra severity white women who gave birth to mulatto children. Because a child took on the status of the mother, mulattoes born to white mothers were free. But these children were treated more harshly than free Black children; those with white mothers were generally required to become indentured servants until they reached thirty years of age. Unlike the racially mixed children of Black women, they represented a corruption of the *white* race.

Antimiscegenation laws also made sure that white women bore genetic offspring for white husbands. As W. J. Cash explained in *The Mind of the South* in 1941, whites enacted laws against interracial marriage to protect "the right of their sons in the legitimate line, through all the generations to come, to be born to the great heritage of the white race."[98] It was only in 1967 that the U.S. Supreme Court in *Loving v. Virginia*[99] ruled that antimiscegenation laws, designed to keep the races from intermingling, were unconstitutional. To this day, one's social status in America is determined by the presence or absence of a genetic tie to a Black parent. Conversely, the white genetic tie—if free from any trace of blackness—is an extremely valuable attribute entitling a child to a privileged status, what legal scholar Cheryl Harris calls the "property interest in whiteness."[100] Ensuring genetic relatedness is important for many reasons, but, in America, one of the most important reasons has been to preserve white racial purity.

CREATING WHITE BABIES:
THE VALUE OF BIOTECHNICAL CHILDREN

The new reproduction also graphically discloses the disparate values placed on children of different races. By trading genes on the market, these technologies lay bare the high value placed on whiteness and the worthlessness accorded blackness. New reproductive technologies are so popular in American culture not simply because of the value placed on the genetic tie, but because of the value placed on the *white* genetic tie. The monumental effort, expense, and technological invention that goes into the new reproduction marks the children produced as especially valuable. It proclaims the unmistakable message that white children merit the spending of billions of dollars toward their creation. Black children, on the other hand, are the object of welfare reform measures designed to discourage poor women's procreation.

The panic over white infertility is not only a private tragedy. True, part of the desperation childless white women feel comes from their personal longing to be a parent. But the high-tech frenzy to conceive has been whipped up by alarm over the falling birthrate of white career women. Feminist author Susan Faludi documents a new pronatalism in the 1980s that was part of a backlash against women's gains in the workplace.[101] In February 1982, newspapers, magazines, and television shows gave top billing to a medical study claiming that women between the ages of thirty and thirty-five risked a nearly 40 percent chance of being infertile. Practically overnight, the media created an infertility epidemic plaguing middle-class America. This figure became the basis for paternalistic editorials and self-help books chastising the women's movement for creating "a sisterhood of the infertile" and exhorting women to stop postponing motherhood. Childless middle-aged women were programmed to feel their "biological clocks" ticking.

The media paid little attention to a federal study released three years later that showed a far lower (13.6 percent) infertility rate for the same age group. Instead, women's careers were erroneously blamed for high rates of endometriosis, miscarriage, and abnormal babies. (In fact, Faludi astutely points out, "women's quest for economic and educational equality has only *improved* reproductive health and fertility.")[102] While the media portray irresponsible Black women as overly fertile, they depict selfish, career-seeking white women as not fertile enough. As a result, white couples flock to high-tech treatment in record numbers, despite no evidence of an increase in the incidence of infertility over the last several decades.[103]

The renewed focus on white women's fertility has eugenic overtones as well. Ben Wattenberg's *The Birth Dearth*, for example, predicted that reproduction in the industrialized world could not keep pace with population growth in the Third World unless American women took measures to have more children.[104] "I believe demographic and immigration patterns inherent in the Birth Dearth will yield an ever smaller proportion of Americans of white European stock," Wattenberg warned, making it "difficult to promote and defend liberty in the Western nations and in the rest of the modernizing world." Television evangelist and Republican presidential contender Pat Robertson agreed that "depopulation of the West" constituted "genetic suicide" and "threatens the power of Western industrialized democracies."[105]

The Bell Curve presented the 1990s domestic version of this argument. Instead of predicting a global imbalance, Charles Murray and Richard Herrnstein foretold increasing social disparities within the United States owing to the higher birthrates of groups with inherently lower intelligence. Like the backlash against professional women's advances, this new form of eugenics interprets the problem of infertility as the shortage of white babies. Thus, the backdrop of infertility that fuels the high-tech fertility business is already dominated by race.

The public's affection for the white babies that are produced by reproductive technologies further legitimates their use. Noel Keane, the lawyer who in 1978 arranged the first public surrogacy adoption, described how this affection influenced the public's attitude toward his clients' arrangement.[106] Although the first television appearance of the contracting parents, George and Debbie, and the surrogate mother, Sue, generated hostility, a second appearance on the *Phil Donahue Show* with two-month-old Elizabeth Anne changed the tide of public opinion. According to Keane, "this time there was only one focal point: Elizabeth Anne, blond-haired, blue-eyed, and as real as a baby's yell." He concludes, "The show was one of Donahue's highest-rated ever and the audience came down firmly on the side of what Debbie, Sue, and George had done to bring Elizabeth Anne into the world." I suspect that a similar display of a curly-haired, brown-skinned baby would not have had the same transformative effect on the viewing public. Imagine a multi-billion-dollar industry designed to create Black children!

Recall the white woman's lawsuit against a fertility clinic for mistakenly giving her a Black man's sperm. The case not only evidences disdain for the technological creation of Black babies; it also highlights the critical importance of producing a genetically pure white child. The clinic's racial mix-up negated the value of the mother's genetic tie. I do not mean to depreciate the woman's personal loss. She wanted a child with her *husband*, who subsequently died of cancer. But receiving the wrong *white* child would have been a far less devastating experience. In the American market, a Black baby is indisputably an inferior product.

While the botched inseminations of white women are presented as tragedies, the reverse racial blunder was the premise for a Hollywood comedy. In *Made in America*, Whoopi Goldberg plays an Afrocentric single mother whose teenage daughter was conceived through artificial insemination. Determined to track down her roots, the daughter raids the sperm bank computer only to discover that she was fathered by a white man (Ted Danson) as the result of a mix-up. Glossing over the race issue, the movie finds comic relief in the unlikely romance between the mother, an eccentric Black bookstore owner, and the sperm donor, a crass white car salesman.

How could this racial intermingling be so easily dismissed when the other sperm bank mix-ups seem so serious? Returning to the colonists' distaste for mulatto children provides a clue. Like the repudiated colonial women, the white women given the wrong sperm bore mulattoes "when they could be producing white children." The same loss did not occur when Black women delivered mulattoes: their children would be Black slaves in any case.

In the film, in contrast to the real-life sperm bank case, the daughter's racial composition is inconsequential: she is Black regardless of which race the sperm depositor turns out to be. Finding out the father's racial identity has no effect on the mother's (or society's) view of the child whatsoever. After all, it is not so uncommon for a Black child to discover a white man somewhere in the family tree. More important, giving a Black woman the wrong sperm does not deprive society of a white child. With so little at stake, American audiences could accept this interracial scenario as a nonthreatening romantic sitcom.

THE COMPLICATIONS OF TRANSRACIAL ADOPTIONS

Whites have sometimes disputed my claims about the value of white genetic ties by pointing to barriers to transracial adoptions. Infertile whites are forced to rely on high-tech means, they argue, because of the difficulties they face in adopting children, including race-matching policies. This contention distorts the reality of the adoption market in two ways. First, most white couples who use IVF resort to adoption as a second-best alternative only after they fail to conceive a genetically related child.[107] Those who cannot afford IVF often try less expensive infertility treatment before pursuing adoption. Consider Dierdre Kearney's decision to adopt after trying to conceive for four of five years of marriage, recounted in *Barren in the Promised Land*:

> "I think we experienced every emotion and feeling one can in dealing with this situation. We have also been through every fertility test there is." Her husband was on medication for three years, and his problem was corrected. She had four surgeries, medication, fertility drugs, and artificial insemination using her husband's semen. "The only option left for us is IVF. We do not have the money; what savings we have is going toward adoption."[108]

Lydia Sommer, a white account specialist married to an attorney, told a similar story. For six of their seven years of marriage, the couple tried infertility treatment, but they "stopped short of IVF, 'drained emotionally and financially.' " They finally abandoned high-tech solutions and adopted a daughter.[109] Sommer's adoption took a peculiar twist, akin to the sperm bank mix-ups. Two months after bringing the baby home, the couple realized she was biracial (the white birth mother had lied about the father's race). The couple promptly returned the child to the adoption agency for a refund.

Could these couples have afforded IVF, they probably would have tried it before resigning themselves to adoption. My point is not that that all infertile whites, or even a majority of them, use reproduction-assisting technologies. It is that the people who do use these high-tech means of conception typically view them, and not adoption, as their preferred way of becoming parents.

Second, the debate over transracial adoption should not over-shadow the predominant preference for white children. The vast majority of white adoptive parents are only willing to take a white child. Even when they adopt outside their race, whites generally prefer non-Black children with Asian or Latin American heritage.[110] "Of dozens of white adopting parents I have interviewed in three years," reported Mary Jo McConahay in the *Los Angeles Times*, "almost all said they would consider adopting a Latino child abroad before a black child at home."[111]

Interracial adoptions, which make up less than 10 percent of all adoptions, are primarily of children *who are not either Black or white*.[112] The international adoption trade is thriving, and fraught with charges of Western brokers' exploitation of Third World women and children.[113] The current recruitment of white couples to adopt Black children stems from the shortage of adoptable white babies, whose soaring price tag reflects their market value. In America, a white child can cost twice as much to adopt as a Black child. In Latin American countries, the price of an adoption depends on the baby's eye color, skin shade, and hair texture. In short, genetically related, white children remain most Americans' first choice.

Besides, white support for transracial adoptions does not fundamentally alter the rules governing claims to white and Black children. All of the literature advocating the elimination of racial considerations in child placements focuses on making it easier for white parents to adopt children of color. A leading book on the subject, for example, states that "[i]n the case of transracial adoption the children are non-white and the adoptive parents are white."[114] (This definition completely ignores adoptions of white children by parents of other races, constituting 2 percent of all adoptions.)[115] Until fairly recently, the law in some states explicitly prohibited Black parents from adopting white children, while allowing white parents to adopt Black children. A South Carolina statute, for example, provided:

> It shall be unlawful for any parent, relative, or other white person in this State, having the control or custody of any white child by right to guardianship, natural or acquired or otherwise, to dispose of, give or surrender such white child permanently into the custody, control, maintenance or support of a Negro.[116]

This bias results partly from the disproportionate number of Black children available for adoption and of white couples seeking to adopt. A report on a major state foster care system, for example, shows that 54 percent of children available for adoption are nonwhite while 87 percent of prospective adoptive parents are white.[117] Because the number of Black children awaiting placement far exceeds the number of available Black adoptive families, there is more pressure for white couples to take in Black children than for Blacks to adopt white children. These statistics, however, reflect only formal adoptions and overlook the prevalence of informal adoptions in the Black community. Black families who attempt to use formal adoption services face numerous institutional barriers, including financial requirements and the cultural insensitivity of predominantly white, middle-class social workers.[118] In fact, middle-income Black couples adopt at a higher rate than similar white couples.[119] These statistics also raise the question why there are so many Black children wallowing in foster care in the first place.

With so many Black children in need of a home, it is not surprising that Black families adopt within their race. Indeed, the 1987 National Health Interview Survey found not a single instance of interracial adoption by a Black mother.[120] Still, the very thought of a Black family adopting a white child seems beyond our cultural imagination. A system that truly assigns children to adoptive parents without regard to race is unthinkable, not because Black children would be placed in white homes, but because white children would be given to Black parents.

Adoption of a Black child by a white family is viewed as an improvement in the Black child's social status and lifestyle and as a positive gesture of racial inclusion. A Black family's dominion over a white child, on the other hand, is seen as an unseemly relationship and an injury to the child. As a judge recognized forty years ago, allowing the adoption of a white child by his mother's Black husband would unfairly cause the child to "lose the social status of a white man."[121] Even today, "it is virtually unheard of for an adoption agency to offer a healthy, able-bodied white child to Black parents for adoption."[122]

Claims about the benefits of racial assimilation are only made about the advantages Black children will presumably experience by living in white homes. In her book *Family Bonds*, for example, adoption advocate Elizabeth Bartholet argues that race-matching policies damage Black children by denying them placements with white adoptive parents. She dismisses, on the other hand, the contention that Black children belong with Black parents. Bartholet reaches this conclusion not only because "there is no evidence that black parents do a better job than white parents of raising black children with a sense of pride in their racial background," but also because Black children reap substantial advantages from a white environment. Unlike Black children "living in a state of relative isolation or exclusion from the white world," Bartholet reasons, "black children raised in white homes are comfortable with their blackness and also uniquely comfortable in dealing with whites."[123]

Bartholet also acknowledges the benefits white parents gain from transracial adoptions. White adoptive families develop a new awareness of racial issues and commitment to a multicultural world that transcends racial differences. She writes passionately of how the Peruvian children she adopted enhanced her life: "I revel in the brown skin and thick black hair and dark eyes and Peruvian features that I could not have produced." Bartholet implies that Black children are *better off* in white homes and that white parents are enriched by raising nonwhite children; but she finds nothing positive to say about growing up with Black parents.

Bartholet advocates a "no-preference" policy that "would remove adoption agencies from the business of promoting same-race placement."[124] The Multiethnic Placement Act of 1994 prohibited agencies that receive federal funding from placing children according to race but not from taking race into account. In 1996, Congress changed the law to eliminate any consideration of race after critics argued that agencies retained too much discretion to continue the preference for race-matching. But a "no-preference" policy with respect to race is in effect a regime that always prefers a white family and accommodates white families' preferences. Although this policy eliminates the preference for Black parents in adoptions of Black children, it retains the preference for white parents in adoptions of white children. Thus, even advocates of transracial adoptions ultimately favor "a system in which white children are reserved for white families."[125] Their policies perpetuate a system designed to provide childless white couples with babies and with the type of babies they prefer.

When I was a fellow at Harvard University, I passed a playground in the Cambridge Common every day on my way to my office overlooking Harvard Square. The diverse group of adults and children playing in the park appeared at first to represent the multicultural mix of the university community. But on closer inspection I discovered a disturbing pattern. It seemed as if all of the minority children had white mothers—probably, in most cases, the result of transracial adoptions. Many of the white children, on the other hand, were tended by Black women—not their mothers, but nannies hired by their white mothers. Despite all the racial intermingling going on, the scene still represented a clear demarcation between the status of white and Black women and their claims to children.

Although transracial adoption is painted as a catalyst for racial harmony, in Bartholet's words "a model of how we might better learn to live with one another in this society," it does not threaten the supremacist code of white superiority. It does nothing to diminish the devaluation of Black childbearing. Nor does it violate the taboo against interracial sex that might lead to a fertile white woman bearing a Black child. The fertility business mirrors the adoption market in catering to the preferences of childless white couples. What is objectionable about both these systems is not so much white people's desire for a particular child as the way these markets are structured solely to fulfill that desire.

RACE AND THE HARM IN SURROGACY

The devaluation of the Black genetic tie helps to explain the harm in surrogacy. Some feminists have denounced contract pregnancy arrangements because they exploit women and commodify women's reproductive capacity. People who hire surrogates are usually wealthier than the women who provide the service. An adopting couple must be fairly well off to afford the costs of a surrogacy arrangement—typically at least $25,000.[126] Surrogacy is appealing to some low-income women because it pays better than other unskilled employment and because it is one of the few available jobs that do not require leaving home. But what is exploitative about paying a surrogate mother a sum of money she would not be able to obtain at other work? What distinguishes activities poor women are induced to perform for money that are exploitative from those that are not? Economic necessity in general pressures poor women to accept occupations rich women would not tolerate. Wealthy people hire poor, unskilled women, for example, to clean their homes and offices.

The claim that poor women are coerced into entering surrogacy contracts by the promise of large sums of money is meaningless by itself. For instance, would it be more or less exploitative to increase the fee paid to surrogate mothers? It has been argued that unpaid surrogacy may be more coercive than an arm's-length commercial arrangement with a stranger; yet increasing the payment would heighten the pressure on a potential surrogate to press her womb into service for the payer.[127] The woman's decision to enter into the surrogacy arrangement at least shows that she found it preferable to her other options for work. Her decision may be evidence that surrogacy is less exploitative than other services wealthier people could buy from her—services which the law does not prohibit despite their harmful or degrading qualities and the parties' unequal bargaining power.

At bottom, the argument against surrogacy rests on the peculiar nature of childbearing that makes its sale immoral. Legal theorist Margaret Jane Radin and other scholars argue that surrogacy impermissibly alienates a fundamental aspect of one's personhood and treats it as a marketable commodity. In Radin's words, "Market-inalienability might be grounded in a judgment that commodification of women's reproductive capacity is harmful for the identity aspect of their personhood and in a judgment that the closeness of paid surrogacy to baby-selling harms our self-conception too deeply."[128] Philosopher Elizabeth Anderson argues that using surrogates' bodies, rather than respecting them, fails to value women in an appropriate way.[129] Surrogacy treats women as objects rather than as valuable human beings by selling their capacity to bear children for a price. The practice places a specific dollar value on the surrogate's personal traits. Directories display photographs of and vital information (height, hair color, racial origins) about women willing to be hired to gestate a baby. Barbara Katz Rothman notes how the term "product of conception," often used to describe the fertilized egg to be implanted in a surrogate mother, reflects this commodification: "It is an ideology that enables us to see not motherhood, not parenthood, but the creation of a commodity, a baby."[130]

Moreover, pregnancy impresses a surrogate's body into paid service to a degree distinct from other work. Unlike most paid laborers, the surrogate mother cannot separate herself from the service she performs. As Kelly Oliver puts it, "Surrogacy is a twenty-four-hour-a-day job which involves every aspect of the surrogate's life. . . . Her body becomes the machinery of production over which the contractor has ultimate control."[131] Commercial surrogacy can be seen as liberating when liberation is measured by the individual's freedom and ability to buy and sell products and labor on the market. But women's wombs and pregnancy are not ordinary products or labor. Like children, organs, or sexual intimacy, women's reproductive capacities should not be bartered in the market.

The relationship between race and reproduction further illuminates this market inalienability. It demonstrates how surrogacy both misvalues and devalues human beings. First, Anderson and Radin argue that surrogacy values women and children in the wrong way. Why do they conclude that paying women for their gestational services will produce this harmful conception of women and their reproductive capacity? It is also possible, as John Robertson suggests, that we could view gestators as "worthy collaborators in a joint reproductive enterprise from which all parties gain, with money being one way that the infertile couple pays its debt or obligation to the surrogate."[132] Anderson's and Radin's sense of the immorality of commercial surrogacy may arise from the features it shares with the American institution of slavery. The experience of surrogate mothers is not equivalent to slavery's horrors, dehumanization, and absolute denial of self-determination. Yet our understanding of the evils inherent in marketing human beings stems in part from the reduction of enslaved Blacks to their physical service to whites.[133]

The quintessential commodification of human beings was the sale of slaves on the auction block to the highest bidder. Slaves were totally and permanently commodified. Slaves bore all of the legal attributes of property: just like a horse, a necklace, or a piece of furniture, they could be "transferred, assigned, inherited, or posted as collateral."[134] In the words of a slave, he was a "flesh and blood commodity, which money could so easily procure in our vaunted land of freedom."[135] Surrogacy's use of women's wombs is reminiscent of Baby Suggs's admonition in *Beloved* about slavery's objectification of Africans: "And O my people they do not love your hands. Those they only use, tie, bind, chop off and leave empty."[136]

Slave women were treated as surrogate mothers in the sense that they lacked any claim to the children whom they bore and whom they delivered to the masters who owned both mother and child. As the contemporary surrogate mother takes the place of an infertile wife, the economic appropriation of slave women's childbearing was the only way for the slave economy to produce and reproduce its laborers.[137] It is the enslavement of Blacks that enables us to imagine the commodification of human beings, and that makes the vision of fungible breeder women so real.

The issue of race illuminates the harm of surrogacy in a second way. The feminist arguments against surrogacy focus on the commodification of women's wombs. Just as critical, however, is the commodification of the genetic tie, based on a valuation of its worth. In his discussion of egg donation, John Robertson defends recipients' desire to "receive good genes" from women who "appear to be of good stock."[138] He advocates perfecting the technology of egg donation because it will "enhance the ability to influence the genetic makeup of offspring." "Eugenic considerations are unavoidable," Robertson concludes, "and not inappropriate when one is seeking gametes from an unknown third party." Although this process devalues all women, it devalues Black women in a particular way.

Feminist opponents of surrogacy miss an important aspect of the practice when they criticize it for treating women as *fungible* commodities. A Black surrogate is not exchangeable for a white one. In one sense, Anderson and Radin are right that marketing babies misdescribes the way that we value people. Surrogacy, however, is so troubling precisely because its commercial essence lays bare how our society actually *does* value people. We must assess both the liberating and the oppressive potential of surrogacy, not in the abstract realm of reproductive choice, but in the real world that devalues certain human lives with the law's approval.

THE BLACK GESTATIONAL SURROGATE

Gestational surrogacy separates the biological connection between mother and child into two parts—the gestational tie and the genetic tie.[139] In gestational surrogacy, the hired gestator is implanted with an embryo produced by fertilizing the contracting mother's egg with the contracting father's sperm using IVF. The child therefore inherits the genes of both contracting parents and is genetically unrelated to her birth mother. This type of surrogate is treated even more like an "incubator" or "womb for rent" than paid gestators who contribute an egg to the deal. Gestational surrogacy disconnects the parents' valuable genes from the gestator's exploited reproductive capacity.

Gestational surrogacy allows a radical possibility that is at once very convenient and very dangerous: a Black woman can give birth to a white child. White men need no longer rely on white surrogates to produce their valuable white genetic inheritance. This possibility reverses the traditional presumptions about a mother's biological connection to her children. The law has always understood legal parentage to arise definitively from female, but not male, biology.[140]

The European-American tradition identifies a child's mother by the biological act of giving birth: at common law, a woman was the legal mother of the child she bore. But Black gestational surrogacy makes it imperative to legitimate the genetic tie between the (white) father and the child, rather than the biological, nongenetic tie between the (Black) birth mother and the child.

In *Johnson v. Calvert*, a gestational surrogacy dispute, the court legitimated the genetic relationship and denied the gestational one in order to reject a Black woman's bond with the child.[141] The birth mother, Anna Johnson, was a former welfare recipient and a single mother of a three-year-old daughter. The genetic mother, Crispina Calvert, was Filipina, and the father, Mark Calvert, was white. The press, however, paid far more attention to Anna Johnson's race than to that of Crispina Calvert. It also portrayed the baby as white. During her pregnancy, Anna changed her mind about relinquishing the baby and both Anna and the Calverts filed lawsuits to gain parental rights to the child.

Judge Richard N. Parslow, Jr., framed the critical issue as determining the baby's "natural mother." Johnson's attorney relied on the historical presumption that the woman who gives birth to a child is the child's natural, and legal, mother. All states except Arkansas and Nevada apply an irrebuttable presumption of legal parenthood in favor of the birth mother.[142] Yet Judge Parslow held that Johnson had no standing to sue for custody or visitation rights, and granted the Calverts sole custody of the baby. His reasoning centered on genetics. Judge Parslow described the Calverts as "desperate and longing for their own genetic product."[143] He noted the need for genetically related children and compared gestation to a foster parent's temporary care for a child who is not genetically hers. (Robertson has similarly argued that the gestational surrogate is a "trustee" for the embryo and should be kept to "her promise to honor the genetic bond.")[144]

Judge Parslow also equated a child's identity with her genetic composition: "We know more and more about traits now, how you walk, talk, and everything else, all sorts of things that develop out of your genes."[145] On appeal, the California court of appeals also saw genetics as "a powerful factor in human relationships," writing, "The fact that another person is, literally, developed from a part of oneself can furnish the basis for a profound psychological bond. Heredity can provide a basis of connection between two individuals for the duration of their lives."[146] The California Supreme Court affirmed this view, reducing the legal significance of gestation to mere evidence of the determinative *genetic* connection between mother and child.

The California courts reduced legal motherhood to the contribution of an egg to the procreative process. But the law need not place such primacy on genetic relatedness. There is little doubt, for example, that a court would not consider a woman who donated her eggs to an infertile couple to be the legal mother, despite her genetic connection to the child. By relying on the genetic tie to determine legal parenthood, the courts in the *Johnson* case ensured that a Black woman would not be the "natural mother" of a white child.

In Europe, different circumstances have also produced controversy concerning a Black woman bearing a white child. Black women in England and Italy have been implanted with a white woman's eggs in order to bear a child of their own. It was reported that the British woman used a white woman's eggs because of the shortage of Black women who donate their eggs to infertile couples. She resorted to eggs of a different race only after waiting four years for a Black donor. In her mind, the egg donor's race was not determinative: because the father was of mixed racial heritage, the child would be of mixed race as well—regardless of the egg donor's race. As the clinic director noted, "all you are going to do by having a white woman's egg is have a slightly paler shade of coffee colour rather than a darker shade of coffee colour."[147]

In Italy, an African woman's choice of a white woman's egg was far more momentous. Because her husband, whose sperm fertilized the egg, was white, her baby was also white. The second woman deliberately selected the donor's race because she believed that "the child would have a better future if it were white."[148] Unlike gestational surrogacy, egg donation and marriage to the father gave this woman a solid legal claim to the white child she bore. Yet the shock of a Black woman giving birth to her own white child was great enough to make international news and to send experts pondering about the ethics of such "designer babies." A wide spectrum of commentators condemned even the British woman's selection of a white egg donor. Conservative British politician Jill Knight maintained that choosing a child's ethnic identity was "plain and unvarnished genetic engineering."[149] The chairman of the British Medical Association's ethics committee called for Parliament to debate the issue. And a spokeman for the Catholic media center stated that "the Catholic Church would be opposed to such interference with the natural processes."[150]

It is regrettable that the woman in Italy refused to give birth to a

Black child. Seduced by the misleading allure of the new reproduction, she unfortunately sought a technological solution to the problem of racism. On the other hand, the furor over her racial selection of eggs overlooked the fact that most white couples also choose to have a white child when they select the race of a sperm or egg donor or surrogate mother. Race is the sperm donor characteristic most likely to be matched to recipient specifications, and virtually all sperm banks are willing to meet this request.[151] It was most hypocritical for white ethicists and politicians to lash out at this Black woman for picking the most popular type of donor eggs.

Gestational surrogacy invokes the possibility that white middle-class couples will use Black women to gestate their babies. Since contracting couples need not be concerned about the gestator's genetic qualities (most important, her race), they may favor hiring the most economically vulnerable women in order to secure the lowest price for their services. Black gestators would be doubly disadvantaged in any custody dispute: besides being less able to afford a court battle, they are unlikely to win custody of the white child they bear, as the *Johnson* case demonstrates. Writer Katha Pollitt speculates that this legal advantage might have been the Calverts' motive for choosing a Black gestational surrogate in the first place. "Black women have, after all, always raised white children without acquiring any rights to them," Pollitt notes. "Now they can breed them, too."[152]

Some writers had already predicted a caste of breeders, composed of women of color whose primary function would be to gestate the embryos of more valuable white women.[153] These breeders, whose own genetic progeny would be considered worthless, might be sterilized. The vision of Black women's wombs in the service of white men conjures up images from slavery. Slave women were similarly compelled to breed children who would be owned by their masters and to breast-feed their masters' white infants, while neglecting their own children. In fact, Anna Johnson's lawyer likened the arrangement Johnson made with the Calverts to "a slave contract."[154]

Some white feminists present these images of Black women's degradation in order to enhance the potential horror of reproductive technology's oppression of women. But a strictly gender-focused analysis fails to confront the racism that makes these images a real possibility. In Gena Corea's futuristic scenario, for example, white women are equally exploited as compulsory egg donors in the reproductive brothel.[155] Corea does not question whether white middle-class women might collude in their husbands' use of Black women's bodies to produce their own white, genetically related children.

MAGNIFYING RACIAL INEQUITIES

So far I have argued that use of new reproductive technologies reflects an already existing racial caste system. High-tech means of procreation may also magnify racial inequities by enhancing the power of privileged whites and contributing to the devaluation of Blacks. With only 40,000 babies in the United States conceived through IVF since 1981,[156] the racial disparity in its use will hardly alter the demographic composition of the country. Rather, the harm occurs at the ideological level — the message it sends about the relative value of Blacks and whites in America. But this is not an imaginary harm: ideology has a real effect on social policy and consequently on the material conditions of people's lives. By strengthening the ideology that white people deserve to procreate while Black people do not, the new reproduction may worsen racial inequality.

We should not dismiss the possibility of more tangible harms, however. The ability to select or improve the genetic features of one's offspring carries material as well as symbolic advantages. Modern genetic technologies allow parents who can afford them to secure the health and physical abilities of their children. Without government subsidies, this could produce a society where only the poor bear children with genetic disorders. Concentrating the power of genetic enhancement in the hands of an already privileged class would exacerbate differences in the status and welfare of social groups.

While birth control has been the tool for imposing negative eugenics, the new reproduction is the instrument for achieving positive eugenics — increasing the number of births from superior parents. According to Noel Keane, the doctor who assisted in the first public surrogacy arrangement explained his participation in terms of eugenics: "I performed the insemination because there are enough unwanted children and children of poor genetic background in the world."[157]

The March 1934 issue of *Scientific American* reported that each year between 1,000 and 3,000 American women requested sperm for artificial insemination, a procedure used by women with sterile husbands since the mid-nineteenth century. Noting that the women usually wanted the most biologically fit donors, the article extolled the eugenic potential of this reproductive technology: "Some 10,000 to 20,000 babies [could] be born every year from selected sources, while less than 500 babies per year are now being born to the men of real talent in our country. What will be the eugenic effect on the race, if this same tendency grows?"[158]

The eugenic possibilities of artificial insemination were explored most notably by Hermann J. Muller, a zoologist who won the Nobel Prize in 1946 for his discovery that radiation causes gene mutations. Muller believed that mankind should take control of the evolutionary process in order to transform society for the better. In his 1935 classic, *Out of the Night: A Biologist's View of the Future*, Muller estimated that artificial insemination could enable 50,000 children to inherit the genes of a single "transcendently estimable man" and the majority of the population to possess the innate qualities of such men as Lenin, Newton, Pasteur, Beethoven, and Marx.[159] Unlike most eugenicists, Muller rejected the notion that socially lower classes or less advanced races had genetically inferior intelligence, attributing differences among groups to their environment. In fact, Muller condemned social inequalities for hindering eugenic progress; he advocated a classless society with equal opportunity for education and welfare that would reveal the population's true genetic variation.

Muller revived his vision of improving mankind's genetic quality through artificial insemination in a paper presented at a 1959 University of Chicago conference celebrating the hundred-year anniversary of Darwin's *Origin of Species*. In 1971, four years after Muller's death, a right-wing millionaire named Robert K. Graham realized Muller's fantasy by establishing the Hermann J. Muller Repository for Germinal Choice. (Muller had disavowed the repository prior to his death because of his concern about biased solicitations.) Graham originally stocked the bank with sperm donated exclusively by Nobel laureates, including William Shockley, but later began accepting donations from other scientists.[160]

Singapore provides a contemporary example of a positive eugenics program. The Singapore government responded to the country's falling birthrate by investing in the rapid development of new reproductive technologies, including the world's first egg bank and micro-insemination sperm transplant (MIST), a technique used to increase a man's sperm count.[161] Fueled by concern over Singapore's growing Malay and Indian populations, the program aims at increasing the fertility of the educated elite, particularly those of Chinese ancestry.

The tax laws as well as employment and social security benefits provide added incentives for the affluent to have more children. The state-run Social Development Unit helps female university graduates find suitable husbands. Singapore's policy has succeeded in boosting fertility 3.5 percent over the past decade.[162]

WHAT SHOULD WE DO?

What does it mean that we live in a country in which white women disproportionately undergo expensive technologies to enable them to bear children, while Black women disproportionately undergo surgery that prevents them from being able to bear any? Surely this contradiction must play a critical part in our deliberations about the morality of these technologies. What exactly does race mean for our understanding of the new reproduction?

Let us consider three possible responses for social policy. First, we might acknowledge that race influences the use of reproductive technologies, but decide this does not justify interfering with individuals' liberty to use them. Second, we could work to ensure greater access to these technologies by providing public assistance or including them in insurance plans. Finally, we might determine that these technologies are harmful and that their use should therefore be discouraged.

The Liberal Response: Setting Aside Social Justice

One response to this racial disparity is to note that it stems from the economic and social structure, not from individuals' use of reproductive technologies. Protection of individuals' procreative liberty should prohibit government intervention in the choice to use IVF and other high-tech services, as long as that choice itself does not harm anyone. Because protecting individual liberty from state intrusion is so central to liberal philosophy, I call this the liberal response.[163] Currently, there is little government supervision of reproduction-assisting technologies, and many proponents fear legal regulation of these new means of reproduction. In their view, financial and social barriers to IVF are unfortunate but inappropriate reasons to interfere with those fortunate enough to have access to this technology. Nor, according to the liberal response, does the right to use these technologies entail any government obligation to provide access to them. Just as current constitutional jurisprudence recognizes no right to public funding of abortions or other reproductive health services, there is no constitutional right to government subsidies for high-tech fertility treatment. Some prominent liberal thinkers, such as John Rawls and Ronald Dworkin, have addressed economic inequality in their accounts of political liberalism. But most, including a majority of U.S. Supreme Court justices, set aside such concerns. Furthermore, if for cultural reasons Blacks choose not to use these technologies, this is no reason to deny them to people who have different cultural values.

Perhaps we should not question infertile couples' motives for wanting genetically related children. After all, people who have children the old-fashioned way may also practice this type of genetic selection when they choose a mate. It would be hypocritical to condemn people who resort to new reproductive technologies for having the same desires for their children as more conventional parents, whose decisions are not so scrutinized. The desire to share genetic traits with our children may not reflect the eugenic notion that these particular traits are *superior* to others; rather, as Barbara Berg notes, "these characteristics may simply symbolize to the parents the child's connection to past generations and the ability to extend that lineage forward into the future."[164] Several people have responded to my concerns about race by explaining to me, "White couples want white children not because of any belief in racial superiority, but because they want children who are like them."

Moreover, the danger of government scrutiny of people's motives for their reproductive decisions may override concerns about racism. This danger leads some commentators who oppose the practice of using abortion as a sex-selection technique to nevertheless oppose its legal prohibition.[165] As Tabitha Powledge put it, "To forbid women to use prenatal diagnostic techniques as a way of picking the sexes of their babies is to begin to delineate acceptable and unacceptable reasons to have an abortion. . . . I hate these technologies, but I do not want to see them legally regulated because, quite simply, I do not want to provide an opening wedge for legal regulation of reproduction in general."[166] It would similarly be unwise to permit the government to question individuals' reasons for deciding to use reproduction-assisting technologies.

The Distributive Solution

We need not question individuals' reasons in order to question the societal impact of a practice.[167] My purpose is not to judge individuals' motivations, but to scrutinize the legal and political context which helps to both create and give meaning to individuals' motivations. Another approach to procreative liberty places more importance on reproduction's social context than does the liberal focus on the fulfillment of individual desires. Procreative liberty cannot be separated from concerns about equality. In fact, the very meaning of reproductive liberty is inextricably intertwined with issues of social justice. Policies governing reproduction not only affect an individual's personal identity; they also shape the way we value each other and interpret social problems. The social harm that stems from confining the new reproduction largely in the hands of wealthy white couples might be a reason to demand equalized access to these technologies.

This view also recognizes the social constraints on individuals' ability to make reproductive decisions. The concept of the already autonomous individual who acts freely without government intrusion is a fallacy that privileges decisionmaking by the most wealthy and powerful members of society. It ignores the communities and social systems that both help and hinder an individual in determining her reproductive life.

Obviously, the unequal distribution of wealth in our society prevents the less well off from buying countless goods and services that wealthy people can afford. But there may be a reason why we should be especially concerned about this result when it applies to reproduction. The same reasons that lead liberals to protect the rights of privileged individuals to use expensive reproductive technologies counsel in favor of paying closer attention to reproduction's social consequences.

Reproduction is special. Government policy concerning reproduction has tremendous power to affect the status of entire groups of people. This is why the Supreme Court in *Skinner v. Oklahoma* declared the right to bear children to be "one of the basic civil rights of man."[168] This is why in their *Planned Parenthood v. Casey* opinion Supreme Court Justices O'Connor, Kennedy, and Souter stressed the importance that the right to an abortion had for women's equal social status. It is precisely the connection between reproduction and human dignity that makes a system of procreative liberty that privileges the wealthy and powerful particularly disturbing.

Because procreative liberty is such an important right, so central to "personal identity, to dignity, and to the meaning of one's life,"[169] its infringement by forces other than the state should also be addressed. Why must we adopt the baseline of existing inequalities? Why should the deepening of these inequalities not weigh heavily in balancing the benefits and harms of assisted reproduction? Procreative liberty's importance to human dignity is a compelling reason to guarantee the equal distribution of procreative resources in society. Moreover, addressing the power of unequal access to these resources to entrench unjust social hierarchies is no less important than allowing wealthy individuals alone to fulfill expensive procreative choices. We might therefore address the racial disparity in the use of reproductive technologies by ensuring through public spending that their use is not concentrated among affluent white people. Government subsidies, such as Medicaid, and legislation mandating health insurance coverage of fertility services would allow more diverse and widespread enjoyment of the new reproduction.

Should We Discourage the New Reproduction?

If these technologies are in some ways positively harmful, will expanding the distribution of fertility services solve the problem? Will distributing more of the technologies be enough to redress the racist social arrangements that make these technologies dangerous? Political philosopher Iris Marion Young criticizes liberal theories of distributional justice for ignoring the institutional context that inhibits people from determining their actions and that helps to guide distributive patterns.[170] This distributive approach restricts the meaning of social justice to the morally proper allocation of material goods among society's members. Although the more equalized distribution of resources would alleviate many social problems, it alone cannot eliminate oppressive social structures. My racial critique of the new reproduction is more unsettling than its exposure of the maldistribution of technologies. It also challenges the importance that we place on genetics and genetic ties. Eradicating the harmful aspects of new reproductive technologies, then, may require deterring people from using them.

But can we limit individuals' access to these technologies without

critically trampling on individual freedom from unwarranted government intrusion? After all, government has perpetrated much injustice
on the theory that individual interests must be sacrificed for the public good. This was the rationale justifying the eugenic sterilization
laws enacted earlier in this century. According to eugenicists, the law
could restrict the reproductive liberty of the unfit in the interest of improving the genetic quality of the nation.

Even for liberals, individuals' freedom to use reproductive technologies is not absolute. Most liberals would place some limit on their
use, perhaps by identifying the legitimate reasons for procreation.
John Robertson, for example, concedes that the state may prevent
parents from cloning offspring or using genetic screening to intentionally diminish the health of their children (intentionally bearing a
deaf child, for example).[171] He justifies this restriction by arguing that
these uses of reproduction-assisting technologies do not further the
core value of procreation of producing "normal, healthy children" for
rearing.[172] If such a core view of reproduction can limit individuals'
personal procreative decisions, then why not consider a view that
takes into account the new reproduction's role in social arrangements
of wealth and power? If the harm to an individual child or even to a
core notion of procreation can justify barring parents from using the
technique of their choice, then why not the new reproduction's potential for worsening group inequality? The magnitude of harm that can
result from the unequal use of these technologies, an inequality rooted
partly in racism, justifies government regulation.

Some have concluded that the harms caused by certain reproduction-assisting practices even justify their prohibition. In 1985, for example, the United Kingdom passed the Surrogacy Arrangements Act
banning commercial contract pregnancy arrangements and imposing
fines and/or imprisonment on the brokers who negotiate these agreements.[173] The authors of the act reasoned that "[e]ven in compelling
medical circumstances the dangers of exploitation of one human
being by another appears [*sic*] to the majority of us far to outweigh
the potential benefits, in almost every case."[174] Some Marxist and radical feminists agree that paid pregnancy contracts should be criminalized to prevent their exploitation and commodification of women and
children.[175] Surrogacy contracts are void and unenforceable in five
states in this country; three others prohibit commercial surrogacy.

On the other hand, the government need not depart at all from the
liberal noninterference model of rights in order to discourage or
refuse to support practices that contribute to social injustice.[176] Even

the negative view of liberty that protects procreative choice from government intrusion leaves the state free to decide *not* to lend assistance to the fertility business or its clients. Indeed, liberals who argue that the state *must* facilitate the use of these technologies, by enforcing paid pregnancy contracts for instance, contradict their own precepts.

We should therefore question a system that channels millions of dollars into the fertility business, rather than spending similar amounts on programs that would provide more extensive benefits to infertile people. *New York Times* reporter Trip Gabriel describes the "$350 million-a-year" fertility business as "a virtually free-market branch of medicine . . . largely exempt from government regulation and from the downward pressure on costs that insurance companies exert."[177] The fact that new reproductive technologies facilitate procreative decisions is not reason enough to exempt them from government supervision; obstetrics and abortion services are subject to regulation. Taking these social justice concerns more seriously would justify government efforts to reallocate resources away from expensive reproductive technologies toward activities that would benefit a wider range of people.

Indeed, we can no longer avoid these concerns about the social costs and benefits of IVF. Such calculations are now part of the debate surrounding the advisability of state laws requiring insurance companies to include the cost of fertility treatment in their coverage. One as yet unsuccessful couple reported that "insurance has paid for everything at about $100,000 a year (three years now)."[178] Covering the costs of expensive high-tech procedures means raising the price of insurance for everyone. The Massachusetts Association of Health Maintenance Organizations says its members pay $40 million more in premiums to cover infertility treatment for 2,000 couples.[179] The federal Office of Technology Assessment estimates that it would cost $25 million to extend coverage for IVF under the plan that insures the nation's 3 million civilian employees of the federal government.[180] Moreover, providing insurance for expensive fertility treatments but not adoption (which can also cost thousands of dollars) ironically makes these technologies the only alternative some people can afford.

A study recently reported in the *New England Journal of Medicine* calculated the real cost of IVF at approximately $67,000 to $114,000 per successful delivery.[181] For older couples with more complicated conditions, the cost rose to $800,000. Unlike the $8,000 cost per IVF cycle, these figures refer to the costs involved in the birth of at least one live baby as a result of IVF, including the cost of treatment, delivery, and neonatal intensive care. (The high incidence of risky multiple births with IVF dramatically boosts hospital charges.) The authors concluded that the debate about insurance coverage must take into account these economic implications of IVF, as well as ethical and social judgments about resource allocation. Yes, insurance coverage increases access to these technologies to some degree. But can we justify devoting such exorbitant sums to a risky, nontherapeutic procedure with an 80 percent failure rate when so many basic health needs go unmet?

Research designed to reduce infertility, programs that facilitate adoption, and the general provision of basic human needs are examples of expenditures that would help a far broader range of people than IVF.[182] The federal government has done little to combat the epidemic spread of chlamydia, an STD that affects millions of people and contributes to especially high infertility rates among young Black women. It must be remembered that most high-tech interventions such as IVF do not cure infertility; the couples who use them remain biologically unable to bear a child without technological assistance. The medical establishment has much more to gain from developing expensive technological interventions that foster a dependent clientele than from research directed at the causes and prevention of infertility. The IVF clinic at New York Hospital–Cornell Medical Center, for example, generates a $2 million annual surplus for the Cornell Medical College that enables its physicians to earn up to $1 million a year.[183] This kind of profit creates a strong incentive to push infertile couples toward repeated attempts at a high-tech solution, despite abysmal success rates that only drop with each try.

Black women in particular would be better served by a focus on the improvement of basic conditions that lead to infertility, such as occupational and environmental hazards, diseases, and complications following childbirth or abortion. Increasing access to preventive health care and treatment for STDs would yield a far bigger payoff than increasing access to expensive fertility treatment. Yet the relative modesty of financial rewards, combined with disinterest in increasing Black birthrates, steers medical ventures off this more promising course. Indeed, as we saw in Chapter 3, more resources are directed toward developing long-term contraceptives for poor women of color in the United States and abroad that may lead to an even higher incidence of infertility-causing STDs and other health problems.

The concentration of effort on the new reproduction diverts attention from the interests of poorer Black women in another, more subtle way. Although the "biological clock" metaphor is grossly exaggerated, one reason for infertility among white, educated, high-income women is their postponement of childbearing in order to pursue a career.[184] The cause of these women's infertility is not biological; rather, it is a workplace that makes it virtually impossible for women to combine employment and child-rearing. These women can avoid this social problem by seeking expensive fertility treatment after achieving some status in the office. In other words, they can afford to bypass the structural unfairness to mothers through technological intervention. Similarly, many affluent white women gained entry to the male-dominated workplace by assigning female domestic tasks to low-paid dark-skinned nannies.[185] These luxuries, which most Black women cannot afford, take the place of widespread reforms that would increase *all* women's employment options. Relying on expensive interventions to resolve the tension between child-raising and work destroys the possibility of unity in women's struggle for fundamental change in the sexual division of labor.

This reliance on high-tech intervention rather than improving basic health and workplace conditions hurts not only Black women but all women and, ultimately, all of our society. We would all benefit from a health policy that redirected the billions of dollars currently spent on fertility treatment toward eradicating the causes of infertility. We would all benefit from a view of family that valued loving relationships, however created, rather than genes traded on the market. We would all benefit from a work world that appreciated mothers' care for children. Once again, America's unwillingness to attend to the needs of Black citizens stymies the potential for widespread change that would enrich everyone's life.

∞

There is no question that the way we view the freedom to create children technologically, as well as "naturally," is shaped by race. Racial injustice infects the use of new reproductive technologies no less than it infects the use of birth control. While too much fertility is seen as a Black woman's problem that must be curbed through welfare policy, too little fertility is seen as a white woman's problem to be cured through high-tech interventions. The new reproduction is designed for the creation of white babies.

We must address the contribution that this disparity makes to racial injustice in America. Staunch civil libertarians object that intervening might unfairly limit the choices of wealthy white people. I, too, am wary of state interference in reproductive decisionmaking; after all, Black women are the most vulnerable to such government abuse. But our vision of procreative liberty must include the eradication of group oppression, and not just a concern for protecting the reproductive choices of the most privileged. It is to that reconception of reproductive liberty that I now turn.

THE MEANING OF LIBERTY

If Americans' reproductive decisions are protected by the Constitution, how is it possible that Black women's reproduction has been subjected to so much degradation and intrusion? The Supreme Court has elevated reproductive liberty to the level of a fundamental right against government interference deserving of the highest judicial scrutiny. But Black women's reproductive choices seem to fall outside this sphere of protection that is supposed to apply to all citizens. There is something drastically wrong with a conception of reproductive freedom that allows this wholesale exclusion of the most disadvantaged from its reach. We need a way of rethinking the meaning of liberty so that it protects all citizens equally. I propose that focusing on the connection between reproductive rights and racial equality is the place to start.

WHOM LIBERTY LEAVES OUT

The dominant view of liberty reserves most of its protection only for the most privileged members of society. This approach superimposes liberty on an already unjust social structure, which it seeks to preserve against unwarranted government interference. Liberty protects all citizens' choices from the most direct and egregious abuses of government power, but it does nothing to dismantle social arrangements that make it impossible for some people to make a choice in the first place. Liberty guards against government intrusion; it does not guarantee social justice.

Three tenets of this version of liberal philosophy support the exclusion of social justice concerns from the meaning of liberty. Liberty is understood as a guarantee of government neutrality, as limited only to tangible harms, and as a negative right. Liberals require the state to remain neutral as to competing conceptions of value and human relationships so that each individual is free to choose her own moral understanding of justice.[1] Liberty allows each individual to live by her own understanding of procreation, as long as she causes no harm to others. While government neutrality protects citizens against imposition of state orthodoxy, it also means that the definition of liberty must take a color-blind stance in regard to reproductive policies. Critical thinkers have demonstrated that the liberal reliance on seemingly neutral principles actually legitimates the interests and experiences of white people.[2] Government neutrality conceals the racist origins of social practices that do not overtly discriminate on the basis of race. It ignores the way that the degrading mythology about Black mothers influences public policy as long as government officials do not explicitly act on the basis of race.

Liberal theory assumes that people are rational, autonomous beings who make procreative decisions of their own free will. Any state intrusion in these decisions would violate the command of neutrality. But this conception of individuals does not take into account the background social conditions that may have constrained their decisions. In this view, an indigent mother's reliance on government benefits to survive does not diminish the voluntariness of her agreement to use Norplant in exchange for welfare payments. Nor do the limited range of women's economic opportunities or the parties' unequal social and economic positions diminish the voluntariness of a surrogate's agreement to sell her reproductive labor. Indeed, liberals believe that refusing to uphold surrogacy arrangements or to allow poor women to "choose" Norplant "undermines the notion that women are free, autonomous actors."[3]

Some liberals also dismiss social justice concerns by characterizing them as "symbolic" or "intangible." Liberty only commands that the government stay out of people's decisions, which individuals are free to make as long as they do not cause *tangible* harm. This means that the government need not be concerned with social practices that create such vague injuries as the devaluation of Black mothers. By this logic, the claim that a practice may adversely impact the social status of all women or reinforce the subordination of Black people is less important than the claim of personal loss to an individual citizen. But policies that degrade the value of Black women's childbearing really do harm people. What distinguishes the traditional view of liberty from an approach that takes social justice into account is not the latter's failure to require actual effects. I am concerned with a different type of effect—the effect on social and political relationships, rather than simply on individual choices. Social harms such as these can have a far more widespread and devastating impact on people's lives.

Finally, the negative view of liberty privileges the choices of those who have the means to realize them. The Supreme Court interprets reproductive liberty as a negative right against state interference, not a positive right to the resources needed to procreate or to prevent procreation. "It means that a person violates no moral duty in making a procreative choice," explains John Robertson in his influential *Children of Choice*, but "does not imply the duty of others to provide the resources or services necessary to exercise one's procreative liberty despite plausible moral arguments for governmental assistance."[4] Liberals frame the issue of access to abortion or reproductive technologies, for example, as freedom from government interference with private decisions to use them, rather than a claim to public resources to make these options truly available.

If reproductive freedom is important enough to human dignity to protect from government interference, then its infringement by forces other than the state should also be addressed. Liberals' defense of reproductive liberty as a "moral right" central to "personal identity, meaning, and dignity"[5] is a compelling reason to ensure the equal distribution of procreative resources in society. Liberals give no good reason why our understanding of procreative liberty must adopt a baseline of existing inequalities or why the deepening of these inequalities should not weigh heavily in our deliberations about policies affecting reproduction.

Many feminists have similarly renounced privacy doctrine on the grounds that government nonintervention into the private sphere permits women's subordination rather than promoting women's autonomy.[6] They point out that the private realm of the family has long operated as a site of violence and male domination. Catharine MacKinnon, for example, argues that privacy serves as "a means of subordinating women's collective needs to the imperatives of male supremacy" because "the legal concept of privacy can and has shielded the place of battery, marital rape, and women's exploited labor; has preserved the central institutions whereby women are deprived of identity, autonomy, control, and definition; and has protected the primary activity through which male supremacy is expressed and enforced."[7] As another legal scholar, Fran Olsen, puts it, "Privacy is most enjoyed by those with power."[8] These theorists have criticized the Supreme Court's view of women's right to abortion as a privacy right, arguing that a gender equality approach to reproductive freedom would have advanced women's interests far better.

The negative view of reproductive liberty not only disregards "private" obstacles to reproductive decisionmaking, such as social prejudices, racist business practices, and the maldistribution of wealth, but it also disregards certain instances of state interference in poor people's reproductive decisions. It allows the state to exploit poor women's dependence on government funds to influence their reproductive choices. Even prohibition of very coercive measures, such as criminal sanctions for refusing to use birth control, leaves ample room for the state to constrain poor women's reproductive decisionmaking by placing conditions on welfare benefits. Incentive programs give adequate protection to autonomy under the traditional approach because they allow welfare mothers to make a choice. Because this view sees poor women's waiver of their right to procreate as voluntary, it does not require the government to justify its deliberate effort to deter these women from having children.

This view recognizes the violation in a statute that bans a white, middle-class woman from taking the procreative option she wishes (a law that absolutely prohibits abortion or a method of birth control, for example). But it disregards how poverty, racism, sexism, and other systems of power — often facilitated by government action — also impair many people's decisions about procreation. Liberals cannot tell us why their theory of reproductive liberty, which invalidates virtually every hindrance to affluent people's procreative options, should so easily permit much more coercive government programs targeting poor people. Far from being impartial, this view of reproductive liberty privileges the choices of the wealthiest and most powerful members of society.

Not only does this concept of liberty leave inequality intact, but it overlooks and sometimes precludes efforts to eradicate inequality. Once liberty is set up to protect only the interests of the most privileged, it then excludes the equality claims of the dispossessed. Most liberals would probably refuse to consider, for example, the possibility I raised in the previous chapter that social justice might require that the government restrict the availability of new reproductive technologies for wealthy people. "As troubled as we might be by differential access," John Robertson contends, "the demands of equality should not bar access for those fortunate enough to have the means." Nor does Robertson view new reproductive technologies' capacity to intensify already existing inequalities as a serious consideration. He dismisses the possibility that genetic enhancement might exacerbate race and class disparities as "simply another instance in which wealth gives advantages."[9]

This notion of liberty rests on the assumption that privileging individual autonomy over social justice is essential to human freedom. The primacy of liberty, which shifts the burden of persuasion to those seeking to limit individual choice, does not allow for the possibility that other concerns might have equal constitutional or moral importance. This way of thinking separates social justice from the meaning and realization of individual liberty. It operates like blinders that obscure issues of social power that determine the significance of reproductive freedom and control. It obscures them, not by ignoring them altogether, but by claiming to achieve individual freedom without the need to rectify social inequalities. In his analysis of procreative liberty, for example, Robertson views the question of the state's obligation to alleviate social and economic circumstances that constrain reproductive decisionmaking as a "*separate* issue of social justice."[10] While the state is obligated to protect procreative liberty as a matter of *rights*, Robertson argues, it remains free to decide whether or not to address economic and social inequities as a matter of *social policy*. This is the identical position taken by the Supreme Court in the abortion-funding cases when it attributed women's inability to pay for abortions to their poverty rather than to any constitutionally recognizable state action.

The primacy of liberty over equality, then, accepts the possibility that inequality may be inevitable in a liberal society. Although the pursuit of equality, once liberty is assured, is commendable, liberalism cannot guarantee its realization. Proponents of this view hold that adequate protection of individual liberty may simply make substantive equality a pipe dream. Inequality is the price we may have to pay for freedom. For this reason, philosopher William Galston defends liberalism as the best accommodation of human differences we can hope for: "It is 'repressive' not in comparison with available alternatives but only in relation to *unattainable* fantasies of perfect liberation."[11] "Face it," these theorists seem to admonish, "seriously protecting individual liberty means relinquishing the fantasy of complete racial equality."

The preference for liberty over equality is ingrained in America's constitutional history. While the Constitution's framers protected their private property and personal expression from government power, they neglected to mention equality in the Constitution. When the founding fathers were confronted with the contradiction of creating a new government dedicated to individual liberty that also permitted the enslavement of Africans, "they decided that protecting the property of slaveowners must have priority over black freedom."[12] The Constitution's guarantees of liberty existed alongside its recognition and protection of slavery for nearly a century.

After the Civil War and the Reconstruction amendments abolished slavery and its vestiges, white Americans continued to rely on the Constitution's protection of their liberty to safeguard their position of power. The Supreme Court's 1896 decision in *Plessy v. Ferguson*, which upheld Louisiana's segregation of railroad cars, affirmed the state's power under the Constitution to make formal legal distinctions between the white and colored races. But it was Justice John Marshall Harlan's dissenting opinion that set forth the conservative notion of liberty that was to outlive the holding in *Plessy*:

> The white race deems itself to be the dominant race in this country. And so it is, in prestige, in achievements, in education, in wealth, and in power. So, I doubt not, it will continue to be for all time, if it remains true to its great heritage, and *holds fast to the principles of constitutional liberty*.

Although *Plessy*'s separate-but-equal doctrine was repudiated six decades later in *Brown v. Board of Education*, the doctrine that holds fast to liberty at the expense of racial equality remains a principal means of realizing Justice Harlan's prediction.

Defenders of this approach celebrate liberalism's advantages over totalitarian or communitarian regimes for protecting personal autonomy. "Without the protection of rights," Robertson points out, "important aspects of individual dignity and integrity have no protection from legislative majorities or policymakers."[13] Liberalism's protection of individual autonomy against totalitarian power is a monumental advance over systems of raw governmental domination. But liberalism has failed to deliver on its promise of freedom for all citizens.

THE NARROW FOCUS OF REPRODUCTIVE RIGHTS

It is not just white male academics who have neglected Black women's procreative interests, but also the mainstream women's movement. The birth control movement in the early part of this century renounced its feminist objectives to collaborate with the eugenics movement, eventually adopting the philosophy of population control. Female crusaders during that period advocated birth control, not as a means of self-determination for all women, but as a tool of social control by the white elite. The first publicly funded birth control clinics were established in the South to lower welfare costs. Decades later, the mainstream opposition to sterilization reform again collided with Black women's interests. When the Committee to End Sterilization Abuse introduced guidelines to end the sterilization abuse of poor minority women, Planned Parenthood and the National Abortion Rights Action League opposed them on the grounds that they restricted white, middle-class women's access to sterilization. In addition, the pro-choice movement remained relatively complacent about the effective denial of access to abortions for poor women by the Supreme Court's decisions in the abortion-funding cases. The movement's belated mobilization triggered by the fear that the Supreme Court might overrule *Roe v. Wade* seemed motivated by the threat to the reproductive rights of affluent women.

Another aspect of the mainstream reproductive rights agenda that eclipses Black women's needs is its focus on abortion. The struggle for judicial recognition of a constitutional right to abortion has consumed the bulk of the movement's energy. This is changing as the leading reproductive rights organizations begin to incorporate issues beyond abortion and as Black women's own organizations gain greater prominence. But to most Americans, "reproductive rights" is still synonymous with "the right to an abortion." The narrow focus on abortion rights reflects the traditional interpretation of liberty. The primary concern of white, middle-class women centers on laws that restrict choices otherwise available to them, such as statutes that make it more difficult to obtain an abortion.

Black women, on the other hand, especially those who are poor, must deal with a whole range of forces that impair their choices. Their reproductive freedom, for example, is limited not only by the denial of access to safe abortions, but also by the lack of resources necessary for a healthy pregnancy and parenting relationship. Their choices are limited not only by direct government interference in their decisions, but also by government's failure to facilitate them. A racist mythology that casts them as unfit to be mothers skews the way that doctors, caseworkers, and judges treat their decision to have children. The focus of reproductive rights discourse on abortion neglects this broader range of reproductive health issues. Addressing the particular concerns of Black women helps to expand our vision of reproductive freedom to include the full scope of what it means to have control over one's reproductive life.

Another problem with the focus on abortion is that it does not respond to policies that regulate pregnancy or that seek to deter it altogether. If abortion is the heart of women's reproductive rights, then state policies that do not interfere with that right seem acceptable. If the full extent of reproductive freedom is the right to have an abortion, then a policy that encourages abortion—such as the prosecution of crack-addicted mothers or the denial of benefits to welfare mothers—does not interfere with that freedom.

A broader understanding of reproductive freedom does not reject abortion rights in favor of a right to procreate. Rather, it sees the right to terminate a pregnancy as one part of a broader right to autonomy over one's body and one's reproductive decisionmaking. It also recognizes the connection between schemes that deny public funding for abortion yet pay for long-term contraceptives such as Norplant and Depo-Provera. Women who cannot be assured of abortion in emergency situations will feel greater pressure to take permanent steps to prevent conception. In this way, subsidizing permanent or temporary sterilization and refusing to pay for abortions go hand in hand. Betsy Hartmann makes a similar point about population control policies that seek to reduce birthrates of Third World women:

> The population control and antiabortion philosophies, although diametrically opposed, share one thing in common: They are both antichoice. Population control advocates impose contraception and sterilization on women; the so-called Right-to-Life movement denies women the basic right of access to abortion and birth control. Neither takes the interests and rights of the individual woman as their starting point. Both approaches attempt to control women, instead of letting women control their bodies themselves.[14]

Black women's advocacy against sterilization and Norplant abuse calls for an alternative approach to reproductive freedom that challenges both the population control and antiabortion positions, one that ensures women access to safe, effective birth control methods as well as protection from coercive birth control policies.

Angela Davis insightfully describes the difference between minority women's support of abortion rights and the endorsement of abortion:

> When Black and Latina women resort to abortions in such large numbers, the stories they tell are not so much about the desire to be free of their pregnancy, but rather about the miserable social conditions which dissuade them from bringing new lives into the world. . . . During the early abortion rights campaign, it was too frequently assumed that legal abortions provided a viable alternative to the myriad problems posed by poverty. As if having fewer children could create more jobs, higher wages, better schools, etc. This assumption reflected the tendency to blur the distinction between *abortion rights* and the general advocacy of *abortion*. The campaign often failed to provide a voice for women who wanted the *right* to legal abortions while deploring the social conditions that prohibited them from bearing more children.[15]

Black women's experiences, then, demand not only a rejection of the singular preoccupation with abortion rights, but also a reassessment of the meaning of abortion rights and its place in a broader vision of reproductive freedom.

CLAIMING REPRODUCTIVE LIBERTY FOR BLACK WOMEN

Despite the serious flaws in the dominant view of liberty, it would be a mistake to abandon the notion of liberty altogether. We should not relinquish its important values for the sake of promoting equality. I see two benefits of liberty for advocating Black women's reproductive rights: liberty stresses the value of self-definition, and it protects against the totalitarian abuse of government power.

First, affirming the constitutional claim to personhood is particularly important to Black women because they have historically been denied the dignity of their full humanity and identity. The principle of self-definition has special significance for Black women. Legal scholar Angela Harris recognizes in the writings of Zora Neale Hurston an insistence on a "conception of identity as a construction, not an essence. . . . [B]lack women have had to learn to construct themselves in a society that denied them full selves."[16] Black women's willful self-definition is an adaptation to a history of social denigration. Rejected from the dominant society's norm of womanhood, Black women have turned to their own internal resources. Harris contrasts this process of affirmative self-definition with the paradigm of women as passive victims. Black women willfully create their own identities out of "fragments of experience, not discovered in one's body or unveiled after male domination is eliminated."

The concept of personhood embodied in liberty can be used to affirm the role of will and creativity in Black women's construction of their own identities. Relying on the concept of self-definition celebrates the legacy of Black women who have survived and transcended conditions of oppression. The process of defining one's self and declaring one's personhood defies the denial of self-ownership inherent in slavery. This affirmation of personhood is especially suited for challenging the devaluation of Black motherhood underlying the regulation of Black reproduction.

This argument for claiming reproductive liberty is similar to the reason why critical race scholars, such as Patricia Williams, disagreed with critics of rights discourse. Critical legal studies theorists rejected rights discourse in part because of its stereotyping of human experience. But Williams argued that this is a lesser historical evil than having been ignored altogether. "The black experience of anonymity, the estrangement of being without a name, has been one of living in the oblivion of society's inverse, beyond the dimension of any consideration at all," writes Williams.[17]

By asserting rights, then, dispossessed people rebel against this social degradation and demand social recognition. "For the historically disempowered, the conferring of rights is symbolic of all the denied aspects of their humanity," Williams contends, for "rights imply a respect that places one in the referential range of self and others, that elevates one's status from human body to social being." It is not Blacks' assertion of their rights such as reproductive liberty but America's lack of commitment to these rights that has perpetuated the oppressive regulation of reproduction.

Another important element of liberty is its delineation of the limits of governmental power. Constitutional law professor Jed Rubenfeld, for example, advances an interpretation of the right of privacy that focuses on the affirmative consequences of laws challenged on the basis of privacy claims.[18] According to Rubenfeld, it is the "totalitarian" intervention of government into a person's life that the right of privacy protects against. The right of privacy, then, means "the right not to have the course of one's life dictated by the state."

Liberty's protection against government abuse makes it a valuable concept for guarding Black women's reproductive decisions. Although government policies do not account for the full extent of the obstacles they face, Black women are especially vulnerable to government control over their decisions. The problem has been that traditional notions of liberty have overlooked these abuses by devaluing the importance of Black women's autonomy and pretending that the government has not acted at all. We can correct these flaws by attending to the essential relationship between liberty and equality.

GOVERNMENT STANDARDS FOR PROCREATION: THE OVERLAP OF LIBERTY AND EQUALITY

The concepts of liberty and equality provide the basis for two separate constitutional challenges to government regulation of Black women's reproduction. A liberty theory addresses the government's interference in Black women's autonomy over their reproductive decisions. An equality theory addresses the ways in which government policy perpetuates the inferior status of Black women. The government's regulation reflects a long history of denigration of Black mothers dating back to slavery, and it serves to perpetuate that legacy of unequal respect.

There is also a powerful argument to be made that the current denial of Black women's reproductive autonomy is a badge of slavery that violates the Thirteenth Amendment. For decades, the Thirteenth Amendment has been relegated to the annals of history, ignored by contemporary civil rights advocates as a potential ground for challenging racially discriminatory laws and practices. But the amendment has enjoyed a recent renaissance in legal scholarship. Some scholars have used the Thirteenth Amendment to seek aggressive federal remedies for current violations of Black citizens' liberties, such as white supremacist speech and violence.[19] Others have extended the Thirteenth Amendment's reach beyond issues involving race to a variety of gender, class, and human rights problems.[20]

Focusing on the Thirteenth Amendment has several benefits: it ties present-day practices that injure Black Americans to the nation's history of racial injustice; it centers attention on the constitutional value of freedom from enslavement; and it authorizes government action to combat both public and private acts of repression. The Thirteenth Amendment claim links together slave masters' control of Black women's childbearing and contemporary policies that penalize Black women for having babies. While slave masters had the power to compel compliance with their procreative mandates through force, current policies more often achieve their ends through the manipulation of government benefits. While slaveowners profited from encouraging slave women to bear many children, modern-day taxpayers believe they save money by discouraging poor Black women from having children. But these practices share the common theme of denying a woman's freedom to control her own reproductive life because of her race. This is the essence of the injury imposed by both slave-breeding and coerced birth control.

I would like to advance a notion of reproductive freedom that combines the values captured by both liberty and equality. The policies I describe in this book combine in a single government action several wrongs prohibited by both constitutional doctrines, grounded in the due process and equal protection clauses of the Fourteenth Amendment, also in the Constitution's antislavery provisions. Black mothers are denied autonomy over procreative decisions because of their race. The government's denial of Black women's fundamental right to choose to bear children serves to perpetuate the legacy of racial discrimination embodied in the devaluation of Black motherhood. The full scope of the government's violation can be better understood, then, by a constitutional theory that acknowledges the complementary and overlapping qualities of the Constitution's guarantees of equality and liberty. Viewing policies that regulate Black reproduction as imposing a racist government standard for procreation uses this approach.

Poor crack addicts and welfare mothers are punished for having babies because they fail to measure up to the state's ideal of motherhood. These women are not penalized simply because they may harm their unborn children or because their childbearing will cost taxpayers money. They are penalized because the combination of their poverty, race, and marital status is seen to make them unworthy of procreating.

Governmental standards for procreation implicate both equality and privacy interests by denying human dignity. The right to bear children goes to the heart of what it means to be human. The value we place on individuals determines whether we see them as entitled to perpetuate themselves in their children. Denying someone the right to bear children—or punishing her for exercising that right—deprives her of a basic part of her humanity. When this denial is based on race, it also functions to preserve a racial hierarchy that essentially disregards Black humanity.

The abuse of sterilization laws designed to effect eugenic policy demonstrates the potential danger of governmental standards for procreation. The salient feature of the eugenic sterilization laws is their brutal imposition of society's restrictive norms for childbearing. Governmental control of reproduction in the name of science masks racist and classist judgments about who deserves to have children. It is grounded on the premise that people who depart from social norms do not deserve to procreate. Carrie Buck, for example, was punished by sterilization not because of any mental disability, but because she was poor and became pregnant out of wedlock.

Explanations of the eugenic rationale reveal this underlying moral standard for procreation. One eugenicist, for example, justified his extreme approach of putting the socially inadequate to death as "the surest, the simplest, the kindest, and most humane means for preventing reproduction among those *whom we deem unworthy of the high privilege.*"[21] Dr. Albert J. Priddy, superintendent of the Virginia Colony for Epileptics and Feebleminded, similarly explained the necessity of eugenic sterilization in one of his annual reports: the "sexual immorality" of "anti-social morons" made them "wholly unfit for exercising the *right of motherhood.*"[22]

These arguments view citizens as instruments of the state. In his book *Human Nature and the Social Order*, published in 1940, Columbia University professor Edward L. Thorndike proposed that women's wombs should be placed "at the disposal of the state" in order that their reproduction serve society in more useful ways.[23] When people deemed undeserving of procreation defy their state-prescribed role by bearing children, they are considered enemies of society. Jacob Landman, a professor at City College in New York, explained this thinking in the introduction to *Human Sterilization*:

> Society has been brought to a greater realization than ever of the evils that attend the presence of the growing number of the socially undesirable people in our population. The mentally diseased, the feebleminded, the idiots, the morons, and the criminals are regarded as the *Nemeses of our civilization* and the prohibition of their propagation is considered the salvation of society and the race.[24]

In this way, procreation by those unfit for motherhood becomes a crime—both literally, as in the case of the prosecution of drug-

addicted mothers or imposition of Norplant as a condition of probation, and figuratively.

Women deemed unworthy of procreation may remain members of
society only if they do not bear children. A 1928 Wisconsin study of
women who were discharged after being sterilized in institutions for
the feebleminded found: "Many mentally deficient persons by consenting to the operation are permitted to return, under supervision, to
society where they become self-supporting social units and *acceptable
citizens*. Those inmates unwilling to consent to the operation remain
segregated for social protection as well as individual welfare."[25] Their
social acceptability was contingent on their consent to sterilization.
This is the effect of proposals to require welfare mothers to be implanted with Norplant or, less directly, of child exclusion policies that
penalize welfare mothers who have additional children. Like the feebleminded women in the 1920s, these deviant mothers are entitled to
social participation only if they agree not to reproduce.

Fourteen years after *Buck v. Bell*, the Supreme Court acknowledged
the danger of eugenic policies. Justice William Douglas recognized
both the fundamental quality of the right to procreate and its connection to equality in *Skinner v. Oklahoma*.[26] *Skinner* considered the constitutionality of the Oklahoma Habitual Criminal Sterilization Act
authorizing the sterilization of persons convicted two or more times
for "felonies involving moral turpitude." An Oklahoma court had ordered Skinner to undergo a vasectomy after he was convicted once of
stealing chickens and twice of robbery with firearms. The statute, the
Court found, treated unequally criminals who had committed the
same kind of offense. For example, men who had committed grand
larceny three times were sterilized, but embezzlers were not. A contemporary version of the Oklahoma statute might be one that imposed sterilization for smoking crack, but not marijuana, during
pregnancy.

The Supreme Court struck down the statute as a violation of the
equal protection clause. Declaring the right to bear children to be
"one of the basic civil rights of man," the Court applied strict scrutiny
to the classification and held that the government failed to demonstrate that the statute's classifications were justified by eugenics or the
inheritability of criminal traits.

Skinner rested on grounds that linked equal protection doctrine and
the right to procreate. Justice Douglas framed the legal question as "a
sensitive and important area of human rights." The reason for the
Court's elevation of the right to procreate was its recognition of the

serious risk of discrimination inherent in state intervention in reproduction. The Court also understood the genocidal implications of a
government standard for procreation: "In evil or reckless hands [the
government's power to sterilize] can cause races or types which are
inimical to the dominant group to wither and disappear."

The critical role of procreation in human survival and the invidious
potential for government discrimination against disfavored groups
make heightened protection crucial. Justice Douglas believed that
the government's biased use of the power to sterilize was just as invidious "as if it had selected a particular race or nationality for oppressive treatment." Justice Robert Jackson's concurrence alluded to the
particular danger inherent in linking this oppressive treatment to
criminal punishment: "There are limits to the extent to which a leg-
islatively represented majority may conduct biological experiments at
the expense of the dignity and personality and natural powers of a minority—even those who have been guilty of what the majority defines
as crimes."

Although the reasons advanced for the sterilization of chicken
thieves and the prosecution of drug-addicted mothers or schemes to
induce welfare mothers to use Norplant are different, these practices
are dangerous for similar reasons. They impose racist governmental
judgments that certain members of society do not deserve to have
children. As the Court recognized in *Skinner*, the enforcement of a
government standard for childbearing denies the disfavored group a
critical aspect of human dignity. When this denial is based on race,
the violation is especially heinous. Governmental policies that perpetuate racial subordination through the denial of procreative rights,
which threaten both racial equality and privacy at once, should be
subject to the most intense scrutiny.

TOWARD A NEW MEANING OF REPRODUCTIVE LIBERTY

Imagine that courts and legislatures have accepted the argument that
the prosecution of crack-addicted mothers violates their right of privacy. All pending indictments for drug use during pregnancy are dismissed and bills proposing fetal abuse laws are discarded. Would
there be any perceptible change in these women's existence? Most of
these women would still live in miserable conditions of poverty, find it
difficult to get drug treatment, and receive inadequate prenatal care.
If they are on welfare, they may be denied any additional benefits for

the new baby. Although these women are especially vulnerable to government regulation, they are also especially vulnerable to the government's accommodation of social forces that degrade them.

As a negative right, liberty is inadequate to eliminate the subordination of Black women. In this section, I will suggest two approaches that I believe are necessary for theories of reproductive liberty to contribute to the end of racial injustice. First, we need to adopt a positive view of liberty. Second, the law must recognize the connection between the right to liberty and racial equality.

The abstract freedom to choose is of meager value without meaningful options from which to choose and the ability to effectuate one's choice. The traditional concept of liberty makes the false presumption that the right to choose is contained entirely within the individual and not circumscribed by the material conditions of the individual's life. Moreover, the abstract freedom of self-definition is of little help to someone who lacks the resources to realize the identity she envisions or whose emergent self is continually beaten down by social forces. Defining the guarantee of personhood as no more than shielding a sphere of personal decisions from the reach of government—merely ensuring the individual's "right to be let alone"—is inadequate to protect the dignity and autonomy of the poor and oppressed.

The definition of liberty as a purely negative right serves to exempt the state from any obligation to ensure the social conditions and resources necessary for self-determination and autonomous decision-making. Based on this narrow view of liberty, the Supreme Court has denied a variety of claims to government aid. Catharine MacKinnon notes that "[i]t is apparently a very short step from that which the government has a duty not to intervene in to that which it has no duty to intervene in." An alternative notion of liberty need not make the step between these two propositions. "Ultimately, the affirmative duties of government cannot be severed from its obligations to refrain from certain forms of control," notes Laurence Tribe, for "both must respond to a substantive vision of the needs of human personality."[27]

This concept of liberty includes not only the negative proscription against government coercion, but also the affirmative duty of government to protect the individual's personhood from degradation and to facilitate the processes of choice and self-determination. This approach shifts the focus of liberty theory from state nonintervention to an affirmative guarantee of personhood and autonomy. Under this postliberal doctrine, the government is not only prohibited from penalizing welfare mothers or crack-dependent women for choosing to bear children; it is also required to provide subsistence benefits, drug treatment, and medical care. Ultimately, the state should facilitate, not block, citizens' efforts to install more just and egalitarian economic, social, and political systems. Legal scholar Robin West has eloquently captured this progressive ideal of liberty as "an individual life free of illegitimate social coercion facilitated by hierarchies of class, gender, or race. The goal is an affirmatively autonomous existence: a meaningfully flourishing, independent, enriched individual life."[28]

This affirmative view of liberty is not a free-for-all, extending to disempowered groups the right of privileged people to do whatever they want with their bodies. It is grounded in the understanding that protecting the human dignity of all citizens requires affirmative steps to destroy unjust institutions and practices. This objective also requires limiting private citizens' ability to exploit others. Janice Raymond contends that a human rights approach to reproductive freedom supports a ban on surrogacy arrangements and reproductive technologies. Because international human rights are based on the dignity and integrity of human beings, she explains, "whatever violates a person's dignity or integrity—economic exploitation, medical experimentation, and the trafficking in women's bodies for sexual or reproductive purposes—is not a right, either for the persons who say they choose to engage in these acts or for those who induce them to participate."[29] As I suggested in Chapter 6, for example, a social justice approach would justify prohibiting private fertility clinics from discriminating against Black women or even restricting the amount of business they do.

This affirmative view of liberty takes on a new dimension by recognizing the connection between liberty and racial equality. The government's duty to guarantee personhood and autonomy stems not only from the needs of the individual but also from the needs of the entire community. The harm caused by restrictive policies is not simply the incursion on each individual welfare mother's decisionmaking; it is the perpetuation of a degraded image that affects the status of an entire race. The devaluation of a poor crack addict's decision to bear a child is tied to the dominant society's disregard for the motherhood of all Black women. The diminished value placed on Black motherhood, in turn, is a badge of racial inferiority worn by all Black people. The social justice approach to liberty recognizes the connection between the dehumanization of the individual and the subordination of the group.

The reason that legislatures should reject laws that punish Black women's reproductive decisions is not an absolute and isolated notion of individual autonomy. Rather, legislatures should reject these laws as a critical step toward eradicating a system that has historically demeaned Black motherhood. Respecting Black women's decisions to bear children is a necessary ingredient of a community that affirms the personhood of all of its members. The right to reproductive autonomy is in this way linked to the goal of racial equality and the broader pursuit of a just society. This broader dimension of liberty's guarantees also provides a stronger claim to government's affirmative responsibilities. The state should act both to address private conduct and to transform social circumstances that preclude Black women's reproductive autonomy because of this important link between reproduction and racial equality.

Thus, I advocate that race take center stage in our deliberations about reproductive health policy. The quest for racial equality is a compelling reason to eradicate practices that blatantly disrespect Black women's procreative decisions. It is also a compelling reason to scrutinize every policy concerning reproduction to determine its impact on Blacks. As prior chapters disclosed, race has profoundly influenced every aspect of childbearing in America, helping to shape the very meaning of reproductive freedom. America's definition of and preoccupation with race inextricably ties reproductive politics to racial politics. There is good cause to suspect a racial agenda behind programs that affect reproduction and to be concerned about these programs' effect on the status of Black people.

The result of this new race consciousness will not only be to improve Black women's lives—although this alone would be a monumental achievement. It will be to free our understanding of reproductive liberty from racism's corrupting influence, so that we may set about the task of creating a society in which each citizen is equally respected. Racism has stunted Americans' imagination of reproductive freedom and stymied development of liberating reproductive policies that would benefit everyone. Only by exploding racism's hold can we hope to envision and achieve reproductive justice.

Liberals are right in that protecting procreative liberty is crucial to ensuring human dignity and freedom. But a vision of procreative liberty that sets aside considerations of social justice and equality will achieve just the opposite: it will reinforce social hierarchies that deny many individuals the ability to be self-determining human beings. Once we understand liberty as requiring the eradication of oppressive structures rather than opposing these changes, it makes no sense to privilege liberty over equality. A far better approach for theorists committed to protecting individual autonomy is to explore how social justice could be made central to their conception of rights, of harms, and of the value of procreation.

Under this alternative view, procreation's special status stems as much from its role in social structure and political relations as from its meaning to individuals. Seeing the value of procreation centered in this social context changes our understanding of both private choices and state conduct relating to reproduction. Social justice becomes a critical, rather than a separable, concern in judging the value of individuals' procreative decisions and the legitimacy of government actions and inactions that affect these decisions. These concerns would invalidate government conditions on welfare benefits that discourage recipients from having children. Furthermore, they would call for government action that steers resources away from expensive reproductive technologies and long-term contraceptives and toward research that improves women's health.

I see the main effect of a social justice approach as promoting liberty rather than restricting it. My objective is not to deny wealthy people's options because others do not have them. Rather, my vision of liberty seeks to ensure that dispossessed and disempowered groups share the means to be self-determining and valued members of society. For too long, Black women's struggle against the most degrading repression has been left out of the official story of reproductive rights in America. But it is their struggle that highlights the poverty of current notions of reproductive freedom. It is also their struggle that can lead to a more radical vision of reproductive justice. As I have tried to show throughout this book, a vision of liberty that respects the reproductive integrity of Black women is a critical step toward a just society for everyone.

Notes

Preface to the Vintage Books Edition (2017)

1. Stacy Buckingham-Howes et al., "Systematic Review of Prenatal Cocaine Exposure and Adolescent Development," *Pediatrics* 131, no. 6 (June 2013); Katie McDonough, "Long-term Study Debunks Myth of the 'Crack Baby,'" *Salon*, July 23, 2013.
2. Lynn M. Paltrow and Jeanne Flavin, "Arrests of and Forced Interventions on Pregnant Women in the United States, 1973–2005: Implications for Women's Legal Status and Public Health," *Journal of Health Politics, Policy & Law* 38, no. 2 (April 2013), pp. 299–343.
3. Michele Goodwin, "Fetal Protection Laws: Moral Panic and the New Constitutional Battlefront," *California Law Review* 102, no. 4 (August 2014), pp. 781–875.
4. Nina Liss-Schultz, "Tennessee's War on Women Is Sending New Mothers to Jail," *Mother Jones*, March 14, 2016.
5. Guttmacher Institute, "Last Five Years Account for More Than One-Quarter of All Abortion Restrictions Enacted Since Roe," January 13, 2016.
6. Karen Pazol et al., *Abortion Surveillance—United States, 2009*, available at http://www.cdc.gov/mmwr/preview/mmwrhtml/ss6108a1.htm?s_cid=ss6108a1_x.
7. Amnesty International, *Deadly Delivery: The Maternal Health Care Crisis in the USA* (London: Amnesty International Secretariat, 2010); Marian MacDorman et al., "Recent Increases in the U.S. Maternal Mortality Rate: Disentangling Trends from Measurement Issues," *Obstetrics & Gynecology* 128, no. 3 (September 2016), pp. 447–55.
8. Lynette Holloway, "New York Latest Target of Black Anti-Abortion Billboards," *The Root*, February 24, 2011; Miriam Zoila Pérez, "Past and Present Collide as the Black Anti-Abortion Movement Grows," *Colorlines*, March 3, 2011.
9. SisterSong Policy Report, *Race, Gender and Abortion: How Reproductive Justice Activists Won in Georgia* (Atlanta, Ga., October 2010).
10. "Against Their Will," five-part series, *Winston-Salem Journal*, December 2002. http://www.journalnow.com/specialreports/againsttheirwill/.
11. Corey Johnson, "Female Inmates Sterilized in California Prisons Without Approval," The Center for Investigative Reporting, July 7, 2013.
12. Dorothy Roberts, *Shattered Bonds: The Color of Child Welfare* (New York: Basic Civitas, 2001); Dorothy Roberts, "Complicating the Triangle of Race, Class, and State: The Insights of Black Feminists," *Ethnic & Racial Studies* 37, no. 10 (2014), pp. 1776–82; Dorothy Roberts, "Prison, Foster Care, and the Systemic Punishment of Black Mothers," *UCLA Law Review* 59 (2012), pp. 1474–500.
13. Gwendolyn Mink, *Welfare's End* (Ithaca, N.Y.: Cornell University Press, 2002); Anna Marie Smith, *Welfare and Sexual Regulation* (New York: Cambridge University Press, 2007); Kaaryn S. Gustafson, *Cheating Welfare: Pubic Assistance and the Criminalization of Poverty* (New York: New York University Press, 2011).
14. Rebekah J. Smith, "Family Caps in Welfare Reform: Their Coercive Effects and Damaging Consequences," *Harvard Journal of Law & Gender* 29 (2006), pp. 170, 179.
15. Editorial Board, "Good Riddance to a Repugnant California Cap on Family Aid," *LA Times*, June 16, 2016.
16. Roberts, *Shattered Bonds*; Angela Y. Davis, *Are Prisons Obsolete?* (New York: Seven Stories Press, 2003); Michelle Alexander, *The New Jim Crow: Mass Incarceration in the*

Age of Colorblindness (New York: The New Press, 2010); Beth Richie, *Arrested Justice: Black Women, Violence, and America's Prison Nation* (New York: New York University Press, 2012).

17. Priscilla A. Ocen, "Punishing Pregnancy: Race, Incarceration, and the Shackling of Pregnant Prisoners," *California Law Review* 100, no. 5 (2012), pp. 1239–311. See generally *Mothers Behind Bars: A State-by-State Report Card and Analysis of Federal Policies on Conditions of Confinement for Pregnant and Parenting Women and the Effect on Their Children* (Washington, D.C.: Rebecca Project for Human Rights and National Women's Law Center, 2010).

18. Nakima Levy-Pounds, "Beaten by the System and Down for the Count: Why Poor Women of Color and Children Don't Stand a Chance Against U.S. Drug-Sentencing Policy," *University of St. Thomas Law Journal* 3, no. 2 (2006), pp. 462–98; George Lipsitz, "'In an Avalanche Every Snowflake Pleads Not Guilty': The Collateral Consequences of Mass Incarceration and Impediments to Women's Fair Housing Rights," *UCLA Law Review* 59 (2012), pp. 1746–809; Geneva Brown, "The Intersectionality of Race, Gender, and Reentry: Challenges for African-American Women," issue brief (Washington, D.C.: American Constitution Society, November 2010).

19. Dorothy Roberts, "Privatization and Punishment in the New Age of Reprogenetics," *Emory Law Journal* 54, no. 3 (July 2005), pp. 1343–60.

20. Dorothy Roberts, *Fatal Invention: How Science, Politics, and Big Business Re-create Race in the Twenty-first Century* (New York: The New Press, 2011); Dorothy Roberts, "Race, Gender, and Genetic Technologies: A New Reproductive Dystopia?," *Signs* 34, no. 4 (Summer 2009), pp. 783–804.

21. Lindsey Bever, "White Woman Sues Sperm Bank After She Mistakenly Gets Black Donor's Sperm," *The Washington Post*, October 2, 2014.

22. Jael Silliman et al., *Undivided Rights: Women of Color Organize for Reproductive Justice* (Cambridge, Mass.: South End Press, 2004).

23. I wrote about this experience in Dorothy Roberts, "Reproductive Justice, Not Just Rights," *Dissent*, Fall 2015.

24. Zakiya Luna and Kristin Luker, "Reproductive Justice," *Annual Review of Law & Social Science* 9 (November 2013), p. 330.

25. Kimala Price, "What Is Reproductive Justice?: How Women of Color Activists Are Redefining the Pro-choice Paradigm," *Meridians* 10, no. 2 (April 2010), p. 61.

26. Aline C. Gubrium et al., "Realizing Reproductive Health Equity Needs More Than Long-Acting Reversible Contraception (LARC)," *American Journal of Public Health* 106, no. 1 (2016), pp. 18–19.

27. Dorothy Roberts and Sujatha Jesudason, "Movement Intersectionality: The Case of Race, Gender, Disability, and Genetic Technologies," *DuBois Review* 10, no. 1 (October 2013), pp. 313–28.

Introduction

1. Quoted in Bert James Loewenberg and Ruth Bogin, eds., *Black Women in Nineteenth-Century American Life* (University Park: Pennsylvania State University Press, 1976), p. 329. Free Black women purchased their daughters and sisters from white slave masters to enable them to escape sexual abuse. A fee simple title gives the holder absolute ownership of property.

2. Herbert G. Gutman, *The Black Family in Slavery and Freedom, 1750–1925* (New York: Pantheon, 1976), p. 541.

3. George Frederickson, *The Black Image in the White Mind* (Middletown, Mass.: Wesleyan University Press, 1971); Winthrop D. Jordan, *White over Black: American Attitudes Toward the Negro, 1550–1812* (Chapel Hill: University of North Carolina Press, 1969).

4. Ronald T. Takaki, *Iron Cages: Race and Culture in Nineteenth-Century America* (New York: Knopf, 1979).

5. Cornel West, *Race Matters* (Boston: Beacon Press, 1993), pp. 85–86.

6. Kimberlé Crenshaw, "Race, Reform, and Retrenchment: Transformation and Legitimation in Antidiscrimination Law," *Harvard Law Review* 101 (1988), pp. 1331, 1381.

7. Nancy Stepan, *The Idea of Race in Science: Great Britain, 1800–1960* (Hamden, Conn.: Archon, 1982); Stephen Jay Gould, *The Mismeasure of Man* (New York: Norton, 1981); Barbara Jeanne Fields, "Slavery, Race, and Ideology in the United States of America," *New Left Review* 181 (1990), p. 95.

8. Frederickson, *Black Image in the White Mind*, p. 255.

9. Simone de Beauvoir, *The Second Sex* (New York: Knopf, 1952), p. 171.

10. Angela Y. Davis, *Women, Race, and Class* (New York: Vintage, 1983), pp. 5–7; bell hooks, *Ain't I a Woman? Black Women and Feminism* (Boston: South End Press, 1981); Beverly Guy-Sheftall, *Daughters of Sorrow: Attitudes Toward Black Women, 1880–1920* (Brooklyn, N.Y.: Carlson, 1990), p. 10; Patricia Morton, *Disfigured Images: The Historical Assault on Afro-American Women* (Westport, Conn.: Greenwood, 1991).

11. Davis, *Women, Race, and Class*, p. 5.

12. Deborah Gray White, *Ar'n't I a Woman? Female Slaves in the Plantation South* (New York: Norton, 1985), pp. 28–29.

13. Quoted in Guy-Sheftall, *Daughters of Sorrow*, p. 46.

14. Gerda Lerner, ed., *Black Women in White America: A Documentary History* (New York: Vintage, 1973), pp. 163–71; Paula Giddings, *When and Where I Enter: The Impact of Black Women on Race and Sex in America* (New York: Bantam, 1984), pp. 85–89; hooks, *Ain't I a Woman?* pp. 55–60.

15. Lerner, *Black Women in White America*, pp. 163–64.

16. On Bruce and regressionist ideology, see Gutman, *Black Family in Slavery and Freedom*, pp. 531–44.

17. Philip A. Bruce, *The Plantation Negro as a Freeman* (Williamston, Mass.: Corner House, 1889), pp. 84–85.

18. Quoted in Guy-Sheftall, *Daughters of Sorrow*, pp. 11–12.

19. Howard Odum, *Social and Mental Traits of the Negro: Research into the Conditions of the Negro Race in Southern Towns* (New York: Macmillan Co., 1910), p. 165.

20. Paul H. Gebhard et al., *Pregnancy, Birth, and Abortion* (New York: Harper, 1958), p. 154.

21. J. Philippe Rushton, *Race, Evolution, and Behavior: A Life History Perspective* (New Brunswick, N.J.: Transaction, 1994).

22. Adam Miller, "Professors of Hate," *Rolling Stone*, Oct. 20, 1994, p. 7.

23. hooks, *Ain't I a Woman?* p. 85.

24. Elizabeth Fox-Genovese, *Within the Plantation Household: Black and White Women of the Old South* (Chapel Hill: University of North Carolina Press, 1988), p. 292; Ann Ferguson, "On Conceiving Motherhood and Sexuality: A Feminist Materialist Approach," in Joyce Treblicot, ed., *Mothering Essays in Feminist Theory* (Totowa, N.J.: Rowman, 1983), pp. 153, 171.

25. June O. Patton, "Moonlight and Magnolias in Southern Education: The 'Black Mammy Memorial' Institute," *Journal of Negro History* 65 (1980), pp. 149, 153.

26. Brent Staples, "Aunt Jemina Gets a Makeover," *New York Times*, Oct. 19, 1994, p. A22.

27. Edward Mapp, "Black Women in Films," *Black Scholar* 4 (1973), p. 42; Donald Bogle, *Toms, Coons, Mulattoes, Mammies, and Bucks: An Interpretive History of Blacks in American Films* (New York: Viking, 1973); Morton, *Disfigured Images*, pp. 7–8.

28. Michael P. Johnson, "Smothered Slave Infants: Were Slave Mothers at Fault?" *Journal of Southern History* 47 (1981), p. 493, quoting South Carolina Mortality Schedules, 1850, Abbeville District.

29. Ibid., pp. 496–508; Todd L. Savitt, "Smothering and Overlaying of Virginia Slave

Children: A Suggested Explanation," *Bulletin of the History of Medicine* 49 (1975), p. 400.

30. Quoted in Guy-Sheftall, *Daughters of Sorrow*, p. 44.

31. Jacqueline Jones, *Labor of Love, Labor of Sorrow: Black Women, Work, and the Family from Slavery to the Present* (New York: Vintage, 1986).

32. Ibid., p. 63.

33. Ibid., pp. 127–29.

34. W. E. B. Du Bois, "The Black Mother," *The Crisis* 5 (Dec. 1912), p. 78.

35. See, for example, John Dollard, *Caste and Class in a Southern Town* (New York: Harper, 1937); Charles S. Johnson, *Growing Up in the Black Belt: Negro Youth in the Rural South* (Washington, D.C.: American Council on Education, 1941); Allison Davis and John Dollard, *The Personality Development of Negro Youth in the Urban South* (Washington, D.C.: American Youth Commission, 1962 [1940]).

36. E. Franklin Frazier, *The Negro Family in the United States* (Chicago: University of Chicago Press, 1939).

37. Department of Labor, Office of Planning and Policy Research, *The Negro Family: The Case for National Action* (Washington, D.C., 1965).

38. Jewell Hardy Gresham, "The Politics of Family in America," *The Nation*, July 24–31, 1989, p. 116.

39. Charles Murray, "The Coming White Underclass," *Wall Street Journal*, Oct. 29, 1993, p. A14.

40. House Subcommittee on Human Resources, *Illegitimacy and Welfare: Hearings on H.R. 4*, 104th Cong., 1st sess., Jan. 20, 1995 (written testimony of William J. Bennett).

41. Lee Smith, "The New Wave of Illegitimacy," *Fortune*, April 18, 1994, p. 81.

42. Rickie Solinger, *Wake Up Little Susie: Single Pregnancy and Race Before Roe v. Wade* (New York: Routledge, 1992), pp. 24–25.

43. Murray, "The Coming White Underclass."

44. Tom W. Smith, *Ethnic Images* (Chicago: National Opinion Research Center, University of Chicago, 1990), p. 9.

45. Milwaukee County Welfare Rights Organization, *Welfare Mothers Speak Out*, ed. Thomas Howard Tarantino and Dismass Becker (New York: Norton, 1972), p. 72.

46. Philip Gourevitch, "Dial Hate," *New York Magazine*, Oct. 24, 1994, pp. 28, 30.

47. Charles Murray, *Losing Ground: American Social Policy, 1950–1980* (New York: Basic Books, 1984).

48. Wahneema Lubiano, "Black Ladies, Welfare Queens, and State Minstrels," in Toni Morrison, ed., *Race-ing Justice, En-Gendering Power: Essays on Anita Hill, Clarence Thomas and the Construction of Social Reality* (New York: Pantheon, 1992), pp. 323, 339.

49. Lucy A. Williams, "Race, Rat Bites, and Unfit Mothers: How Media Discourse Informs Welfare Legislation Debate," *Fordham Urban Law Journal* 22 (1995), pp. 1159, 1164–66.

50. See, e.g., Rich Cornell, "The Hidden Devastation of Crack," *Los Angeles Times*, Dec. 18, 1994, p. A1; Judith Kleinfeld, "Crack-Impaired Children Show Strange Behavior in School," *Anchorage Daily News*, Feb. 20, 1995, p. B8; Sheila Simmons, "Greater Cleveland's First Crack Babies Are Now in School; How Are They Doing? And at What Cost to Society?" *Plain Dealer*, Dec. 11, 1994, p. 8.

51. Ted Weisenburger, "Who's Protecting Our Children?" *Arizona Republic*, Sept. 18, 1994, p. E1.

52. Tony Tague, Muskegon County Prosecutor, *Protection of Pregnant Addicts and Drug-Affected Infants in Muskegon County, Michigan* (Muskegon, Mich.: Muskegon County Prosecutor's Office, 1991), p. 3.

53. Katharine Greider, "Crackpot Ideas; Exaggerated Reports of Damage Done to Babies Born to Mothers Who Use Crack Cocaine," *Mother Jones* 20 (July 1995), p. 52, quoting columnist Charles Krauthammer.

54. Ibid.

55. Marilyn Gardner, "Crack Babies Disadvantaged from Day 1," *Houston Post*, Jan. 14, 1990, p. F1 (emphasis added).

56. Jeff Dickerson, "Crack Babies Cost Us a Lot More Than $504 Million," *Atlanta Journal*, Sept. 20, 1991, p. A18.

Chapter 1. Reproduction in Bondage

1. Herbert G. Gutman, *The Black Family in Slavery and Freedom, 1750–1925* (New York: Pantheon, 1976), pp. 84–85.

2. Henry Louis Gates, Jr., "To be Raped, Bred, or Abused," *New York Times Book Review*, Nov. 22, 1987, p. 12, reviewing Harriet Jacobs, *Incidents in the Life of a Slave Girl* (1987).

3. A. Leon Higginbotham, Jr., *In the Matter of Color: Race and the American Legal Process; The Colonial Period* (New York: Oxford University Press, 1978), pp. 42–45, 252.

4. Gutman, *Black Family in Slavery and Freedom*, pp. 77–78.

5. W. E. B. Du Bois, *Black Reconstruction in America, 1860–1880*, ed. August Meier (New York: Atheneum, 1985 [1935]), p. 44.

6. Wilma King, *Stolen Childhood: Slave Youth in Nineteenth-Century America* (Bloomington: Indiana University Press, 1995), p. xvii.

7. Bernard Schwartz, ed., *Statutory History of the United States*, vol. 1, *Civil Rights* (New York: Chelsea House, 1970), p. 83.

8. Claire Robertson, "Africa into the Americas? Slavery and Women, the Family, and the Gender Division of Labor," in David Barry Gasper and Darlene Clark Hine, eds., *More Than Chattel: Black Women and Slavery in the Americas* (Bloomington: Indiana University Press, 1996), pp. 3, 27.

9. Thomas Jefferson to John W. Eppes, June 30, 1820, in Edwin Morris Betts, ed., *Thomas Jefferson's Farm Book: With Commentary and Relevant Extracts from Other Writings* (Princeton: Princeton University Press, 1953), p. 46.

10. Gutman, *Black Family in Slavery and Freedom*, p. 77.

11. George P. Rawick, ed., *The American Slave: A Composite Autobiography*, supp. series 1, vol. 8 (Westport, Conn.: Greenwood, 1977), p. 1075.

12. Richard H. Steckel, "Women, Work, and Health Under Plantation Slavery in the United States," in Gaspar and Hine, *More Than Chattel*, pp. 43, 55.

13. Gutman, *Black Family in Slavery and Freedom*, p. 50.

14. bell hooks, *Ain't I a Woman? Black Women and Feminism* (Boston: South End Press, 1981), pp. 40–41.

15. Robert William Fogel and Stanley L. Engerman, *Time on the Cross: The Economics of American Negro Slavery* (Boston: Little, Brown, 1974), p. 78.

16. Thelma Jennings, "Us Colored Women Had to Go Through a Plenty," *Journal of Women's History* 1 (Winter 1990), pp. 45, 49–74.

17. Frederick Douglass, *Life and Times of Frederick Douglass* (New York: Crowell, 1966), pp. 118–19.

18. Quoted in George P. Rawick, *From Sundown to Sunup: The Making of the Black Community* (Westport, Conn.: Greenwood, 1972), p. 88.

19. Jacqueline Jones, *Labor of Love, Labor of Sorrow: Black Women, Work, and the Family from Slavery to the Present* (New York: Vintage, 1986), p. 34.

20. Catherine Clinton, "Caught in the Web of the Big House: Women and Slavery," in Walter Raser, R. Frank Saunders, and John L. Wakelyn, eds., *The Web of Southern Social Relations: Women, Family, and Education* (Athens: University of Georgia Press, 1985), pp. 19, 23.

21. Quoted in Rawick, *From Sundown to Sunup*, p. 88.

22. Clinton, "Caught in the Web of the Big House," p. 24.

23. Jones, *Labor of Love, Labor of Sorrow*, p. 37. Robert Fogel and Stanley Engerman estimate that "the share of Negro children fathered by whites on slave plantations probably averaged between 1 and 2 percent." *Time on the Cross*, p. 133.

24. Quoted in Beverly Guy-Sheftall, *Daughters of Sorrow: Attitudes Toward Black Women, 1880–1920* (Brooklyn, N.Y.: Carlson, 1990), p. 60.

25. Angela Y. Davis, *Women, Race, and Class* (New York: Vintage, 1983), pp. 23–24.

26. Robertson, "Africa into the Americas?" p. 25.

27. Quoted in Angela P. Harris, "Race and Essentialism in Feminist Legal Theory," *Stanford Law Review* 42 (1990), pp. 581, 600.

28. See Jacquelyn Dowd Hall, "'The Mind That Burns in Each Body': Women, Rape, and Racial Violence," in Ann Snitow et al., eds., *Powers of Desire: The Politics of Sexuality* (New York: Monthly Review Press, 1983), pp. 328, 332–33.

29. Caroline D. Krass, "Bringing the Perpetrators of Rape in the Balkans to Justice: Time for an International Criminal Court," *Denver Journal of International Law and Policy* 22 (Spring 1994), pp. 317, 320.

30. Judith Kelleher Schafer, "The Long Arm of the Law: Slave Criminals and the Supreme Court in Antebellum Louisiana," *Tulane Law Review* 60 (1986), pp. 1247, 1265.

31. A. Leon Higginbotham Jr. and Anne F. Jacobs, "The 'Law Only as an Enemy': The Legitimization of Racial Powerlessness Through the Colonial and Antebellum Criminal Laws of Virginia," *North Carolina Law Review* 70 (1992), pp. 969, 1055–56.

32. See A. Leon Higginbotham, *In the Matter of Color: Race and the American Legal Process* (New York: Oxford University Press, 1978), p. 146.

33. *George v. State*, 37 Miss. 316 (1859).

34. Martha Minow, "Forming Underneath Everything That Grows: Toward a History of Family Law," *Wisconsin Law Review*, 1985, pp. 819, 862.

35. Dorothy Sterling, ed., *We Are Your Sisters: Black Women in the Nineteenth Century* (New York: Norton, 1984), p. 26.

36. Ibid.; Gutman, *Black Family in Slavery and Freedom*, p. 80.

37. Quoted in Eugene D. Genovese, *Roll, Jordan, Roll: The World the Slaves Made* (New York: Pantheon, 1976), pp. 426–27.

38. Elizabeth Fox-Genovese, *Within the Plantation Household: Black and White Women of the Old South* (Chapel Hill: University of North Carolina Press, 1988), p. 334.

39. Sterling, *We Are Your Sisters*, p. 25.

40. Clinton, "Caught in the Web of the Big House," pp. 30–31; hooks, *Ain't I a Woman?* pp. 36–37.

41. Davis, *Women, Race, and Class*, p. 7.

42. Kenneth M. Stampp, *The Peculiar Institution: Slavery in the Ante-Bellum South* (New York: Vintage, 1956), p. 205. On the law governing bequests of slaves not yet born, see Thomas D. Morris, *Southern Slavery and the Law, 1619–1860* (Chapel Hill: University of North Carolina Press, 1996), pp. 89–93.

43. *Banks' Administrator v. Marksberry*, 3 Littell's Rep. 275 (1823).

44. Ibid., p. 280.

45. Quoted in Davis, *Women, Race, and Class*, p. 7.

46. Toni Morrison, *Beloved* (New York: Plume, 1987), p. 23.

47. Stampp, *The Peculiar Institution*, p. 239; Herbert Gutman and Richard Sutch, "The Slave Family: Protected Agent of Capitalist Masters or Victim of the Slave Trade?" in Paul A. David et al., *Reckoning with Slavery* (New York: Oxford University Press, 1976), p. 94; Michael Tadman, *Speculators and Slaves: Masters, Traders, and Slaves in the Old South* (Madison: University of Wisconsin Press, 1989).

48. Thomas D. Russell, "South Carolina's Largest Slave Auctioneering Firm," *Chicago-Kent Law Review* 68 (1993), p. 1241.

49. Ibid.

50. Josiah Henson, *Father Henson's Story of His Own Life* (New York: Corinth Books, 1962), pp. 12–13, quoted in Julius Lester, *To Be a Slave* (New York: Laurel Leaf Library, 1976), pp. 48–49.

51. Wilma King, "'Suffer with Them till Death': Slave Women and Their Children in Nineteenth-Century America," in Gaspar and Hine, *More Than Chattel*, pp. 147, 152.

52. Octavia Albert, *The House of Bondage; or, Charlotte Brooks and Other Stories* (1890), pp. 3–4.

53. Jones, *Labor of Love, Labor of Sorrow*, p. 35.

54. Ibid., p. 14.

55. Quoted in Lester, *To Be a Slave*, p. 38.

56. King, *Stolen Childhood*, p. xx.

57. Stampp, *The Peculiar Institution*, p. 57; Steckel, "Women, Work, and Health," p. 44.

58. Margaret A. Burnham, "An Impossible Marriage: Slave Law and Family Law," *Law and Inequality* 5 (1987), pp. 187, 194.

59. *State v. Mann*, 13 N.C. 263 (1829).

60. Lester, *To Be a Slave*, p. 77.

61. Herbert Gutman devotes an entire chapter to slave naming practices. See "Somebody Knew My Name," in *Black Family in Slavery and Freedom*, pp. 230–56.

62. Peggy Cooper Davis, "Contested Images of Family Values: The Role of the State," *Harvard Law Review* 107 (1994), p. 1348. In *Neglected Stories: The Constitution and Family Values* (New York: Hill and Wang, 1997), Professor Davis demonstrates how the stories of enslaved families influenced the development of the United States Supreme Court's family rights jurisprudence. Despite legal constraints, Davis argues, slaves formed family relationships in which they created their own moral meanings.

63. *Narrative of Lunsford Lane* (1842), reprinted in William L. Katz, ed., *Five Slave Narratives* (New York: Arno Press, 1968), p. 8.

64. Schwartz, *Civil Rights*, p. 72.

65. Peggy Cooper Davis, "Neglected Stories and the Lawfulness of *Roe v. Wade*," *Harvard Civil Rights—Civil Liberties Law Review* 28 (1993), pp. 299, 309.

66. Davis, "Contested Images," p. 1362.

67. Jones, *Labor of Love, Labor of Sorrow*, p. 19.

68. Michael P. Johnson, "Smothered Slave Infants: Were Slave Mothers at Fault?" *Journal of Southern History* 47 (1981), pp. 493, 513.

69. E. Ann Kaplan, "Sex, Work, and Motherhood: The Impossible Triangle," *Journal of Sex Research* 27 (1990), pp. 409, 417.

70. Rayna Rapp, "Constructing Amniocentesis: Maternal and Medical Discourses," in Faye Ginsburg and Anna Loewenhaupt Tsing, eds., *Uncertain Terms: Negotiating Gender in American Culture* (Boston: Beacon Press, 1990), p. 33.

71. Cheryll Ann Cody, "Cycles of Work and of Childbearing: Seasonality in Women's Lives on Low-Country Plantations," in Gasper and Hine, *More Than Chattel*, p. 61. Ann Patton Malone discovered a similar seasonality in her study of 989 slave births from 15 Louisiana plantations recorded from 1822 through 1861. Ann Patton Malone, *Sweet Chariot: Slave Family and Household Structure in Nineteenth-Century Louisiana* (Chapel Hill: University of North Carolina Press, 1992), pp. 232–33.

72. Cody, "Cycles of Work and of Childbearing," p. 69.

73. King, "Suffer with Them till Death," p. 152.

74. Cody, "Cycles of Work and of Childbearing," p. 72.

75. Richard H. Steckel, "A Dreadful Childhood: The Excess Mortality of American Slaves," *Social Science History* 10 (1986), p. 427.

76. Deborah Gray White, *Ar'n't I a Woman? Female Slaves in the Plantation South* (New York: Norton, 1985), p. 70.

77. Ibid., p. 74.

78. Ibid., p. 71.

79. Betty Wood, "Some Aspects of Female Resistance to Chattel Slavery in Low-Country Georgia, 1763–1815," *Historical Journal* (1987), pp. 603, 610 n.24, quoting *Georgia Gazette,* April 20, 1786.

80. Fox-Genovese, *Within the Plantation Household,* p. 323.

81. Ibid., p. 321.

82. Linda Brent (Harriet Jacobs), *Incidents in the Life of a Slave Girl,* ed. L. Maria Child (New York: Harcourt Brace Jovanovich, 1973), p. 96.

83. Ibid., pp. 91–92.

84. Orlando Patterson, *Slavery and Social Death: A Comparative Study* (Cambridge: Harvard University Press, 1982), pp. 5–7.

85. Darlene Hine and Kate Wittenstein, "Female Slave Resistance: The Economics of Sex," in Filomina C. Steady, ed., *The Black Woman Cross-Culturally* (Rochester, Vt.: Schenkman, 1981), pp. 289, 296. See also Stephanie Shaw, "Mothering Under Slavery in the Antebellum South," in Evelyn Nakano Glenn, Grace Chang, and Linda Rennie Forcey, eds., *Mothering: Ideology, Experience, and Agency* (New York: Routledge, 1993), p. 237.

86. Gutman, *Black Family in Slavery and Freedom,* p. 80.

87. Brenda E. Stevenson, "Gender Convention, Ideals, and Identity Among Antebellum Virginia Slave Women," in Gaspar and Hine, *More Than Chattel,* pp. 169, 171.

88. Charles L. Perdue, Thomas E. Barden, and Robert K. Phillips, eds., *Weevils in the Wheat: Interview with Virginia Ex-Slaves* (Charlottesville: University Press of Virginia, 1976), pp. 48–49.

89. Stampp, *The Peculiar Institution,* p. 104.

90. White, *Ar'n't I a Woman?* p. 80.

91. Ibid., pp. 80–81.

92. Ibid., p. 84.

93. Gutman, *Black Family in Slavery and Freedom,* p. 80.

94. Ibid., p. 81.

95. White, *Ar'n't I a Woman?* pp. 125–26.

96. Ibid., p. 87.

97. Quoted in ibid., p. 147.

98. Henry Bibb, *Narrative of the Life and Adventures of Henry Bibb, an American Slave,* 3d ed. (Miami: Mnemosyne, 1969 [1850]), p. 44.

99. *Jane (a slave) v. The State,* 3 Mo. 45 (1831).

100. A. Leon Higginbotham, Jr., "Race, Sex, Education, and Missouri Jurisprudence: *Shelley v. Kramer* in Historical Perspective," *Washington University Law Quarterly* 67 (1989), pp. 673, 694–95.

101. Elizabeth Fox-Genovese, "Strategies and Forms of Resistance: Focus on Slave Women in the United States," in Gary Y. Okihiro, ed., *In Resistance: Studies in African, Caribbean, and Afro-American History* (Amherst: University of Massachusetts Press, 1986), pp. 143, 158.

102. Fogel and Engerman, *Time on the Cross,* pp. 124–25.

103. Higginbotham and Jacobs, "The 'Law Only as an Enemy,'" p. 1042.

104. Fogel and Engerman, *Time on the Cross,* p. 124.

105. Todd L. Savitt, "Smothering and Overlaying of Virginia Slave Children: A Suggested Explanation," *Bulletin of the History of Medicine* 49 (1975), p. 400.

106. Richard H. Steckel, "A Peculiar Population: The Nutrition, Health, and Mortality of American Slaves from Childhood to Maturity," *Journal of Economic History* 46 (Sept. 1986), pp. 721–41.

107. Lester, *To Be a Slave,* p. 40.

108. Morrison, *Beloved,* p. 164.

109. Gutman, *Black Family in Slavery and Freedom,* p. 355. Gutman does not explain how Tucker's slaves learned to read and write. Criminal laws prior to the Civil War prohibited such instruction (Higginbotham, *In the Matter of Color,* p. 198), but a tiny percentage of slaves were literate.

110. Stampp. *The Peculiar Institution*, p. 97. Stampp explains how a few slaves (usually skilled ones who lived in towns) were able to purchase freedom for themselves or their loved ones:

> Occasionally, they earned the necessary Funds by working nights and Sundays. More often, they hired their own time. Either way, they gradually accumulated enough money to pay their masters an amount equal to their value and thus obtained deeds of emancipation. Benevolent masters helped ambitious bondsmen by permitting them to make the payments in installments over a period of years or by accepting a sum lower than the market price.

Ibid., p. 96.

111. Quoted in Bert James Loewenberg and Ruth Bogin, eds., *Black Women in Nineteenth-Century American Life* (University Park: Pennsylvania State University Press, 1976), p. 329.

112. See Anita L. Allen, "Surrogacy, Slavery, and the Ownership of Life," *Harvard Journal of Law and Public Policy* 13 (1990), pp. 139, 142–44.

113. Edmund S. Morgan, *Virginians at Home: Family Life in the Eighteenth Century* (Williamsburg, Va.: Colonial Williamsburg, 1952), quoted in Gutman, *Black Family in Slavery and Freedom*, p. 352.

114. Gutman, *Black Family in Slavery and Freedom*, p. 51. This conclusion was confirmed by Robert Fogel and Stanley Engerman in *Time on the Cross*, pp. 126–44. Fogel and Engerman further assert that "the high fertility rate of slave women was not the consequence of the wanton impregnation of very young unmarried women by either white or black men, but of the frequency of conception after first birth." Ibid., p. 137.

115. Malone, *Sweet Chariot*.

116. Ibid., pp. 1–2.

117. Gutman, *Black Family in Slavery and Freedom*, p. 276.

118. Fox-Genovese, *Within the Plantation Household*, p. 48.

119. Stevenson, "Gender Convention, Ideals, and Identity," p. 178.

120. Gutman, *Black Family in Slavery and Freedom*, pp. 196–229.

121. Ibid., p. 222.

122. Ibid., p. 217 (emphasis deleted).

123. Ibid., pp. 226–27.

124. Malone, *Sweet Chariot*, p. 258.

125. See, e.g., Andrew Billingsley, *Climbing Jacob's Ladder: The Enduring Legacy of African American Families* (New York: Simon and Schuster, 1992); Robert Hill, *Informal Adoption Among Black Families* (Washington, D.C.: National Urban League Research Department, 1977); Elmer P. Martin and Joanne Mitchell Martin, *The Black Extended Family* (Chicago: University of Chicago Press, 1978); Carol B. Stack, *All Our Kin: Strategies for Survival in a Black Community* (New York: Harper, 1975).

126. See Billingsley, *Climbing Jacob's Ladder*, p. 30.

127. See Patricia Hill Collins, *Black Feminist Thought: Knowledge, Consciousness, and the Politics of Empowerment* (Boston: Unwin Hyman, 1990), pp. 120–21.

128. Billingsley, *Climbing Jacob's Ladder*, p. 31.

129. Jacqueline Jones, "'My Mother Was Much of a Woman': Black Women, Work, and the Family Under Slavery," *Feminist Studies* 8 (1982), pp. 235, 252–61.

130. Jones, *Labor of Love, Labor of Sorrow*, pp. 12–13.

131. Davis, *Women, Race, and Class*, p. 17, quoting Angela Y. Davis, "The Black Woman's Role in the Community of Slaves," *Black Scholar* 3 (Dec. 1971). Davis amended this statement to acknowledge that men also performed domestic tasks important to the slave community.

Chapter 2. The Dark Side of Birth Control

1. *Griswold v. Connecticut*, 381 U.S. 479 (1965).
2. David M. Kennedy, *Birth Control in America: The Career of Margaret Sanger* (New Haven: Yale University Press, 1970); Ellen Chesler, *Woman of Valor: Margaret Sanger and the Birth Control Movement in America* (New York: Simon and Schuster, 1992).
3. Margaret Sanger, *Woman and the New Race* (New York: Brentano's, 1920), p. 94.
4. See, e.g., Carole R. McCann, *Birth Control Politics in the United States, 1916–1945* (Ithaca, N.Y.: Cornell University Press, 1994); Linda Gordon, *Woman's Body, Woman's Right: A Social History of Birth Control in America* (New York: Grossman, 1976).
5. Angela Davis, "Racism, Birth Control, and Reproductive Rights," in Marlene Gerber Fried, ed., *From Abortion to Reproductive Freedom: Transforming a Movement* (Boston: South End Press, 1990), pp. 15, 20.
6. Historian Carole McCann criticizes accounts of the birth control movement written by Linda Gordon, David Kennedy, Ellen Chesler, and others for representing the development of the movement as a consequence of Margaret Sanger's will, independent of its historical context. McCann, *Birth Control Politics in the United States*, pp. 3–4.
7. Daniel J. Kevles, *In the Name of Eugenics: Genetics and the Uses of Human Heredity* (New York: Knopf, 1985), p. 8.
8. Francis Galton, *Eugenics: Its Definition, Scope and Aims* (London: Macmillan, 1905), p. 50.
9. Francis Galton, *Inquiries into the Human Faculty* (New York: Macmillan, 1883), pp. 24–25.
10. Francis Galton, "Hereditary Talent and Character," *Macmillan's Magazine* 12 (1865), pp. 157, 165.
11. Francis Galton, "The Possible Improvement of the Human Breed Under the Existing Conditions of Law and Sentiment," *Nature* 64 (1901), pp. 659, 663.
12. Francis Galton, "Hereditary Improvement," *Fraser's Magazine* 7 (1873), quoted by William H. Tucker, *The Science and Politics of Racial Research* (Urbana: University of Illinois Press, 1994), p. 48.
13. Galton, "Hereditary Talent and Character," pp. 318, 320.
14. Ibid., p. 321.
15. President Theodore Roosevelt, "Sixth Annual Message to Congress," Dec. 3, 1903, quoted in Elaine Tyler May, *Barren in the Promised Land: Childless Americans and the Pursuit of Happiness* (New York: Basic Books, 1995), p. 61.
16. Davis, "Racism, Birth Control, and Reproductive Rights," p. 20.
17. Sven Lindqvist, *Exterminate All the Brutes* (New York: New Press, 1996).
18. Charles B. Davenport, *Heredity in Relation to Eugenics* (New York: Holt, 1911).
19. Kevles, *In the Name of Eugenics*, pp. 45–47.
20. Ibid., p. 56; Philip R. Reilly, *The Surgical Solution: A History of Involuntary Sterilization in the United States* (Baltimore: Johns Hopkins University Press, 1991), pp. 19–20.
21. Reilly, *The Surgical Solution*, p. 18.
22. Stephen Jay Gould, *The Mismeasure of Man* (New York: Norton, 1981), pp. 175–77.
23. Tucker, *Science and Politics of Racial Research*, pp. 72–73.
24. Henry H. Goddard, *The Kallikak Family: A Study in the Heredity of Feeblemindedness* (New York: Macmillan, 1912); Henry H. Goddard, *Feeble-mindedness: Its Causes and Consequences* (New York: Macmillan, 1914).
25. Tucker, *Science and Politics of Racial Research*, pp. 80–81; Kevles, *In the Name of Eugenics*, p. 81.
26. C. C. Brigham, *A Study of American Intelligence* (Princeton: Princeton University Press, 1923).
27. Ibid., p. 197.

28. Madison Grant, *The Passing of the Great Race* (New York: Scribner, 1923).

29. Ibid., p. 60.

30. Tucker, *Science and Politics of Racial Research*, pp. 91–93.

31. Ibid., p. 93, quoting "The Great American Myth," editorial, *Saturday Evening Post*, May 7, 1921.

32. Ibid., p. 93, quoting *Eugenical News* 18 (1933), p. 111.

33. Ibid., pp. 91–92, quoting E. Huntington, "Heredity and Responsibility," *Yale Review* 6 (1917), p. 305.

34. Ibid., pp. 106–9. See, for example, Lewis M. Terman, *The Measurement of Intelligence* (Cambridge, Mass.: Riverside, 1916).

35. E. M. East, *Heredity and Human Affairs* (New York: Scribner, 1929), p. 306.

36. Quoted in Reilly, *The Surgical Solution*, p. 77.

37. H. H. Goddard, *Human Efficiency and Levels of Intelligence* (Princeton: Princeton University Press, 1920), p. 99.

38. Stephen Trombley, *The Right to Reproduce: The History of Coercive Sterilization* (London: Weidenfeld, 1988), p. 49.

39. Quoted in Reilly, *The Surgical Solution*, p. 28.

40. Quoted in ibid., p. 32.

41. Kevles, *In the Name of Eugenics*, p. 93; Reilly, *The Surgical Solution*, p. 35.

42. Reilly, *The Surgical Solution*, p. 35.

43. G. Frank Lydston, *Diseases of Society* (Philadelphia: Lippincott, 1906), p. 564.

44. Quoted in Reilly, *The Surgical Solution*, p. 46.

45. Harry Hamilton Laughlin, *The Legal and Administrative Aspects of Sterilization: Report of Committee to Study and to Report on the Best Practical Means of Cutting Off the Defective Germ-Plasm in the American Population*, 2 vols. (Cold Springs Harbor, N.Y.: Eugenics Record Office, 1914).

46. In his 1929 report *The Legal Status of Eugenical Sterilization*, Laughlin defined the "socially inadequate" as:

> (1) feeble-minded; (2) insane (including the psychopathic); (3) criminalistic (including the delinquent and wayward); (4) epileptic; (5) inebriate (including drug-habitués); (6) diseased (including the tuberculous, the syphilitic, the leprous, and others with chronic, infectious and legally segregable diseases); (7) blind (including those with seriously impaired vision); (8) deaf (including those with seriously impaired hearing); (9) deformed (including the crippled); and (10) dependent (including orphans, ne'er-do-wells, the homeless, tramps and paupers).

Ibid., p. 65.

47. Reilly, *The Surgical Solution*, pp. 64–65.

48. Kevles, *In the Name of Eugenics*, p. 118.

49. Robert J. Cynkar, *"Buck v. Bell:* 'Felt Necessities' v. Fundamental Values?" *Columbia Law Review* 81 (1981), pp. 1418, 1438.

50. *Buck v. Bell*, 274 U.S. 200 (1927).

51. Holmes wrote in a 1915 law review article: "I believe that the wholesale social regeneration . . . cannot be affected appreciably by tinkering with the institution of property, but only by taking in hand life and trying to build a race." Oliver Wendell Holmes, "Ideals and Doubts," *Illinois Law Review* 10 (1915), pp. 1, 3.

52. Reilly, *The Surgical Solution*, pp. 94–95.

53. Ibid., p. 98.

54. Kevles, *In the Name of Eugenics*, p. 108.

55. Herbert Aptheker, "Sterilization, Experimentation, and Imperialism," *Political Affairs* 53 (1974), p. 45.

56. Quoted in May, *Barren in the Promised Land*, p. 101.

57. Stephen Jay Gould, "Carrie Buck's Daughter," *Constitutional Commentary* 2 (1985), pp. 331, 336.

58. May, *Barren in the Promised Land*, p. 110.

59. Kevles, *In the Name of Eugenics*, p. 116, quoting *Richmond Times-Dispatch*, April 6, 1980.

60. Beverly Guy-Sheftall, *Daughters of Sorrow: Attitudes Toward Black Women, 1880–1920* (Brooklyn, N.Y.: Carlson, 1990), pp. 20–21.

61. Thurman B. Rice, *Racial Hygiene: A Practical Discussion of Eugenics and Race Culture* (New York: Macmillan, 1929), pp. 318–20, 368.

62. Reilly, *The Surgical Solution*, p. 72.

63. Gordon, *Woman's Body, Woman's Right*, pp. 277–78, quoting Michael G. Guyer, *Being Well-Born* (Indianapolis: Bobbs-Merrill Co., 1916).

64. Quoted in Reilly, *The Surgical Solution*, p. 74.

65. Donald K. Pickens, *Eugenics and the Progressives* (Nashville, Tenn.: Vanderbilt University Press, 1968), p. 67.

66. Ibid., p. 97.

67. Allan Chase, *The Legacy of Malthus: The Social Costs of the New Scientific Racism* (Urbana: University of Illinois Press, 1980), pp. 299–300.

68. Tucker, *Science and Politics of Racial Research*, p. 134; see E. S. Cox, "Repatriation of the American Negro," *Eugenical News* 21 (1936), pp. 133–38.

69. McCann, *Birth Control Politics in the United States*, p. 58.

70. Ibid., p. 100.

71. Margaret Sanger, "Dangers of Cradle Competition," in *The Pivot of Civilization* (New York: Brentano's, 1922), pp. 170–89.

72. Ibid., p. 175.

73. Ibid., pp. 177–78.

74. Margaret Sanger, *An Autobiography* (New York: Dover, 1971 [1938]), p. 375.

75. Sanger, *Pivot of Civilization*, p. 187.

76. Sanger, *Autobiography*, pp. 374–75.

77. Sanger, *Pivot of Civilization*, p. 189.

78. Paul Popenoe, "Birth Control and Eugenics," *Birth Control Review* 1 (March 1917), p. 6.

79. McCann, *Birth Control Politics in the United States*, p. 180.

80. "Principles and Aims of the American Birth Control League," appendix to Sanger, *Pivot of Civilization*, p. 277.

81. Kevles, *In the Name of Eugenics*, pp. 64–66.

82. Havelock Ellis, *The Task of Social Hygiene* (Boston: Houghton Mifflin, 1912), pp. 46–47.

83. Gordon, *Woman's Body, Woman's Right*, p. 332.

84. W. E. B. Du Bois, "Black Folk and Birth Control," *Birth Control Review* 16 (June 1932), p. 166.

85. Gordon, *Woman's Body, Woman's Right*, p. 332.

86. Margaret Sanger to Clarence J. Gamble, Dec. 10, 1939, p. 2.

87. Gordon, *Woman's Body, Woman's Right*, p. 332.

88. Quoted in ibid., p. 333.

89. "Birth Control: South Carolina Uses It for Public Health," *Life*, May 6, 1940, pp. 64–68.

90. Otto Klineberg, *Negro Intelligence and Selective Migration* (New York: Columbia University Press, 1935), p. 59.

91. James Reed, *The Birth Control Movement and American Society: From Private Vice to Public Virtue* (Princeton: Princeton University Press, 1978); Charles Valenza, "Was Margaret Sanger a Racist?" *Family Planning Perspectives* 17 (Jan.–Feb. 1985), p. 44.

92. McCann, *Birth Control Politics in the United States*, pp. 58, 99–134.

93. Chesler, *Woman of Valor*, pp. 214–15.

94. Valenza, "Was Margaret Sanger a Racist?" p. 44.

95. Sanger, "Racial Betterment," p. 12.

96. McCann, *Birth Control Politics in the United States*, p. 112; Valenza, "Was Margaret Sanger a Racist?" pp. 44–46.

97. Donald K. Pickens also asserts that "Margaret Sanger was not a racist like Madison Grant." Pickens, *Eugenics and the Progressives*, p. 84.

98. Margaret Sanger to Albert Lasker, July 9, 1942, quoted in Valenza, "Was Margaret Sanger a Racist?" p. 46.

99. Kevles, *In the Name of Eugenics*, p. 118.

100. Jessie M. Rodrique, "The Black Community and the Birth-Control Movement," in Ellen Carol DuBois and Vicki L. Ruiz, eds., *Unequal Sisters: A Multicultural Reader in U.S. Women's History* (New York: Routledge, 1990), p. 333.

101. Ibid., p. 334; Loretta J. Ross, "African-American Women and Abortion: 1800–1970," in Stanlie M. James and Abena P. A. Busia, eds., *Theorizing Black Feminisms: The Visionary Pragmatism of Black Women* (London: Routledge, 1993), pp. 141, 145; Joseph McFalls and George Masnick, "Birth Control and the Fertility of the U.S. Black Population, 1880 to 1980," *Journal of Family History* 6 (Spring 1981), pp. 89–106.

102. Rodrique, "The Black Community and the Birth-Control Movement," p. 334.

103. George S. Schuyler, "Quantity or Quality," *Birth Control Review* 16 (June 1932), pp. 165, 166.

104. McFalls and Masnick, "Birth Control and the Fertility of the U.S. Black Population," p. 100.

105. Ibid., p. 90.

106. Ibid., pp. 91–93. McFalls and Masnick concur that birth control was an important variable in Blacks' declining fertility rate from 1880 to 1940, along with "a decrease in the proportion of time blacks spent in stable unions and an increase in subfecundity." Ibid., p. 104.

107. Rodrique, "The Black Community and the Birth-Control Movement," pp. 335–38; Robert G. Weisbord, *Genocide? Birth Control and the Black American* (Westport, Conn.: Greenwood and Two Continents, 1975), pp. 44–45; Vanessa N. Gamble and Judith A. Houck, "'A High-Voltage Sensitivity: A History of African Americans and Birth Control," paper presented to the Institute of Medicine, June 1994.

108. Quoted in Weisbord, *Genocide?* p. 43.

109. Guy-Sheftall, *Daughters of Sorrow*, pp. 13, 34.

110. W. E. B. Du Bois, "Darkwater: Voices Within the Veil," in Eric J. Sundquist, ed., *The Oxford W. E. B. Du Bois Reader* (New York: Oxford University Press, 1996), p. 481.

111. Ibid., p. 565.

112. W. E. B. Du Bois, "Opinion," *The Crisis* 24 (Oct. 22, 1922), pp. 247–53.

113. Gilbert Osofsky, *Harlem: The Making of a Ghetto* (New York: Harper, 1971).

114. Du Bois, "Black Folk and Birth Control," p. 167.

115. Newell Sims, "Hostages to the White Man," *Birth Control Review* 16 (July–Aug. 1932), p. 214.

116. Elmer A. Carter, "Eugenics for the Negro," *Birth Control Review* 16 (June 1932), p. 169.

117. Lucien Brown, "Keeping Fit," *New York Amsterdam News*, Nov. 28, 1932, quoted in McCann, *Birth Control Politics in the United States*, p. 155.

118. Pickens, *Eugenics and the Progressives*, p. 84.

119. Quoted in Rodrique, "The Black Community and the Birth-Control Movement," p. 338.

120. Lemuel T. Sewell, "The Negro Wants Birth Control," *Birth Control Review* 17 (May 1933), p. 131.

121. Rodrique, "The Black Community and the Birth-Control Movement," pp. 338–39.

122. McCann, *Birth Control Politics in the United States*, p. 139.

123. Ibid., pp. 141–42.

124. Quoted in ibid., p. 142.

125. Ibid., p. 139.

126. Ibid., p. 151, quoting Margaret Sanger to Julius Rosenwald, Oct. 9, 1929.

127. Ibid., p. 156.

128. Ibid., p. 158, quoting Mabel Staupers to Margaret Sanger, April 2, 1935.

129. See Reilly, *The Surgical Solution*, pp. 111–27.

130. Ibid., p. 101.

131. See George Smith, "Limitations on Reproductive Autonomy for the Mentally Handicapped," *Journal of Contemporary Health Law and Policy* 4 (1988), pp. 71, 77 n.35. See also Reilly, *The Surgical Solution*, p. 2, stating that between 1907 and 1960 more than 60,000 retarded and mentally ill persons were sterilized without their consent.

132. Aptheker, "Sterilization, Experimentation, and Imperialism," pp. 41–42.

133. Reilly, *The Surgical Solution*, p. 138.

134. Davis, "Racism, Birth Control, and Reproductive Rights," p. 22.

135. Moya Woodside, *Sterilization in North Carolina: A Sociological and Psychological Study* (Chapel Hill: University of North Carolina Press, 1950), pp. 31–33.

136. Thomas M. Shapiro, *Population Control Politics: Women, Sterilization, and Reproductive Choice* (Philadelphia: Temple University Press, 1985).

137. Joann Rodgers, "Rush to Surgery," *New York Times Magazine*, Sept. 21, 1975, p. 34.

138. Julius Paul, "The Return of Punitive Sterilization Proposals: Current Attacks on Illegitimacy and the AFDC Program," *Law and Society Review* 3 (1968), pp. 77, 92.

139. Carl M. Cobb, "Students Charge BCH's Obstetrics Unit with 'Excessive Surgery,'" *Boston Globe*, April 29, 1972, p. 1.

140. Ibid., p. 6.

141. Quoted in Betsy Hartmann, *Reproductive Rights and Wrongs: The Global Politics of Population Control* (Boston: South End Press, 1995), p. 255.

142. Quoted in Aptheker, "Sterilization, Experimentation, and Imperialism," p. 41.

143. "Stresses and Strains of Black Women," *Ebony*, June 1974, pp. 33, 36.

144. Claudia Dreifus, "Sterilizing the Poor," in Claudia Dreifus, ed., *Seizing Our Bodies: The Politics of Women's Health* (New York: Vintage, 1978), p. 105.

145. Jack Jones, "Negro Doctors Fear Birth Control Genocide," *Los Angeles Times*, Sept. 30, 1968, p. B2.

146. Gena Corea, *The Hidden Malpractice: How American Medicine Treats Women as Patients and Professionals* (New York: Morrow, 1973), pp. 180–81.

147. Ibid., p. 181.

148. "Sterilization Charges Grow," *Washington Post*, July 24, 1973, p. A12.

149. Nancy Hicks, "Sterilization of Black Mother of 3 Stirs Aiken, S.C.," *New York Times*, Aug. 1, 1973, p. 27. See also *Walker v. Pierce*, 560 F.2d 609 (4th Cir. 1977), *cert. denied*, 434 U.S. 1075 (1978). The U.S. Court of Appeals ruled against two patients who sued Dr. Pierce for violations of their civil rights, finding that Dr. Pierce secured adequate consents and was not acting under color of state law.

150. Weisbord, *Genocide?* pp. 159–61; Aptheker, "Sterilization, Experimentation, and Imperialism," p. 40. See also *Cox v. Stanton*, 529 F2d 47 (4th Cir. 1975).

151. *Relf v. Weinberger*, 372 F.Supp. 1196, 1199 (D.D.C. 1974), on remand sub nom. *Relf v. Mathews*, 403 F.Supp. 1235 (D.D.C. 1975), vacated sub nom. *Relf v. Weinberger*, 565 F.2d 722 (D.C. Cir. 1977).

152. Chase, *Legacy of Malthus*, p. 16.

153. 42 C.F.R. §§ 50.201–207 (1978).

154. Paul, "Return of Punitive Sterilization Proposals."

155. Ibid., p. 101.

156. Hartmann, *Reproductive Rights and Wrongs*, pp. 247–48.

157. Annette B. Ramirez de Arellano and Conrad Seipp, *Colonialism, Catholicism, and Contraception* (Chapel Hill: University of North Carolina Press, 1983), pp. 96–104.

158. Connie Uri, quoted in May, *Barren in the Promised Land*, p. 119.

159. Ibid., p. 113.

160. Ruth Colker, "Feminism, Theology, and Abortion: Toward Love, Compassion, and Wisdom," *California Law Review* 77 (1989), pp. 1011, 1067 n.196.

161. Rosalind Petchesky, "Reproduction, Ethics, and Public Policy: The Federal Sterilization Regulations," *Hastings Center Report* 9 (1979), pp. 29, 35–39, discusses reasons for opposition to the sterilization regulations.

162. Reilly, *The Surgical Solution,* p. 147.

163. May, *Barren in the Promised Land,* p. 112.

164. Laurie Nsiah-Jefferson, "Reproductive Laws, Women of Color, and Low-Income Women," in Sherrill Cohen and Nadine Taub, eds., *Reproductive Laws for the 1990s,* (Clifton, N.J.: Humana, 1989), pp. 23, 46.

165. Linda S. Peterson, *Contraceptive Use in the United States: 1982–90,* National Center for Health Statistics, Advance Data, no. 260 (Feb. 14, 1995), p. 8.

166. Charlotte Rutherford, "Reproductive Freedoms and African-American Women," *Yale Journal of Law and Feminism* 4 (1992), pp. 255, 273. Only 0.5% of Black men are contraceptively sterile, compared to 8.4% of white men and 24% of Black women. Felicia Halpert, "Birth Control for Him," *Essence,* Nov. 1990, p. 20. Halpert surmises that Black men's "big fear about vasectomy" derives from its association with castration rather than its prevention of genetically related offspring. These statistics also indicate that Black women are far more vulnerable than Black men to government control of reproduction.

167. Judith Levin and Nadine Taub, "Reproductive Rights," in Carol Lefcourt, ed., *Women and the Law* (1989), sec. 10A.07[3][b]. p. 10A-28.

168. Frank F. Furstenberg, Jr., et al., *Adolescent Mothers in Later Life* (New York: Cambridge University Press, 1987).

169. Petchesky, "Reproduction, Ethics, and Public Policy," p. 39.

170. Julian Lewis, "Is Birth Control a Menace to Negroes?" *Jet,* Aug. 1954, pp. 52–55, quoted in Weisbord, *Genocide?* p. 53.

171. Dick Gregory, "My Answer to Genocide," *Ebony,* Oct. 1971, p. 66, quoted in Weisbord, *Genocide?* p. 91.

172. William A. Darity and Castellano B. Turner, "Family Planning, Race Consciousness, and the Fear of Race Genocide," *American Journal of Public Health* 62 (1972), p. 1454; William A. Darity and Castellano B. Turner, "Fears of Genocide Among Black Americans as Related to Age, Sex, and Region," *American Journal of Public Health* 63 (1973), p. 1029.

173. *Muhammad Speaks,* Aug. 29, 1969, quoted in Weisbord, *Genocide?* p. 103.

174. Ross, "African-American Women and Abortion," p. 153.

175. Quoted in Vanessa Northington Gamble, "Race, Class, and the Pill: A History," in Sarah E. Samuels and Mark D. Smith, eds., *The Pill: From Prescription to Over the Counter* (Menlo Park, Calif.: Kaiser Family Foundation, 1994), pp. 21, 30.

176. Kay Mills, *This Little Light of Mine: The Life of Fannie Lou Hamer* (New York: Plume, 1994), p. 274.

177. Quoted in Ross, "African-American Women and Abortion," p. 153.

178. Weisbord, *Genocide?* p. 47.

179. Quoted in Rodrique, "The Black Community and the Birth-Control Movement," p. 341.

180. Toni Cade, "The Pill: Genocide or Liberation," in Toni Cade, ed., *The Black Woman: An Anthology* (New York: Signet, 1970), p. 163.

181. Quoted in Ross, "African-American Women and Abortion," p. 156.

182. Ibid., pp. 153–56; Weisbord, *Genocide?* pp. 120–21; Ralph Z. Hallow, "The Blacks Cry Genocide," *The Nation,* April 28, 1969, p. 535.

183. Quoted in Ross, "African-American Women and Abortion," p. 155.

184. Donald J. Bogue, "Family Planning in Negro Ghettos of Chicago," *Milbank Memorial Fund Quarterly,* April 1970, pt. 2, p. 283. An analysis of data from the 1965 National Fertility Study found "very little difference . . . between large city blacks and whites

in the proportions who have ever used contraception (78 per cent of the blacks and 80 per cent of the whites)." Charles F. Westoff and Norman B. Ryder, "Contraceptive Practice Among Urban Blacks in the United States, 1965," *Milbank Memorial Fund Quarterly*, April 1970, pt. 2, pp. 215, 218. Blacks, however, were less likely to be currently using contraceptives.

185. Weisbord, *Genocide?* p. 116.

186. Ross, "African-American Women and Abortion," p. 151.

187. Ibid., p. 141.

188. *Webster's Third New International Dictionary*, p. 947.

189. Weisbord, *Genocide?* pp. 11–12.

190. Donald A. MacKenzie, *Statistics in Britain, 1865–1930: The Social Construction of Scientific Knowledge* (Edinburgh: Edinburgh University Press, 1981), p. 18.

191. John R. Kramer, "Introduction to Symposium: Criminal Law, Criminal Justice, and Race," *Tulane Law Review* 67 (1993), pp. 1725, 1733–34.

192. See Benno Muller-Hill, *Murderous Science: Elimination by Scientific Selection of Jews, Gypsies, and Others, Germany 1933–1945* (New York: Oxford University Press, 1988), pp. 28–38; Robert Proctor, *Racial Hygiene: Medicine Under the Nazis* (Cambridge: Harvard University Press, 1988), pp. 95–117.

Chapter 3. From Norplant to the Contraceptive Vaccine

1. *Skin Deep* (September 1994), a documentary produced by Deb Ellis and Alexandra Halkin.

2. Lynn Smith and Nina J. Easton, "The Dilemma of Desire," *Los Angeles Times Magazine*, Sept. 26, 1993, p. 24.

3. American Medical Association Board of Trustees Report, "Requirements or Incentives by Government for the Use of Long-Acting Contraceptives," *Journal of the American Medical Association* 267 (April 1, 1992), p. 1818.

4. Albert G. Thomas, Jr., and Stephanie M. LeMelle, "The Norplant System: Where Are We in 1995?" *Journal of Family Practice* 40 (1995), p. 125.

5. Donald Kimelman, "Poverty and Norplant: Can Contraception Reduce the Underclass?" *Philadelphia Inquirer*, Dec. 12, 1990, p. A18.

6. Ibid.

7. Sheldon J. Segal. "Norplant Developed for All Women, Not Just the Well-to-Do," *New York Times*, Dec. 29, 1990, p. A18.

8. David R. Boldt, "A 'Racist Pig' Offers Some Final Thoughts on Norplant," *Philadelphia Inquirer*, Dec. 30, 1990, p. F7.

9. Steve Lopez, "A Difference of Opinion," *Philadelphia Inquirer*, Nov. 16, 1990, p. B1.

10. Boldt, "A 'Racist Pig' Offers Some Final Thoughts on Norplant," p. F7.

11. Jonathan Alter, "One Well-Read Editorial," *Newsweek*, Dec. 31, 1990, pp. 85, 86.

12. "Journalistic Thought Police," *Richmond Times-Dispatch*, Dec. 27, 1990, p. A12.

13. Matthew Rees, "Shot in the Arm: The Use and Abuse of Norplant; Involuntary Contraception and Public Policy," *New Republic*, Dec. 9, 1991, p. 16.

14. David Frankel, Letter to the Editor, *Washington Post*, Dec. 29, 1990, p. A18.

15. Quoted in Sally Quinn, "Childhood's End," *Washington Post*, Nov. 27, 1994, p. C1.

16. Deborah L. Shelton, "Complications of Birth; Norplant Contraceptive," *American Medical News* 38 (Feb. 20, 1995), p. 15.

17. Planned Parenthood Federation of America, *Survey of Planned Parenthood Affiliates on Provision of Norplant* (December 1992).

18. Smith and Easton, "Dilemma of Desire."

19. Ibid.

20. Rees, "Shot in the Arm," p. 16.

21. Quoted in Alan Harper, "Racism Suggested in Payments to Poor for Norplant

Implants," *New York Beacon*, March 4, 1994 (available on Ethnic News Watch, Softline Information, Inc.).

22. Quoted in William H. Tucker, *The Science and Politics of Racial Research* (Urbana: University of Illinois Press, 1994), p. 294.

23. Quoted in Craig Flourney, "Duke Says He's Proud of Years as Klan Chief," *Dallas Morning News*, June 17, 1992, pp. A1, A16.

24. Dwight J. Ingle, *Who Should Have Children? An Environmental and Genetic Approach* (Indianapolis and New York: Bobbs-Merrill, 1973).

25. Tucker, *Science and Politics of Racial Research*, p. 193.

26. Staff of House Committee on Ways and Means, House of Representatives, *Overview of Entitlement Programs 1994 Green Book*, 103d Cong., 2d sess., 1994, pp. 402, 444; Teresa L. Amott, "Black Women and AFDC: Making Entitlements Out of Necessity," in Linda Gordon, ed., *Women, the State, and Welfare* (Madison: University of Wisconsin Press: 1990), p. 280.

27. Nadja Zolokar, *The Economic Status of Black Women* (Washington, D.C.: U.S. Commission on Civil Rights, 1990), p. 1.

28. Clint Bolick, "Clinton's Quota Queens," *Wall Street Journal*, April 30, 1993, p. A12.

29. William Henry, "Beyond the Melting Pot," *Time*, April 9, 1990, pp. 28–31.

30. Smith and Easton, "Dilemma of Desire," p. 24.

31. Department of Health and Human Services, *Annual Health Profile Release*, Public Health Report 110 (Sept.–Oct. 1995), p. 645.

32. Charles Murray, "The Coming White Underclass," *Wall Street Journal*, Oct. 29, 1993, p. A14.

33. Congressional Budget Office, *Sources of Support for Adolescent Mothers* (Washington, D.C., 1990), p. 52.

34. Quoted in Jean Hopfensperger, "The Great Welfare Debate: Overhaul Proposals Are the Next Item on the GOP Agenda," *Minneapolis Star Tribune*, Feb. 11, 1995, p. 7A.

35. "For High School Girls, Norplant Debate Hits Home," *New York Times*, March 7, 1993, p. A28.

36. Esther Oxford, "What They Learn at Laurence Paquin School," *The Independent*, Oct. 28, 1993, p. 25.

37. Tracey Kaplan and John Johnson, "Birth Control Implants at Valley School Defended," *Los Angeles Times*, March 26, 1993, p. A1; Colin McMahon and Carol Jouzaitis, "Taboos Leave Many Teens Unprotected," *Chicago Tribune*, May 24, 1994, p. N1.

38. Clergy United for the Renewal of East Baltimore, *Information on and Concerns about Norplant in the Black Community* (January 1993). See also Laura M. Litvan, "Norplant Program Assailed; Poor Black Girls Seen as Targets," *Washington Times*, Dec. 4, 1992, p. Bl. When the all-Black DuSable High School in one of Chicago's poorest neighborhoods recently started a family-planning program in its clinic, 13 ministers from local churches filed a lawsuit to shut it down. They charged that the clinic was a "calculated and pernicious effort to destroy the very fabric of family life among black parents and their children." Barbara Kantrowitz et al., "Kids and Contraceptives," *Newsweek*, Feb. 16, 1987, p. 54.

39. Pilita Clark, "USA: Contraception or Genocide?" *The Age* (Melbourne), July 14, 1993, p. 14.

40. Paul W. Valentine, "In Baltimore, a Tumultuous Hearing on Norplant," *Washington Post*, Feb. 10, 1993, p. D5.

41. Clark. "USA: Contraception or Genocide?" p. 14.

42. "The Right Prescription for Birth Control?" *Crossfire*, CNN Transcript no. 789, March 15, 1993.

43. McMahon and Jouzaitis, "Taboos Leave Many Teens Unprotected." Elders expressed similar views in an interview in the *San Francisco Chronicle*, Evelyn C.

White, "Grace Under Fire: Joycelyn Elders Recounts the Events Leading to Her Resignation as Surgeon General," *San Francisco Chronicle*, May 21, 1995, sec. 7, p. 1.

44. Paul D. Blumenthal et al., "Contraceptive Outcomes Among Post-partum and Post-abortal Adolescents," *Contraception* 50 (1994), pp. 451, 452.

45. McMahon and Jouzaitis, "Taboos Leave Many Teens Unprotected."

46. Smith and Easton, "Dilemma of Desire."

47. Margaret Polaneczky et al., "The Use of Levonorgestrel Implants (Norplant) for Contraception in Adolescent Mothers," *New England Journal of Medicine* 331 (1994), p. 1201.

48. Ibid., p. 1204.

49. Blumenthal et al., "Contraceptive Outcomes," p. 451. For another similar survey, see Linda Dinerman et al., "Outcomes of Adolescents Using Levonorgestrel Implants vs. Oral Contraceptives or Other Contraceptive Methods," *Archives of Pediatrics and Adolescent Medicine* 149 (1995), p. 967.

50. Blumenthal et al., "Contraceptive Outcomes," pp. 456–57.

51. Abbey B. Berenson and Constance M. Wiemann, "Patient Satisfaction and Side Effects with Levonorgestrel Implant (Norplant) Use in Adolescents 18 Years of Age or Younger," *Pediatrics* 92 (1993), pp. 257, 260. See also Lorraine Dugoff et al., "Assessing the Acceptability of Norplant Contraceptive in Four Patient Populations," *Contraception* 52 (1995), p. 283, reaching a similar conclusion. Another study comparing Baltimore patients who chose Norplant to those who chose the pill, however, found that Norplant was selected more often by women who were spacing their children or discontinuing childbearing than by adolescents who were postponing childbearing. Carol S. Weisman et al., "Comparison of Contraceptive Implant Adopters and Pill Users in a Family Planning Clinic in Baltimore," *Family Planning Perspectives* 25 (1993), pp. 224, 226.

52. Centers for Disease Control and Prevention, *Adolescent Pregnancy in the United States, 1980–1990* (1996); Alison M. Spitz et al., "Pregnancy, Abortion, and Birth Rates Among U.S. Adolescents—1980, 1985, and 1990," *Journal of the American Medical Association* 275 (April 1996), pp. 989, 991.

53. Centers for Disease Control, *Adolescent Pregnancy in the United States*, p. 2; Spitz et al., "Pregnancy, Abortion, and Birth Rates Among U.S. Adolescents," p. 991.

54. Centers for Disease Control, *Adolescent Pregnancy in the United States*, p. 3.

55. Kristin Luker, *Dubious Conceptions: The Politics of Teenage Pregnancy* (Cambridge: Harvard University Press, 1996), pp. 81–108; Deborah L. Rhode, "Adolescent Pregnancy and Public Policy," in Annette Lawson and Deborah L. Rhode, eds., *The Politics of Pregnancy: Adolescent Sexuality and Public Policy* (New Haven: Yale University Press, 1993), p. 301.

56. Blumenthal et al., "Contraceptive Outcomes," p. 452.

57. Mireya Navarro, "Teen-Age Mothers Viewed as Abused Prey of Older Men," *New York Times*, May 19, 1996, p. A1; Mike Males, "Poverty, Rape, Adult/Teen Sex: Why 'Pregnancy Prevention' Programs Don't Work," *Phi Delta Kappan* 75 (Jan. 1994), p. 407; Mike Males, "School-Age Pregnancy: Why Hasn't Prevention Worked?" *Journal of School Health* 63 (Dec. 1993), p. 429.

58. Martha C. Ward, "Early Childbearing: What Is the Problem and Who Owns It?" in Faye D. Ginsburg and Rayna Rapp, eds., *Conceiving the New World Order: The Global Politics of Reproduction* (Berkeley: University of California Press, 1995), pp. 140, 147; Luker, *Dubious Conceptions*, p. 145.

59. Spitz et al., "Pregnancy, Abortion, and Birth Rates Among U.S. Adolescents," p. 989.

60. Lee Smith, "The New Wave of Illegitimacy," *Fortune*, April 18, 1994, p. 81.

61. Erika Nolph Ringdahl, "The Role of the Family Physician in Preventing Teenage Pregnancy," *Family Physician* 45 (1992), p. 2215. Since half of adolescent pregnancies occur in the first six months after initiation of sexual activity, that delay is critical. Paula K. Braverman and Victor C. Strasburger, "Contraception," *Clinical Pediatrics*

(Dec. 1993), p. 725. In a study of over 2,000 sexually active female adolescents in the inner city, only 63% sought contraceptive services within the last year. Blumenthal et al., "Contraceptive Outcomes," p. 452.

62. McMahon and Jouzaitis, "Taboos Leave Many Teens Unprotected," p. N1.

63. Braverman and Strasburger, "Contraception," p. 725.

64. Sherrill Cohen and Estelle H. Rogers, "Under Siege: Sexuality Education in the Public Schools," *ACLU Reproductive Rights Update*, Sept. 1994, p. 2. Only 375 middle or high schools in the United States distribute condoms or other forms of birth control according to a 1993 survey.

65. Males, "Poverty, Rape, Adult/Teen Sex."

66. J. G. Dryfoos, "Using Existing Research to Develop a Comprehensive Pregnancy Prevention Program," *Family Planning Perspectives* 22 (1988), p. 211.

67. Jacqueline Trescott, "While the Plight of Young Males Tops the Black Agenda, Girls Face Crises of Lost Self-Esteem and Dreams," *Emerge*, March 1995, pp. 35, 37.

68. Males, "Poverty, Rape, Adult/Teen Sex." See generally Luker, *Dubious Conceptions*.

69. Margaret L. Usdansky, "Crisis: Teens as Parents," *USA Today*, Feb. 22, 1994, p. A1.

70. Rhode, "Adolescent Pregnancy," p. 314, citing Arline Geronimus, "On Teenage Childbearing and Neonatal Mortality in the United States," *Population and Development Review* 13 (1987), p. 245; Mary G. Edwards, "Teenage Childbearing: Redefining the Problem for Public Policy," paper delivered August 30, 1990, before the American Political Science Association; Mark Testa, "Racial Variation in the Early Life Course of Adolescent Welfare Mothers," in Margaret K. Rosenheim and Mark Testa, eds., *Early Parenthood and Coming of Age in the 1990s* (New Brunswick, N.J.: Rutgers University Press, 1992). See also Arline Geroninus, "The Weathering Hypothesis and the Health of African-American Women and Infants: Implications for Reproductive Strategies and Policy Analysis," in Gita Sen and Rachel C. Snow, eds., *Power and Decision: The Social Control of Reproduction* (Boston: Harvard School of Public Health, 1994), p. 79.

71. Frank Furstenberg, Jr., Jeanne Brooks-Gunn, and S. Philip Morgan, *Adolescent Mothers in Later Life* (Cambridge: Cambridge University Press, 1987), pp. 21–47. For a recent analysis of this study see Kathleen Mullan Harris, *Teen Mothers and the Revolving Welfare Door* (Philadelphia: Temple University Press, 1997).

72. Spitz et al., "Pregnancy, Abortion, and Birth Rates Among U.S. Adolescents," p. 989. But see Deborah Jones Merritt, "Ending Poverty by Cutting Teenaged Births: Promise, Failure, and Paths to the Future," *Ohio State Law Journal* 57 (1996), pp. 441, 455–61, discussing studies that suggest that early maternal age alone does not significantly impair child health.

73. Quoted in Smith and Easton, "Dilemma of Desire."

74. Usdansky, "Crisis: Teens as Parents"; Centers for Disease Control, *Adolescent Pregnancy in the United States*, p. 3.

75. Usdansky, "Crisis: Teens as Parents."

76. Jim Ash, Gannett News Service, Jan. 22, 1993.

77. Regina Austin, "Sapphire Bound!" *Wisconsin Law Review* (1989), pp. 539, 565–66. See also Harris, *Teen Mothers and the Revolving Welfare Door*, pp. 80–94, 133–34; William Julius Wilson, *The Truly Disadvantaged: The Inner City, the Underclass, and Public Policy* (Chicago: University of Chicago Press, 1987).

78. Murray, "The Coming White Underclass," p. A14.

79. Ellis and Halkin, *Skin Deep.*

80. Bill Sloat and Keith Epstein, "Many Find Side Effects of Norplant Intolerable; Contraceptive Often Removed, but Its Defenders Maintain Implants Still Safe," *Plain Dealer*, June 18, 1995, p. A1.

81. Gina Kolata, "Will the Lawyers Kill Off Norplant?" *New York Times*, May 28, 1995, p. C1; "American Home Faces Suits by Users of Norplant Device," *Wall Street Journal*, July 28, 1994, p. B14.

82. Andrew Campbell and Nachman Brautbar, "Norplant: Systemic Immunological Complications—Case Report," *Toxicology and Industrial Health* 11 (1995), p. 41.

83. G. W. Bardin, "Norplant Contraceptive Implants," *Obstetrics and Gynecology Report* 2 (1990), pp. 96, 98, and tab. 2.

84. "For High School Girls, Norplant Hits Home," *New York Times*, March 7, 1993, p. A28.

85. Vanessa Cullins et al., "Comparison of Adolescent and Adult Experiences with Norplant Levonorgestrel Contraceptive Implants," *Obstetric Gynecology* 83 (1994), pp. 1026, 1031.

86. Berenson and Wiemann, "Patient Satisfaction and Side Effects," p. 260.

87. Margaret L. Frank et al., "One-Year Experience with Subdermal Contraceptive Implants in the United States," *Contraception* 48 (1993), p. 229; Vanessa E. Cullins, "Preliminary Experience with Norplant in an Inner-City Population," *Contraception* 47 (1993), p. 193.

88. Anita Hardon and Lenny Achthoven, "Norplant: A Critical Review," *Women and Pharmaceuticals Bulletin* 14 (Nov. 1990), pp. 14, 17.

89. "Norplant Approval for U.S. Near; Surveillance Study Planned to Investigate Safety, Delivery Issues," *Network News*, Nov.–Dec. 1989, p. 4.

90. *Letter of Dr. Judith Weisz and Dr. Paul D. Stolley to Frank Young, Commissioner, Food and Drug Administration*, Aug. 4, 1989.

91. Janice G. Raymond, *Women as Wombs: Reproductive Technologies and the Battle over Women's Freedom* (San Francisco: HarperCollins, 1993), pp. 16–18; "Norplant: 'The Five-Year Needle'; An Investigation of the Bangladesh Trial," *Radical Journal of Health*, March 1988, p. 101; "Bangladesh: Norplant on Trial?" *HAI News*, April 1989 (available from the National Women's Health Network, Washington, D.C.).

92. Carmen Barroso and Sonia Correa, "Public Servants, Professionals, and Feminists: The Politics of Contraceptive Research in Brazil," in Ginsburg and Rapp, *Conceiving the New World Order*, p. 292; Raymond, *Women as Wombs*, pp. 15–16.

93. Margaret L. Frank et al., "Characteristics and Attitudes of Early Contraceptive Implant Acceptors in Texas," *Family Planning Perspectives* 24 (1992), pp. 208, 212.

94. Ibid.

95. Douglas J. Besharov, "A Moral Choice: Would Norplant Simply Stop Unwanted Pregnancies—or Increase Destructive Teen Sex?" *National Review* 45 (Aug. 9, 1993), p. 50.

96. Ibid.

97. Ibid.

98. Rita Rubin, "Stopping This Birth Control Can Hurt: Removing Norplant Capsules Takes Skill," *U.S. News and World Report*, July 25, 1994, p. 59.

99. Associated Press, "Brimfield Woman Among Group Suing Sellers of Norplant," *Telegram and Gazette* (Worcester, Mass.), July 6, 1994, p. A6.

100. Sarah Henry, "Norplant: New Questions About the 'Dream' Contraceptive," *McCall's*, July 1995, p. 52.

101. Smith and Easton, "Dilemma of Desire."

102. Laura Duncan, "Norplant: The Next Mass Tort," *American Bar Association Journal* 81 (Nov. 1995), p. 16.

103. "Plaintiffs Allege Exploitation of Low-Income Women," *Mealey's, Litigation Report: Norplant*, Nov. 17, 1994, p. 6; "Complaint: Norplant Marketed to Disadvantaged Women," *Mealey's Litigation Report: Norplant*, Nov. 3, 1994, p. 17.

104. Kolata, "Will the Lawyers Kill Off Norplant?"

105. Sally Jacobs, "Norplant Draws Concerns over Risks, Coercion," *Boston Globe*, Dec. 21, 1992, p. 1.

106. Catherine Musham, Eva G. Darr, and Mary L. Strossner, "A Qualitative Study of the Perceptions of Dissatisfied Norplant Users," *Journal of Family Practice* 40 (1995), p. 465.

107. Ibid.

108. Telephone interview with Judith Scully, July 8, 1996.

109. Sloat and Epstein, "Many Find Side Effects of Norplant Intolerable."

110. Telephone interview with Judith Scully, July 8, 1996.

111. *Letter from Raymond Haddock, Division Administrator for Medical Services, State of Oklahoma Department of Human Services, to Physicians,* Jan. 20, 1993.

112. Nancie L. Katz, "Around World, Women Forced into Birth Control." *Atlanta Journal and Constitution,* Feb. 4, 1996, p. A19.

113. Ibid.

114. Alexander Cockburn, "Norplant and the Social Cleansers, Part II," *The Nation,* July 25, 1994, p. 116.

115. Memorandum Brief in Opposition to Plaintiff's Motion For Restraining Order, *Tippah County Department of Human Services v. James Sexton & Rose Sexton,* Cause No. YC-448 (Tippah County, MS Youth Court, filed Aug. 6, 1993).

116. Musham, Darr, and Strossner, "Qualitative Study of the Perceptions of Dissatisfied Norplant Users."

117. Ibid.

118. Annette Dula, "African-Americans' Suspicion of the Healthcare System Is Justified: What Do We Do About It?" *Cambridge Quarterly of Healthcare Ethics* 3 (1994), p. 347.

119. Smith and Easton, "Dilemma of Desire." See also P. D. Darney et al., "Acceptance and Perceptions of Norplant Among Users in San Francisco, U.S.A.," *Studies in Family Planning* 21 (1990), p. 152.

120. Smith and Easton, "Dilemma of Desire."

121. Weisman et al., "Comparison of Contraceptive Implant Adopters and Pill Users," pp. 224, 225.

122. Jennifer Frost, "The Availability and Accessibility of the Contraceptive Implant from Family Planning Agencies in the United States, 1991–1992," *Family Planning Perspectives* 26 (Jan.–Feb. 1994), pp. 4, 10.

123. Kaplan and Johnson, "Birth Control Implants at Valley School Defended."

124. Quoted in Rees, "Shot in the Arm," p. 17. Planned Parenthood of Denver sponsored a "Dollar-a-Day" program in an attempt to reduce the repeat pregnancy rate of teens who had become pregnant before age 16. The girls in the program attended a weekly meeting where they received $7, paid in $1 bills, if they succeeded in avoiding pregnancy. Girls who became pregnant were dropped from the program.

125. *60 Minutes: Norplant,* CBS television broadcast, Nov. 10, 1991.

126. Quoted in Fawn Vrazo, "Ease and Secrecy Draw Women to Quarterly Contraceptive Shot," *Charleston Gazette,* Nov. 14, 1994, pp. A1, A20.

127. 42 U.S.C. Sec. 300a-8.

128. American Medical Association, "Board of Trustees Report, Requirements or Incentives by Government for the Use of Long-Acting Contraceptives," p. 1818.

129. Bonnie Steinbock, "Coercion and Long-Term Contraceptives," Special Supplement, *Hastings Center Report* 25 (Jan.–Feb. 1995), pp. S19, S21.

130. Nancy Ehrenreich, "Surrogacy as Resistance? The Misplaced Focus on Choice in the Surrogacy and Abortion Funding Contexts," *DePaul Law Review* 41 (1992), p. 1369; Stephen J. Schulhofer, "Taking Sexual Autonomy Seriously: Rape Law and Beyond," *Law and Philosophy* 11 (1992), p. 35.

131. Annette Will, quoted in Judith Richter, *Vaccination Against Pregnancy; Miracle or Menace?* (Melbourne: Spinifex Press, 1996), p. 126.

132. Richard John Neuhaus, "The Wrong Way to Go," *National Review* 45 (Feb. 1, 1993), p. 53.

133. Ellen H. Moskowitz, Bruce Jennings, and Daniel Callahan, "Long-Acting Contraceptives: Ethical Guidance for Policymakers and Health Care Providers," Special Supplement, *Hastings Center Report* 25 (Jan.–Feb. 1995), pp. S1, S3. The authors conclude, however, that conditioning public assistance payments on the use of long-acting contraceptives wrongly influences use. Ibid., p. S5.

134. George F. Will, "Teenagers and Norplant," *Washington Post,* March 18, 1993, p. A27.

135. Katz, "Around World, Women Forced into Birth Control," p. A19.

136. Leah Makabenta, "Indonesia: Population Success Story Has Shady Side," *Inter Press Service*, Nov. 5, 1992.

137. Arthur Caplan, "The Norplant Safaris: Birth Control Implant Leads to Population Control by Governments," *Seattle Times*, July 7, 1991, p. A13; Dave Todd, "Walking Time Bombs," *Toronto Star*, Dec. 28, 1991, p. H10.

138. Mac Van Dinther, "Population: Drug Implant a Controversial Over-Population Remedy," *Inter Press Service*, Nov. 8, 1989.

139. Sheila J. Ward et al., *Service Delivery Systems and Quality of Care in the Implementation of Norplant in Indonesia* (New York: Population Council, Feb. 1990).

140. "Norplant: 'The Five-Year Needle,'" p. 102.

141. Raymond, *Women as Wombs*, p. 17.

142. Shayam Thapa, "Discontinuation of Norplant Implants in Bangladesh," paper presented at the Annual Meeting of the American Public Health Association, 1990 (abstract available from the National Women's Health Network). For another report of removal problems in Bangladesh, see Karen Hardee et al., "Contraceptive Implant Users and Their Access to Removal Services in Bangladesh," *International Family Planning Perspectives* 20 (1994), p. 59.

143. "Norplant: 'The Five-Year Needle,'" p. 107.

144. Laura Punnett, "The Politics of Menstrual Extraction," in Marlene Gerber Fried, ed., *From Abortion to Reproductive Freedom: Transforming a Movement* (Boston: South End Press, 1990), p. 105. Feminist critiques of international population policy include Betsy Hartmann, *Reproductive Rights and Wrongs: The Global Politics of Population Control*, 2d ed. (Boston: South End Press, 1995); Ruth Dixon-Mueller, *Population Policy and Women's Rights: Transforming Reproductive Choice* (Westport, Conn.: Praeger, 1993); and Sonia Correa, *Population and Reproductive Rights: Feminist Perspectives from the South* (London: Zed Books, 1994).

145. Hartmann, *Reproductive Rights and Wrongs*, p. xix.

146. Ibid., p. 119. See also Richter, *Vaccination Against Pregnancy*, pp. 116–17.

147. Hartmann, *Reproductive Rights and Wrongs*, p. 119.

148. Mary Meehan, "A Secret War Against the Poor," *Our Sunday Visitor*, Jan. 21, 1996, pp. 6–7. Meehan obtained quotations of Frederick Osborn from the Frederick Osborn Papers and the American Eugenics Society Papers at the American Philosophical Society Library, Philadelphia, Pa.

149. Hartmann, *Reproductive Rights and Wrongs*, p. 69.

150. Quoted in ibid., p. 68.

151. Ibid., p. 71.

152. Shelton, "Complications of Birth," p. 15.

153. Anita Allen, the chairperson of Planned Parenthood of Metropolitan Washington, D.C., reported this at a feminist symposium held at Northwestern University Law School in April 1995. See also Tom Bethell, "Norplant Is Welfare State's New Opiate," *Los Angeles Times*, Jan. 24, 1993, p. M5, reporting teens' reluctance to use Norplant.

154. Sharon Cohen, "Norplant Lawsuits Flourish Along with Women's Reports of Problems," *Los Angeles Times*, Oct. 8, 1995, p. A4.

155. Oxford, "What They Learn at Laurence Paquin School," p. 25.

156. Sloat and Epstein, "Many Find Side Effects of Norplant Intolerable." The authors' conclusion is based on data from state health officials assembled by the *Plain Dealer;* the federal government does not compile data on Norplant insertions and removals.

157. Vrazo, "Ease and Secrecy Draw Women to Quarterly Contraceptive Shot," p. A20.

158. "State Report—Maryland: State Contraceptive Program Exceeds Expectations," *Abortion Report*, Dec. 15, 1993, p. 5.

159. "State OKs Depo-Provera Contract," *Grand Rapids Press*, March 2, 1994, p. B4.

160. Hartmann, *Reproductive Rights and Wrongs*, p. 204; Raymond, *Women as Wombs*, p. 117.

161. Hartmann, *Reproductive Rights and Wrongs*, p. 206; Monica Kuumba, "Perpetuating Neo-Colonialism Through Population Control: South Africa and the United States," *Africa Today* 40 (Jan. 1, 1993), p. 79.

162. Vrazo, "Ease and Secrecy Draw Women to Quarterly Contraceptive Shot," p. A20.

163. For a more detailed description of a variety of contraceptive vaccines, see Angeline Faye Schrater, "Contraceptive Vaccines: Promises and Problems," in Helen Bequaert Holmes, ed., *Issues in Reproductive Technology I: An Anthology* (New York: Garland, 1992), p. 31.

164. Richter, *Vaccination Against Pregnancy.*

165. George F. Brown, "Long-Acting Contraceptives: Rationale, Current Development, and Ethical Implications," Special Supplement, *Hastings Center Report* 25 (Jan.–Feb. 1995), p. S12; Schrater, "Contraceptive Vaccines," pp. 37–41.

166. Hartmann, *Reproductive Rights and Wrongs*, p. 280.

167. Daniel Fisher, "Birth Control Vaccine Firm's Goal: Seeks Chunk of Contraceptive Mark," *Houston Post*, April 10, 1994, p. D1.

168. Malcolm W. Browne, "New Animal Vaccines Spread Like Diseases," *New York Times*, Nov. 26, 1991, pp. C1, C6.

169. Bernard Berelson, "Beyond Family Planning," *Science* 163 (Feb. 7, 1969), p. 533.

170. Richter, *Vaccination Against Pregnancy*, p. 110; Marie Cocking, "Anti-Vaccine Lobby Gets Shot in the Arm," *Horizons* 9 (Sept. 1, 1995), p. 8. Richter gives a detailed account of the global campaign against research on immunological contraceptives. Richter, *Vaccination Against Pregnancy*, pp. 110–40.

171. "Call for a Stop to Research on Antifertility 'Vaccines' (Immunological Contraceptives)," reprinted in Richter, *Vaccination Against Pregnancy*, app. 3, pp. 149–52.

172. H. L. K. Gabelnick, director of the Contraceptive Research and Development Program, Norfolk, Va., quoted in Richter, *Vaccination Against Pregnancy*, p. 118.

Chapter 4. Making Reproduction a Crime

1. Transcript of Record, *State of South Carolina v. Whitner*, No. 92-GS-39-670 (Court of General Sessions, April 20, 1992).

2. Judgment Proceedings, *People v. Johnson*, No. 29390 (Cal. Super. Ct. Jan. 2, 1991); William Booth, "Judge Orders Birth Control Implant in Defendant," *Washington Post*, Jan. 5, 1991. p. A1; Michael Lev, "Judge Is Firm on Forced Contraception, but Welcomes an Appeal," *New York Times*, Jan. 11. 1991, p. A17.

3. Judgment Proceedings, *People v. Johnson*, pp. 6–7.

4. Motion to Modify Sentence, *People v. Johnson* (Jan. 10, 1991), p. 18.

5. "Birth Curb Order Is Declared Moot," *New York Times*, April 15, 1992, p. A23.

6. Lynn M. Paltrow, *Criminal Prosecutions Against Pregnant Women: National Update and Overview* (New York: Reproductive Freedom Project, ACLU Foundation, 1992).

7. *Primetime Live: The Most Innocent*, ABC television broadcast, Sept. 7, 1989.

8. See "Key Battle in War on Drugs: Saving Pregnant Women, Endangered Babies," *State Health Notes*, George Washington University Intergovernmental Health Policy Project, June 1990, p. 1.

9. Paul Marcotte, "Crime and Pregnancy," *American Bar Association Journal*, Aug. 1989, p. 14.

10. Susan LaCroix, "Jailing Mothers for Drug Abuse," *The Nation*, May 1, 1989, p. 585; Patrick Reardon, "Drugs and Pregnancy Debate Far from Resolved," *Chicago Tribune*, May 28, 1989, p. B1; Jeffrey A. Parness, "Arming the Pregnancy Police: More Outlandish Concoctions?" *Louisiana Law Review* 53 (1992), p. 427.

11. *Rivera Live*, CNBC television broadcast, July 16, 1996, interviewing Lynn Paltrow.

12. James A. Inciardi, Dorothy Lockwood, and Anne E. Pottieger, *Women and Crack-Cocaine* (New York: Macmillan, 1993), pp. 1–13.

13. Donna Boundy, "Program for Cocaine Abuse Under Way," *New York Times,* Nov. 17, 1985, p. B12.

14. Inciardi et al., *Women and Crack-Cocaine;* Craig Reinarman and Harry G. Levine, "The Crack Attack: Politics and Media in America's Latest Drug Scare," in Joel Best, ed., *Images and Issues: Current Perspectives on Social Problems* (New York: Aldine de Gruyter, 1989).

15. Richard M. Smith, "The Plague Among Us," *Newsweek,* June 16, 1986, p. 15.

16. Diane Alters, "Women and Crack: Equal Addiction, Unequal Care," *Boston Globe,* Nov. 1, 1989, p. 1; Gina Kolata, "On Streets Ruled by Crack, Families Die," *New York Times,* Aug. 11, 1989, p. A13. See also Inciardi et al., *Women and Crack-Cocaine,* pp. 36–39, refuting the claim of crack's special appeal to women.

17. See Jean Davidson, "Drug Babies Push Issue of Fetal Rights," *Los Angeles Times,* April 25, 1989, p. A3.

18. See Douglas Besharov, "Crack Babies: The Worst Threat Is Mom Herself," *Washington Post,* Aug. 6, 1989, p. B1; Kathleen Nolan, "Protecting Fetuses from Prenatal Hazards: Whose Crimes? What Punishment?" *Criminal Justice Ethics* 9 (1990), pp. 13, 14.

19. Jean Davidson, "Newborn Drug Exposure Conviction a 'Drastic' First," *Los Angeles Times,* July 31. 1989, p. A1.

20. Department of Health and Human Services, Office of Evaluation and Inspections, *Crack Babies* (Washington D.C., 1990); Lou Carlozo, "Moms' Arrests Rekindle Issue of Drug Babies," *Chicago Tribune,* Jan. 27, 1995, Metro Lake section, p. 1.

21. "Ignoring Wails of Babies," *Rocky Mountain News,* July 1, 1995, p. A58.

22. Rich Connell, "The Hidden Devastation of Crack," *Los Angeles Times,* Dec. 18, 1994, p. A1, beginning a series entitled "The Real Cost of Crack."

23. Jane E. Brody, "Widespread Abuse of Drugs by Pregnant Women Is Found," *New York Times,* Aug. 30, 1988, p. C1.

24. Cathy Trost, "Born to Lose: Babies of Crack Users Crowd Hospitals, Break Everybody's Heart," *Wall Street Journal,* July 18, 1989, p. A1.

25. Cynthia R. Daniels, *At Women's Expense: State Power and the Politics of Fetal Rights* (Cambridge: Harvard University Press, 1993), p. 116.

26. Connell, "Hidden Devastation of Crack," p. A1; "Crack Babies Overwhelm Child Welfare System, Senate Says," *Brown University Child Behavior and Development Letter* 6 (April 1990), p. 6.

27. Ira J. Chasnoff, "Cocaine, Pregnancy and the Neonate," *Women and Health* 15 (1989), pp. 23, 32–33; Ira J. Chasnoff et al., "Cocaine Use in Pregnancy," *New England Journal of Medicine* 313 (1985), p. 666.

28. Judith Kleinfeld, "Crack-Impaired Children Show Strange Behavior in School," *Anchorage Daily News,* Feb. 20, 1995, p. B8.

29. Ira J. Chasnoff et al., "Temporal Patterns of Cocaine Use in Pregnancy: Perinatal Outcome," *Journal of the American Medical Association* 261 (March 23/31, 1989), p. 1741; Mark G. Neerhof et al., "Cocaine Abuse During Pregnancy: Peripartum Prevalence and Perinatal Outcome," *American Journal of Obstetrics and Gynecology* 161 (1989), p. 633; Diana B. Petitti and Charlotte Coleman, "Cocaine and the Risk of Low Birth Weight," *American Journal of Public Health* 80 (1990), p. 25.

30. Linda C. Mayes et al., "The Problem of Prenatal Cocaine Exposure: A Rush to Judgment," *Journal of the American Medical Association* 267 (Jan. 1992), p. 406; Barry Zuckerman and Deborah A. Frank, "'Crack Kids': Not Broken," *Pediatrics* 89 (Feb. 1992), p. 337; Robert Mathias, "'Crack Babies': Not a Lost Generation, Researchers Say," *NIDA Notes,* Jan.–Feb., 1992, p. 16.

31. Marvin Dicker and Eldin A. Leighton, "Trends in the U.S. Prevalence of Drug-Using Parturient Women and Drug-Affected Newborns, 1979 Through 1990," *American Journal of Public Health* 84 (Sept. 1994), p. 1433. An article by a team of research physicians concluded that "available evidence from the newborn period is far too slim and fragmented to allow any clear predictions about the effects of

intrauterine exposure to cocaine on the course and outcome of child growth and development." Mayes et al., "Problem of Prenatal Cocaine Exposure," p. 406.

32. Bonnie Baird Wilford and Jacqueline Morgan, *Families at Risk: Analysis of State Initiatives to Aid Drug-Exposed Infants and Their Families* (Washington, D.C.: George Washington University, 1993), p. 11; Ira J. Chasnoff et al., "Cocaine/Polydrug Use in Pregnancy: Two-Year Follow-up," *Pediatrics* 89 (1992), p. 337; Robert Mathias, "Developmental Effects of Prenatal Drug Exposure May Be Overcome by Postnatal Environment," *NIDA Notes*, Jan.–Feb. 1992, p. 14.

33. See Scott MacGregor et al., "Cocaine Abuse During Pregnancy: Correlation Between Prenatal Care and Perinatal Outcome," *Obstetrics and Gynecology* 74 (1989), pp. 882, 885.

34. Nesrin Bingol et al., "The Influence of Socioeconomic Factors on the Occurrence of Fetal Alcohol Syndrome," *Advances in Alcohol and Substance Abuse* 6 (1987), p. 105.

35. Gideon Koren et al., "Bias Against the Null Hypothesis: The Reproductive Hazards of Cocaine," *Lancet*, Dec. 16, 1989, p. 1440.

36. Laura E. Gomez, *Misconceiving Mothers: Legislators, Prosecutors, and the Politics of Prenatal Drug Exposure* (Philadelphia: Temple University Press, 1997).

37. Ibid., quoting Nancy L. Day and Gale A. Richardson, "Cocaine Use and Crack Babies: Science, the Media, and Miscommunication," *Neurotoxicology and Teratology* 15 (1993), p. 293.

38. Michelle Oberman, "Sex, Drugs, Pregnancy, and the Law: Rethinking the Problems of Pregnant Women Who Use Drugs," *Hastings Law Journal* 43 (1992), p. 505; Rorie Sherman, "Keeping Babies Free of Drugs," *National Law Journal*, Oct. 16, 1989, p. 1; Bonnie I. Robin-Vergeer, "The Problem of the Drug-Exposed Newborn: A Return to Principled Intervention," *Stanford Law Review* 42 (1990), p. 745.

39. J. R. Fink, "Reported Effects of Crack Cocaine on Infants," *Youth Law News* 11 (1990), p. 37.

40. Daniel R. Neuspiel "Custody of Cocaine-Exposed Newborns: Determinants of Discharge Decisions," *American Journal of Public Health* 83 (Dec. 1993), p. 1726.

41. Joe Sexton, "Officials Seek Wider Powers to Seize Children in Drug Homes," *New York Times*, March 12, 1996, p. B1. Agnes Palazzeti, "Agencies Fight Rise in Drug Births," *Buffalo News*, March 3, 1996, p. C1.

42. Quoted in Oberman, "Sex, Drugs, Pregnancy, and the Law," p. 525.

43. Matt O'Connor, "State Sued on Cocaine Baby Care," *Chicago Tribune*, Sept. 27, 1991, p. B1; Jennifer Preston, "State Agrees to Speed Help to Infants Without Homes," *New York Times*, Dec. 21, 1996, p. A30.

44. A. M. Rosenthal, "On My Mind: The Poisoned Babies," *New York Times*, Jan. 16, 1996, p. A17.

45. *United States v. Vaughn*, Crim. No. F 2172-88 B (D.C. Super. Ct. Aug. 23, 1988); Kary L. Moss, "Pregnant? Go Directly to Jail," *American Bar Association Journal*, Nov. 1, 1988, p. 20; Richard Cohen, "When a Fetus Has More Rights Than the Mother," *Washington Post*, July 28, 1988, p. A21.

46. Marianne Taylor, " 'Addicted' Fetus Sparks Court Battle," *Chicago Tribune*, April 9, 1984, p. A1.

47. Mary Beth Murphy, "Protecting the Fetus at What Cost? Medical, Legal Issues Raised By Detention," *Milwaukee Journal-Sentinel*, Sept. 18, 1995, p. 1. The Wisconsin Supreme Court—the first high court to decide this issue—held that a fetus is not a child under the state's child welfare laws. Tamar Lewin, "Detention of Pregnant Women for Drug Use Is Struck Down," *New York Times*, April 23, 1997, p. A16.

48. *Cox v. Court*, 42 Ohio App. 3d 171, 173, 537 N.E.2d 721, 723 (1988) (reversing juvenile court order).

49. *State v. Johnson*, No. E89-890-CFA, slip opinion, p. 1 (Fla. Cir. Ct. July 13, 1989), aff'd, No. 89-1765 (Fla. Dist. Ct. App. April 18, 1991).

50. Trial Transcript, *State v. Johnson*, pp. 20–24, 32.

51. Ibid., pp. 57–60.

52. Ibid., p. 155.

53. Patricia Barnett Christensen, "The Criminal Prosecution of Mothers of Drug-Exposed Neonates: A Case Study of a Policy Dilemma," Ph.D. dissertation, School of Graduate Studies, Medical College of Georgia, 1992, citing *Greenville News*, Aug. 25, 1989.

54. Plaintiffs' Memorandum in Support of Their Partial Cross-Motion for Summary Judgment and in Opposition to Defendants' Motion for Summary Judgment, *Ferguson v. City of Charleston*, No. 2:93-2624-2 (D.S.C. Oct. 1995).

55. Medical University of South Carolina, Policy II-7 Management of Drug Abuse During Pregnancy (Oct. 1989), quoted in Philip H. Jos, Mary Faith Marshall, and Martin Perlmutter, "The Charleston Policy on Cocaine Use During Pregnancy: A Cautionary Tale," *Journal of Law, Medicine and Ethics* 23 (Summer 1995), p. 120.

56. Jos et al., "Charleston Policy on Cocaine Use During Pregnancy," p. 122.

57. Barry Siegel, "In the Name of the Children: Get Treatment or Go to Jail, One South Carolina Hospital Tells Drug-Abusing Pregnant Women," *Los Angeles Times Magazine*, Aug. 7, 1994, p. 14.

58. Plaintiffs' Memorandum, *Ferguson v. City of Charleston*, p. 19 n.25.

59. Center for Reproductive Law and Policy, *Punishing Women for Their Behavior During Pregnancy: An Approach That Undermines Women's Health and Children's Interests*, Feb. 14, 1996, p. 4; Plaintiffs' Memorandum, *Ferguson v. City of Charleston*, pp. 26–27; Philip J. Hilts, "Hospital Is Accused of Illegal Drug Testing," *New York Times*, Jan. 21, 1994, p. A12.

60. Siegel, "In the Name of the Children," p. 14.

61. Plaintiffs' Memorandum, *Ferguson v. City of Charleston*, p. 27.

62. *Johnson v. State*, 602 So.2d 1288 (Fla. 1992).

63. *Ferguson v. City of Charleston*, No. 2-93-26242-2 (D.S.C. filed Oct. 5, 1993).

64. Philip J. Hilts, "Hospital Put on Probation over Tests on Poor Women," *New York Times*, Oct. 5, 1994, p. B9.

65. Charles Molony Condon, "Clinton's Cocaine Babies: Why Won't the Administration Let Us Save Our Children?" *Policy Review*, Spring 1995, p. 12.

66. *Whitner v. South Carolina*, No. 24468 (S.C. July 15, 1996). John Heilprin, "Drug Users Face Fetal Abuse Charge," *Post and Courier* (Charleston, S.C.), July 16, 1996, p. A1; Lisa Greene, "Court Rules Drug Use Is Fetal Abuse," *The State*, July 16, 1996, p. A1.

67. See Lynn Paltrow and Suzanne Shende, "State by State Case Summary of Criminal Prosecutions Against Pregnant Women," unpublished memorandum to ACLU affiliates and interested parties, Oct. 29, 1990. I confirmed the race of some of the defendants by telephone calls to their attorneys. Telephone interviews with Joseph Merkin, attorney for Sharon Peters (Jan. 7, 1991); James Shields, North Carolina ACLU (Jan. 7, 1991); and Patrick Young, attorney for Brenda Yurchak (Jan. 7, 1991). See also Gina Kolata, "Bias Seen Against Pregnant Addicts," *New York Times*, July 20, 1990, p. A13, indicating that of 60 women charged, 80% were minorities.

68. Paltrow and Shende, *Criminal Prosecutions Against Pregnant Women*; Plaintiffs' Memorandum, *Ferguson v. City of Charleston*, pp. 32–35. Of the 109 women the Greenville solicitor charged with child neglect, 101 were addicted to crack. Not surprisingly, 86 of these women were Black. Christensen, "Criminal Prosecution of Mothers of Drug-Exposed Neonates," pp. 91–92.

69. Maternal, Infant, and Child Health Council, *South Carolina Prevalence of Drug Use Among Women Giving Birth* (Columbia, S.C.: Office of the Governor, 1991), pp. 7–8.

70. Molly McNulty, "Pregnancy Police: The Health Policy and Legal Implications of Punishing Pregnant Women for Harm to Their Fetuses," *New York University Review of Law and Social Change* 16 (1988), pp. 277, 319.

71. Plaintiffs' Memorandum, *Ferguson v. City of Charleston*, p. 32.

72. Condon, "Clinton's Cocaine Babies," p. 14.

73. Christensen, "Criminal Prosecution of Mothers of Drug-Exposed Neonates," p. 104.

74. U.S. General Accounting Office, *Report to the Chairman, Committee on Finance, U.S. Senate, Drug-Exposed Infants: A Generation at Risk,* GAO/HRO-90-138 (Washington, D.C., June 1990).

75. Ira J. Chasnoff, Harvey J. Landress, and Mark E. Barrett, "The Prevalence of Illicit-Drug or Alcohol Use During Pregnancy and Discrepancies in Mandatory Reporting in Pinellas County, Florida," *New England Journal of Medicine* 322 (1990), pp. 1202–6; Carol Angel, "Addicted Babies: Legal System's Response Unclear," *Los Angeles Daily Journal,* Feb. 29, 1988, p. 1.

76. Robin-Vergeer, "Problem of the Drug-Exposed Newborn," pp. 798–99.

77. Mayes et al., "Problem of Prenatal Cocaine Exposure," p. 406; Chasnoff et al., "Prevalence of Illicit-Drug or Alcohol Use During Pregnancy," p. 1206; Robin-Vergeer, "Problem of the Drug-Exposed Newborn," p. 754 and n.36.

78. Christensen, "Criminal Prosecution of Mothers of Drug-Exposed Neonates," pp. 116–18.

79. Lisa Maher, "Punishment and Welfare: Crack Cocaine and the Regulation of Mothering" in Clarice Feinman, ed., *The Criminalization of a Woman's Body* (New York: Harrington Park Press, 1992), pp. 157, 180.

80. Plaintiffs' Memorandum, *Ferguson v. City of Charleston,* pp. 33–34.

81. Chasnoff et al., "Prevalence of Illicit-Drug or Alcohol Use During Pregnancy."

82. Ibid., p. 1204.

83. See, e.g., Helaine Olen, "Racial Tinge to Drug Testing of New Moms," *Chicago Tribune,* Dec. 19, 1991, p. C14, report on study finding Black women more likely than white to be tested and reported to child welfare authorities in Illinois.

84. I elaborate this point in Dorothy E. Roberts, "Reconstructing the Patient: Starting with Women of Color," in Susan M. Wolf, ed., *Feminism and Bioethics: Beyond Reproduction* (New York: Oxford University Press, 1996), p. 116.

85. Janet Gallagher, "Prenatal Invasions and Interventions: What's Wrong with Fetal Rights," *Harvard Women's Law Journal* 10 (1987), p. 9.

86. Veronika E. B. Kolder, Janet Gallagher, and Michael T. Parsons, "Court-Ordered Obstetrical Interventions," *New England Journal of Medicine* 316 (1987), p. 1192.

87. Sara Rosenbaum et al., *The Health of America's Children* (Washington, D.C.: Children's Defense Fund, 1988), pp. 35–37; Institute of Medicine, *Preventing Low Birthweight* (Washington, D.C.: National Academy Press, 1985), pp. 65–72.

88. Ann Pytkowicz Streissguth et al., "Fetal Alcohol Syndrome in Adolescents and Adults," *Journal of the American Medical Association* 265 (April 17, 1991), p. 1961.

89. Barry Zuckerman et al., "Effects of Maternal Marijuana and Cocaine Use on Fetal Growth," *New England Journal of Medicine* 320 (1989), p. 762.

90. See Sandra Blakeslee, "Parents Fight for a Future for Infants Born to Drugs," *New York Times,* May 19, 1990, p. A1.

91. Elizabeth Rosenthal, "When a Pregnant Woman Drinks," *New York Times Magazine,* Feb. 4, 1990, pp. 30, 49; Deanna S. Gomby and Patricia H. Shiono, "Estimating the Number of Substance-Exposed Infants," *The Future of Children* 1 (1991), pp. 17, 23.

92. Barry Zuckerman, "Marijuana and Cigarette Smoking During Pregnancy: Neonatal Effects," in Ira J. Chasnoff, ed., *Drugs, Alcohol, Pregnancy and Parenting* (London: Kluwer, 1988), p. 73.

93. Jeff Lancashire, *U.S. Department of Health and Human Services: Public Health Report,* Jan.–Feb. 1995, p. 105.

94. Carey Goldberg, "Way Out West and Under the Influence," *New York Times,* March 16, 1997, p. A16.

95. Andrew Malcolm, "Crack, Bane of Inner City, Is Now Gripping Suburbs," *New York Times,* Oct. 1, 1989, p. A1.

96. Quoted in Siegel, "In the Name of the Children," p. 14.

97. Quoted in Susan Faludi, *Backlash: The Undeclared War Against American Women* (New York: Anchor Books, 1992), p. 427.

98. Motion for Rehearing and Sentencing, *State v. Johnson*, No. E89-890-CFA (Fla. Cir. Ct. Aug. 25, 1989), p. 12 (emphasis added).

99. Jan Hoffman, "Pregnant, Addicted—And Guilty?" *New York Times Magazine*, Aug. 19, 1990, p. 44.

100. *People v. Stewart*, No. M508197, slip opinion, p. 4 (Cal. Mun. Ct. Feb. 26, 1987); Angela Bonavoglia, "The Ordeal of Pamela Rae Stewart," *Ms.*, July–Aug. 1987, p. 92.

101. Gail Stewart Hand, "Women or Children First?" *Grand Forks Herald*, July 12, 1992, p. 1.

102. Trial Transcript, *State v. Johnson*, p. 364.

103. Jed Rubenfeld, "The Right of Privacy," *Harvard Law Review* 102 (1989), p. 737.

104. See, e.g., *Roe v. Wade*, 410 U.S. 113 (1973) (right to choose whether to terminate a pregnancy); *Griswold v. Connecticut*, 381 U.S. 479, 485 (1965) (right to decide whether to use contraceptives).

105. Eisenstadt v. Baird, 405 U.S. 438, 453 (1972).

106. Myron Wegman, "Annual Summary of Vital Statistics—1991," *Pediatrics* 90 (Dec. 1992), p. 835, Ann Scott Tyson, "Counseling for Moms Aids Inner-City Infants," *Christian Science Monitor*, Oct. 15, 1996, p. A3.

107. Francis G. Caro, Debra Kalmuss, and Iris Lopez, *Barriers to Prenatal Care* (New York: Community Service Society, 1988), p. 1.

108. Michael Abramovitz, "Infant Mortality Soars Here," *Washington Post*, Sept. 30, 1989, p. A1.

109. Donald B. Binsacca et al., "Factors Associated with Low Birthweight in an Inner-City Population: The Role of Financial Problems," *American Journal of Public Health* 77 (1987), p. 505; Kenneth J. Leveno et al., "Prenatal Care and the Low Birth Weight Infant," *Obstetrics and Gynecology* 66 (1985), p. 599.

110. Caro et al., *Barriers to Prenatal Care*; Mary Ann Curry, "Nonfinancial Barriers to Prenatal Care," *Women and Health* 15 (1989), pp. 85–87; Marilyn Poland, Joel Ager, and Jane Olson, "Barriers to Receiving Adequate Prenatal Care," *American Journal of Obstetrics and Gynecology* 157 (1987), pp. 297–303; Ruth Zambrana, "A Research Agenda on Issues Affecting Poor and Minority Women: A Model for Understanding Their Health Needs," in Cesar Perales and Lauren S. Young, eds., *Too Little, Too Late: Dealing with the Health Needs of Women in Poverty* (New York: Harrington Park Press, 1988), p. 137.

111. Myron Wegman, "Annual Summary of Vital Statistics—1993," *Pediatrics* 94 (Dec. 1994), p. 792; Rosenbaum et al., *Children's Defense Fund: The Health of America's Children*, p. 4, tab. 1.1.

112. Sarah B. Brown, ed., Committee to Study Outreach for Prenatal Care, Institute of Medicine, *Prenatal Care: Reaching Mothers, Reaching Infants* (1988).

113. Lorna McBarnette, "Women and Poverty: The Effects on Reproductive Status," in Perales and Young, *Too Little, Too Late*, pp. 55, 57.

114. Pamela Short et al., "Health Insurance for Minorities in the United States," *Journal of Health Care for the Poor and Underserved* 1 (1990), p. 9.

115. The percentage of Black women receiving prenatal care in the first three months of pregnancy declined from a high of 62.7 in 1980 to 61.1 in 1988. The percentage of babies born to Black women getting no prenatal care increased from 8.8 in 1980 to 11.0 in 1988. Philip Hilts, "Life Expectancy for Blacks in U.S. Shows Sharp Drop," *New York Times*, Nov. 29, 1990, p. B17.

116. Robert Pear, "Study Says U.S. Needs to Attack Infant Mortality," *New York Times*, Aug. 6, 1990, p. B9.

117. Randall Kennedy, "The State, Criminal Law, and Racial Discrimination: A Comment," *Harvard Law Review* 107 (1994), pp. 1255, 1274 n. 82, 1256.

118. Quoted in Condon, "Clinton's Cocaine Babies," p. 14.

119. Nicole H. Rafter, *Partial Justice: Women, Prisons, and Social Control* (New Brunswick, N.J.: Transaction, 1990), p. 134.

120. Ibid.

121. Michael Tonry, *Malign Neglect: Race, Crime, and Punishment in America* (New York: Oxford University Press, 1995); John A. Powell and Eileen B. Hershenov, "Hostage to the Drug War: The National Purse, the Constitution, and the Black Community," *U. C. Davis Law Review* 24 (1991), pp. 557, 610.

122. Jos et al., "Charleston Policy on Cocaine Use During Pregnancy," p. 124.

123. Christensen, "Criminal Prosecution of Mothers of Drug-Exposed Neonates," pp. 151, 160, 190.

124. Wendy Chavkin, "Drug Addiction and Pregnancy: Policy Crossroads," *American Journal of Public Health* 80 (1990), p. 483; Molly McNulty, "Combatting Pregnancy Discrimination in Access to Substance Abuse Treatment for Low-Income Women," *Clearinghouse Review* 23 (1989), p. 21.

125. Chavkin, "Drug Addiction and Pregnancy," p. 485

126. National Association of State Alcohol and Drug Abuse Directors, *Survey of State Alcohol and Drug Agency Use FY 1989 Federal and State Funds* (Washington, D.C., 1990), tab. 2.

127. Wendy Chavkin, "Help, Don't Jail, Addicted Mothers," *New York Times,* July 18, 1989, p. A21.

128. Donna R. Weston et al., "Drug Exposed Babies: Research and Clinical Issues," in Jeree Pawl. ed., *Zero to Three* (Washington, D.C.: National Center for Clinical Infant Programs, 1989), p. 4.

129. Chavkin, "Help, Don't Jail, Addicted Mothers," p. A21.

130. Oberman, "Sex, Drugs, Pregnancy, and the Law," p. 517.

131. *Elaine W. v. Joint Diseases North General Hospital,* 613 N.E.2d 523 (N.Y. 1993).

132. Dorothy E. Roberts, *Women, Pregnancy, and Substance Abuse* (Washington, D.C.: Center for Women Policy Studies, 1991); Chavkin, "Drug Addiction and Pregnancy," p. 485; Vicki Breitbart, Wendy Chavkin, Christine Layton, and Paul Wise, "Model Programs Addressing Perinatal Drug Exposure and Human Immunodeficiency Virus Infection: Integrating Women's and Children's Needs," *Bulletin of the New York Academy of Medicine* 71 (Winter 1994), p. 236.

133. Telephone interview with Adrienne Edmonson-Smith, advocate with the Maternal-Child Health Advocacy Project, Wayne State University, July 25, 1990.

134. American Medical Association, "Report of the Board of Trustees on Legal Interventions During Pregnancy: Court Ordered Medical Treatments and Legal Penalties for Potentially Harmful Behavior by Pregnant Women," *Journal of the American Medical Association* 264 (November 28, 1990), p. 2663.

135. American Academy of Pediatrics, Committee on Substance Abuse, "Drug-Exposed Infants," *Pediatrics* 86 (1990), pp. 639, 641.

136. *State v. Johnson,* Trial Transcript, pp. 85–86.

137. Ibid., p. 144.

138. Kary Moss, "Legal Issues: Drug Testing of Postpartum Women and Newborns as the Basis for Civil and Criminal Proceedings," *Clearinghouse Review* 23 (1990), pp. 1406, 1411–12.

139. Oberman, "Sex, Drugs, Pregnancy, and the Law," p. 540.

140. U.S. General Accounting Office Report to the Chairman, House Subcommittee on Health and the Environment, Committee on Energy and Commerce, ADMS Block Grant, *Women's Set Aside Does Not Assure Drug Treatment for Pregnant Women,* GAO/HRO-91-80 (May 1991), p. 20.

141. U.S. General Accounting Office Report to the Chairman, Senate Committee on Finance, *Drug-Exposed Infants: A Generation at Risk,* GAO/HRO-90-138 (June 1990), p. 39.

142. Marilyn L. Poland et al., "Punishing Pregnant Drug Users: Enhancing the Flight from Care," *Drug and Alcohol Dependence* 31 (1993), pp. 199, 202.

143. Personal Responsibility and Work Opportunity Reconciliation Act of 1996, Pub. L. No. 104-193, 110 Stat. 2105 (1996).

144. See, e.g., Daniel R. Neuspiel and Ernest Drucker, "Separating Crack Mothers from Children Does More Harm," letter to editor, *New York Times*, Jan. 16, 1996, p. A16.

145. Hoffman, "Pregnant, Addicted — And Guilty?" p. 34.

146. Stacey L. Arthur, "The Norplant Prescription: Birth Control, Woman Control, or Crime Control?" *UCLA Law Review* 40 (1992), p. 1.

147. See, e.g., *Smith v. Superior Court*, 725 P.2d 1101, 1104 (Ariz. 1986) (en banc) (striking sterilization in exchange for reduced sentence for child abuse); *People v. Pointer*, 199 Cal. Rptr. 357, 366 (Ct. App. 1984) (reversing portion of judgment prohibiting conception as a condition of probation imposed on woman convicted of child endangerment for placing her children on a strict microbiotic diet); *Thomas v. State*, 519 So. 2d 1113, 1114 (Fla. Dist. Ct. App. 1988) (striking probation condition forbidding defendant convicted of stealing from becoming pregnant out of wedlock).

148. Mark A. Stein, "Judge Stirs Debate with Ordering of Birth Control," *Los Angeles Times*, Jan. 10, 1991, p. A3.

149. Martin Gunerson, "Birth Control as a Condition of Probation or Parole," in James M. Humber and Robert F. Almeder, *Biomedical Ethics Reviews: 1992* (Totowa, N.J.: Humana, 1993), p. 83.

150. Of course, all of these justifications apply equally to men; there is no excuse for judges to require the use of contraceptives only in the case of female defendants. Judges have more rarely imposed limits on male defendants' procreative capacity. See, e.g., *People v. Gauntlett*, 352 N.W.2d 310 (Mich. App. 1984) (striking condition requiring probationer to take experimental drug to cause "chemical castration"); *Howland v. State*, 420 S.2d 918 (Fla. App. 1st Dist., 1982) (striking condition prohibiting probationer convicted of child abuse from "fathering" a child); Roberto Sura, "Amid Controversy, Castration Plan in Texas Rape Case Collapses," *New York Times*, March 17, 1992, p. A16.

151. Melissa Burke, "The Constitutionality of the Use of the Norplant Contraceptive Device as a Condition of Probation," *Hastings Constitutional Law Quarterly* 20 (1992), pp. 207, 241. See "Abusive Mother Accepts Contraceptive Implant," *Chicago Tribune*, Feb. 10, 1993, p. A3 (Lisa Smith in Illinois); John Makeig, "Surgical Deterrent: Mom Convicted of Child Abuse Picks Birth-Control Implant over Prison," *Houston Chronicle*, March 6, 1992, p. A1 (Ida Jean Tovar in Texas); "Judge Orders Woman to Be Given Contraceptive," *UPI*, Sept. 6, 1991 (Cathy Lanel Knighten in Texas); "Nebraska," *USA Today*, April 23, 1991, p. A6 (Michelle Carlton in Nebraska); *People v. Johnson*, No. 29390 (Cal. Super. Ct. Tulare County 1990) (Darlene Johnson in California).

152. Stephen Trombley, *The Right to Reproduce: The History of Coercive Sterilization* (London: Weidenfeld, 1988), p. 176.

153. Gunderson, "Birth Control as a Condition of Probation or Parole," p. 94.

154. McClatchy News Service, "Mother Gets 4-Year Term in Abuse Case," *Sacramento Bee*, June 18, 1991, p. B3.

155. Ronald C. Dozier, "Comments on Norplant Case," typewritten memo, April 28, 1993, p. 1.

156. See Appellant's Opening Brief, *People v. Johnson* No. F015316 (Cal. Ct. App. 5th App. Dt., filed April 24, 1991), pp. 25–26, citing *People v. Rylaarsdam*, 130 Cal. App. 3d Supp. 1 (1982); *In re White*, 97 Cal. App. 3d 141 (1979); *People v. Norris*, 88 Cal. App. 3d Supp. 32 (1978).

157. Judgment Proceedings, *People v. Johnson* (Jan. 2, 1991), pp. 6–7.

158. *People v. Zaring*, 10 Cal. Rptr 2d 263, 267 (1992).

159. Bill Ainsworth, "Tulare's Target of Controversy: Judge Howard Broadman's Creative Sentences Have Won Both Plaudits and Condemnation; One Almost Earned Him a Bullet in the Head," *Recorder*, March 28, 1991, p. 1.

160. See *People v. Dominguez*, 64 Cal. Rptr 290 (Ct. App. 1967) (reversing order revoking probation when the defendant became pregnant without being married).

161. See, e.g., *People v. Blankenship*, 16 Cal. App. 2d 606 (1936).

162. Gertrude C. Davenport, "Hereditary Crime," *American Journal of Sociology* 13 (1907), p. 402, reprinted in Nicole H. Rafter, ed., *White Trash: The Eugenic Family Studies* (Boston: Northeastern University Press, 1988), pp. 66, 68.

163. Alexander Cockburn, "Welfare, Norplant, and the Nazis," *The Nation*, July 18, 1994, pp. 79, 80.

Chapter 5. The Welfare Debate: Who Pays for Procreation?

1. Personal Responsibility and Work Opportunity Reconciliation Act of 1996, Title III, Pub. L. No. 104-193, 110 Stat. 2105 (1996).

2. Bob Herbert, "The Mouths of Babes," *New York Times*, July 22, 1996, p. A19.

3. Books demonstrating these flaws in the American welfare system include Frances Fox Piven and Richard A. Cloward, *Regulating the Poor: The Functions of Public Welfare* (New York: Pantheon, 1971); Mimi Abramovitz, *Regulating the Lives of Women: Social Welfare Policy from Colonial Times to the Present* (Boston: South End Press, 1988); Jill Quadagno, *The Color of Welfare: How Racism Undermined the War on Poverty* (New York: Oxford University Press, 1994).

4. Linda Gordon, *Pitied but Not Entitled: Single Mothers and the History of Welfare* (New York: Free Press, 1994). Other important histories of the American welfare system include Gwendolyn Mink, *The Wages of Motherhood: Inequality in the Welfare State, 1917–1942* (Ithaca N.Y.: Cornell University Press, 1995), and Theda Skocpol. *Protecting Soldiers and Mothers: The Political Origins of Social Policy in the United States* (Cambridge: Harvard University Press, 1992).

5. Gordon, *Pitied but Not Entitled*, p. 53.

6. Ibid., p. 48; Abramovitz, *Regulating the Lives of Women*, p. 201; Joel F. Handler and Yeheskel Hasenfeld, *The Moral Construction of Poverty; Welfare Reform in America* (Newbury Park. Calif.: Sage, 1991), pp. 25–27.

7. Michael W. McConnell, "Originalism and the Desegregation Decisions," *Virginia Law Review* 81 (1995), pp. 947, 1131 n.856.

8. Gordon, *Pitied but Not Entitled*, p. 87. See also Mink, *Wages of Motherhood*, p. 120.

9. Gordon, *Pitied but Not Entitled*, pp. 111–43.

10. Eileen Boris, "The Power of Motherhood: Black and White Activist Women Redefine the 'Political,'" *Yale Journal of Law and Feminism* 2 (1989), pp. 25, 26.

11. Gordon, *Pitied but Not Entitled*, p. 295.

12. Ibid., p. 282.

13. Ibid., pp. 276–77; Quadagno, *The Color of Welfare*, p. 21; Piven and Cloward, *Regulating the Poor*, pp. 130–45.

14. Abramovitz, *Regulating the Lives of Women*, p. 344 n.22.

15. Gordon, *Pitied but Not Entitled*, p. 276.

16. Gwendolyn Mink, "Welfare Reform in Historical Perspective," *Connecticut Law Review* 26 (1994), pp. 879, 891.

17. Quadagno, *The Color of Welfare*, pp. 28–31; Piven and Cloward, *Regulating the Poor*, pp. 248–338.

18. Gordon, *Pitied but Not Entitled*, p. 5.

19. Mink, "Welfare Reform in Historical Perspective," pp. 891–92.

20. Quoted in Lucy A. Williams, "Race, Rat Bites, and Unfit Mothers: How Media Discourse Informs the Welfare Legislation Debate," *Fordham Urban Law Journal* 22 (1995), pp. 1159, 1183.

21. Julius Paul, "The Return of Punitive Sterilization Proposals: Current Attacks on Illegitimacy and the AFDC Program," *Law and Society Review* 3 (1968), pp. 77, 103 n.42.

22. Quadagno, *The Color of Welfare*, p. 4.
23. Marcia Coyle and Harvey Berkman, "Welfare Entitlements Face Erosion," *National Law Journal* 18 (June 17, 1996), p. A1.
24. See, e.g., Handler and Hasenfeld, *Moral Construction of Poverty*; Michael B. Katz, *The Undeserving Poor: From the War on Poverty to the War on Welfare* (New York: Pantheon, 1989).
25. *The Personal Responsibility Act of 1995*, H.R. 4, 104th Cong., 1st sess., 1995; "GOP Welfare Plan Would Take Cash from Unwed Mothers to Aid Adoptions," *Chicago Tribune*, Nov. 14, 1994, p. A7.
26. Nancy Gibbs, "The Vicious Cycle," *Time*, June 20, 1994, p. 24.
27. "Senate Finance Committee Hearing," *Federal News Service*, July 13, 1994, in the News Section, p. 1.
28. Nina Perales, "A 'Tangle of Pathology': Racial Myth and the New Jersey Family Development Act," in Martha A. Fineman and Isabel Karpin, eds., *Mothers in Law: Feminist Theory and the Legal Regulation of Motherhood* (New York: Columbia University Press, 1995), pp. 250, 263.
29. David Whitman, "War on Welfare Dependency: A New Crackdown Is Great Politics, but the Results May Not Thrill Taxpayers," *U.S. News and World Report*, April 20, 1996, pp. 37, 40.
30. Statement of Assemblyman Wayne Bryant, New Jersey Assembly Bill 4703 (1990).
31. James R. Kelly, "Why Republican and New Democrat Welfare Changes Need Legal Abortion," *America* 173 (Dec. 30, 1995), p. 7; Iver Peterson, "Abortions Up Slightly for Welfare Mothers," *New York Times*, May 17, 1995, p. B7.
32. *60 Minutes: $64 Question*, CBS television broadcast, May 15, 1994.
33. Plaintiff's Brief in Opposition to Federal Defendant's Motion for Summary Judgment, *C.K. v. Shalala*, 883 F. Supp. 991 (D.N.J. 1995), aff'd sub nom. *C.K. v. New Jersey Dep't of Health & Human Servs.*, 92 F.3d 171 (3d Cir. 1996), Exhibit C; Barbara Vobejda, "N.J. Welfare 'Cap' Has No Effect on Births, Study Finds," *Washington Post*, June 21, 1995, p. A3. One analysis of New Jersey welfare and hospital records contends that "since the implementation of the reform, births to welfare mothers and welfare caseloads have declined significantly." Ted G. Goertzel and Gary S. Young, "New Jersey's Experiment in Welfare Reform," *Public Interest*, Fall 1996, pp. 72, 73.
34. Testimony of Assemblyman Wayne Bryant, 1991 public hearing before New Jersey Assembly Health and Human Services Committee, quoted in Perales, "Tangle of Pathology," p. 257.
35. Brief Amici Curiae for Women's Legal Defense Fund et al., *C.K. v. New Jersey Dep't of Health & Human Servs.*, 92 F. 3d 171 (3d Cir. 1996), p. 26 n.18.
36. Paul, "Return of Punitive Sterilization Proposals," p. 89.
37. Quoted in Edgar May, *The Wasted Americans: Cost of Our Welfare Dilemma* (New York: Harper, 1964), p. 14.
38. Paul, "Return of Punitive Sterilization Proposals," p. 90 n.20.
39. Ibid., p. 89 n.17.
40. Public Hearings before Assembly Health and Human Services Committee, New Jersey Assembly Bills Nos. 4700–4705 (Oct. 22, 1991).
41. Lally Weymouth, "Building Self-Sufficiency," *Washington Post*, March 27, 1992, p. A21.
42. Quoted in Perales, "Tangle of Pathology," p. 262.
43. *Personal Responsibility Act*, H.R. 4, sec. 100.
44. Carl Rowan, "Duplicitous Newt a Bigot-in-Denial," *Chicago Sun-Times*, Editorial Section, June 21, 1995, p. 39; DeWayne Wickham, "Gingrich Blames Poor for 'Self-Made' Poverty," *USA Today*, July 3, 1995, p. A11.
45. Staff of House Committee on Ways and Means, *Overview of Entitlement Programs: 1994 Green Book* 103d Cong., 2d sess., 1994, pp. 402, 444; Teresa L. Amott, "Black Women

and AFDC: Making Entitlement Out of Necessity," in Linda Gordon, ed., *Women, the State, and Welfare* (Madison: University of Wisconsin Press, 1990), p. 280.

46. Richard L. Dugdale, *The Jukes* (1891; New York: Arno Press, 1970), p. 167.

47. Charles B. Davenport, *Heredity in Relation to Eugenics* (New York: Holt, 1911).

48. Quoted in Alexander Cockburn, "Eugenic Nuts Would Have Loved Norplant: The Coercion of Women on Welfare to Avoid Child-bearing Smells of '30s Social Cleansing," *Los Angeles Times*, June 30, 1994, p. B7.

49. Daniel J. Kevles, *In the Name of Eugenics: Genetics and the Uses of Human Heredity* (New York: Knopf, 1985), p. 183, quoting Ronald A. Fisher, "Family Allowances in the Contemporary Economic Situation" (1932).

50. Ibid.

51. Ibid., p. 184.

52. Charles Murray, *Losing Ground: American Social Policy, 1950-1980* (New York: Basic Books, 1984), pp. 154-66.

53. Charles Murray, "The Coming White Underclass," *Wall Street Journal*, Oct. 29, 1993, p. A14.

54. Richard J. Herrnstein and Charles Murray, *The Bell Curve: Intelligence and Class Structure in American Life* (New York: Free Press, 1994).

55. Paul Starr, "Who Owns the Future?" *American Prospect*, Spring 1995, p. 6.

56. *Congressional Record* S11783 (daily ed., Aug. 7, 1995) (statement of Sen. Faircloth).

57. *Congressional Record* H11515 (daily ed., Dec. 16, 1987) (statement of Rep. Roukema).

58. See, e.g., Mickey Kaus, *The End of Equality* (New York: Basic Books, 1992); Lawrence M. Mead, *The New Politics of Poverty: The Nonworking Poor in America* (New York: Basic Books, 1992); Murray, *Losing Ground*.

59. Gregory Acs, "Does Welfare Promote Out-of-Wedlock Childbearing?" in Isabel Sawhill, ed., *Welfare Reform: An Analysis of the Issues* (Washington, D.C.: Urban Institute, May 15, 1995), pp. 51, 53; David Ellwood, *Poor Support: Poverty in the American Family* (New York: Basic Books, 1988), p. 72.

60. Marian Wright Edelman, *Families in Peril: An Agenda for Social Change* (Cambridge: Harvard University Press, 1987), pp. 70-71. See also Mark R. Rank, "Fertility Among Women on Welfare: Incidence and Determinants," *American Society Review* 54 (1989), pp. 296, 298-300, finding that AFDC mothers have lower fertility rates than the general public.

61. Staff of House Committee on Ways and Means, *Overview of Entitlement Programs: Background Material and Data on Programs within the Jurisdiction of the Committee on Ways and Means* 102d Cong., 2d sess., 1992, p. 669.

62. Theresa Funiciello, *Tyranny of Kindness: Dismantling the Welfare System to End Poverty in America* (New York: Atlantic Monthly Press, 1993), p. 57.

63. Kaus, *The End of Equality*, p. 117.

64. Clarence Page, "Thomas' Sister's Life Gives Lie to His Welfare Fable," *Chicago Tribune*, July 24, 1991, p. A19.

65. Ibid.

66. Funiciello, *Tyranny of Kindness*, p. 9.

67. Nancy Fraser and Linda Gordon, "A Genealogy of Dependency: Tracing a Keyword of the U.S. Welfare State," *Signs* 19 (1994), pp. 309, 311.

68. Handler and Hasenfeld, *Moral Construction of Poverty*, p. 19; Eric R. Kingson and Edward D. Berkowitz, *Social Security and Medicare: A Policy Primer* (Westport, Conn.: Greenwood, 1993), pp. 23-25; Gilbert Y. Steiner, *The State of Welfare* (Washington, D.C.: Brookings Institution, 1971), p. 3.

69. Fraser and Gordon, "Genealogy of Dependency," p. 322.

70. Stephen D. Sugarman, "Reforming Welfare Through Social Security," *University of Michigan Journal of Law Reform* 26 (1993), pp. 817, 819-21.

71. Gordon, *Pitied but Not Entitled*, p. 2.

72. David E. Rosenbaum, "Answer: Cut Entitlements. Question: But How?" *New York Times*, June 8, 1993, p. A22.

73. Theodore R. Marmor, Jerry L. Mashaw, and Philip L. Harvey, *America's Misunderstood Welfare State: Persistent Myths, Enduring Realities* (New York: Basic Books, 1990), p. 86.

74. Mink, "Welfare Reform in Historical Perspective," p. 882; Kathryn Edin and Laura Lein, *Making Ends Meet* (New York: Russell Sage Foundation, 1997); Kathryn Edin and Christopher Jencks, "Reforming Welfare," in Christopher Jencks, *Rethinking Social Policy: Race, Poverty and the Underclass* (Cambridge: Harvard University Press, 1992), p. 204, 205–11, describing how poor mothers in Illinois combine work and welfare in order to survive; Kathryn Edin, "Surviving the Welfare System: How AFDC Recipients Make Ends Meet in Chicago," *Social Problems* 38 (1991), p. 462.

75. Sara Rimer, "Jobs Program Participants: Still Poor and in Need of Aid," *New York Times*, April 10, 1995, pp. A1, B10.

76. Alan Finder, "Welfare Clients Outnumber Jobs They Might Fill," *New York Times*, Aug. 25, 1996, p. A1.

77. William Julius Wilson, "Work," *New York Times Magazine*, Aug. 18, 1996, p. 26.

78. U.S. Department of Commerce, Bureau of the Census, *Statistical Abstract of the United States 1993* (Washington, D.C., 1993), p. 470 tab. 737.

79. See, e.g., Donald J. Hernandez, *America's Children: Resources from Family, Government and the Economy* (New York: Russell Sage, 1993), pp. 290, 325; Mary Jo Bane, "Household Composition and Poverty: Which Comes First?" in Sheldon H. Danziger and Daniel H. Weinberg, eds., *Fighting Poverty: What Works and What Doesn't* (Cambridge: Harvard University Press, 1986), pp. 209, 321.

80. William A. Darity and Samuel L. Myers, "Does Welfare Dependency Cause Female Headship? The Case of the Black Family," *Journal of Marriage and the Family* 46 (1984), pp. 765, 773. See also Amott, "Black Women and AFDC," pp. 282–84, examining the factors leading to the rise of single-parent families in the black community.

81. Jencks, *Rethinking Social Policy*, p. 227.

82. Martha F. Davis and Susan K. Kraham, "Beaten, Then Robbed," *New York Times*, Jan. 13, 1995, p. A31.

83. See Martha Fineman, "Masking Dependency: The Political Role of Family Rhetoric," *Virginia Law Review* 81 (1995), p. 2181.

84. Margaret C. Simms, "Black Women Who Head Families: An Economic Struggle," in Margaret C. Simms and Julianne Malveaux, eds., *Slipping Through the Cracks: The Status of Black Women* (New Brunswick, N.J.: Transaction, 1986), pp. 141, 142.

85. Bane, "Household Composition and Poverty," pp. 227–28, 231 tabl. 9.6.

86. Greg J. Duncan and Willard Rodgers, "Longitudinal Aspects of Children's Poverty," *Journal of Marriage and the Family* 50 (1988), pp. 1007, 1012.

87. Andrea H. Beller and John W. Graham, *Small Change: The Economics of Child Support* (New Haven: Yale University Press, 1993).

88. Johanna Brenner, "Towards a Feminist Perspective on Welfare Reform," *Yale Journal of Law and Feminism* 2 (1989), pp. 99, 123.

89. Irwin Garfinkel, Daniel R. Meyer, and Gary D. Sandefur, "The Effects of Alternative Child Support Systems on Blacks, Hispanics, and Non-Hispanic Whites," *Social Service Review* 66 (1992), pp. 505, 518 tab. 3.

90. Perales, "Tangle of Pathology," pp. 252–53.

91. Ibid.

92. See Martha Albertson Fineman, *The Neutered Mother, the Sexual Family, and Other Twentieth-Century Tragedies* (New York: Routledge, 1995), for a critique of the nuclear-family norm that leaves women with the burden of caretaking while denying them adequate government support and stigmatizing those who do not depend on husbands.

93. Susan Bennett and Kathleen A. Sullivan, "Disentitling the Poor: Waivers and Welfare 'Reform,'" *University of Michigan Journal of Law Reform* 26 (1993), p. 741.

94. Lucy A. Williams, "The Ideology of Division: Behavior Modification Welfare Reform Proposal," *Yale Law Journal 102* (1992), p. 719.

95. Rosemary L. Bray, "So How Did I Get Here?" *New York Times Magazine,* Nov. 8, 1992, pp. 35, 40.

96. Funiciello, *Tyranny of Kindness,* p. 24.

97. Brenda Clegg Gray, *Black Female Domestics During the Depression in New York City, 1930–1940* (New York: Garland, 1993), p. 103, quoted in Gordon, *Pitied but Not Entitled,* p. 192.

98. Quoted in Lucie E. White, "No Exit: Rethinking 'Welfare Dependency' from a Different Ground," *Georgetown Law Journal* 81 (1993), pp. 1961, 1973.

99. Patrick J. Horvath, "Has Harassment Become the Plan for Reducing Welfare Rolls?" *New York Times,* Aug. 15, 1995, p. A16 (letter to editor).

100. See, e.g., *Bowen v. Gilliard,* 483 U.S. 587 (1987); *Lyng v. Castillo,* 477 U.S. 635 (1986). The Supreme Court invalidated, however, early welfare eligibility requirements such as AFDC's "man in the house" rule. *Lewis v. Martin,* 397 U.S. 552 (1970) (holding unconstitutional a regulation allocating to mother for purposes of AFDC elibility income of man who shares her home with no legal obligation to provide support); *King v. Smith,* 392 U.S. 309 (1968) (invalidating Alabama's regulation disqualifying from AFDC any mother living with man who was not obligated to provide support).

101. *Anderson v. Edwards,* 115 S. Ct. 1291 (1995).

102. *Wyman v. James,* 400 U.S. 309 (1971).

103. *Roe v. Norton,* 422 U.S. 391 (1975).

104. *Allen v. Eichler,* No. 89A-FE-4, 1990 WL 58223 (Del. Super. Ct. April 3, 1990).

105. Laurie Nsiah-Jefferson, "Reproductive Laws, Women of Color, and Low-Income Women," in Nadine Taub and Sherrill Cohen, eds., *Reproductive Laws of the 1990s* (Clifton, N.J.: Humana, 1989), p. 23 (discussing limitations on access to abortion services and new reproductive technologies); Ruth Colker, "An Equal Protection Analysis of United States Reproductive Health Policy: Gender, Race, Age, and Class," *Duke Law Journal* (1991), pp. 324, 340–50 (describing the unavailability of contraception and sex education, prenatal care, and abortion for poor or adolescent females); Dorothy E. Roberts, "The Future of Reproductive Choice for Poor Women and Women of Color," *Women's Rights Law Reporter* 12 (1990), p. 59 (describing the constraints on the reproductive choices of a hypothetical pregnant woman in the inner city).

106. Jacquelyne Johnson Jackson, "Urban Black Americans," in *Ethnicity and Medical Care* (Cambridge: Harvard University Press, 1981), p. 37; Ruth Zambrana, "A Research Agenda on Issues Affecting Poor and Minority Women for Understanding Their Health Needs," in Cesar A. Perales and Lauren Young, eds., *Too Little, Too Late: Dealing with the Health Needs of Women in Poverty* (New York: Harrington Park Press, 1988), p. 137.

107. Charles Reich, "The New Property," *Yale Law Journal* 73 (1964), p. 733.

108. *Sherbert v. Verner,* 374 U.S. 398 (1963).

109. *Maher v. Roe,* 432 U.S. 464 (1977).

110. Ibid.

111. *Harris v. McRae,* 448 U.S. 297 (1980).

112. Susan Frelich Appleton, "Standards for Constitutional Review of Privacy-Invading Welfare Reforms: Distinguishing the Abortion-Funding Cases and Redeeming the Undue Burden Test," *Vanderbilt Law Review,* 49 (1996), pp. 1, 20. For more on baselines, see Seth F. Kreimer, "Allocational Sanctions: The Problem of Negative Rights in a Positive State," *University of Pennsylvania Law Review* 132 (1984), pp. 1293, 1358–74; Cass R. Sunstein, "Neutrality in Constitutional Law (With Special Reference to Pornography, Abortion, and Surrogacy)," *Columbia Law Review* 92 (1992), p. 1.

113. 111 S. Ct. 1759 (1991). For a more thorough discussion of the *Rust v. Sullivan* deci-

sion, see Dorothy E. Roberts, *"Rust v. Sullivan* and the Control of Knowledge," *George Washington Law Review* 61 (1993), p. 201.

114. Brief of Amici Curiae, The American Public Health Association, The American College of Physicians, et al., in Support of Petitioners, *Rust v. Sullivan* (declaration of Dr. David A. Grimes).

115. William D. Mosher, "Use of Family-Planning Services in the United States: 1982 and 1988," *National Center for Health Statistics, Advance Data*, no. 184 (April 11, 1990), pp. 2–3.

116. Angela Y. Davis, "Sick and Tired of Being Sick and Tired: The Politics of Black Women's Health," in Evelyn C. White, ed., *The Black Women's Health Book: Speaking for Ourselves* (Seattle: Seal Press, 1990), pp. 18, 23.

117. Mosher, "Use of Family Planning Services in the United States," pp. 2–3.

118. Francis G. Caro, Debra Kalmuss, and Iris Lopez, *Barriers to Prenatal Care* (New York: Community Service Society, 1988), p. 1.

119. Zambrana, "Research Agenda on Issues Affecting Poor and Minority Women," p. 150.

120. *Rust v. Sullivan*, p. 1772.

121. Ibid., p. 1776.

122. Ibid., p. 1782 n.3 (Blackmun, J., dissenting).

123. Brief for Petitioners, *Rust v. Sullivan*, p. 12.

124. *New York v. Sullivan*, 889 F.2d 401, 413–14 (2d Cir. 1989).

125. Keith Goldschmidt, "Tallahassee: Fear, Panic and Frustration Lurk Capitol Halls," *Gannett News Service*, Feb. 25, 1994.

126. *C.K. v. Shalala*, 883 F. Supp. 991 (D.N.J. 1995), aff'd sub nom. *C.K. v. New Jersey Dep't of Health & Human Servs.*, 92 F.3d 171 (3d Cir. 1996).

127. Ibid., p. 997.

128. Ibid., pp. 1007–8.

129. Dandridge v. Williams, 397 U.S. 471 (1970).

130. *C.K. v. Shalala*, pp. 486–87.

131. See, e.g., *Plyer v. Doe*, 457 U.S. 202 (1982) (invalidating Texas law withholding funding for education of children not legally admitted to U.S.); *New Jersey Welfare Rights Organization v. Cahill*, 411 U.S. 619 (1973) (holding statute limiting welfare benefits to married parents denied equal protection to children born out of wedlock).

132. *C.K. v. Shalala*, pp. 1013–14.

133. *Planned Parenthood v. Casey*, 112 S. Ct. 2791, 2811 (1992).

134. On opposition to welfare reform policies on the grounds that they will increase abortion rates, see Tamar Lewin, "Abortion Foes Worry About Welfare Cutoffs," *New York Times*, March 19, 1995, p. D4; Cheryl Wetzstein, "Abortion Tops 'Family Cap' Debate: Policy Feared as Coercion to End Pregnancy," *Washington Times*, May 1, 1995, p. A6. Susan Frelich Appleton discusses the constitutional implications of family caps' promotion of abortion in "When Welfare Reforms Promote Abortion: 'Personal Responsibility,' 'Family Values,' and the Right to Choose," *Georgetown Law Journal* 85 (1996), p. 155.

135. Appleton, "Standards for Constitutional Review," pp. 57–58.

136. Ibid., pp. 62–64.

137. *C.K. v. Shalala*, p. 1015.

138. *Primetime Live: End of Innocence*, ABC television broadcast, Sept. 9, 1993.

139. Gaston Rimlinger, *Welfare Policy and Industrialization in Europe, America, and Russia* (New York: Wiley, 1971), p. 62, quoted in Quadagno, *The Color of Welfare*, p. 5.

140. Quadagno, *The Color of Welfare*, pp. 5–6.

141. Robert L. Heilbroner, "The Roots of Social Neglect in the United States," in Eugene V. Rostow, ed., *Is Law Dead?* (New York: Simon and Schuster, 1971), pp. 288, 296.

142. W. E. B. Du Bois, *Black Reconstruction in America, 1860–1880*, ed. August Meier (New York: Atheneum, 1992 [1935]), p. 700.

143. Derrick Bell, *Faces at the Bottom of the Well: The Permanence of Racism* (New York: Basic Books, 1992), p. 12.

144. Dirk Johnson, "Duke's Loss Brings Joy Even as It Fans Anger," *New York Times*, Nov. 18, 1991, p. B7.

145. Harold Cruse, *Rebellion or Revolution?* (New York: Morrow, 1968), p. 104.

Chapter 6. Race and the New Reproduction

1. For descriptions of new reproductive technologies, see Lori B. Andrews, *New Conceptions: A Consumer's Guide to the Newest Infertility Treatments, Including In Vitro Fertilization, Artificial Insemination, and Surrogate Motherhood* (New York: St. Martin's, 1984), pp. 4–7, 120–263; John A. Robertson, *Children of Choice: Freedom and the New Reproductive Technologies* (Princeton: Princeton University Press, 1995); Susan Sherwin, *No Longer Patient: Feminist Ethics and Health Care* (Philadelphia: Temple University Press, 1992), p. 117.

2. See generally John Lawrence Hill, "What Does It Mean to Be a 'Parent'? The Claims of Biology as the Basis for Parental Rights," *New York University Law Review* 66 (1991), p. 357; Note, "Redefining Mother: A Legal Matrix for New Reproductive Technologies," *Yale Law Journal* 96 (1986), p. 187.

3. Robertson, *Children of Choice*, p. 3.

4. Ruth Hubbard and Elijah Wald, *Exploding the Gene Myth* (Boston: Beacon Press, 1993), pp. 108–16.

5. See Nancy Polikoff, "This Child Does Have Two Mothers: Redefining Parenthood to Meet the Needs of Children in Lesbian-Mother and Other Nontraditional Families," *Georgetown Law Journal* 78 (1990), p. 459; Sharon Elizabeth Rush, "Breaking with Tradition: Surrogacy and Gay Fathers," in Diana Tietjens Meyers, Kenneth Kipnis, and Cornelius F. Murphy, Jr., eds., *Kindred Matters: Rethinking the Philosophy of the Family* (Ithaca, N.Y.: Cornell University Press, 1993), p. 102.

6. Daniel Wikler and Norma J. Wikler, "Turkey-Baster Babies: The Demedicalization of Artificial Insemination," *Milbank Quarterly* 69 (1991), p. 5; Juliette Zipper and Selma Sevenhuijsen, "Surrogacy: Feminist Notions of Motherhood Reconsidered," in Michelle Stanworth, ed., *Reproductive Technologies: Gender, Motherhood, and Medicine* (Minneapolis: University of Minnesota Press, 1987), pp. 118, 137–38.

7. Robertson, *Children of Choice*, p. 145, noting that assisted reproduction furthers the "primary aim to provide a couple with a child to live and rear in a two-parent family."

8. Wikler and Wikler, "Turkey-Baster Babies," pp. 13–16.

9. Sherwin, *No Longer Patient*, p. 127; Office of Technology Assessment, *Artificial Insemination: Practice in the United States*, OTA-BP-BA-48 (Washington, D.C.: Government Printing Office, 1988), pp. 9, 11. Most IVF clinics accept only heterosexual married couples as clients. Thomas A. Shannon, "In Vitro Fertilization: Ethical Issues," in Elaine Hoffman Baruch, Amadeo F. D'Adamo, Jr., and Joni Seager, eds., *Embryos, Ethics, and Women's Rights: Exploring the New Reproductive Technologies* (New York: Harrington Park Press, 1988), pp. 155, 163.

10. Martha A. Field, *Surrogate Motherhood* (Cambridge: Harvard University Press, 1988), p. 116.

11. See, e.g., Janice G. Raymond, *Women as Wombs: Reproductive Technologies and the Battle over Women's Freedom* (San Francisco: HarperCollins, 1993); Barbara Katz Rothman, *Re-creating Motherhood: Ideology and Technology in a Patriarchal Society* (New York: Norton, 1989); Sherwin, *No Longer Patient*, p. 127.

12. Carol Smart, "'There is of course the distinction dictated by nature': Law and the Problem of Paternity," in Stanworth, *Reproductive Technologies*, pp. 98, 100.

13. See, e.g., Gena Corea, *The Mother Machine: Reproductive Technologies from Artificial Insemination to Artificial Wombs* (New York: Harper, 1985), pp. 166–85; Rothman,

Re-creating Motherhood, pp. 29–47; Sherwin, *No Longer Patient*, p. 132; Judith Lorber, "Choice, Gift or Patriarchal Bargain? Women's Consent to In Vitro Fertilization in Male Infertility," in Helen Bequaert Holmes and Laura M. Purdy, eds., *Feminist Perspectives in Medical Ethics* (Bloomington: University of Indiana Press, 1992), p. 169.

14. See Richard Saltus, "Genetic Test Helps Find Abnormal Eggs in Test-Tube Fertilization," *Boston Globe*, Nov. 5, 1996, p. A3 (reporting live-delivery success rate of 20.7%); Robert Pear, "Fertility Clinics Face Crackdown: U.S. Says Success Rates Are Overstated and Wins Ban Against Such Claims," *New York Times*, Oct 26, 1992, p. A15 (less than 15% success rate per procedure); Michael R. Soules, "The In Vitro Fertilization Pregnancy Rate: Let's Be Honest with One Another," *Fertility and Sterility* 43 (1985), pp. 511–513 (criticizing widespread practice of exaggerating IVF pregnancy rates).

15. Elaine Tyler May, *Barren in the Promised Land: Childless Americans and the Pursuit of Happiness* (New York: Basic Books, 1995), pp. 211–59; Christine Crowe, "'Women Want It': In-Vitro Fertilization and Women's Motivations for Participation," *Women's Studies International Forum* 8 (1985), pp. 547, 551; Kirsten Kozolanka, "Giving Up: The Choice That Isn't," in Renate D. Klein, ed., *Infertility: Women Speak Out About Their Experiences of Reproductive Medicine* (New York: Pandora, 1989), p. 121 ("I have never taken seriously the idea of giving up. You see, giving up, for the infertile, is not really an option at all").

16. Raymond, *Women as Wombs*, p. 6 ("Between 23 and 60% of women undergo IVF treatment because of their male partners' infertility"); Lorber, "Choice, Gift, or Patriarchal Bargain?" p. 171 (noting that mostly women undergo infertility treatments even though they are responsible for less than 40% of infertility); Judith Lorber, "In Vitro Fertilization and Gender Politics," in Baruch et al., *Embryos, Ethics, and Women's Rights*, p. 124.

17. Raymond, *Women as Wombs*, pp. xix–xx.

18. Robert Hanley, "Reporter's Notebook: Grief Over Baby M," *New York Times*, Jan. 12, 1987, p. B1. See also *In the Matter of Baby M*, 537 A.2d 1227, 1235 (N.J. 1988).

19. *Matter of Baby M*, 525 A.2d 1128, 1139 (N.J. Super. Ct. Ch. Div. 1987), rev'd, 537 A.2d 1227 (N.J. 1988). As this citation indicates, the trial court's decision was reversed by the New Jersey Supreme Court.

20. Field, *Surrogate Motherhood*, p. 51. See also Margaret Jane Radin, "Market Inalienability," *Harvard Law Review* 100 (1987), pp. 1849, 1930: "[W]omen—their reproductive capacities, attributes, and genes—are fungible in carrying on the male genetic line."

21. *Matter of Baby M*, 537 A.2d, p. 1266 (emphasis added).

22. Robertson, *Children of Choice*, pp. 131–32.

23. See Kelly Oliver, "Marxism and Surrogacy," in Holmes and Purdy, *Feminist Perspectives in Medical Ethics*, pp. 266, 270–73.

24. Office of Technology Assessment, *Infertility: Medical and Social Choices*, OTA-BA-358 (Washington, D.C., 1988), pp. 7, 54.

25. Lynne S. Wilcox and William D. Mosher, "Use of Infertility Services in the United States," *Obstetrics and Gynecology* 82 (July 1993), pp. 122, 124–25.

26. Trip Gabriel, "High-Tech Pregnancies Test Hope's Limit," *New York Times*, Jan. 7, 1996, pp. A1, 18.

27. Geoffrey Cowley, "The Biology of Beauty," *Newsweek*, June 3, 1996, p. 60.

28. Robin Schatz, "Sperm Bank Mixup Claim; Woman Sues Doctor, Bank; Says Wrong Deposit Used," *Newsday*, March 9, 1990, p. 5; Ronald Sullivan, "Mother Accuses Sperm Bank of Mixup," *New York Times*, March 9, 1990, p. B1.

29. Barbara Kantrowitz and David Kaplan, "Not the Right Father," *Newsweek*, March 19, 1990, p. 50.

30. Dorinda Elliot and Friso Endt, "Twins—with Two Fathers; The Netherlands: A Fertility Clinic's Startling Error," *Newsweek*, July 3, 1995, p. 38.

31. Ibid.

32. Office of Technology Assessment, *Infertility*, p. 51.

33. Susan Faludi, *Backlash: The Undeclared War Against American Women* (New York: Anchor Books, 1991), p. 31.

34. Office of Technology Assessment, *Infertility*, p. 56; Sevgi O. Aral and Willard Cates, Jr., "The Increasing Concern with Infertility: Why Now?" *Journal of the American Medical Association* 250 (November 4, 1983), p. 2327.

35. Joan C. Callahan, "Introduction," in Joan C. Callahan, ed., *Reproduction, Ethics, and the Law: Feminist Perspectives* (Bloomington: University of Indiana Press, 1995), pp. 24–25.

36. Office of Technology Assessment, *Infertility*, p. 145.

37. Terry Sollom, "State Actions on Reproductive Health Issues in 1994," *Family Planning Perspectives* 27 (March 1, 1995), p. 83.

38. George J. Annas, "Fairy Tales Surrogate Mothers Tell," *Law, Medicine, and Health Care* 16 (1988), pp. 27, 28.

39. Sollum, "State Actions on Reproductive Health Issues."

40. Ellen Goodman, "Government Gone Awry: Poor People Given Fertility Treatments," *Arizona Republic*, March 22, 1994, p. B7.

41. Monique Burns, "A Sexual Time Bomb: The Declining Fertility Rate of the Black Middle Class," *Ebony*, May 1995, p. 74.

42. Rayna Rapp, "Moral Pioneers: Women, Men and Fetuses on a Frontier of Reproductive Technology," lecture delivered in Storrs, Conn., 1987, quoted in Laurie Nsiah-Jefferson and Elaine J. Hall, "Reproductive Technology: Perspectives and Implications for Low-Income Women and Women of Color," in Kathryn Strother Ratcliff et al., eds., *Healing Technology: Feminist Perspectives* (Ann Arbor: University of Michigan Press, 1989), pp. 93, 105.

43. Patricia A. King, "The Past as Prologue: Race, Class, and Gene Discrimination," in George J. Annas and Sherman Elias, eds., *Gene Mapping: Using Law and Ethics as Guides* (New York: Oxford University Press, 1992), pp. 94, 103. See also Nsiah-Jefferson and Hall, "Reproductive Technology," p. 109.

44. Quoted in Faludi, *Backlash*, p. 29.

45. Donald L. Chatman, "Endometriosis in the Black Woman," *American Journal of Obstetrics and Gynecology* 125 (1976), p. 987.

46. Ibid.

47. Elizabeth Heitman, "Infertility as a Public Health Problem: Why Assisted Reproductive Technologies Are Not the Answer," *Stanford Law and Policy Review* 6 (1995), pp. 89, 94.

48. Cooper Center for IVF, "Cooper Center for IVF Responds to the Fertility Market," *New York Times*, Jan. 14, 1996, p. A16 (advertisement).

49. Hubbard and Wald, *Exploding the Gene Myth*, p. 33.

50. James E. Bowman, "Genetic Screening: Toward a New Eugenics?" in Annette Dula and Sara Goering, eds., *It Just Ain't Fair; The Ethics of Health Care for African Americans* (Westport, Conn.: Praeger, 1994), pp. 165, 167; Annette Dula, "African Americans' Suspicion of the Healthcare System Is Justified: What Do We Do About It?" *Cambridge Quarterly of Healthcare Ethics* 3 (1994), pp. 347, 349; Hubbard and Wald, *Exploding the Gene Myth*, p. 34.

51. Troy Duster, *Back Door to Eugenics* (New York: Routledge, 1990), p. 26.

52. Arthur T. Fort et al., "Counseling the Patient with Sickle-Cell Disease About Reproduction: Pregnancy Outcome Does Not Justify the Maternal Risk," *American Journal of Obstetrics and Gynecology* 11 (1971), p. 324.

53. Ibid., p. 327. A North Carolina woman with sickle-cell trait sued the county board of health after its nurses and doctor wrongfully convinced her to be sterilized. See *Avery v. County of Burke*, 660 F.2d 111 (4th Cir., 1981).

54. Henry W. Foster, Jr., "Clinical Management: Sickle-Cell State and Pregnancy," *Urban Health* 6 (1977), p. 20.

55. Martha Southgate, "Coping with Infertility," *Essence*, Sept. 1994, p. 28.

56. Ibid.
57. May, *Barren in the Promised Land*, p. 18.
58. Ibid., p. 211.
59. Arthur L. Greil, *Not Yet Pregnant: Infertile Couples in Contemporary America* (New Brunswick, N.J.: Rutgers University Press, 1991), p. 159.
60. Heitman, "Infertility as a Public Health Problem," p. 94.
61. Rayna Rapp, "Women's Responses to Prenatal Diagnosis: A Sociocultural Perspective on Diversity," in Karen H. Rothenberg and Elizabeth J. Thomson, eds., *Women and Prenatal Testing: Facing the Challenges of Genetic Technology* (Columbus: Ohio State University Press, 1994), pp. 219, 224. See also Jeff Stryker, "Tuskegee's Long Arm Still Touches a Nerve," *New York Times*, April 13, 1997, sec. 4, p. 4, reporting that "[so] great is the mistrust that grew out of the [Tuskegee syphilis] study that it is continuing to interfere with attempts to fight AIDS in certain black neighborhoods."
62. For studies finding that Blacks were more likely than whites to want life-prolonging treatment, see P. V. Caralis et al., "The Influence of Ethnicity and Race on Attitudes Toward Advance Directives, Life-Prolonging Treatments, and Euthanasia," *Journal of Clinical Ethics* 4 (1993), p. 165; Jill Klessig, "The Effect of Values and Culture on Life-Support Decisions," *Western Journal of Medicine* 157 (1992), p. 316; F. K. Port et al., "Discontinuation of Dialysis Therapy as a Cause of Death," *American Journal of Nephrology* 9 (1989), p. 9.
63. See, e.g., Burns, "Sexual Time Bomb," p. 74; Southgate, "Coping with Infertility," p. 28.
64. Richard J. Herrnstein and Charles Murray, *The Bell Curve: Intelligence and Class Structure in American Life* (New York: Free Press, 1994).
65. A. Leon Higginbotham, Jr., and Barbara K. Kopytoff, "Racial Purity and Interracial Sex in the Law of Colonial and Antebellum Virginia," *Georgetown Law Journal* 77 (1989), pp. 1967, 1968. See also Winthrop Jordan, *White over Black: American Attitudes Toward the Negro, 1550–1812* (Chapel Hill: University of North Carolina Press, 1969), p. 108, noting that colonial slave codes were paradoxically aimed at disciplining whites to ensure maintenance of a "private tyranny" over slaves.
66. David Gordon Nielson, *Black Ethos: Northern Urban Negro Life and Thought, 1890–1930* (Westport, Conn.: Greenwood, 1977), pp. xv–xvi.
67. Anthony Flint, "Black Academics Split on Afrocentrism," *Boston Globe*, Sept. 27, 1994, p. 1.
68. See Ana Mari Cauce et al., "Between a Rock and a Hard Place: Social Adjustment of Biracial Youth," in Maria P. P. Root, ed., *Racially Mixed People in America* (Newbury Park, Calif.: Sage, 1992), pp. 207, 213; Robert E. T. Roberts, "Self-Identification and Social Status of Children of Black-White Marriages in Chicago," paper presented at 9th International Congress of Anthropological and Ethnological Sciences, Aug. 20, 1983, p. 27 tab. 14.
69. Stephen L. Carter, "The Black Table, the Empty Seat, and the Tie," in Gerald Early, ed., *Lure and Loathing: Essays on Race, Identity, and the Ambivalence of Assimilation* (New York: Penguin, 1994), pp. 55, 64.
70. See generally, Twila L. Perry, "The Transracial Adoption Controversy: An Analysis of Discourse and Subordination," *New York University Review of Law and Social Change* 21 (1993–94), p. 33.
71. Position paper developed at the National Association of Black Social \Yorkers' conference in Nashville, Tenn., April 4–9, 1972, reprinted in part in Rita James Simon and Howard Altstein, *Transracial Adoption* (New York: Wiley, 1977), p. 50.
72. See Suzanne C. Carothers, "Catching Sense: Learning from Our Mothers to Be Black and Female," in Faye Ginsburg and Anna Lowenhaupt Tsing, eds., *Uncertain Terms: Negotiating Gender in American Culture* (Boston: Beacon Press, 1990), pp. 232, 239–40; Patricia Hill Collins, "The Meaning of Motherhood in Black Culture and Black Mother/Daughter Relationships," *Sage* 3 (Fall 1987), p. 7.

73. Janice Hale, "The Black Woman and Child Rearing," in La Frances Rodgers-Rose, ed., *The Black Woman* (Beverly Hills: Sage, 1980), pp. 79, 80.

74. Sociologist Joyce Ladner describes "Black survival techniques" as a "broad repertoire of psychological attitudes and behavioral acts on the overt and covert level." See Joyce A. Ladner, *Mixed Families: Adopting Across Racial Boundaries* (Garden City, N.Y.: Anchor Books, 1977), p. 80. See also Joyce A. Ladner, "Mixed Families: White Parents and Black Children," *Society*, Sept.–Oct. 1977, pp. 70, 77–78, discussing difficulties white parents are likely to experience in raising emotionally healthy Black children.

75. See Nielson, *Black Ethos*, pp. 157–72; Kathy Russell, Midge Wilson, and Ronald Hall, *The Color Complex: The Politics of Skin Color Among African Americans* (New York: Harcourt Brace Jovanovich, 1992), pp. 24–29. See also E. Franklin Frazier, *The Negro Church in America* (New York: Schocken, 1963), pp. 30–31, observing that in post–Civil War Black Methodist and Baptist denominations, there were separate organizations based on distinctions of color.

76. Cornel West writes about these two forms of "hybridity" in Black American life. He notes, e.g., the "cultural hybridity" of Black religion and music, "in which the complex mixture of African, European, and Amerindian elements are constitutive of something that is new and black in the modern world." Cornel West, *Race Matters* (Boston: Beacon Press, 1993), p. 101. He also refers to Malcolm X's "personal hybridity," due to Malcolm's white grandfather, "which blurred the very boundaries so rigidly policed by white supremacist authorities." Ibid., p. 103.

77. Laurence H. Tribe, "Technology Assessment and the Fourth Discontinuity: The Limits of Instrumental Rationality," *Southern California Law Review* 46 (1973), pp. 617, 648.

78. Lerone Bennett, Jr., *The Negro Mood and Other Essays* (New York: Ballantine, 1964), p. 84.

79. W. E. B. Du Bois, *The Souls of Black Folk* (New York: Signet, 1969), p. 45.

80. See Joyce Pettis, "Self-Definition and Redefinition in Paule Marshall's *Praisesong for the Widow*," in Harry B. Shaw, ed., *Perspectives of Black Popular Culture* (Bowling Green, Ohio: Bowling Green Press, 1990), p. 93. Examples of Black female fictional characters who invent themselves are Toni Morrison's Pilate in *Song of Solomon* and her protagonist in *Sula*, and Alice Walker's Shug Avery and Celie in *The Color Purple*. See Toni Morrison, *Song of Solomon* (New York: Knopf, 1977); Toni Morrison, *Sula* (New York: Knopf, 1974); Alice Walker, *The Color Purple* (New York: Harcourt Brace Jovanovich, 1982).

81. Patricia J. Williams, *The Alchemy of Race and Rights* (Cambridge: Harvard University Press, 1991), p. 183. See also Mary Helen Washington, *Invented Lives: Narratives of Black Women 1860–1960* (New York: Anchor Books, 1987).

82. John Steinbeck, *Burning Bright* (New York: Viking, 1950), p. 29.

83. Sarah Franklin, "Deconstructing 'Desperateness': The Social Construction of Infertility in Popular Representations of New Reproductive Technologies," in Maureen McNeil, Ian Varcoe, and Steven Yearley, eds., *The New Reproductive Technologies* (New York: St. Martin's, 1990), pp. 200, 207.

84. See, e.g., Lori B. Andrews and Lisa Douglass, "Alternative Reproduction," *Southern California Law Review* 65 (1991), p. 640 n.56; Robertson, *Children of Choice*, pp. 29–34.

85. See, e.g., several books and articles by Betty Jean Lifton: *Journey of the Adopted Self: A Quest for Wholeness* (New York: Basic Books, 1994); *Lost and Found: The Adoption Experience* (New York: Bantam, 1981); "Brave New Baby in the Brave New World," in Baruch et al., *Embryos, Ethics, and Women's Rights*, pp. 149, 151.

86. Lifton, "Brave New Baby," p. 150.

87. Margaret R. Brown, "Whose Eyes Are These, Whose Nose?" *Newsweek*, March 7, 1994, p. 12. Peggy Orenstein, "Looking for a Donor to Call Dad," *New York Times Magazine*, June 18, 1995, p. 28, describes several peoples' search for their sperm donor fathers.

88. Jerry E. Bishop and Michael Waldholz, *Genome* (New York: Simon and Schuster, 1990), p. 218, quoting Professor Walter Gilbert.

89. See *New York Times Book Review*, Oct 16, 1994, p. 1.

90. Duster, *Backdoor to Eugenics*, p. 164; Carl F. Cranor, ed., *Are Genes Us? The Social Consequences of the New Genetics* (New Brunswick, N.J.: Rutgers University Press, 1994); Rochelle Cooper Dreyfuss and Dorothy Nelkin, "The Jurisprudence of Genetics," *Vanderbilt Law Review* 45 (1992), pp. 313, 320–21; Abby Lippman, "Prenatal Genetic Testing and Screening: Constructing Needs and Reinforcing Inequities," *American Journal of Law and Medicine* 17 (1991), pp. 15, 19; Susan M. Wolf, "Beyond 'Genetic Discrimination': Toward the Broader Harm of Geneticism," *Journal of Law, Medicine, and Ethics* 23 (1995), p. 345.

91. Dreyfuss and Nelkin, "Jurisprudence of Genetics," pp. 320–21.

92. U.S. Department of Health and Human Services and U.S. Department of Energy, *Understanding Our Genetic Inheritance: The U.S. Human Genome Project: The First Five Years FY 1991–1995* (Washington, D.C., 1990), p. ix.

93. Daniel Goleman, "Forget Money: Nothing Can Buy Happiness, Some Researchers Say," *New York Times*, July 16, 1996, p. C1.

94. Callahan, "Introduction," p. 11, citing Rothman, *Re-creating Motherhood*. See also Raymond, *Women as Wombs*, p. 30, describing "ejaculatory fatherhood," a "new norm of fatherhood grounded in male gametes and genes."

95. Noel P. Keane and Dennis L. Breo, *The Surrogate Mother* (New York: Everest House, 1981), p. 30. Larry Greil found, however, that the infertile wives he interviewed were more affected by infertility than their husbands. Greil, *Not Yet Pregnant*, pp. 68–69. Men are far less likely than women to be sterilized, either voluntarily or coercively: in 1982, 19% of the 54 million American women ages 15 to 44 had had tubal ligations or hysterectomies, while only 6% had husbands with vasectomies. William D. Mosher, "Fecundity and Infertility in the United States," *American Journal of Public Health* 78 (1988), pp. 181, 182. Another reason why men are less likely to be sterilized than women may be that fathers are given less responsibility for children than mothers.

96. William B. Smith, *The Color Line: A Brief in Behalf of the Unborn* (New York: McClure, Phillips and Co., 1905), p. 15.

97. Higginbotham and Kopytoff, "Racial Purity and Interracial Sex in the Law of Colonial and Antebellum Virginia," p. 1997.

98. W. J. Cash, *The Mind of the South* (New York: Knopf 1941), p. 116.

99. *Loving v. Virginia*, 388 U.S. 1 (1967).

100. Cheryl I. Harris, "Whiteness as Property," *Harvard Law Review* 106 (1993), p. 1707.

101. Faludi, *Backlash*, pp. 27–35.

102. Ibid., p. 30.

103. Office of Technology Assessment, *Infertility*, pp. 4–5.

104. Ben J. Wattenberg, *The Birth Dearth* (New York: Pharos Books, 1987).

105. Quoted in Ezra Bowen, "Battling Over Birth Policy: Is It Racist to Urge the West to Have More Babies?" *Time*, Aug. 24, 1987, p. 58.

106. Keane and Breo, *The Surrogate Mother*, pp. 95–96. See also Michelle Stanworth, "Reproductive Technologies and the Deconstruction of Motherhood," in Stanworth, *Reproductive Technologies*, pp. 10, 27.

107. Elizabeth Bartholet, *Family Bonds: Adoption and the Politics of Parenting* (Boston: Houghton Mifflin, 1993), pp. 24–38, describing how society makes adoption the last resort for infertile couples who want children; pp. 187–98, describing the author's own efforts to become pregnant through in vitro fertilization before pursuing adoption.

108. May, *Barren in the Promised Land*, p. 233.

109. Ibid., p. 249.

110. Zanita E. Fenton, "In a World Not Their Own: The Adoption of Black Children," *Harvard Blackletter Journal* 10 (1993), pp. 39, 51–54.

111. Mary Jo McConahay, "The Baby Trade: Where There Is Poverty in the Third

World and a Baby Shortage in the First, Children Become a Commodity," *Los Angeles Times Magazine*, Dec. 16, 1990, p. 12.

112. Christine Bachrach et al., *Adoption in the 1980's*, National Center for Health Statistics, *Advance Data from Vital and Health Statistics*, no. 181 (Jan. 5, 1990), pp. 1–2.

113. Raymond, *Women as Wombs*, pp. 144–54.

114. Simon and Altstein, *Transracial Adoption*, p. 9.

115. Bachrach et al., *Adoption in the 1980's*, p. 6.

116. SC Code Ann. § 16-17-460 (Law Co-op 1976), repealed by 1981 SC Acts No. 71 § 3. Other states prohibited transracial adoptions by either race. On past statutory prohibitions of transracial adoptions, see Susan J. Grossman, "A Child of a Different Color: Race as a Factor in Adoption and Custody Proceedings," *Buffalo Law Review* 17 (1968), pp. 303, 308–9. Courts have struck down statutory bans on transracial adoptions as unconstitutional. See, e.g., *Compos v. McKeithen*, 341 F. Supp 264 (E. D. La. 1972), holding that a Louisiana statute prohibiting transracial adoption violated the Equal Protection Clause. In *Palmore v. Sidoti*, 466 U.S. 429 (1984), the Supreme Court reversed a decision removing a white child from her biological mother because the mother had married a Black man.

117. Bartholet, *Family Bonds*, pp. 95–96. See also Rita J. Simon and Howard Altstein, *Transracial Adoption: A Follow-Up* (Lexington, Mass.: Lexington Books, 1981), p. 67.

118. See Dawn Day, *The Adoption of Black Children: Counteracting Institutional Discrimination* (Lexington, Mass.: Lexington Books, 1979), p. 85; Fenton, "In a World Not Their Own," pp. 44–46. On the historical exclusion or neglect of Black children by formal adoption institutions, see Andrew Billingsley and Jeanne M. Giovannoni, *Children of the Storm: Black Children and American Child Welfare* (New York: Harcourt Brace Jovanovich, 1972).

119. Andrew Billingsley, *Climbing Jacob's Ladder: The Enduring Legacy of African-American Families* (New York: Simon and Schuster, 1992), pp. 29–30.

120. Bachrach et al., *Adoption in the 1980's*, p. 7.

121. *In re Adoption of a Minor*, 228 F.2d 446, 447 (D.C. Cir. 1955) (reversing trial judge's denial of adoption of white child by his Black stepfather). Even the reversing appellate court agreed that "[t]here may be reasons why a difference in race, or religion, may have relevance in adoption proceedings," although the court did not find such reasons dispositive in this case. Ibid., p. 448.

122. Anita Allen, "The Black Surrogate Mother," *Harvard Blackletter Journal* 8 (1991), pp. 17, 23 n.51.

123. Bartholet, *Family Bonds*, pp. 104–6.

124. Ibid., p. 115.

125. Perry, "The Transracial Adoption Controversy," p. 104.

126. Field, *Surrogate Motherhood*, p. 25.

127. Andrews and Douglass, "Alternative Reproduction," pp. 672–73; Ruth Macklin, "Is There Anything Wrong with Surrogate Motherhood? An Ethical Analysis," *Law, Medicine, and Health Care* 16 (1988), pp. 57, 62.

128. Radin, "Market Inalienability," p. 1932.

129. Elizabeth S. Anderson, "Is Women's Labor a Commodity?" *Philosophy and Public Affairs* 19 (1990), pp. 71, 80–87.

130. Barbara Katz Rothman, "Reproductive Technology and the Commodification of Life," in Baruch et al., *Embryos, Ethics, and Women's Rights*, pp. 95, 96.

131. Oliver, "Marxism and Surrogacy," pp. 274–75.

132. John A. Robertson, "Procreative Liberty and the State's Burden of Proof in Regulating Noncoital Reproduction," *Law, Medicine, and Health Care* 16 (1988), p. 22.

133. See Anita L. Allen, "Surrogacy, Slavery, and the Ownership of Life," *Harvard Journal of Law and Public Policy* 13 (1990), p. 139; Sarah S. Boone, "Slavery and Contract Motherhood: A 'Racialized' Objection to the Autonomy Arguments," in Helen Bequaert Holmes, ed., *Issues in . . . Reproductive Technology I: An Anthology* (New York: Garland, 1992), pp. 349, 351, arguing that "African-American female enslavement

and [commercialized contract motherhood] are two very different social expressions of the same underlying ideological forms."

134. Harris, "Whiteness as Property," p. 1720. See generally Kenneth M. Stampp, *The Peculiar Institution: Slavery in the Ante-Bellum South* (New York: Vintage, 1956), pp. 192–236, discussing the legal status of slaves as chattel property.

135. Lucy A. Delaney, "From the Darkness Cometh the Light; or, Struggles for Freedom," reprinted in Henry Louis Gates, Jr., ed., *Six Women's Slave Narratives, 1831–1909* (New York: Oxford University Press, 1988), p. 10.

136. Toni Morrison, *Beloved* (New York: Plume, 1987), p. 88. In her autobiography, Sallie Bingham, a wealthy white heiress, makes a similar observation about the Black servants who lived in her Kentucky home: "Blacks, I realized, were simply invisible to most white people, except as a pair of hands offering a drink on a silver tray." Sallie Bingham, *Passion and Prejudice: A Family Memoir* (New York: Applause Theatre Book Pubs., 1991), p. 270.

137. Angela Y. Davis, "Surrogates and Outcast Mothers: Racism and Reproductive Politics," in Dula and Goering, *It Just Ain't Fair*, pp. 41, 43.

138. John A. Robertson, "Technology and Motherhood: Legal and Ethical Issues in Human Egg Donation," *Case Western Reserve Law Review* 39 (1988–89), pp. 1, 31.

139. See Note, "Redefining Mother," p. 193.

140. Janet L. Dolgin, "Just a Gene: Judicial Assumptions About Parenthood," *UCLA Law Review* 40 (1993), p. 637. For historical accounts of American law governing rights to children, see Michael Grossberg, *Governing the Hearth: Law and the Family in Nineteenth-Century America* (Chapel Hill: University of North Carolina Press, 1985), pp. 196–285; Mary Ann Mason, *From Father's Property to Children's Rights: The History of Child Custody in the United States* (New York: Columbia University Press, 1994), p. 70.

141. 5 Cal. 4th 84, 19 Cal. Rptr 2d 494 (1993), *cert. denied*, 114 S. Ct. 206 (1993). See Philip Hager, "State High Court to Rule in Child Surrogacy Case," *Los Angeles Times*, Jan. 24, 1992, p. A1.

142. Hill, "What Does It Mean to Be a 'Parent'?" pp. 371–72.

143. *Johnson v. Calvert*, No. X-633190, slip opinion, p. 21 (Cal. App. Dept. Super. Ct. Oct. 22, 1990), aff'd, *Anna J. v. Mark C.*, 12 Cal. App. 4th 977, 286 Cal. Rptr 369 (1991), aff'd, *Johnson v. Calvert*, 5 Cal. 4th 84, 19 Cal. Rptr 494 (1993), *cert. denied*, 114 S. Ct. 206 (1993).

144. John A. Robertson, "Embryos, Families, and Procreative Liberty: The Legal Structure of the New Reproduction," *Southern California Law Review* 59 (1986), pp. 942, 1015.

145. *Johnson v. Calvert*, slip opinion, p. 8.

146. *Anna J. v. Mark C.*

147. Jill Serjeant, "Clinic Blames Shortage of Black Eggs for Baby Row," *Reuters World Service*, Dec. 31, 1994.

148. Abbie Jones, "Fertility Doctors *Try* to Egg On Donors," *Chicago Tribune*, March 6, 1994, p. F1.

149. David Fletcher et al., "Black Woman Awaits Implant to Have Mixed-Race Baby," *Daily Telegraph*, Dec. 31, 1993, p. 1.

150. Ibid.

151. Office of Technology Assessment, *Artificial Insemination*, pp. 40–41, 65.

152. Katha Pollitt, "Checkbook Maternity: When Is a Mother Not a Mother?" *The Nation*, Dec. 31, 1990, pp. 825, 842.

153. See, e.g., Corea, *The Mother Machine*, p. 276 (describing a "reproductive brothel"); Raymond, *Women as Wombs*, pp. 143–44 (describing the growth of reproductive clinics in developing countries that specialize in sex predetermination and foreshadow the use of Third World women as gestational surrogates); Rothman, "Reproductive Technology," p. 100 ("Can we look forward to baby farms, with white embryos grown in young and poor Third-World mothers?").

154. David Behrens, "It's a Boy! But Whose? Surrogate and Genetic Parents in Tug-of-War," *New York Newsday*, Sept. 21, 1990, pp. 1, 15.

155. See Corea, *The Mother Machine*, p. 276; Gena Corea, "The Reproductive Brothel," in Gena Corea et al., eds., *Man-Made Women: How New Reproductive Technologies Affect Women* (Bloomington: Indiana University Press, 1987), pp. 38, 45.

156. Gabriel, "High-Tech Pregnancies Test Hope's Limit," p. 18.

157. Keane and Breo, *The Surrogate Mother*, p. 36.

158. John Harvey Caldwell, "Babies by Scientific Selection," *Scientific American* 150 (March 1934), pp. 124–25.

159. Hermann J. Muller, *Out of the Night: A Biologist's View of the Future* (New York: Vanguard, 1935).

160. Daniel J. Kevles, *In the Name of Eugenics: Genetics and the Uses of Human Heredity* (New York: Knopf, 1985), pp. 262–63.

161. Raymond, *Women as Wombs*, pp. 70–71; Nicholas D. Kristof, "Singapore Decides It Wants Lots of Children After All," *New York Times*, Dec. 7, 1986, sec.4, p. 3.

162. Sonia Correa, *Population and Reproductive Rights: Feminist Perspectives from the South* (London: Zed Books, 1994), p. 43.

163. See generally Robertson, *Children of Choice*. Important books by contemporary liberal philosophers include John Rawls, *A Theory of Justice* (Cambridge: Harvard University Press, 1971); Ronald Dworkin, *A Matter of Principle* (Cambridge: Harvard University Press, 1985).

164. Barbara J. Berg, "Listening to the Voices of the Infertile," in Callahan, ed., *Reproduction, Ethics, and the Law*, pp. 80, 82.

165. Joan C. Callahan, "Introduction to Part II: Prenatal and Postnatal Authority," in Callahan, *Reproduction, Ethics, and the Law*, pp. 133, 134.

166. Tabitha M. Powledge, "Unnatural Selection: On Choosing Children's Sex," in Helen B. Holmes et al., eds., *The Custom-Made Child? Women-Centered Perspectives* (Totowa, N.J.: Humana, 1981), pp. 193, 197.

167. Christine Overall, *Ethics and Human Reproduction: A Feminist Analysis* (Winchester, Mass.: Unwin Hyman, 1987), pp. 17–39.

168. *Skinner v. Oklahoma*, 316 U.S. 535, 541 (1942).

169. Robertson, *Children of Choice*, p. 24.

170. Iris Marion Young, *Justice and the Politics of Difference* (Princeton: Princeton University Press, 1990), pp. 15–38.

171. Robertson, *Children of Choice*, pp. 167–69.

172. Ibid, p. 167.

173. Rosemarie Tong, "Feminist Perspectives on Gestational Motherhood: The Search for a Unified Focus," in Callahan, *Reproduction, Ethics, and the Law*, pp. 55, 58, citing Surrogacy Arrangements Act, 1985, United Kingdom, chap. 49, p. 2 (1) (a) (b) (c).

174. Ibid., p. 64.

175. Ibid., pp. 64–68.

176. Joan C. Callahan and Dorothy E. Roberts, "A Feminist Social Justice Approach to Reproduction-Assisting Technologies: A Case Study on the Limits of Liberal Theory," *Kentucky Law Review* 84 (1996), p. 1197.

177. Gabriel, "High-Tech Pregnancies Test Hope's Limit," p. 18.

178. May, *Barren in the Promised Land*, pp. 234–35.

179. *ABC World News Tonight*, Transcript #6038, Feb. 22, 1996.

180. Office of Technology Assessment, *Infertility*, p. 11.

181. Peter J. Neuman et al., "The Cost of a Successful Delivery with In Vitro Fertilization," *New England Journal of Medicine* 331 (1994), p. 239.

182. Bartholet, *Family Bonds*; Nsiah-Jefferson and Hall, "Reproductive Technology," pp. 112–113; Heitman, "Infertility as a Public Health Problem," pp. 96–98; Nadine Taub, "Surrogacy: A Preferred Treatment for Infertility?" *Law, Medicine, and Health Care* 16 (1988), p. 89.

183. Gabriel, "High-Tech Pregnancies Test Hope's Limit," p. 1.

184. Aral and Cates, "Increasing Concern with Infertility," pp. 2328-29; Berg, "Listening to the Voices of the Infertile," p. 93.

185. Kimberlé Crenshaw, "Demarginalizing the Intersection of Race and Sex: A Black Feminist Critique of Antidiscrimination Doctrine, Feminist Theory, and Antiracist Politics," *University of Chicago Legal Forum*, 1989, pp. 139, 154 n.35.

Chapter 7. The Meaning of Liberty

1. Michael J. Sandel, *Liberalism and the Limits of Justice* (Cambridge: Cambridge University Press, 1982).

2. See, e.g., Patricia J. Williams, "The Obliging Shell (an Informal Essay on Formal Equal Opportunity)," in *Alchemy of Race and Rights* (Cambridge: Harvard University Press, 1991), p. 98; Richard Delgado, *Rodrigo's Chronicles* (New York: New York University Press, 1995).

3. John A. Robertson, *Children of Choice: Freedom and the New Reproductive Technologies* (Princeton: Princeton University Press, 1995), p. 257 n.35.

4. Ibid., p. 23.

5. Ibid., p. 30.

6. See, e.g., Ruth Colker, *Abortion and Dialogue: Pro-Choice and American Law* (Bloomington: Indiana University Press, 1992); Catharine A. MacKinnon, *Feminism Unmodified: Discourses on Life and Law* (Cambridge: Harvard University Press, 1987); Sylvia A. Law, "Rethinking Sex and the Constitution," *University of Pennsylvania Law Review* 132 (1984), p. 955; Elizabeth M. Schneider, "The Violence of Privacy," *Connecticut Law Review* 23 (1991), p. 973.

7. Catharine A. MacKinnon, "*Roe v. Wade*: A Study in Male Ideology," in Jay L. Garfield and Patricia Hennessey, eds., *Abortion: Moral and Legal Perspectives* (Amherst: University of Massachusetts Press, 1984), pp. 45, 53.

8. Frances Olsen, "Constitutional Law: Feminist Critiques of the Public/Private Distinction," *Constitutional Commentary* 10 (1993), p. 325.

9. Robertson, *Children of Choice*, pp. 226, 166.

10. Ibid., p. 23 (emphasis added).

11. William A. Galston, *Liberal Purposes: Goods, Virtues, and Diversity in the Liberal State* (Cambridge: Cambridge University Press, 1991), p. 4 (emphasis added).

12. Derrick Bell, "Black History and America's Future," *Valparaiso Law Review* 29 (1995), pp. 1179, 1183. Derrick Bell describes the accommodation of slavery in "The Chronicle of the Constitutional Contradiction," in *And We Are Not Saved: The Elusive Quest for Racial Justice* (New York: Basic Books, 1987), p. 26.

13. Robertson, *Children of Choice*, p. 224.

14. Betsy Hartmann, *Reproductive Rights and Wrongs: The Global Politics of Population Control and Contraceptive Choice* (New York: Harper, 1987), p. xii.

15. Angela Davis, "Racism, Birth Control, and Reproductive Rights," in Marlene Gerber Fried, ed., *From Abortion to Reproductive Freedom: Transforming a Movement* (Boston: South End Press, 1990), pp. 15, 17.

16. Angela Harris, "Race and Essentialism in Feminist Legal Theory," *Stanford Law Review* 42 (1990), pp. 581, 613.

17. Williams, *Alchemy of Race and Rights*, pp. 153-54.

18. Jed Rubenfeld, "The Right of Privacy," *Harvard Law Review* 102 (1989), p. 737.

19. See, e.g., Charles H. Jones, "An Argument for Federal Protection Against Racially Motivated Crimes: 18 U.S.C. Sec. 241 and the Thirteenth Amendment," *Harvard Civil Rights-Civil Liberties Law Review* 21 (1986), p. 689.

20. Legal scholars have argued, e.g., that the amendment protects a woman's right to an abortion because compelled pregnancy is a form of involuntary servitude. Andrew Koppelman, "Forced Labor: A Thirteenth Amendment Defense of Abortion," *Northwestern Law Review* 84 (1990), p. 480. They have argued that it prohibits programs

requiring welfare recipients to work for the government. Julie A. Nice, "Welfare Servitude," *Georgetown Journal on Fighting Poverty* 1 (1993), p. 340. And they have argued that it requires the state to protect children from the domination of an abusive parent. Akhil R. Amar and Daniel Widawsky, "Child Abuse as Slavery: A Thirteenth Amendment Response to *DeShaney*," *Harvard Law Review* 105 (1992), p. 1359.

21. Mark H. Haller, *Eugenics: Hereditarian Attitudes in American Thought* (New Brunswick, N.J.: Rutgers University Press, 1984), p. 42, quoting eugenicist W. Duncan McKim (emphasis added).

22. Paul A. Lombardo, "Three Generations, No Imbeciles: New Light on *Buck v. Bell*," *New York University Law Review* 60 (1985), pp. 30, 46, quoting *Report of the Virginia State Epileptic Colony* (1922–23), p. 27 (emphasis added).

23. Edward L. Thorndike, *Human Nature and the Social Order* (New York: Macmillan, 1940).

24. Jacob H. Landman, *Human Sterilization: The History of the Sexual Sterilization Movement* (New York: Macmillan, 1932), p. vii (emphasis added).

25. Quoted in Philip R. Reilly, *The Surgical Solution: A History of Involuntary Sterilization in the United States* (Baltimore: Johns Hopkins University Press, 1991), pp. 101–2 (emphasis added).

26. *Skinner v. Oklahoma*, 316 U.S. 535 (1942).

27. Laurence Tribe, *American Constitutional Law*, 2d ed. (Mineola, N.Y.: Foundation Press, 1988), p. 1305.

28. Robin West, "Progressive and Conservative Constitutionalism," *Michigan Law Review* 87 (1989), pp. 641, 707.

29. Janice G. Raymond, *Women as Wombs: Reproductive Technologies and the Battle over Women's Freedom* (San Francisco: HarperCollins, 1993), p. 194.

Index